The Complete Idiot's Reference Card

10 Essential Elvis Dates

January 8, 1935: Born in Tupelo, Mississippi
September 12, 1948: Moves to Memphis, Tennessee
July 5-6, 1954: Records "That's All Right (Mama)" at Sun Studios
March 24, 1958: Enters the Army
August 14, 1958: Mother Gladys dies
March 5, 1960: Discharged from the Army
May 1, 1967: Marries Priscilla Beaulieu in Las Vegas
February 1, 1968: Only child, Lisa Marie Presley, born
October 9, 1973: Divorced from Priscilla Presley
August 16, 1977: Dies at Graceland, age 42

Elvis Firsts

First car: 1942 Lincoln Zephyr, March 1953
First commercial recording: Sun Studios, Memphis, July 5, 1954 ("Harbor Lights")
First commercial release: "That's All Right (Mama)"/"Blue Moon of Kentucky," July 19, 1954
First concert appearance: Overton Park Shell, Memphis, July 30, 1954
First radio appearance: Interview with Dewey Phillips on WHBQ, Memphis, July 7, 1954
First nightclub appearance: Eagle's Nest, Memphis, August 7, 1954
First riot after an Elvis concert: Jacksonville, FL, May 13, 1955
First contract: with manager Tom Parker August 15, 1955
First national television appearance: The Dorsey brothers' *Stage Show*, January 28, 1956
First album: *Elvis Presley*, RCA, March 13, 1956
First house: 1034 Audubon Dr., Memphis, $40,000; the family moved in on May 11, 1956.
First appearance on *The Ed Sullivan Show*: September 9, 1956
First movie: *Love Me Tender*, which opened November 15, 1956
First Gold Record: "Heartbreak Hotel," April 11, 1956

10 Touchstone Performances

October 16, 1954: First appearance on the Louisiana Hayride.
December 4, 1956: Legendary Million-Dollar-Quartet session at Sun Studios (with Carl Perkins, Johnny Cash, Jerry Lee Lewis).
September 26, 1956: Mississippi-Alabama Fair and Dairy Show, Tupelo, MS; triumphant return home at show where he first performed at age 10.
March 25, 1961: USS *Arizona* Memorial Fund Concert, Honolulu, Hawaii; last concert until 1968.
December 3, 1968: "Comeback Special," NBC Television, first live performance in seven years.
July 31, 1969: International Hotel, Las Vegas, NV; first appearance in Las Vegas in 13 years.
January 14, 1973: "Elvis: Aloha from Hawaii," first world-wide satellite broadcast.
December 31, 1975: Pontiac Silverdome, Detroit, MI; set record for single performance gate receipts, $816,000.
June 9-11, 1972: Madison Square Garden, New York, NY; Elvis' only live NY city concerts.
June 26, 1977: Market Square Arena, Indianapolis, IN; Elvis' last concert.

Top Ten #1 Singles

"All Shook Up" (8 weeks)

"Heartbreak Hotel" (7 weeks)

"Don't Be Cruel" (7 weeks)

"Teddy Bear" (7 weeks)

"Jailhouse Rock" (6 weeks)

"Are You Lonesome Tonight?" (6 weeks)

"It's Now or Never" (5 weeks)

"Love Me Tender" (4 weeks)

"Stuck On You" (4 weeks)

"A Big Hunk O' Love" (2 weeks)

Albums That Reached #1

Blue Hawaii (20 weeks)

Elvis Presley (10 weeks)

Loving You (10 weeks)

G.I. Blues (10 weeks)

Elvis (5 weeks)

Elvis' Christmas Album (4 weeks)

Something for Everybody (3 weeks)

Roustabout (1 week)

Aloha from Hawaii via Satellite (1 week)

Elvis' Vital Stats

Height: 6'0"

Weight: 168-250

Neck: 15–16

Waist: 32-40

Chest: 39

Shoes Size: 11D

Eyes: Blue

Hair: "Dirty" Blond (dyed black)

Blood Type: O Positive

alpha
books

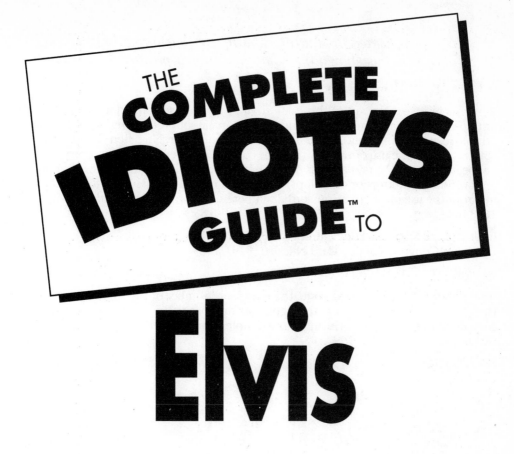

THE COMPLETE IDIOT'S GUIDE™ TO

Elvis

by Frank Coffey

alpha
books

A Division of Macmillan Reference USA
A Simon & Schuster Macmillan Company
1633 Broadway New York, NY 10019-6705

This book is dedicated to Stuart Graham, my cousin and brother (he loved Elvis first), who has shown me what grace under pressure is all about.

©1997 by Frank Coffey

International Standard Book Number: 0-02-861873-4
Library of Congress Catalog Card Number: 97-071189

99 98 97   4 3 2 1

Interpretation of the printing code: the rightmost number of the first series of numbers is the year of the book's printing; the rightmost number of the second series of numbers is the number of the book's printing. For example, a printing code of 97-1 shows that the first printing occurred in 1997.

Printed in the United States of America

Editorial Manager
Gretchen Henderson

Director of Editorial Services
Brian Phair

Executive Editor
Gary M. Krebs

Production Editor
Phil Kitchel

Technical Editor
Jim Donovan

Illustrator
Judd Winick

Designer
Glenn Larsen

Indexers
Nadia Ibrahim
Tim Tate

Production Team
Angela Calvert
Kim Cofer
Mary Hunt
Daniela Raderstorf
Megan Wade
Maureen West

Contents at a Glance

Contents

Foreword

Elvis and idiocy go a long way back.

In fact, you could make a pretty fair case that it was Idiots—more than hound dogs, Sam Phillips, Scotty Moore, Bill Black, Chet Atkins, D.J. Fontana, black pegged slacks, blue suede shoes, pink Cadillacs, or even screaming teens (well...)—who were Elvis' greatest accomplices in becoming so famous he dang near ruled the known universe.

This does not, I hasten to add, mean that Elvis' discoverers, accompanists, or fans (who number among them, alongside so many other worthies, me) are Idiots. Far from it. Elvis' fans are the non-Idiots in the Presliad. They figured him out right away. In fact, they got it quicker than even Elvis himself did. (But he was put in such a ridiculous situation that he got right off.)

No, the Idiots are the people who did not and do not love Elvis and what he symbolizes.

Of such Idiots, we could make a long list, beginning with people like Jim Denny of the Grand Ole Opry; comedian Steve Allen; Ed Sullivan before he saw the light; music critics, schoolmarms, and Hollywood producers; and going on to include every benighted jazzbo with a grudge against the sort of low-rent rockabilly cool-cat Elvis represented *in excelsis*.

You could make a case for Idiots far from Elvis (Nixon, not knowing what to do with him when the Big E himself literally turned up on the White House doorstep) and Idiots close to him (Colonel Tom Parker, going to his grave under the delusion that he'd pulled off a carny hustle, when what he'd really done was spend three decades selling True Genius short). You could even call Mick Jagger an Idiot for being unimpressed the last time he saw him, and having the temerity to say so out loud in *Rolling Stone*. Father, forgive him, for I ain't about to.

But why bother with any such enumeration of villains and morons? Time—no, not just time, history, in all its disdainful glory—has passed them by. Elvis, today, is known far and wide for what he truly was (or *is*—see Chapters 2 and 23). A prophet of our culture, a man so much bigger than our time that he, and he alone, came to *define* it, in all its ghostly, gutter-level glamour.

There are still Idiots who do not understand this aspect of Elvis, but that's OK. The remedy is at hand...actually, it's physically in your hand, in the shape of this book. Considering what you might be holding—a pink and black brickbat, a copy of the *Girls! Girls! Girls!* soundtrack featuring "Song of the Shrimp," or both—that's a relief. Rather than reviling these Idiots as ignorant stooges, or casting them into the outer darkness where reside Kenny G, Michael Bolton, and all their kith and kin, we can now hope to rescue them from the fetters of their Idiocy.

Tackling such a thing is a fearsome task, for the devil of Idiocy sometimes infests minds surprisingly strong in their ability to resist the Truth, which is that Elvis did not come to save us, but to show us how to save ourselves. The Truth, as Frank Coffey demonstrates in these pages, is not in the sneer, but in the South. And this Truth will, indeed, set you free.

Upon this rock (and roll), Elvis and those who loved him and followed his example—from Buddy Holly and John Lennon on up to today—built not a church but an entire world. It was a world radically altered in almost every respect from the one Elvis found when he separated from Jesse Garon. That old world did not nurture him, but tried instead to strangle him with its fables about what boys from the dust and dirt of Tupelo, who lived in housing projects, might achieve. In response, Elvis did not tell us another fable—he *became* another fable. The man from Tupelo lived a life that was a fairy-tale incarnate (albeit not one with a particularly happy ending)—and if you doubt this, you need to stop reading this filibuster and turn immediately to Brother Coffey's main text.

Now that we've got the Sinners out of the room, we can complete the thought: Elvis was a big man and a brave man. He was not afraid to tell the truth about himself in songs such as "A Fool Such as I" and "I Can Help." ("Have a laugh on me/I can help"—he's the only one who sang that line, because he was the only one who had the nerve to think of it.) Pay attention to the sound Elvis spread 'round the world, and I promise: He will rescue you from all pomposity and pretense, he will free your soul and your mind will follow, and you will find yourself left with every preconception all shook up.

Like the good Christian American he was, Elvis believed we should all have more than one chance. If his 30-some movies, 99 charted albums, and innumerable hit singles have not yet done it for you, there's always *The Complete Idiot's Guide to Elvis* to give you a running jump at salvation, one last prayerful leap onto the mystery train that's been pulling out of the station these past four decades.

But if you don't Get It this time, then you have been certified as not only an Idiot but an Irredeemable Idiot, and there's only one thing left to do: Return to Sender.

Now if I were an Idiot, this would frighten me most of all, for when we Return to Sender, who exactly do you figure will be seated at his or her left hand, playing guitar, wiggling his hips, sneering his sneer, and trying to drum up enough buddies for a touch-football game, offering everybody on the winning side a pink Cadillac convertible?

—Dave Marsh
A Fool but No Idiot
April 29, 1997

Introduction

Like millions of other breathless adolescent baby boomers, I was introduced to Elvis Aron Presley in 1956—on Sunday, October 28, to be exact. The man who brought him to America's attention was Ed Sullivan—the stiffest bore on television, as far as I was concerned.

On Sunday nights at 8:00, I usually watched *The Steve Allen Show*—"Steverino" was funny and, for the time, edgy—but this night I made an exception. It was the second of Elvis' three appearances on *The Ed Sullivan Show*, but this marked the first time he shared the stage with Ed himself. (Sullivan was involved in an auto accident, leaving distinguished British character-actor Charles Laughton, of all people, to guest host on Elvis' debut on the show six weeks before), and I distinctly remember how profoundly uncomfortable Sullivan looked when he introduced Elvis.

I remember, too, how uncomfortable my mother—a minister's daughter—looked when Elvis started singing and swiveling (not until the third broadcast did the self-appointed defenders of decent American values manage to pressure CBS into showing Elvis only from the waist up). My father, on the other hand, didn't look uncomfortable at all; why, he was so outraged the "bum" was on the tube at all that he left the room.

Like every other kid in America, I instantly *got* Elvis and understood what he was about: he was free, unrestrained, wild, and, like *Mad* magazine, communicated to grown-ups that they were living in Squaresville and that we had our own cool world now, thankyuverymuch. Elvis was the Pied Piper. I signed up. Millions of other kids did, too. Not that we knew it, but a youth and rock and roll revolution, destined to change the world, had just started.

Elvis' timing couldn't have been more perfect in square, post-World War II times: He was *different*. And he was *hip*. Being hip at that time meant you did things that parents disapproved of—namely, sex. Just *thinking* about sex or a sexy rock star was enough to send a parent into a tizzy.

Today Elvis is everywhere: His records and CDs continue to sell, his face has appeared on a stamp, and you can more easily find Elvis paraphernalia than you can gift items on the Statue of Liberty and the Eiffel Tower combined. This summer, RCA will be releasing *Elvis Presley Platinum: A Life in Music,* a four-CD, 100-song box set that will contain 77 never-before-released songs—including a recently discovered 1953 recording of "I'll Never Stand in Your Way," from Elvis' very first session. Twenty years after his death, the Elvis phenomenon isn't waning—it's growing with every passing year.

Trying to understand the fascination with Elvis—the Cult of Elvis, if you will—is a good part of this book's mission. But it is also an attempt to tell the story of Elvis Aron Presley in a new and different way: This is, quite literally, a how-to book on the King of Rock and Roll. (And, yes, I know that sounds funny, but there's really useful instructional stuff in this book. Honest.) If you have half the fun reading it that I had writing it, I'll be proud and happy. Long live the King!

How To Use This Book

There is so much to say about Elvis that organizing the material in this book became quite a challenge. The organizational choices I've made will allow readers to first get a grasp of the wonder of Elvis, to understand the amazing man we celebrate, and then to delve into his life and career in a logical and natural way.

Part 1, "Everybody Let's Rock!," introduces you to the Elvis Presley phenomenon. I'll talk about why we love him, why we want to know more about him, and how he found himself at ground zero of a cultural explosion. You'll find some essential facts that will be useful as you move through the book, some tips on how best to enjoy the King, and even a test of your Elvis IQ.

Part 2, "Where Did Mr. Sideburns Come From?," steps back in time and explores how Elvis' place and time influenced his music. We'll trace the roots of rock and roll, meet Elvis' family, learn about the culture of Memphis and Tupelo, and get a telling glimpse into the King's hardscrabble childhood. Elvis was a Southern man to the end, and everything about him—from his diet to his manners to his musical tastes—reflected his roots.

Part 3, "Kingdom Coming: The Rise of Elvis," is a fascinating look at Elvis' earliest failures and successes. We'll see a raw, talented kid waltz into Sun Studios and emerge, with breathtaking speed, a star. We'll meet the enigmatic, wily Colonel Tom Parker and get a rundown of Elvis' earliest contractual dealings.

Part 4, "Top of the World, Mama: The Reign of Elvis," captures Elvis at his peak. We'll watch Elvis take America by storm, on TV, in concert, and in the movies. Then, in the midst of huge success, we'll see Elvis drafted into the Army—and do his duty honorably and without complaint. We'll find out about his early loves and meet the legendary Memphis Mafia, that motley group of Elvis' buddies who did anything to protect and serve their King.

Part 5, "Free-Fallin': The Decline of Elvis," tells you everything you need to know about the King's downfall. From his later life's passions (women, karate, and fancy cars) to his bad habits (overeating, addiction to prescription drugs, and a fondness for guns), we'll get a picture of Elvis in his later years: a lonely man who was confused by his staggering success and allowed to go astray by those closest to him. We'll then experience the inevitable: Elvis' tragic death at only 42 years of age and the bizarre turns of events following it. Finally, we'll see how Elvis' death affected his family, friends, fans, and the country at large.

Part 6, "All the King's Things," shows how Elvis continues to be a presence in our personal lives and in society at large. It's also a practical starter's guide on how to collect his records and memorabilia. And, finally, you'll get to "visit" Graceland, from your armchair—and get some tips to get you ready to go for real. That's when you know you've graduated into true Elvis fandom!

Extras

To help you make the most of this book, I've liberally sprinkled throughout the text what we in the publishing business call "sidebars," which appear in boxes with recurring cartoon art. Each type of box contains different information; think of the sidebars as entertaining, informative tidbits that add flavor and spice to the main meal.

For the Record

"Bet you didn't know...." That's what these sidebars are all about; interesting and little known "factoids" that you, as a resident Elvis expert, can trot out to impress friends and family.

Return to Sender
There's always been a lot of misinformation about Elvis; I'll point the finger at some of it in these boxes.

The Word
Think of this as a mini-Elvis dictionary—definitions of words and lingo specific to Elvis and his world.

The King and I
These are quotes from and about Elvis—short, sweet, and always entertaining.

Going for Gold
Here are practical tips for you on listening to or collecting Elvis.

Acknowledgments

All books are works of collaboration. Here are some of the good folks who helped me out and to whom I'd like to say a special thank you:

Carl "Slow Hand" Waldman for his writing, research, organization, and world-class objectivity; there's no one else I'd rather have worked with.

Jim Donovan, literary agent extraordinaire and hopeless Elvis nutcase, for the skilled application of his blue pencil and quick wit.

John Dawson, talented and gracious Texas-based photographer, whose lucid eye and encyclopedic knowledge of Elvis helped make this book come to life.

Jim Barkley, book, sales, and Elvis lover, whose passion and enthusiasm helped create this book.

Maggie Begley, of Maggie Begley Communications, for putting up with me while I hiked in Elvis' shoes.

Phil Kitchel, Elvis expert, gifted copy editor, and calming presence during stormy weather.

Gary M. Krebs, witty e-mailer, rock and roll expert, and consummate editor, who came up with the idea for this book, fought vigorously and relentlessly to make it a reality, kept his lucid eye always focused on the prize, and is the one person most responsible for this book's existence.

Special Thanks from the Publisher to the Technical Reviewer

The Complete Idiot's Guide to Elvis was reviewed by an expert who not only checked the accuracy of what you'll learn in this book, but also provided valuable insight and suggestions to ensure that the most important Elvis tidbits are included herein. Our thanks are extended to Jim Donovan.

Mr. Donovan is a literary agent and editor based in Dallas, Texas. Having worked as a book buyer for a large, independent chain of bookstores, he worked as a senior editor for Taylor Publishing in Dallas from 1987-1993. He has since worked as an agent and freelance editor and writer. Mr. Donovan has also written two books, *Dallas—Shining Star of Texas* and *The Dallas Cowboys Encyclopedia*.

Part 1
Everybody, Let's Rock!

Along with millions of other Americans, I first saw Elvis Aron Presley when he gyrated onto The Ed Sullivan Show *in 1956. We'd never seen anything like him—an uninhibited, unabashed sensualist who was belting out a new kind of music: rock and roll. That music, of course, took us Baby Boomers by storm—creating a sound, a look, and an attitude dramatically different from anything our parents had ever imagined. The music was dangerous, wild, sexy. So was Elvis. Elvis started a cultural revolution, the era of rock and roll. And we had a hero, a leader, our own swivel-hipped cult figure.*

In Part 1 of this book, I'll get you going. I'll give an overview of Elvis the man and Elvis the phenomenon, exploring why he is perhaps the most compelling cultural figure of this century. I'll explain when and how he exploded on the scene. I'll tell you the basic facts of his remarkable life and some tips on how best to enjoy him.

So without further ado—it's one for the money, two for the show, three to get ready, now...

The King and You

This chapter will explain why millions of people the world over love, adore, and flat-out worship Elvis Presley. Of course, most of us know that he's called the King of Rock and Roll. But what, pray tell, does that mean?

Where to start a discussion of Elvis? According to some, he's merely a singer, albeit a legendary one. That's not my attitude. Elvis Presley is one of the most influential human beings of the 20th century. I'll talk about why, in my view, more than any single person, Elvis is responsible for the creation of a new, indigenous American art form: rock and roll music. I'll discuss how Elvis and his music affect the country and the world. And then I'll discuss why, improbably, the King became more famous and more significant after his death.

The Phenomenon of Elvis: Why We Love Him, Why We Study Him

Elvis is called "the King" because he was the flashpoint, the linchpin, the centerpiece of a musical and cultural revolution called rock and roll. It can be said that the rock revolution went on to become the most significant worldwide cultural phenomenon of the 20th century, affecting style, language, art, film, customs, values, ethics, as well as music. Elvis Presley started the revolution.

Elvis Presley made musical and social history by combining heretofore primarily black forms of music—rhythm and blues (R and B) and gospel—with primarily white forms of music—country-western and pop—to create a whole new thing called rock.

Of course, Elvis wasn't the only singer bringing rock to the mass American audience: Fellow musicians Bill Haley ("Rock Around The Clock," 1955), Jerry Lee Lewis ("Great Balls of Fire," 1957), and Chuck Berry ("Maybellene," 1955) became early popularizers too. Legendary singers Fats Domino, Bo Diddley, and Little Richard were there at the beginning. (Richard actually claims that *he* was the King, but despite widespread acknowledgment of his talents and accomplishments, few have echoed the sentiment.)

Early, innocent Elvis in 1957 on the cover of "All Shook Up"/"Teddy Bear."

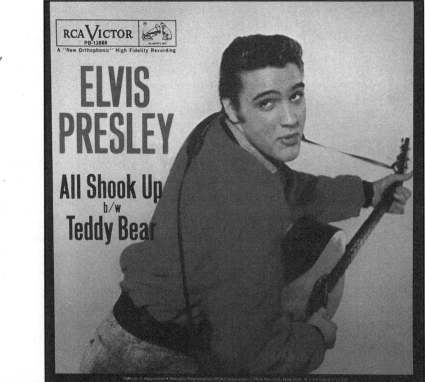

But it was Elvis Presley, preternaturally handsome, sneeringly sexy, with a voice both raw and velvety, who captured the hearts and minds (and loins) of mainstream America. Elvis started out as a pretender to the throne and became the King.

Need another way to get a handle on the King? Think of The Beatles. Like Elvis, the boys from Liverpool (who were huge Elvis fans—even idolizers) radically changed music and culture. Girls swooned, parents raged. Elvis gave us pompadours and sideburns; The Beatles, long locks and facial hair. Elvis was rebellion, '50s style: fast cars and hot nights. The Beatles provided the late '60s/early '70s version: peace, love, and consciousness alteration. But they shared one thing: impact. It's not too grandiose to say that everyone in America was affected by Elvis *and* The Beatles. Everyone. But Elvis was first.

Elvis died early, at age 42. And, subsequently, something highly improbable happened to Elvis Aron Presley: The King became bigger in death than in life. Today, Elvis is ubiquitous. A million fans make an annual pilgrimage to his Memphis home, Graceland. Elvis made more money in the three years after his death than during his entire career. He has sold over one billion records.

Elvis impersonators—fanatical fans making careers out of paying homage—are legion, and have become a cultural phenomenon in their own right. (Comedian Andy Kaufman garnered attention with his uncanny impersonation in the 1970s, and today many impersonators actually make a living doing the King Thing.) Supposed sightings of Elvis alive are regularly reported (and joked about) in the media. Elvis collectibles are among the most expensive and sought-after trophies in high-toned auction houses in New York, Los Angeles, and London. (His American Express card sold for $80,000 dollars!) Elvis Presley Enterprises, run by his ex-wife Priscilla to market his name, is a hugely successful business. Elvis' image is on clocks, calendars, mugs, stamps, plates, toys, you name it. You can't avoid Elvis. Twenty years after his death, he is, as the saying goes, everywhere.

In the beginning, there was Elvis. The father of a generation's music. To know him is to know the most influential art form of the 20th century—rock and

Return to Sender
Don't be fooled into thinking Priscilla Presley was Elvis' beneficiary. In fact, although she was involved in Elvis Presley Enterprises, the marketing branch of the Elvis Presley estate, she wasn't even mentioned in her late ex-husband's will. The sole heirs to Elvis' estate were his daughter, Lisa Marie; his father, Vernon; and his grandmother, Minnie Mae. With her grandfather and great-grandmother deceased, Lisa Marie became sole heir when she turned 25 in 1993.

The King and I
"There have been contenders, but there is only one King."

—Bruce Springsteen

roll. To understand him is to understand the country: innocent and calculating, vibrant and vulnerable, powerful and flawed—envied and admired around the world.

Elvis Presley left this life in 1977 at age 42. But he will never die.

Long live the King.

Elvis Presley, Eye of the Hurricane

Wherever Elvis went, whatever he did, whenever he did it, controversy followed. If asked what his life was all about, Elvis, who by all accounts was not a particularly analytical or introspective man, probably would have answered that his life was about music and rocking the joint. (And, he'd have been partly right.) But it also turned out to be about *morality* and rocking the boat.

The plain truth is that Elvis shook folks up. Early on, he was a white boy singing like a black man, and a lot of people were upset and threatened by that. Why? At the root of it was racism. It was okay for black people to "shake, rattle and roll," to let go, to express their emotions—and sexuality—through their music. But at the time, demure, white-bread America didn't do that. They didn't even know *how*. In addition, there was a certain "class-ism" at work: the cultural/media elite of the North didn't want no redneck Southern boy upsetting their proper social order. There was, and is, a definite Northern prejudice directed at the South that is plainly revealed in some of the criticism of Elvis.

America before Elvis was a culture dominated by Protestant, conservative values: People didn't raise their voices, didn't draw attention to themselves—and didn't have much fun. Maybe it made sense after the Depression, after World War II, and in the midst of the Cold War, with nuclear bombs hanging over the country's head. Much of the music reflected that cautious sensibility: smooth, slow, and safe. *Elvis wasn't safe.* For the generation coming of age after World War II, the baby boomers, who were the first to embrace Elvis, the old music was just that: Old. Boring. The King showed them a different way: Let go. Rock out. Jump and shout. It scared the hell out of Middle America. And what scared them most was…sex.

And Elvis Presley was pure sex. His voice, his moves ("pelvic gyrations"), and his extraordinary looks made girls and women weak in the knees. Boyfriends and husbands had to adapt (or spend their nights alone). Elvis was cool, Elvis was hot. Boys looked at how their girls looked at Elvis and got the message. Clothes changed. Hair got longer. Hip was in, square was out. And parents? When they weren't furious, they were…afraid. Elvis expressed pure, unfettered freedom, and, to middle-of the-road '50s America, freedom was dangerous.

The King and I
"He taught white America to get down."

—James Brown

So great was the fear, so threatening was Elvis to America's sexual standards, that during his early TV appearances, cameramen were ordered to cut him off at the waist. Preachers denounced him from pulpits (unaware that Elvis was a god-fearing boy from a very religious family), as did teachers in classrooms and parents at the dinner table. Newspapers reviled him. A typical spew from early in his career: "His performance was the most disgusting exhibition this reporter has ever seen." Elvis threatened the order of things, and the culture's authority figures—not to mention the show-business powers on both coasts—wanted him gone.

But Elvis Presley wasn't going away. He was going *up*: a rocketing Hillbilly Cat who broke all the rules and watched, in amazement, as America followed him.

There's plenty of irony in the image of Elvis as a radical cultural force because, deep down, he wasn't all that radical. He was religious, a Republican, and, like most young men from his generation, he liked hamburgers, cars, and girls. He had no use for the counter-culture that developed in the '60s and, publicly anyway, denounced drug taking, free love, and the peace movement.

> **The King and I**
> "I've been blamed for just about everything wrong in this country."
> —Elvis

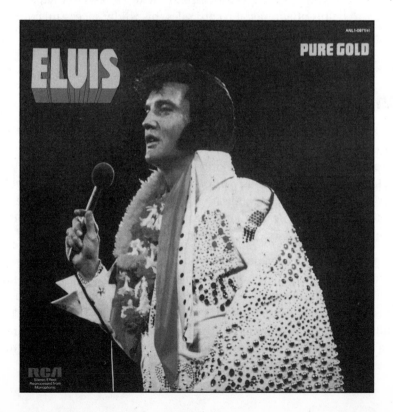

The cover of Elvis: Pure Gold, *released in 1980. Late Elvis, in his Vegas glory.*

Later in life, Elvis' transformation to a Vegas-style performer created another round of controversy for fans. So did his ballooning weight and his use of painkillers and scores of other prescribed drugs. His death and the facts revealed about it shocked the nation. But even in decline and unhappiness, Elvis symbolized America. Elvis was overweight and so was the country. He took too many pills; so did many Americans. He divorced the love of his life, and so did 50 percent of his countrymen. America could look at Elvis and see itself.

So, as you delve into Elvis, remember: If anyone disses you for listening to "Hound Dog" a hundred times in a row... if anyone questions you for renting the movie *Blue Hawaii*... if anyone looks puzzled about your investment in a black-and-white glossy of Elvis... or for surfing endlessly on the Web for Elvis info... or for joining one of the 480 or so Elvis Presley fan clubs... just tell them you are a student of American history—no, make that *world* history! You are not an Elvis nut-case, you are a cultural archivist! And you are not alone.

The King and I

"Elvis Presley was a symbol of the country's vitality, rebelliousness, and good humor."

—President Jimmy Carter

Crowning Glory

Elvis was the King, the "Greatest Entertainer in the World." His meteoric rise to the top attests to that, as do his phenomenal record sales, his wildly successful concert tours, his popular movies, and his many awards. But his accomplishments also can be defined through the impact he had on people's lives.

It All Started with the Music

Early in his career, Elvis paid his musical dues. As the Hillbilly Cat, he toured the South for lousy wages. His first contract for a series of appearances was for $18 a show. Not all early audiences responded to him. Some were offended and showed their disgust. Others—like the kids in *Back To The Future,* listening in horror to Marty McFly (Michael J. Fox) do Chuck Berry—just didn't *get* him, and sat on their hands in stunned silence at the weird anomaly before them. Plus, he got plenty of horrible reviews, and many of his musical peers (think envy here) were very critical of him.

But Elvis Presley was a gyrating spectacle—moves he'd picked up from black entertainers on the seamy side of Memphis, not to mention from god-possessed Pentecostal preachers—and his popularity spread like a gasoline-stoked brushfire. Less than a year after his first commercial recording, Elvis caused his first riot (May 13, 1955 in Jacksonville, Florida)—and it wasn't because the audience didn't like him. In less than two years, Elvis went from being a regional sensation to a national one. He was getting more and more press. His records were selling. His concerts were selling out. His female fans were screaming out.

But there were reality checks in this Cinderella story. Critics still wrote scathing reviews. The *Los Angeles Mirror-Times* called his show a "corruption of the innocent," and "a lesson in pornography." Other entertainers (jealousy?) were often unkind, including superstar Bing Crosby who said, "Elvis Presley has contributed nothing to music." Elvis' first engagement in Las Vegas, scheduled for four weeks, was canceled halfway through because of a poor reception.

Such setbacks proved to be footnotes to his climb to the top. As time and his career moved on, he became so popular and such a money machine, his contribution to music could not be ignored. Even many who previously held him in contempt came to respect him. Even if they didn't like his style of music, they couldn't deny his consummate professionalism and his down-home humility. His polite off-stage personality played a part in his growing success, but it all started with and fed off the music, the look, the act, and the attitude.

The King and I

"Everything happened so blame fast I don't know where I was yesterday and I don't know where I'll be tomorrow."

—Elvis

Award City

The records (I'm talking about the statistical kind here) and accolades piled up quickly. Elvis' lifetime musical achievements are mind-boggling. Check out the following:

➤ 14 number-one records on the Top 100/Hot 100 chart

➤ 11 number-one records on the Country chart

➤ 7 number-one records on the Rhythm and Blues chart

➤ 7 number-one records on the Easy-Listening chart

➤ 21 number-one records on the British chart

➤ 12 records on the Top 100/Hot 100 chart for more than 20 weeks

➤ 25 albums that reached the Top Ten

➤ 4 albums on the charts for a year or more

➤ 6 number-one extended-play albums

➤ 110 titles of albums and singles certified as either gold, platinum, or multi-platinum (U.S. sales)

Because of that last number—about twice as many as The Beatles—Elvis is considered by many to be the greatest recording artist of all time.

For the Record

It is estimated that one billion Elvis record units have sold worldwide. To put that in perspective, that's enough for four albums or singles for every person in the U.S. If all of Elvis' records were put side-by-side, they would stretch around the globe—twice.

Accurate worldwide figures are impossible to obtain, but Elvis received numerous gold record awards from many other countries, including Australia, Belgium, Canada, France, Germany, Japan, the Netherlands, South Africa, Sweden, the United Kingdom, and (the former) Yugoslavia.

During his lifetime, Elvis received many other awards, including 16 Grammy nominations and three Grammy Awards. The latter should have been more, but you know—politics. The Grammy he won in 1967 was the first ever to a true rock and roll artist, although he won it for a sacred/inspirational performance, and his two others in 1972 and 1974 were for sacred music as well.

For the Record

The Rock & Roll Hall of Fame is a museum dedicated to the history of rock and roll. Although it was founded in 1983, it found a permanent home in Cleveland, Ohio, in 1995. In 1986, the first induction ceremony took place in New York City. The first 10 inductees were Elvis Presley, Chuck Berry, Little Richard, The Everly Brothers, James Brown, Sam Cooke, Buddy Holly, Ray Charles, Fats Domino, and Jerry Lee Lewis.

Elvis received hundreds of other awards, such as the Memphis Music Award, the Las Vegas Musical Star of the Year, keys to various cities, and the World Championship Attendance Record (a gold belt from the International Hotel).

Television Triumphs

Concerts and radio led to TV for Elvis. Elvis' talent—and photogenic features—translated perfectly to the small screen. He made his first TV appearance in October 1955—a regional broadcast for the Louisiana Hayride—eight months after his first commercial recording. Eleven months later, he appeared on national TV, the first of six appearances on the Dorsey Brothers's *Stage Show*. Soon afterward came two appearances on *The Milton Berle Show* and one on *The Steve Allen Show*. Then, in September 1956, he was featured on the cover of *TV Guide*, because of his first appearance on *The Ed Sullivan Show*. Eighty percent of American viewers tuned in to watch him—the largest TV audience in history to that time (a record unbroken until The Beatles' appearance on the same show). He appeared two more times on Sullivan; the Elvis musical revolution was on its full-tilt boogie way.

For the Record

On his third and final appearance on *The Ed Sullivan Show*, January 6, 1957, Elvis sang seven songs, including "Hound Dog" and "Don't Be Cruel." The King was shown only from the waist up because of earlier complaints about his licentious moves. The girls screamed anyway. Ed Sullivan congratulated him on the air for being "a real decent, fine boy."

Hollywood Hurrahs

Hollywood soon came calling. Less than seven months after his first national TV appearance, Elvis was filming his first movie, *Love Me Tender*. He made a total of 33 movies. Elvis, of course, was a box-office success, his films grossing a reported $150 million. (In those days, that was stellar.) He was listed in the theater owners' Money-Making Stars poll seven times:

- ➤ 1957, ranking 4th
- ➤ 1961, ranking 10th
- ➤ 1962, ranking 5th
- ➤ 1963, ranking 7th
- ➤ 1964, ranking 6th
- ➤ 1965, ranking 6th
- ➤ 1966, ranking 10th

The King and I
"I've been studying the actors the girls like—Jimmy Dean, Humphrey Bogart, Marlon Brando—and they don't smile, never smile. When they do smile, it becomes an event. If I don't smile, I'm gonna get 'em."

—Elvis

His films were not received as favorably by critics as they were by fans. The early ones—*Love Me Tender, Loving You, Jailhouse Rock, King Creole, G.I. Blues, Flaming Star,* and *Wild in the Country*—are generally considered his best performances; and, not coincidentally, were the most autobiographical, exploring poor-boy-makes-good themes. The later movies were pretty much glitzy star vehicles.

All of them, however, spoke to young people—Elvis' roguish charm, inner strength, and individualism emanated from the silver screen, and his music thus had one more outlet for reaching the masses. It is bittersweet irony that Elvis, who initially didn't want to sing in his movies but rather wanted to be a "real actor," sang in every film he ever made.

Elvis: A Cultural Obsession

Elvis Presley is a cultural obsession, no question. He lives in musical references and in artwork and in writing—both literary and tabloid. He symbolizes rebellion, extravagance, celebrity, innocence—and lost innocence. Since the emergence of the public Elvis, people have been trying to explain why Elvis Aron Presley was and is such an American cultural obsession. Why did he have such enormous cultural impact?

For the Record

Currently there are 480 active Elvis fan clubs around the world. No other celebrity comes close.

Of course, the true measure of a person is the effect he or she had on other people's lives. In terms of society, Elvis broke down musical barriers, bringing rock and roll into the lives of many. He broke down racial barriers, making it possible for white people to sing like black people and vice versa. He broke down sexual barriers, making it acceptable to express oneself through dance in public. He broke down regional barriers, bringing Northerners and Southerners together around his music.

In terms of individuals, he affected millions of lives in countless ways. Seeing Elvis in an early concert live or on Ed Sullivan was a defining moment in many lives—an epiphany. For many women, Elvis was the first crush on someone larger than life itself. For many men, Elvis was their first lesson on what it was to be cool and wild at the same time. One Elvis song—"Heartbreak Hotel," "Hound Dog," "Don't Be Cruel," "All Shook Up," "Are You Lonesome Tonight," "Burning Love," or choose your favorite—can bring back a flood of memories of time, place, and people. And, of course, just as with JFK and John Lennon, millions of people remember exactly where they were and what they were doing when they heard the shocking news that Elvis had died at 42.

Perhaps Elvis' greatest effect was on artists of all styles and backgrounds: Elvis embodied freedom, the opportunity—no, the right—to follow your own muse. To do it your way, no matter the consequences. Without such liberation, art dies. Elvis, especially the young Elvis, was free, unfettered by convention, untouched by stricture. He was pure, natural, a force of nature. He transcended his roots, transcended poverty, ignorance, and small-mindedness to create magic for millions. Maybe that's the reason the King lives on so persuasively—for in true freedom there are no boundaries, even those of mortality.

Or maybe he was just a great singer.

The Least You Need to Know

➤ Elvis Presley was the first singer to reach a mass audience performing a new musical form called rock and roll.

➤ By embodying rock—a musical and social revolution—Elvis was perceived as a threat to mainstream America, and became by far the most controversial entertainer of his time.

➤ Elvis Presley in death has become an enduring American cultural obsession.

Elvis 101:
First Fun Lessons

Okay, so your college's course on Elvis was full, or your undergraduate institution didn't *offer* a course on Elvis—imagine that! Or maybe you didn't even go to college (it's too expensive now anyway). What then? How to attack the huge body of material?

Now that you have an understanding, from Chapter 1, of the musical and cultural phenomenon that was Elvis Presley, it's helpful if you get a framework of basic events in which to fit the information. This chapter will do that for you.

Just keep in mind that much of Elvis—his music and movies, and much of the hoopla surrounding him since his death—is meant to be fun. I'm drawn to Elvis because he made us feel happy. So enjoy!

So How Much Do You Know About Elvis?

Before I go any further, let's see how much you know. Take this short quiz on *Elvisology* to improve your confidence—or rattle you enough to hit this book hard! Relax. A scholarship doesn't depend on your results. Nor are you on *Jeopardy* with millions watching.

The Word
Elvisology is the official Graceland term for historical and statistical information on the life and career of Elvis.

1. Who's the King of Rock and Roll?

2. What instrument did Elvis play?

3. Where is Graceland?

4. Who was Colonel Tom Parker?

5. Who's the most famous dog in rock and roll history?

6. Who was Elvis' only wife?

7. Who is Elvis' only child?

8. What was the name of the studio where Elvis made his first recording?

9. Who are the Memphis Mafia?

10. Why was Elvis referred to as "Elvis the Pelvis"?

11. In what movie did the jailbirds rock?

12. What's the most famous hotel in rock and roll history?

Answers:

1. Elvis Presley (now how can you miss *that* one?)

2. Guitar (and piano, by the way, but rarely on stage)

Going for Gold
Many colleges, especially in the American Southeast (like the Universities of Mississippi and Tennessee) offer courses on Elvis—both in musicology and sociology. About 300 such courses are now offered worldwide. If you're going to (or back to) college, why not take a course on American royalty?

3. Memphis, Tennessee

4. Elvis' manager

5. "Hound Dog" (the hit song)

6. Priscilla Beaulieu Presley

7. Lisa Marie

8. Sun Studios

9. Elvis' inner circle of friends, bodyguards, and hangers-on

10. Because of his gyrations on stage

11. *Jailhouse Rock*

12. "Heartbreak Hotel" (sorry, not "Hotel California")

So do you know more than you think you did? It's amazing what you pick up from osmosis. Maybe you should ask your teacher for extra credit.

Don't Know Much about History

Here's an overview of Elvis' life and career:

Elvis Presley was a singer, guitarist, and actor. As a rock and roll idol from the '50s through the '70s, he influenced both music and mores for an entire generation. In the words of the historical marker that stands outside the house where he was born: "Presley's career as a singer and entertainer redefined popular music."

Born in humble circumstances in Tupelo, Mississippi, in 1935 to blue-collar parents, Elvis was the survivor of identical twins. When Elvis was 13, Vernon and Gladys Presley moved the family to Memphis, Tennessee, where he was exposed to a variety of musical styles, including rhythm and blues and jazz. He worked as an usher at a movie theater, a truck driver, and a warehouseman before beginning his show-business career, arguably the most remarkable in modern history.

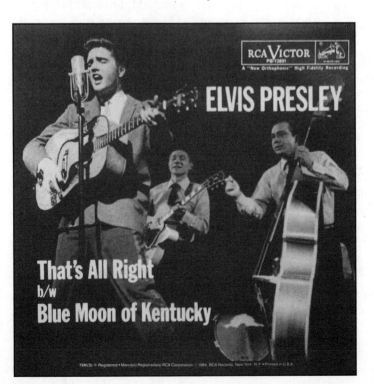

Elvis' very first single from 1954: "That's All Right"/ "Blue Moon of Kentucky." Scotty Moore (l) and Bill Black (r) in the background.

Elvis recorded several singles for Sam Phillips, owner of Memphis' Sun Studio, and first toured locally as the "Hillbilly Cat," singing in a style associated with black musicians like B.B. King. Signed by RCA in 1955, he became an overnight sensation on radio and in concert halls, singing both up-tempo rock songs and haunting ballads. His performance style featured a commanding voice and a charismatic stage presence—sneers, twitches, pelvic gyrations—leading to mass hysteria among teenage audiences and threatening parents and religious leaders.

The King and I

"It's hard to explain rock and roll music. If you feel it, you can't help but move to it. That's what happens to me, I can't help it."

—Elvis

In 1956, Elvis, already a millionaire at 21, began his film career. His 33 movies (the last in 1972), vehicles for his singing and personality, were box-office, if not critical, successes.

Elvis married Priscilla Beaulieu in 1967. The couple had a daughter, Lisa Marie, in 1968, and were divorced in 1973. With the advent of The Beatles and other artists of the so-called British Invasion in the 1960s, Elvis' popularity declined and he cut back dramatically on personal appearances, concentrating on his films. Elvis made a stunning comeback as a rocker with an electrifying TV special, simply titled "Elvis" and broadcast on December 3, 1968. In the early '70s, Elvis resumed touring and achieved great success, especially in Las Vegas. A new generation of fans were won over with a new series of hit records. During his lifetime, he sold some 600 million singles and albums.

Return to Sender

Do you think Elvis was an alcoholic? Because of the later Elvis' stout, bloated appearance, many people assume that he abused alcohol. Nothing could be further from the truth. Elvis, adhering to his God-fearing roots, rarely took a drink of anything alcoholic.

In Elvis' final years, he struggled with a weight problem from a steady diet of junk food. After his death of a heart attack at age 42 in 1977, it was revealed that he had been dependent on stimulants and depressants, many of them prescribed.

Elvis' popularity endured, however, and a culture has arisen surrounding reported sightings and impersonators. His primary home in Memphis, Graceland, has become a shrine to fans, visited by millions.

For the Record

Elvis' estate earned more money in the year after his death than any while he was alive. RCA sold an astonishing 200 million Elvis records during the year after his death—and in the first *three* years after his death, he earned more money than he did in his entire *career*.

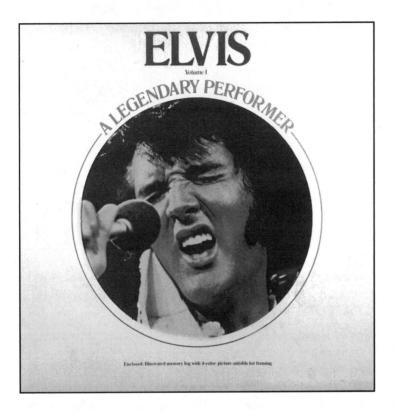

The album cover for Elvis: A Legendary Performer Volume 1. *Elvis in 1976, still singing his heart out.*

Those are the bare bones of Elvis' life and career. It's a starting place, but it doesn't begin to get to the heart of the matter. Read on.

Elvis 101: Highlights of His Life and Career

The human brain can only hold so many dates. No one expects you to memorize the detailed chronology at the end of the book (see Appendix A). But you should know the following dates off the top of your head if you really want to be considered an Elvis authority. This isn't just to impress your friends. This is to be centered, focused, well-rounded. Ready to put your brain cells to work? Here goes…

Royalty Is Born

Elvis' birth in a "shotgun" house in Tupelo, Mississippi has been written about extensively. Think of Abe Lincoln in the log cabin in Kentucky. Think dirt-poor poverty.

January 8, 1935 Elvis Aron Presley is born to Gladys and Vernon Presley of Tupelo. His twin brother, Jesse Garon, is stillborn shortly before and buried in a shoe box in an unmarked grave.

January 8, 1946 Eleven-year-old Elvis, who wants a .22-caliber rifle for his birthday, is given a six-string guitar instead.

September 12, 1948 Vernon Presley, jobless and perhaps one step ahead of the law for moonshining, moves the family to a tiny apartment in Memphis, Tennessee.

A Man of Many Influences

Elvis' early musical influences were eclectic for the time and included country and western, gospel he heard in both black and white Southern churches, and blues and jazz on Memphis' famed Beale Street. The center of the nation's black music, Beale Street hosted all the era's great blues stars, people like Muddy Waters, Roy Brown, Big Bill Broonzy, Big Boy Crudup, Lonnie Johnson, Rufus Thomas, and Johnny Ace. B.B. King, for one, was a regular performer and, in fact, his initials derive from the nickname, "Beale Street Blues Boy."

July 18, 1953 Eighteen-year-old Elvis goes to the Memphis Recording Service and cuts a four-dollar acetate record. Accompanying himself on guitar, he covers two songs by the Ink Spots, "My Happiness" and "That's When Your Heartaches Begin."

July 5, 1954 Elvis joins with guitarist Scotty Moore and bass player Bill Black at Sun Studios to record several songs, his first commercial recording session. Elvis is nervous and the session goes poorly. During a break, Elvis picks up his guitar and riffs on a blues tune called "That's All Right (Mama)," by Arthur Crudup. Scotty and Bill join in. Sam Phillips, owner of Sun and the Memphis Recording Service, overhears the jam session and senses he's found gold—literally.

July 7, 1954 Phillips gives a local DJ, Dewey Phillips, a copy of "That's All Right (Mama)" and the flip side, Bill Monroe's bluegrass song, "Blue Moon of Kentucky," to air on his radio show. Both are performed in a crackling, up-tempo style that becomes the blueprint for rock and roll. Response is so strong that Dewey plays the record at least 14 times.

July 19, 1954 "That's All Right (Mama)" and "Blue Moon of Kentucky" is released by Sun Records (Sun 209), Elvis' first commercial record release.

July 30, 1954 Elvis' first billed concert appearance (he's listed third) is on the Slim Whitman Show at Overton Park Band Shell in Memphis.

Elvis: Deal-Maker and Chart-Topper

Elvis' rise was meteoric. Featuring a cutting-edge look—longish, greasy hair and sideburns—and a powerful, plaintive voice effective for both rock and balladry, he quickly went from being a regional sensation to a national one. His unfettered style generated hysteria and controversy. Newspaper headlines called him "the Prince from Another Planet."

November 20, 1955   Elvis signs a three-year deal with RCA Victor.

January 10, 1956   Elvis records "Heartbreak Hotel" at RCA's Nashville studios. By April, the ballad would be the nation's No. 1 hit, the first of Elvis' 14 Top 100 number-one hits.

Elvis on TV

TV was perfect for a performer with Elvis' photogenic charisma. Displaying a polite, humble personality when off-stage, he began to win over more stubborn audiences. Even some mothers joined their hysterical daughters in Elvis idolatry. Fathers generally needed more time.

January 28, 1956   Elvis (with Bill Black and Scotty Moore) makes his national television debut (he had already appeared on local television) on the Dorsey Brothers' *Stage Show*. Elvis sings "I Got A Woman," "Shake, Rattle and Roll," and "Flip, Flop and Fly."

February 25, 1956   "I Forgot To Remember To Forget" becomes Elvis' first #1 national Country best seller (for two weeks).

March 11, 1956   Colonel Tom Parker, a former carnival and circus promoter, and present manager of a number of country acts, such as Eddie Arnold and Hank Snow, becomes Elvis' official manager for a 25 percent fee. Parker manages Elvis until his death, never representing another artist.

> **The King and I**
> "He can't last. I tell you flatly, he can't last."
> —Jackie Gleason

March 13, 1956   Elvis' first LP, *Elvis Presley*, is released.

Elvis at the Top

In the mid-1950s, no one could match Elvis' string of successful hits or his ability to capture the public's attention, whether on TV or on stage. Almost single-handedly, he sold rock and roll to the American public, followed by a wave of black *and* white performers of the new style.

April 6, 1956   Elvis signs a seven-year deal with Paramount Pictures.

April 11, 1956   "Heartbreak Hotel" becomes Elvis' first million seller.

April 23, 1956   Elvis plays for the first time in Las Vegas at the New Frontier Hotel (with comedian Shecky Green) and bombs. Elvis just couldn't reach the older, middle American audience. (People would have to grow up with Elvis to appreciate him as middle-agers, it seems.) It would be Elvis' last appearance in Vegas for 13 years.

May 11, 1956   Elvis buys his first home at 1034 Audubon Drive in Memphis. It costs $40,000 dollars, which Elvis pays in cash. He lives with Vernon and Gladys.

May 12, 1956   "Heartbreak Hotel" has sold 1,350,000 copies and is moving at the unheard-of rate of 70,000 per week. "Elvis Presley" becomes RCA's best-selling LP ever.

The King and I
"I wouldn't have Elvis Presley on my show at any time."

—Ed Sullivan, 1955

July 13, 1956 RCA releases "Hound Dog"/"Don't Be Cruel," and Ed Sullivan signs Elvis to three appearances for $50,000, making him the highest paid guest star on a variety show in television history.

September 9, 1956 Elvis appears for the first time on *The Ed Sullivan Show*. An estimated 54 million people watch Elvis sing "Hound Dog," "Don't Be Cruel," "Ready Teddy," and "Love Me Tender." Not until The Beatles appeared on Sullivan in 1964 would a larger audience watch a television show.

Elvis in the Movies

With his star rising, Elvis moved on to his fantasy career—in movies. He idolized Marlon Brando and James Dean, and hoped he would be able to convey the same tough-guy cool on the silver screen.

November 15, 1956 *Love Me Tender*, the first of Elvis' 33 movies, premieres.

December 4, 1956 A historic and impromptu recording session at Sun Studios includes Elvis, Jerry Lee Lewis, Carl Perkins, and Johnny Cash. The Million Dollar Quartet—which began with Elvis playing piano and singing "Blueberry Hill"—would be released as a bootleg album in 1980.

Graceland: Home Sweet Home

A King needs a palace, doesn't he?

April 10, 1957 Gladys, Vernon, and Elvis move into Graceland. "All Shook Up" reaches number one on *Billboard*'s Top 100 chart, beginning a run of eight weeks at the top spot, the longest of any Elvis song.

October 17, 1957 The film *Jailhouse Rock* premieres in Memphis.

Elvis in the Army

Kings also have to do battle, or at least be ready to. Elvis was drafted. Many later performers, such as John Lennon, thought he "died" when he joined the Army, meaning that he suddenly stopped being a social threat. There is some truth here: It was hard to consider Elvis a rebel as he followed orders like a good soldier and sported a crew-cut.

March 24, 1958 Elvis is inducted into the United States Army.

August 14, 1958   Gladys Presley dies in Memphis of a heart attack resulting from hepatitis.

March 5, 1960   Sgt. Elvis Presley is discharged from the Army.

Every King Needs a Queen

Elvis loved a lot of women, but he only married once. To most Elvis fans, Priscilla remains the one and only queen—especially since she is mother to Elvis' only child, Lisa Marie.

December 25, 1960   Sixteen-year-old Priscilla Ann Beaulieu, who Elvis met in November of 1958 while stationed in Germany, spends Christmas at Graceland.

October 23, 1961   The *Blue Hawaii* album hits the charts, where it will stay for 79 weeks—20 weeks at #1.

The King and I
"Before Elvis, there was nothing."

—John Lennon

August 27, 1965   The adoring Beatles meet their hero at Elvis' Bel Air (Los Angeles) mansion.

May 1, 1967   Elvis marries Priscilla Beaulieu in Las Vegas.

Princess Lisa Marie

The King and the Queen make a Princess.

February 1, 1968   Lisa Marie Presley, Elvis' only child, is born nine months to the day of her parents' marriage.

December 3, 1968   Elvis appears before a live audience for the first time since 1961 in his own TV special on NBC (the show was actually taped in July).

Vegas Elvis

Elvis reinvents himself onstage in Las Vegas and breathes new life into his musical career. His new persona involves dazzling jumpsuits, a huge stage production, and singing more pop ballads, often with a larger band backing him up.

July 31, 1969   For the first time since 1956, Elvis appears in Las Vegas, at the International Hotel, and is a sensation.

September 20, 1969   Elvis' last number-one hit, "Suspicious Minds," is released.

Elvis' Decline

Elvis had lived in the fast lane too much of his life—it was getting time to pay the piper. There would be impersonators to imitate Elvis, true believers to claim sightings of Elvis, artists to reference him, and a public willing to keep spending money for everything Elvis—from music to memorabilia.

December 21, 1970   Elvis, by now a heavy prescription-drug abuser, visits President Richard Nixon in the White House and receives a U.S. federal narcotics badge, with which he pledges to help fight the battle against drugs.

January 14, 1973   Elvis appears live around the world in a TV special, *Elvis: Aloha from Hawaii*, viewed by an estimated one billion people.

October 9, 1973   Elvis and Priscilla are divorced.

December 31, 1975   In a concert at Pontiac, Michigan, Elvis sets a record for a single performance with $816,000 in gate receipts.

December 12, 1976   Elvis' makes his last Las Vegas appearance, at the Las Vegas Hilton.

August 1, 1977   Elvis' bodyguards, Red and Sonny West, a year after being fired by Vernon Presley, publish a book with Dave Hebler, *Elvis: What Happened?*, which reveals shocking details of Elvis' life and sends him into a deep depression.

Last Rites

Although Elvis passed away before his time, he would endure as a cultural phenomenon.

August 16, 1977   Elvis is found dead in a Graceland bathroom by his girlfriend, Ginger Alden. The official cause of death is listed as cardiac arrhythmia. In fact, Elvis had numerous drugs in his system, including codeine and barbiturates, and likely died of polypharmacy or multiple drug ingestion.

August 18, 1977   Elvis is buried beside his mother in Forest Hill Cemetery, Memphis, Tennessee. (On October 2, 1977, after a bizarre attempted kidnapping of Elvis' body, Elvis and Gladys' bodies are moved and reburied side by side at Graceland.)

Just the Facts...the Essential Ones, That Is

What was the name of Elvis' mother's poodle? Sounds like trivia, doesn't it? However, the answer—"Duke," after John Wayne—sounds more like cultural history, given the rugged individualism and American values John Wayne stands for and the great influence he had over a generation.

In fact, you might make a cultural thesis out of the convergence of Presley and Wayne, something like: "The King and the Duke: American Heroes in an Age of Innocence." Okay, no need to get highfalutin'. You get the point. Studying Elvis is studying Americana. In the case of Elvis, it's really impossible to separate cultural history from trivia, since Elvis' moment in American history symbolizes all our moments.

For example, the fact that Elvis' middle name "Aron" was meant to be "Aaron" but was misspelled by his father says a lot about poverty and education. The fact that Elvis favored books on the spiritual and the occult tells us about his quest for meaning in his life. The fact that his favorite actors were James Dean, Marlon Brando, Tony Curtis, and George C. Scott tells us something about how he got to be the actor he was. The fact that the Elvis commemorative postage stamp is the best-selling commemorative stamp of all time tells us about America's continuing fascination with Elvis.

Elvis' Vital Statistics

> **Born:** January 8, 1935, in Tupelo, Mississippi
> **Died:** August 16, 1977, in Memphis, Tennessee
> **Height:** 6'0"
> **Weight:** 168 (1950s) to 250 (1970s)
> **Eyes:** Blue
> **Hair:** Dishwater blond (dyed black)
> **Neck:** $15^{1}/_{2}$ to 16
> **Waist:** 30 (1950s) to 42 (1970s)
> **Chest:** 39
> **Blood type:** O Positive
> **Shoe size:** 11D

Other informational tidbits, although seemingly trivia, are key facts in music history, such as Elvis' first commercial recording, "That's All Right, (Mama)," and Elvis' first Top 100 single, "Heartbreak Hotel," and his most successful single, "All Shook Up." Similarly, the name of Elvis' first movie, *Love Me Tender*, is cinema history.

For the Record

The Elvis commemorative stamp was released by the U.S. Postal Service in January 1993. A year earlier the public had been surveyed to see which Elvis image they preferred—rockabilly or Vegas (young or old). Young Elvis won and went on to become the best-selling stamp in postal history; 500,000 were printed, twice that of any other commemorative issue.

Ultimately, Elvis became America's looking glass. He is us and we are him. Sometimes the reflected realities are not pleasant. But overall, Elvis Presley reflected much that is good and vibrant in America. His story is prototypically American and the stuff of dreams.

The Least You Need to Know

➤ The amount of information on Elvis—and the demand for that information—is huge and ever-increasing.

➤ Elvis' stardom was immediate: he conquered radio, the charts, live performing, TV, and film by the end of 1956.

➤ When it comes to Elvis, no fact is too trivial for fans.

Chapter 3

Please Don't Stop Loving Me: Appreciating Elvis

In This Chapter

➤ How to listen to Elvis

➤ How to watch Elvis

➤ Entering the debate: Early vs. Late Elvis

Elvis represents moments in time. If you look at him in the context of musical and social history, you can appreciate him for the impact he had at the time—music and society were forever changed by the upstart performer from Mississippi/Tennessee who sang and moved like no one before him. If you choose later moments in his life, you can appreciate him as a Hollywood star or as an extravagant and polished pop performer.

But Elvis also represents something constant, something universal. If you look at his entire career, you can appreciate the body of his entire life-work, and his enduring place in history as a cultural symbol.

This chapter offers some suggestions on listening to and watching Elvis. Don't forget while you're reading this that Elvis doesn't just go to the brain. He reaches other parts of the body. When you've done all the reading you can, put on a CD (or tape or record), turn up the volume, and go with it. Or put in a videocassette of an Elvis movie and sing, dance, or jump along.

The 1962 album cover for 50,000,000 Elvis Fans Can't Be Wrong, Volume 2. When you're listening and watching Elvis, you're never alone.

There Ain't Nothing Like a Song: Listening to Elvis

Elvis' body of musical work is staggering: He recorded 709 songs. He performed countless others live.

He was an interpreter of other people's material, adding his special urgency to them. He is listed as co-writer on a number of songs, but he was not the driving creative force for the material—until it was time to perform.

For the Record

Elvis is listed as co-writer on the following songs: "All Shook Up" (with Otis Blackwell), "Don't Be Cruel" (with Otis Blackwell), "Let Me" (with Vera Matson), "Love Me Tender" (with Vera Matson), "Paralyzed" (with Otis Blackwell), "Poor Boy" (with Vera Matson), "That's Someone You Never Forget" (with Red West), "We're Gonna Move" (with Vera Matson), and "You'll Be Gone" (with Red West and Charlie Hodge).

He is also listed as adapter and/or arranger on the following songs: "Aloha O," "Amazing Grace," "America the Beautiful," "By and By," "Farther Along," "The First Noel," "I Was Born About Ten Thousand Years Ago," "I'll Take You Home Again Kathleen," "I'm Gonna Walk Dem Gold Stairs," "Joshua Fit the Battle," "Milky White Way," "O Come, All Ye Faithful," "Oh Little Town of Bethlehem," "Run On," "Santa Lucia," "So High," "Stand by Me," and "Swing Down, Sweet Chariot" (based on "Swing Low, Sweet Chariot").

Songs evoke memories for all of us. For those of us who grew up with Elvis, we already have strong associations with particular songs. Those of us who are novices perhaps don't have the memories, but we can get them. Go out and buy a CD of Elvis' hit tunes as a good starting place—the *Collector's Gold* set of three CDs, for example—then branch out from there. Your ears will thank you.

For the Record

Elvis' covers of other people's music often left a lasting impression. Bob Dylan, a fan of Elvis, once said, "Elvis recorded a song of mine; that's the recording I treasure most." Dylan was talking about "Don't Think Twice, It's All Right," which Elvis did in 1971. Elvis recorded another Dylan tune, "Tomorrow Is a Long Time," and often sang Dylan songs in concert, including "Blowin' in the Wind," "Mr. Tambourine Man," and "It Ain't Me Babe."

Choosing a favorite song is tough. A top three is a little easier, but still hard. My advice is go for a top 10. Or how about a top 10 Early Elvis, a top 10 Movie Elvis, and a top 10 Late Elvis? There were many great early songs, such as "That's All Right (Mama)," "Mystery Train," "Heartbreak Hotel," "Blue Suede Shoes," "Hound Dog," "Don't Be Cruel," "Love Me Tender," "All Shook Up," "Teddy Bear," "Jailhouse Rock," "Are You Lonesome To-night," "(Marie's the Name) His Latest Flame," and "Return to Sender," to name a few.

And there are great late ones, such as "U.S. Male," "Suspicious Minds," "Kentucky Rain," "Burning Love," and "Hurt."

But I'm being subjective. Find your own. The discography in Appendix D will help you get a sense of Elvis' recording career.

The Needle vs. The Laser

For most of us—all except those diehards who have kept their turntables and record collections—the days of putting a stack of 45s on the record player are long gone. Few of us, even if we've kept our LP collections, bother wiping them off anymore and dealing with that scratchy sound. Fortunately, almost all of Elvis' songs and many of his albums are now available on CD and cassette. Some are re-issues of the old LPs; others are new collections; some even have previously unreleased material. The King has been digitized and he sounds great through top-of-the-line tweeters and woofers.

Going for Gold
To appreciate Elvis' singing prowess, check out how he could sing low (and utterly sincerely) on "Love Me Tender;" how he could reach thrilling high notes on "My Way;" how he could be naughtily playful on "Teddy Bear;" and how he could growl (or is it a purr?) on "All Shook Up."

That said, we mustn't ever forget how wonderful Elvis sounded on those early hi-fi sets that kids had in the '50s and '60s. We mustn't forget how the scratches on the records didn't matter. There was even something fun about a record skipping—about stopping the dancing and walking over to fix it if a good stomp on the floor didn't do the trick.

I cannot emphasize too strongly that whatever format you have or choose, take care of your stuff! Control dust around your collections. Wipe off records and CDs. Put records, tapes, and CDs back into sleeves, jackets, and cases. What you have is a pricey investment. All who neglected to take care of Elvis on vinyl are now kicking themselves since condition is paramount in collectibles (as you'll find out in Part 6).

A Watershed Moment in Music

Elvis' early music doesn't offend or surprise in the 1990s. The mixing of musical styles is now common. But in the 1950s, country, blues, rhythm and blues, gospel, and pop (the crooning variety) had only begun to seek each other out. In any case, the music and image Elvis created became a prototype for everything to follow.

When Elvis started horsing around in Sun Studios on July 5, 1954, and singing the Arthur Crudup blues song "That's All Right (Mama)" with country guitar player Scotty Moore and double bass player Bill Black, a new fusion took place. Elvis attacked the song with breathless intensity and melodic mastery, in a singing style combining all his eclectic influences. Black slapped at his bass strings to get a driving rhythm going, and Moore combined chordal rhythms with single note fills. Producer Sam Phillips added just the right amount of echo. Black and white music came together at that moment—fast blues with a country beat is perhaps the best way to describe it—now termed *rockabilly*. The success of that song and others like it in the months to come tore down musical barriers—a key moment in what would become the larger tradition of *rock and roll*.

That Voice

What is it about Elvis' voice and singing style? First and foremost, he has a good musical ear and hits the right notes with total assurance. Second, he has good lungs and delivers the notes with ease. Third, he has range and can go deep or high. Fourth, he can sing smooth or rough, comfortable in both styles. Fifth, he has attitude and expression in his breathing and phrasing. His singing comes across as uninhibited, passionate, and, perhaps most of all, sincere.

You can hear many influences in Elvis' singing: the sensuality of blues performers, the syncopation of rhythm and blues singers, the passion of gospel singers, the twang of country singers, and the smoothness of crooners. But it's hard to quantify such influences. And Elvis wasn't particularly analytical about it. He listened to music on the radio, in churches, and on street corners. He responded instinctively and created the music he felt. One key ingredient that comes forth is the irrepressible joy of singing and making music. No question, the musical process, like all creative processes, is hard to define. Whatever the causes or the sources, what came forth was all Elvis.

The Word
The phrase **rock and roll**, referring to the hard-driving music that evolved from a combination of styles such as rhythm and blues and jazz, was borrowed by DJ Alan Freed from the 1934 song by the Boswell Sisters called "Rock And Roll," in which it was used as a sexual euphemism. In the 1960s, rock and roll was shortened to **rock**.

The Word
Rockabilly is the fusion of black rhythm and blues and white country music with "rock and roll" and "hillbilly music." It might have been Dewey Phillips, the first DJ to play Elvis, who first used the word. On his Memphis program, he would say: "Man, they're rocking country music. They're rockabillys."

The King and I
"A lot of people ask me where I got my singing style. Well I didn't copy my style from anybody."

—Elvis

Guitar Man

Elvis got his first guitar when he was 11 years old, and his Uncle Vester taught him a few chords. The rest is history. Elvis played rhythm, which is to say he accompanied his songs by strumming chords on an acoustic guitar. He had a strong sense of rhythm, which helped drive other musicians playing with him. He did very little lead work. His sidemen, such as Scotty Moore in the early days and James Burton in the 1970s, played the lead work on his songs.

The King and I
"Elvis was the whole rhythm section on a whole bunch of his first records, the first four at least. Wasn't no drums on there, just him and a bass, with Scotty [Moore] playing lead guitar. Elvis could have been a hell of a musician, I think. But, he just never bothered to learn more chords. He didn't need to, really. He was having a ball—really enjoying it."

—"Cowboy" Jack Clement, Memphis musician

Elvis owned numerous guitars in his lifetime, but gave many of them away (some to audience members during concerts). At the time of his death, he owned 15, now part of the Graceland collection. The oldest one is the 1956 Gibson J200 (now part of the "Sincerely Elvis exhibit"). Elvis used the Gibson in both concerts and movies, and played it in his 1968 TV special "Elvis."

Elvis was not known for his guitar virtuosity, but he was known as a key figure in the history of the instrument; through his image as a guitar-wielding rock and roller, the instrument became inextricably tied to the music. Rockers who followed, notably John Lennon and his British peers, would later admit that Elvis' use of guitar—as both a driving musical force as well as a cool prop—inspired them to play the instrument.

Piano Man Too?

Elvis was actually more proficient on piano than on guitar. He played piano on a number of recordings, including "Trying to Get to You," "My Heart Cried for You," "Write To Me From Naples," "Suppose," "One Night of Sin," "As Long as I Have You," "Beyond the Reef," "Old Shep," "He's Only a Prayer Away," "Lawdy Miss Clawdy," "Wear My Ring Around Your Neck," "I'll Hold You in My Heart," "One-Sided Love Affair," and "Unchained Melody." As part of his later stage shows, he regularly played piano on "Unchained Melody."

For the most part, however, Elvis reserved his piano work for friends and fellow musicians; for example, at Graceland Elvis once played piano (and sang) with James Brown, the "Godfather of Soul," on "Old Blind Barnabas," a traditional gospel song. Other songs Elvis was known to play on piano were "You'll Never Walk Alone," "Blue Eyes Crying in the Rain," and "Danny Boy." He even played two classic pieces, Beethoven's "Moonlight Sonata" and Debussy's "Clair de Lune."

Don't Forget the Sidemen

When listening to Elvis, keep in mind that he was collaborating with other talented musicians. His original sidemen, Scotty Moore on lead guitar and Bill Black on stand-up bass, are legendary for their contributions to Elvis' sound (as is producer Sam Phillips). Moore and Black parted company with Elvis in September of 1957, because of a financial dispute—they weren't making any royalties off his songs, and were still getting paid a flat weekly salary—but Moore returned after two years, doing studio sessions with Elvis, performing in his movies, and playing with him on his "Comeback Special" in 1968. The well-known country and rock guitar player James Burton toured with Elvis' TCB ("Takin' Care of Business") band from 1969 to 1977. Nashville session bass player Bob Moore played on 28 of Elvis' recordings from 1958 to 1966.

The uncredited drummer on a number of Elvis' Sun recordings was Johnny Bernero. D.J. Fontana was Elvis' regular drummer from 1955 to 1969, influencing generations of rock drummers with his powerful, precise backbeat—and that immortal snare roll at the end of every verse of "Hound Dog." Session piano player Floyd Cramer backed Elvis on his Nashville recording sessions from January 1956 to January 1968.

The Jordanaires, sometimes called "The Sound Behind the King," started their association with Elvis on "Hound Dog," "Don't Be Cruel," and "Anyway You Want Me" in July 1956. The members were Gordon Stoker (first tenor), Neal Matthews (second tenor), Hoyt Hawkins (baritone), and Hugh Jarrett (bass). In June 1958, Ray Walker replaced Hugh Jarrett.

The King and I
"It was Scotty Moore's guitar riff [in "I Want You, I Need You, I Love You"] when he was doing *The Steve Allen Show* that got me into rock music."

—Elton John

Other back-up groups to sing with Elvis were:

> The Amigos
> The Anita Kerr Singers
> The Blossoms
> The Carole Lombard Trio/Quartet
> The Imperials
> J.D. Sumner and the Stamps Quartet
> The Jubilee Four
> The Ken Darby Trio
> Lea Jane Berineti Singers
> The Mello Men
> The Nashville Edition
> The Surfers
> The Sweet Inspirations
> Voice

Devil in Disguise: Watching Elvis

To some, Elvis really was the "devil in disguise" (the name of one of his songs), since his dance moves and singing style were sexually explicit for the time. Elvis' choice of clothing and hairstyle also contributed to his perceived sexual "danger." Like James Dean and Marlon Brando, he looked like a hood—and that meant all young daughters were in peril. We now can watch him away from the original context and enjoy the raw talent and attitude behind his act. But, when looking at photographs and watching him on tape, consider him both ways—Elvis as the performer and Elvis as the dangerous groundbreaker and trend-setter.

The King and I
"I jump around because it is the way I feel. In fact, I can't even sing with a beat at all if I stand still."

—Elvis

The King and I
"His performance was the most disgusting exhibition I have ever seen…. He is the male counterpart of a hoochie-coochie dancer in a burlesque show."

—Male newspaper reporter

All Shook Up: Elvis the Dancer

Some called it dancing; others, pelvic gyrations—and worse. Whatever you call it, it was pure Elvis. His body movements were original—no one had seen anything like it before Elvis came along. You can't shake or move like that today without being considered a copycat or parody.

How to put it in words? With a sneer on his face—just this side of a snarl—and his nostrils flaring, Elvis would twitch his head. His legs would be spread wide with his knees pointing inward. The right foot would begin tapping. The legs would twist and a knee would snap. He'd rise to the balls of his feet and raise an arm. He'd wiggle, grind, bump his hips—hence, Elvis the Pelvis. In fact, his whole quivering body would jerk spasmodically from time to time. He'd also swing the guitar wildly. When he put down the guitar, his dancing was more focused, but it still verged on being out of control, as if the whole thing could come unglued at any time. At times it did and he would lie on the stage, writhing. He pushed the physical envelope.

That Smile: Kid Cool

I've mentioned the sneer. When his face was in repose, Elvis had a sulky look that bordered on surly. Part of it was the famous natural curl of his lips. The smile was incandescent and brilliant. Has there ever been a better one? But the smile also revealed awareness—as if he were saying, "I'm putting on a show here, and we both know it."

The Best-Looking Man Ever

Elvis had a fabulous look, no question. Some say he was the best-looking man ever. (It's also been said that Bill Clinton got elected president because he looks and talks just a little like Elvis.) Part of Elvis' great appeal were those dreamy "bedroom" blue eyes. Another part was his full and curling lips. And let us not forget his thick hair, done up oh-so '50s cool (pomade—a thick hair gel—and all) with sideburns. He didn't have to bother dyeing it black (or blond as he did for some movies). The natural sand-color was all anybody could wish for, but let's admire him for always going for something extra.

Elvis Fashion: Hillbilly Cat vs. Vegas Stud

Early on, Elvis showed a taste for stylish, even way-out clothes. Starting in 1952 while he was still in high school, he often shopped at Lansky Brothers, a store on Beale Street in Memphis favored by black entertainers and known for its brightly colored and loose-fitting suits.

At Humes High, Elvis stood out, with his longish hair and flashy clothes. (In fact, future Memphis Mafian Red West cemented his friendship with young Elvis when he defended the fledgling "zoot-suiter" from students who thought he deserved a beating.) As a performer, Elvis started out in baggy suits and long hair greased with pomade (later, when Elvis went to Hollywood, he would dye his hair jet black). At the time, his peers mostly had crew cuts. Over the years his suits began to fit a little better and were color-coordinated. Compared to everyone else, especially everyone white, Elvis Presley was a wild hepcat.

It is said that Elvis copied Tony Curtis' hairstyle, Rudolph Valentino's sideburns, and Roy Orbison's dyed hair. Whatever the influences, Elvis as a whole was an original. By the way, when you watch tapes or look at photos, notice how Elvis' hair messed up so perfectly. How did he do that?

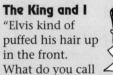

The King and I
"Elvis kind of puffed his hair up in the front. What do you call it? Pompadour. And he always wore unusual clothing. He had good taste, but his clothing was unusual. Just like the day he came to school wearing pink trousers."

—Bill Perry, a boyhood friend

On his TV special on December 3, 1968, his first appearance before a live audience since 1961, Elvis wore black leather, a throwback to the 1950s tough look. But, with his next concerts, beginning in July 1969 in Las Vegas, Elvis reinvented himself. From then on, he favored lavish costumes—flared-leg jumpsuits by designer Bill Belew—a look that was more Liberace than James Dean. He experimented with other lavish costumes, such as two-piece and sleeveless outfits—but the jumpsuits worked best for him. He felt he looked taller in them, and he had the mobility he wanted without having to worry about a shirttail coming out. With the jumpsuits, which were studded and embroidered, he wore elaborate belts, flowing scarves, and even frilly capes.

Some of the names of jumpsuit designs included American Eagle, Black Eagle, Blue Aztec, Blue Braid, Blue Prehistoric Bird, Blue Swirl, Burning Love, Flame, Gypsy, Indian, Inca Gold Leaf, King of Spades, Mad Tiger, Mexican Sundial, Nail Studded Suit, Peacock, Red Eagle, Red Lion, Sundial, Tiffany, White Eagle, and White Prehistoric Bird.

Probably the most famous costume in entertainment history is the gold-lamé tuxedo Elvis wears on the cover of *50,000,000 Fans Can't Be Wrong—Elvis' Gold Records, Volume 2*, released in 1959. The suit, designed in 1957 by Nudie's of Hollywood, can be seen at Graceland.

For some fans, the Elvis look that appealed to them most was the military look. Elvis looked great in a uniform, and no other American soldier in history was as sought out for photos.

Let's not forget Hollywood Elvis. In his films, you can see him in an array of costumes—Hawaiian shirts, black leather, blue denim, grey flannel, bathing suits, and a variety of athletic wear appropriate to boxing, karate, car racing, and boat racing.

Elvis on Film (Rent the Videotapes Now!)

The easiest way to see Elvis is to go out and rent a videotape. If you want to see Elvis' best work, start with the early movies. Later, the movies generally became shameless star vehicles with less attention paid to plot and production values. (A critic once observed that Elvis moved through these later movies with an "amiable disregard" for their shortcomings.)

When watching Elvis' movies, observe the King on a number of levels. Watch him as a talented performer and musician who brings his stage-developed grace, energy, and charisma to bear. But also watch him, especially in his early films, as an untrained actor struggling to find himself in dramatic roles. And watch him just to see him sing songs and perform.

As for the movies themselves, none are recognized as film classics. Some were valiant attempts, and others are charmingly campy, representing a bygone era in movie history. Whatever you make of them, keep in mind that at the time they were among the most commercially successful series of musicals ever produced by Hollywood.

My top three Elvis films? *Jailhouse Rock*, *King Creole*, and *Flaming Star*.

For easy reference, here's the complete Elvis Filmography. (Elvis' movie career—and his Hollywood nights—are discussed in greater detail in Chapter 14. Also, TV specials about him, some of which also have been released on videocassette, are discussed in Chapter 22.)

Love Me Tender (1956)   A Southern family in a post-Civil War setting. See it for Elvis' endearing debut as an actor and for the title song. (In black and white.)

Loving You (1957)   The rise of a gas station attendant to stardom as a country-and-western singer. Elvis sings "Teddy Bear" and wears a famous red-satin shirt with white fringe. The singing group The Jordanaires makes an appearance. And his parents appear as extras in a concert audience. This movie shows Elvis' power on the screen.

Jailhouse Rock (1957)   A jailbird becomes a rock star. The title song, Elvis' favorite production number, really rocks—and Elvis choreographed the terrific dance number. The excellent soundtrack features three Lieber & Stoller songs. A drama that really delivers, don't miss it. (See this film in the original black and white, not the colorized version.)

King Creole (1958)   New Orleans nightclub singer gets caught up in the underworld. Strong performance by the King, based on a novel by Harold Robbins.

G.I. Blues (1960)   Guitar-playing G.I. in West Germany. Elvis sings "Blue Suede Shoes." (In black and white.)

Flaming Star (1960)   Elvis plays a mixed-blood convincingly. The story is remarkably politically correct for its time. Only two songs in this one, none after the first 10 minutes. Intelligently directed by Don Siegel, this is another must-see Elvis movie.

Wild in the Country (1961)   Elvis as a wannabe writer. A good cast and a charming story from a Clifford Odets script. Terrific chemistry between Elvis and Hope Lange. Plus a wonderfully Lolita-like allure from the oh-so-ripe Tuesday Weld.

Blue Hawaii (1961)   Ex-G.I. starts new life with a tourist agency. The first truly lavish Elvis vehicle. Elvis sings "Can't Help Falling in Love" and breaks hearts.

Follow That Dream (1962)   Florida homesteaders get caught up in local politics. Elvis uses his martial-arts skills. Elvis sings the title song with his back to the camera, perhaps his comment on this weak star vehicle.

Kid Galahad (1962)   Remake of a 1932 film about a boxer. Elvis looks good in the ring.

Girls! Girls! Girls! (1962)   A young man struggles to keep his father's fishing boat. Again, a Hawaiian setting. Elvis sings "Return to Sender."

It Happened at the World's Fair (1963)   Elvis is a struggling bush pilot who falls in love at the Seattle World's Fair. Elvis has a moving on-camera rapport with child actress Sue-Lin.

Fun in Acapulco (1963)   Elvis is a lifeguard and singer at an Acapulco resort. Elvis acts opposite Ursula Andress.

Kissin' Cousins (1964)   An army lieutenant assigned to relocate a moonshiner family discovers he's related to them. Elvis plays two different characters, cousins who are spitting images of each other.

Viva Las Vegas (1964)   Elvis is a race-car driver in Las Vegas. The King and Vegas go well together, we learn. So do Elvis and Ann-Margret; E sings a duet with A-M, "The Lady Loves Me." Elvis rocks out brilliantly throughout the film.

Roustabout (1964)   A going-nowhere singer joins up with a carnival. Elvis makes a good roustabout. So does Raquel Welch.

Girl Happy (1965)   A singer gets involved with a mobster's daughter on spring break in Ft. Lauderdale. Shelley Fabares, singer of the hit "Johnny Angel," was Elvis' favorite co-star.

Tickle Me (1965)   A rodeo cowboy and singer works at an all-female ranch and health spa. Elvis and the rodeo fit.

Harum Scarum (1965)   A singer is kidnapped and taken to an Arabian palace where he falls in love with the princess. An unusual setting for Elvis.

Frankie and Johnny (1966)   A riverboat singer and gambler must choose between gambling and the girl he loves. Elvis is convincing as a gambler on a lucky streak.

Paradise, Hawaiian Style (1966)   A charter pilot fights to keep his business. Not as much fun as the earlier *Blue Hawaii*.

Spinout (1966)   A race-car driver who loves the single life is forced to choose between three women he loves (one of them played by Shelley Fabares). He marries them all—to other people—and keeps his freedom. Rent at the same time as *Viva Las Vegas* to compare (he plays race car drivers in both). The Las Vegas setting fits the King better, as far as I'm concerned. On the soundtrack album (not in the movie), Elvis does a beautiful version of Bob Dylan's "Tomorrow Is A Long Time."

Easy Come, Easy Go (1967)   Elvis is a frogman diving for treasure. Check out the novelty song, "Yoga Is As Yoga Does."

Double Trouble (1967)   A singer playing Europe is caught between two women—a sophisticate and an ingenue. Elvis sings "Long Legged Girl (with the Short Dress On)" —not a huge hit, but a real winner.

Clambake (1967)   A millionaire's son changes places with a water-ski instructor. Good chemistry between Elvis and Shelley Fabares again, but not much else.

Stay Away, Joe (1968)   A ne'er-do-well Native American becomes a bull rider. Stereotypical portrayal of contemporary Indians.

Speedway (1968)   A race-car driver takes on the IRS. It's ironic that Elvis played opposite Ol' Blue Eyes' daughter Nancy Sinatra. They sing together on "There Ain't Nothing Like a Song." Indeed.

Live a Little, Love a Little (1968)   A photographer juggles two conflicting jobs. At least Elvis isn't a race-car driver in this one.

Charro! (1968)   A cowpoke takes on his former band of outlaws. The closest Elvis came to a totally dramatic role, with only one song, played as the credits roll. A downbeat Western released when Westerns as a genre were not performing at the box office.

> **The King and I**
> "[Rock and roll is] phony and false, sung, written, and played by cretinous goons."
>
> —Frank Sinatra

The Trouble with Girls (and How to Get Into It) (1969)   The manager of a medicine show in the 1920s unmasks a murderer.

Change of Habit (1969)   A doctor working in an urban ghetto falls in love with a nun. An atypical Elvis vehicle, with a young Mary Tyler Moore opposite him. By no means a good movie, Elvis' last feature film does have touching moments when the King works to heal others.

In addition to the above 31 musicals, two documentaries were made while Elvis was alive. Both are rentable on videocassette.

Elvis, That's the Way It Is (1970)   A documentary about Elvis' appearance at the International Hotel in Las Vegas. See the King perform.

Elvis On Tour (1972)   A documentary about a 15-city Elvis tour. Night after night, the King delivers.

Just so you know: The five most-rented Elvis videos are *Viva Las Vegas*, *Blue Hawaii*, *Love Me Tender*, *G.I. Blues*, and *Jailhouse Rock*.

> **Going for Gold**
> Want to get inside Elvis' head? Rent the films that most inspired him as an actor and as a person. He loved James Dean in *Rebel Without a Cause* and memorized all his dialogue, which he would recite to friends. Elvis also idolized Marlon Brando's work in *The Wild One*.

Television Footage of His Royal Highness

The following is a list of Elvis' TV appearances. Little of this material is readily available for viewing (as Elvis would sing, "Release me!"), but some footage has been used in TV specials on the King (as indicated in the subsequent list).

Television Appearances:

Louisiana Hayride—March 5, 1955
Town and Country Jubilee—March 14, 1955
Grand Prize Saturday Night Jamboree—March 19, 1955
The Roy Orbison Show—May 31, 1955
Stage Show—January 28, 1956
Stage Show—February 4, 1956
Stage Show—February 11, 1956
Stage Show—February 18, 1956
Stage Show—March 17, 1956
Stage Show—March 24, 1956
The Milton Berle Show—April 3, 1956
The Milton Berle Show—June 5, 1956
Dance Party—June 20, 1956
The Steve Allen Show—July 1, 1956
Hy Gardner Calling—July 1, 1956
The Ed Sullivan Show—September 9, 1956
The Ed Sullivan Show—October 28, 1956
Holiday Hop—December 31, 1956
The Ed Sullivan Show—January 6, 1957
American Bandstand—January 8, 1959

Television Specials:

"Welcome Home, Elvis" (Frank Sinatra-Timex special on ABC)—May 12, 1960. Elvis fresh from the army.

"Elvis" (NBC special)—December 3, 1968. Sometimes referred to as the "Comeback" TV show. On videocassette.

"Elvis: Aloha from Hawaii" (NBC special)—Broadcast from Hawaii first to the Far East (January 14, 1973), then to Europe (January 15), then to the U.S. (April 4). First such show ever beamed by satellite this way. Elvis sings 29 songs in the 90-minute special. Wow! On videocassette.

"Elvis in Concert" (CBS special)—October 3, 1977. Aired soon after his death. Elvis sings 14 songs. The King is dead, long live The King.

A number of TV specials have been made on the Big E. Some, as indicated, are on video-cassette. If not, call the networks, call your cable service, be proactive. This is important.

"Memories of Elvis"—NBC special, first broadcast in November 1977. Lots of footage from "Elvis" and "Elvis: Aloha from Hawaii" (see previous list). Hosted by Ann-Margret.

"Nashville Remembers Elvis on his Birthday"—NBC special, first broadcast in January 1978 (later shown as "Elvis Remembered: Nashville to Hollywood"). Other singers doing Elvis, with footage of The King doing "Heartbreak Hotel" and "My Way." Hosted by Jimmy Dean.

"Elvis Memories"—Syndicated special, first broadcast in 1981. Mostly interviews and film clips with some footage of Elvis on "Dance Party" (see previous).

"Disciples of Rock"—Syndicated special (Monticello Productions), first broadcast in 1984. Also known as "Mondo Elvis," this documentary is about Elvis fans.

"Elvis: One Night With You"—HBO special, first broadcast in January 1985. An uncut, live jam session, parts of which were used in "Elvis," the NBC special (see previous). On videocassette.

"Elvis Presley's Graceland"—Showtime special, first broadcast in January 1985. A tour of Graceland, hosted by Priscilla Presley (similar to Jacqueline Kennedy's tour of the White House). On videocassette.

"Elvis: The Echo Will Never Die"—Syndicated special, first broadcast in August 1985. Interviews with Elvis' friends and fellow performers. Hosted by Kasey Kasem. On videocassette.

"Elvis '56"—Cinemax special, first broadcast in August 1987. Vintage clips, home movies, and photographs about 1956, narrated by the drummer of The Band, Levon Helm. Includes recording-session tapes of "Hound Dog" and "Don't Be Cruel." On videocassette.

More Tube Time

The following are other video releases where you can get an audience with the King.

TV Guide *Presents Elvis Presley* (1956)—An interview with Elvis from an August 6, 1956, concert at Lakewood, Florida. Hard to find.

This Is Elvis (1986)—Footage of various concerts, films, and interviews, with reenactments and a pseudo-Elvis narration. (144 minutes)

Young Elvis (1989)—Some early performances, in particular *Stage Show* and *The Milton Berle Show*. (75 minutes)

Elvis (1990)—Newsreel footage and early performances, as well as photos. (45 minutes)

Elvis, the Great Performances: Center Stage (Vol. 1) (52 minutes) and *Elvis, the Great Performances: The Man and His Music* (Vol. 2) (1990) (52 minutes)— Performances and home movies.

Elvis (1991)—Early performances and Hollywood coverage. (3 cassettes, 30 minutes each)

Elvis Lives (1991)—Early TV appearances and movie trailers. (90 minutes)

Elvis and the Colonel: The Untold Story (1993)—NBC TV fictionalized movie.

Elvis, the Lost Performances (Date unavailable)—Early performances.

Early vs. Late Elvis: A Debate

Cats vs. dogs. Yankees vs. Dodgers. Democrat vs. Republican. Come on, these are personal things. Very subjective. There's no definitive answer. Same with Early vs. Late Elvis, Memphis vs. Vegas. It's not the answer to the debate that counts, but the debate itself, and—you as a blossoming Elvis expert—should enter it.

Here are some of the debating points on each side:

Early Elvis: Raw, authentic, sexual, utterly original, cocky, fearless, dangerous, threatening, revolutionary, electric, scandalous. A white man "singing black." A sex object. Lock up your daughters, hide your wife. A prince.

Late Elvis: Polished, sensual, commanding, gaudy, glitzy, larger-than-life, mainstream. Hedonist extraordinaire. A lover. A pop singer. A Vegas entertainer. Rock's answer to Sinatra. Smooth. Powerful. Martial artist. An icon. A living legend. The greatest. The King.

For the Record

Elvis imitators can be divided into two categories: look-alikes and sound-alikes. As for sound-alikes, Early Elvises outnumber Late Elvises. As for look-alikes, Late Elvises outnumber Early. Of course, sometimes the twain meet and we get the whole package. Elvis, it is said, enjoyed his imitators (when they were good). What would he make of the fact that there are now thousands of them, many of them making a pretty decent paycheck for their efforts?

Take your pick. Take a stand. Listen to the early stuff, like "That's All Right (Mama)." Then listen to the late material, like "My Way." Look at the early photos and study those sensual and athletic moves. Check out the late photos to see the consummate, polished pro. Then make your decision. In 1992, the American public voted overwhelmingly for

Early Elvis in balloting held by the U.S. Postal Service. But you can make up your own mind. And, remember, you can always change it.

The Least You Need to Know

➤ Elvis' genius was in his singing and performing; he composed very little and was neither a brilliant guitarist nor pianist.

➤ Elvis' looks and style were controversial and cutting-edge.

➤ Elvis' musicals were certainly not great films, but they contain several excellent performances and were immensely popular and profitable.

➤ Elvis had two distinct periods: Early Elvis was raw and powerful; Late Elvis was polished and dramatic.

Part 2
Where Did Mr. Sideburns Come From?

One of the most fascinating aspects about Elvis Presley is his uniqueness. When he hit, we'd never seen anyone like him. He copied no one. In fact, in one of his first conversations with Sam Phillips, his first producer, Elvis said, "I don't sound like nobody." For a shy, supposedly unsophisticated country boy, that shows a lot of chutzpah.

In Part 2, I will discuss how and why this unprivileged boy became one of the greatest entertainers of all time. What was it like in America, specifically the American South, when Elvis was growing up? Where did his singular sound come from? Would rock and roll have emerged without Elvis Presley? (Which is another way of asking, would there have been another Elvis if the real one had not existed?)

In Part 2, I want to take you back to the future. Elvis Presley—in all his magnificent glamour and magnetism—created *the future* we live in today. Elvis was free… and he showed everyone else how much fun and how much power there was in that freedom.

Wild in the Country: Elvis' Place and Time

In This Chapter

➤ The setting for Elvis' youth

➤ The conditions of Tupelo during Elvis' youth

➤ Current events during Elvis' youth

Born and bred in the Deep South, Elvis was part of that culture, and although his remark-able career took him far and wide, he was always a Southern Man with Southern values—belief in hard work, family, loyalty, religion, and patriotism.

But the age Elvis was born into was the most challenging of the 20th century—poverty, warfare, and the threat of atomic destruction. These national and global concerns, combined with the post-war population boom and developments in media and commu-nications, led to a decreased emphasis on regional differences and the rise of a *shared* American culture. Because of all these factors, and his own electric talent, Elvis was in many ways the first truly national phenomenon.

This chapter will give you a sense of Elvis' Southern background and the events that occurred during his formative years.

The album cover for the 1971 album Elvis Country. Elvis is seen here as a three-year old.

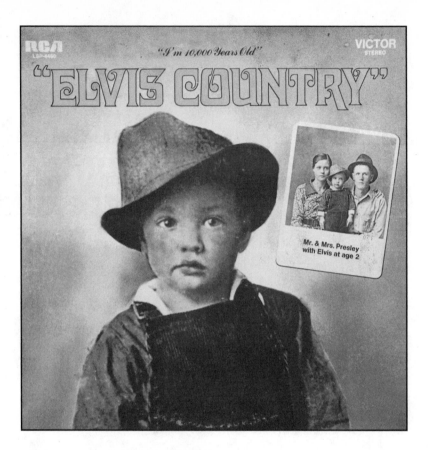

Geography Lesson: Southern Man

The Deep South Elvis knew best was the western part near the Mississippi River. Elvis and Memphis are forever associated with each other. But let's not forget Tupelo, located in the rolling hills of northeastern Mississippi, where Elvis spent the first 13 years of his life.

When the sun shines, it dries up the creekbeds. When the rains come, they come hard and the creeks winding through the hills flood, creating swamplands. Tornadoes wreak havoc upon the land. This was a land of cotton fields and sugar cane plantations. And poverty. Elvis' parents, Vernon Presley and Gladys Love Smith, grew up in sharecropping families, working fields of peas and corn, as well as cotton. Their ancestors originally settled in the Carolinas, then moved westward.

For the Record

Almost exactly one year after the birth of Elvis Aron Presley, a tornado touched down in Tupelo, Mississippi. It only took 32 seconds, but that half-minute was deadly: Hundreds of homes were destroyed, hundreds of people were killed, and thousands were injured. But the Presleys' little shotgun shack in East Tupelo was untouched. The family survived.

Tupelo was a typical small Southern town, and the Presleys were a typical small-town family, who magically found their way up from poverty to…well, in their case, to wealth beyond their wildest dreams.

For poor, small-town people, both black and white, the big city represented opportunity, and the nearest big city was Memphis, 70 miles to the northwest in Tennessee, situated on the Mississippi River. The Old South was still in transition, behind the rest of the country in the change from a rural economy to an industrial, mechanized economy. Comparatively, by the 1940s, multi-racial Memphis (40 percent black) was well on the way to being the New South. Wages for unskilled laborers—Vernon described himself as a "laborer" on Elvis' birth certificate—were four times what one could find in Tupelo, but still below the poverty line at approximately $2,500 a year.

He's a Holy Roller

The glue in Southern communities was the church. The Presleys belonged to the First Assembly of God church, a white Pentecostal sect whose beliefs included faith healing.

The Pentecostals might be called a (poor) white version of black gospel churches, encouraging audience participation through musical and verbal expression, including speaking in tongues. Inside church walls, whites found a spontaneous and sensual release that was frowned upon elsewhere.

The King and I
"During the singing the preachers would cut up all over the place, jumping on the piano, moving every which way. I guess I learned something from that."

—Elvis

The Word
Holy rollers were congregations of fundamentalist churches known for the intensity of their religious expression. Among other things, they were known to rock back and forth in their pews. The etymology is perhaps different from the term "rock and roll," but a connection can be made in the emotion and the physical movement found in both.

Elvis sang with his parents in the Assembly of God Church—not in the choir, but from the pews—starting at age two. Elvis also attended "camp meetings" and "religious revivals," special religious gatherings where behavior was even more demonstrative. The flamboyant preachers, dubbed *holy rollers*, jumped around and wiggled and were even known to leap on a piano. The congregation also would act out, believing themselves possessed by God's spirit.

Across the Great (Cultural) Divide

In America, in the decades before, during, and after World War II, there were many cultural divisions that, looking back now, seem to have been taken for granted by society. Think about the pre-Elvis polarization: Northerners and Southerners were polarized economically, and both groups were guilty of cultural stereotyping. People of Elvis' economic and social background were viewed by some as "trash," or the more specific and degrading "white trash." As for race relations, black people as a group faced legal, educational, and economic disadvantages compared to whites. A generation gap existed as well, with parents threatened by their children's behavior, much of it a reaction to the culture's standard of sexual repression.

Return to Sender
Elvis, a rebel? You'd think someone with his stage persona would have been a wild boy. Not so. His mother, having lost his twin brother, barely let him out of her sight. He stood up whenever adults entered the room and addressed them as "sir" or "ma'am."

Elvis bridged these gaps. He was a Southern boy who became popular way beyond his own backyard. He was a poor boy who made it rich. He was a white man who sang black material. And he was a young man who eventually earned the respect of older folks as well because of his immeasurable talent, his polite manners (hammered into him by Gladys who always wanted something better for her son), and his willingness to serve his country.

Elvis Timeline: What Was Going Down as Elvis Sprung Up

Elvis wasn't raised in a vacuum. Big events were happening during his boyhood, teenage years, and early 20s. The Presleys struggled to survive on a local level. National media was not a part of their daily life. In fact, there was no true mass national culture when Elvis was growing up; regions—North and South, East and West—were distinct and largely disconnected. Elvis' generation was the last to be raised in a regionalized America; today the differences between regions are largely insignificant. In Elvis' time they influenced (and branded) you profoundly.

But there were great shared experiences as well. Elvis was born during the Great Depression. He grew up during World War II, the Korean War, and the Cold War. Moreover, race relations were going through a fundamental transitional period during his boyhood, and those changes accelerated dramatically during his adolescence as the Civil Rights movement began to make itself heard.

The following timeline will give you a sense of what was happening in the world as the young Elvis grew up. Call it context. (But don't worry, you won't be tested!)

Elvis' birth year (1935)   When Elvis is born on January 8, 1935, Franklin Delano Roosevelt is President and the Great Depression is raging. Four days before Elvis' birth, FDR, in his State of the Union address, promises that the federal government will provide jobs for 3.5 million people on welfare. In May, Roosevelt creates the Works Progress Administration (WPA) to provide jobs for needy Americans. One of those needy Americans will be Vernon Presley.

The King and I
"He [Elvis] burst on the scene when the world needed a hero, when everybody needed a sunrise. We'd come through a depression. We'd come through a war. Everybody was ready to give vent to their emotions."

—Janelle McComb, family friend

Elvis at four (1939)   On September 1, 1939, German troops storm Poland. Two days later, Britain and France declare war on Germany and World War II is underway. That same year, John Steinbeck's *The Grapes of Wrath*, a novel about desperate American poverty, is published. Also, *Gone With the Wind*, a film about the Old South, is released.

Elvis at six (1941)   On December 7, 1941, the Japanese bomb Pearl Harbor. The next day, the U.S. declares war on Japan and, on December 11, the U.S. declares war on Germany and Italy.

Elvis at eight (1943)   On May 13, 1943, Italy declares war on its former ally, Germany.

Elvis at 10 (1945)   On May 7, 1945, Germany surrenders. (President Roosevelt died the month before and vice-president Harry S. Truman succeeded him.) On August 29, Japan surrenders. In October 1945—the same month Georgia-born Jackie Robinson becomes the first black player to sign with a Major League Baseball team, the Brooklyn Dodgers—Elvis wins second place in the talent show of the Mississippi-Alabama Fair and Dairy Show.

Elvis at 11 (1946)   Elvis gets his first guitar. On March 5, former British Prime Minister Winston Churchill declares that an Iron Curtain has descended across the European Continent. The Cold War between the West and the Soviet Union is underway. In June of that year, RCA Victor introduces the vinyl plastic phonograph record.

Elvis at 12 (1947)   In a climate of fervent anti-Communism, the House Committee on Un-American Activities attempts to ferret out supposed Communists from Hollywood film-making. On November 25, 1947, the American motion picture industry bars the "Hollywood Ten."

Elvis at 13 (1948) On September 12, Elvis moves to Memphis. The same year Harry S. Truman, a Southerner from Missouri, calls for an end to "Jim Crowism," asking Congress to outlaw lynching and to establish a federal commission on Civil Rights. Truman also calls for an end to discrimination in the armed forces.

Elvis at 14 (1949) Chinese Communists capture Peking from the Nationalists. By year's end, the Nationalist government of China will move its capital to Formosa (now Taiwan). That same year, President Truman makes a frightening announcement: The Soviet Union has developed the atomic bomb. School children, including Elvis, regularly participate in air-raid drills. Fear of a new and terrible war is palpable. Movies offer an escape, which young Elvis eagerly embraces. One film he sees over and over is *City Across The River*, starring Tony Curtis, who sports a "ducktail" haircut that Elvis adopts as his own.

Elvis at 15 (1950) The Korean War begins with the U.S. committing troops to defend South Korea from North Korea. Senator Joseph McCarthy of Wisconsin launches his anti-Red crusade, falsely claiming that 205 members of the State Department are members of the Communist Party. President Truman orders that a hydrogen bomb be built, more powerful than the atom bomb. The University of Tennessee in Memphis defies court rulings and rejects five black candidates. Meanwhile, a report states that children spend as many hours a week (27) watching television as they do attending school.

Elvis at 17 (1952) Dwight D. Eisenhower is elected President, with Richard Nixon as his vice-president. The Supreme Court upholds the decision barring segregation on interstate railways. In October of that year, Sony introduces the pocket-size transistor radio.

Elvis at 18 (1953) Elvis graduates from high school. The same year, Korean armistice begins. It is learned that the Soviet Union has the hydrogen bomb.

Going for Gold
To get an idea of what African-Americans had to overcome to achieve equal opportunity and how whites responded, rent the PBS series *Eyes on the Prize*. Elvis played a part in the integration of African-American and white cultures by introducing heretofore "black" music to mass white audiences.

Elvis at 19 (1954) On July 5, Elvis makes his first commercial recording. On May 17, the Supreme Court reaches a momentous decision in *Brown vs. The Board of Education*, outlawing segregation in America's public schools. The Southern states react angrily: "The South will not abide by nor obey this legislative decision by a political court," a senator from Mississippi angrily proclaims.

Elvis at 20 (1955) On March 5, 1955 Elvis makes his television debut on the Louisiana Hayride. The same year, the U.S. gives $216 million in aid to South Vietnam, the early stage of a growing commitment to that country's autonomy from North Vietnam.

Elvis at 21 (1956) A banner year for Elvis—Colonel Tom Parker becomes his manager, he sings on *The Ed Sullivan Show*, and he stars in his first movie (*Love Me Tender*). The same year, the Supreme Court rules that segregation in public transportation is unconstitutional; Southern bus companies can no longer force blacks to sit at the back of the bus.

Elvis at 22 (1957) Elvis purchases Graceland. The same year, Arkansas defies federal law when state militia block black students from entering all-white Little Rock High School; President Eisenhower sends in troops and federalizes the Arkansas National Guard. In Nashville, Tennessee, a bomb rips a school that admitted blacks. That same year, the Soviets launch the first man-made satellite, Sputnik, into orbit around the earth. Thirteen U.S. servicemen and five civilians are injured by a bomb in Saigon, Vietnam—the first casualties in a war that will eventually claim over 58,000 American lives.

Elvis at 23 (1958) Elvis is inducted into the Army. The same year, the U.S. launches its first satellite, Explorer I, into orbit around the earth.

So now you're getting familiar with Elvis' context—his time and place. In the next chapter, we'll take a look at the music getting airplay during his formative years and where it came from.

The Least You Need to Know

➤ Elvis Presley was part of the last generation of quintessentially old-fashioned Southern men—polite, god-fearing, loyal, and family-oriented.

➤ The Deep South of Elvis' youth was a place of hardship and poverty.

➤ Elvis grew up in unsettled times—depression, war, McCarthyism, racial strife, and the threat of atomic and nuclear weapons—which helped create a climate open to dramatic social change.

Chapter 5

The Royal Family Tree

In This Chapter

➤ All about Elvis' ancestors

➤ Elvis' parents spotlighted

➤ Information on Jesse Garon and other family members

Before we try to get a handle on Elvis, the Legend, let's put Elvis, the Man, in context. He was, after all, flesh and blood, born of other flesh and blood and, as was common in poor Southern families, had lots of relatives. Elvis was a country boy, and the old maxim can certainly be applied to him: You can take Elvis out of the country, but you can't take the country out of Elvis.

His family tree has been traced back as far as David Pressley on his father's side and Richard Mansell on his mother's—all the way to the 1700s. Both his parents came from large, desperately poor families; it is not melodramatic to say that growing up, Elvis really had nothing.

Daddy Vernon's Bloodline

David Pressley arrived from Scotland or Ireland (no one's sure which) in New Bern, North Carolina, with his son Andrew in about 1745. Andrew moved about 200 miles inland to Anson County, where he worked as a blacksmith. His son, Andrew Jr. (1754-1855), was a soldier in the Revolutionary War. Andrew Jr. had a son, Dunnan (1780-1850), in Lancaster County, South Carolina.

Return to Sender
The Presley family tree actually leads back to the name Pressley. The latter spelling of the name conveys the proper pronunciation. With the one "s," the name is often mispronounced "Prezley."

Dunnan moved 300 miles to Madison, Tennessee. His son, Dunnan Jr. (1827-1900), was married four times and served as a Confederate soldier in the Civil War, deserting twice. In Itawamba County, Mississippi, he married his second wife, Martha Jane Wesson. One of their two daughters was Rosella Presley (1862-1924)—note the spelling change. She was a sharecropper who had nine or 10 children out of wedlock. One of them was Jessie D. McClowell Presley (1896-1973). Jessie D. and Minnie Mae Hood (1893-1980), Elvis' paternal grandparents, were married in 1913. One of their seven children was Vernon Elvis Presley, father of the King.

Confused? Read it again tomorrow.

Mama Gladys' Bloodline

Richard Mansell was a Revolutionary War soldier. He had a son William Mansell (1795-1842), who, with Morning Dove White (?-1835), a Cherokee Indian, had a son, John Mansell (1828-?)—hence the statement that Elvis had a smidgen of Native American blood is true. John married Elizabeth Gilmore and had two children, Anna Mansell (1854-1935) and White Mansell (1849-?). Anna was an Alabama widow when she married Milege (Obe) Smith (1837-1909), the son of John Smith of Atlanta. They moved to Saltillo, Mississippi, where they had a son, Robert Lee Smith (?-1932). White married Martha Tacket (1852-1887), daughter of Abner Tacket and Nancy J. Burdine. White Mansell and Martha Tacket had a daughter Octavia (Doll) Mansell (1876-1935) in Missouri. First-cousins Robert and Octavia (Elvis' maternal grandparents) got married and had nine children—one of them Gladys Love Smith, mother of the King.

Cottonpicking, Moonshining Man: Vernon Presley

Vernon Elvis Presley was born in Fulton, Mississippi on April 19, 1916 to Jessie McClowell Presley and Minnie Mae Hood Presley. Vernon grew up in the worst part of poor Tupelo, with little guidance from his hard-drinking, ne'er-do-well father, J.D.

Vernon left school early and, with few skills and little ambition, went through a succession of "dead-end" jobs, including cotton picking, truck driving, and carpentry. He and Gladys eloped when he was 17. Like his father, he was a handsome man, who made sure he enjoyed himself, often with all night carousing and drinking.

Though it is too harsh to say that Vernon was lazy, it is certainly fair to say he lacked ambition. A hardscrabble life? Without question. It would not be until his son found fame that Vernon Presley would achieve any sort of financial security. Because of Elvis, Vernon's sunset years would be comfortable (although not without agitation, due to his son's high-intensity life) until his death in 1979.

That's All Right (Mama): Gladys Love Smith

Gladys Love Smith Presley was born into a family of sharecroppers on April 25, 1912 in Pontotoc County, Mississippi, and was raised in Lee County. The daughter of Robert Lee Smith and Doll Mansell Smith, Gladys grew up in the rural poverty that was common to her place and generation.

With the exception of her father, Gladys' family was a hard-drinking, troubled mix. Her brothers had problems too: one was born deaf and mute; it can be said the other was lazy at best. Gladys herself was known to be a cheerful, bright, and pretty girl who, unlike the rest of her clan, seemed to understand that there was more to life than what was being offered in rural Mississippi during the Great Depression. Gladys' inherent joyousness may well have been forever destroyed when her father died suddenly of pneumonia, throwing the Smiths into terrible financial disarray. Forced to work 12-hour shifts at a garment center, the teenage Gladys took responsibility for her ailing mother.

Gladys' personality was a product of her upbringing: life had been hard and with each new turn, she reacted with fearfulness and superstition. There was little capacity for joy demonstrated, even when her son gained a success beyond Gladys' wildest imaginings. In fact, with Elvis' success, and his inevitable separation from her, Gladys began to abuse both pills and alcohol. In cruel irony, given the terrible deprivations she suffered in her own life, Gladys seemed incapable of enjoying her son's success and died prematurely in 1958 at age 46.

And How's About All Them Aunts, Uncles, and Cousins?

On his father's side, Elvis had six aunts and uncles. Vernon, his father, was the firstborn. Second-born Uncle Vester (no, not Fester from *The Addams Family)* helped teach young Elvis how to play guitar. He worked as the head gate guard at Graceland for years and has co-authored books on Elvis. He married Elvis' mother's sister Clettes Smith, becoming Elvis's double uncle. They had a daughter Patsy. Double-first-cousin Patsy worked as one of Elvis' secretaries and married Marvin (Gee Gee) Gambill, Elvis' chauffeur and valet.

Third-born Aunt Nasval (Nashville) Presley became an ordained minister, serving as pastor at the First Assembly of God church in Walls, Mississippi, a church that Elvis helped finance. She married William Earl Pritchett. Fourth-born Aunt Delta Mae (Peggy) Presley married Pat Biggs, one of Elvis' favorite uncles who he helped buy a nightclub. In 1967, after her husband died, she moved to Graceland and worked as a housekeeper. Fifth-born Gladys Earline Presley ("Little Gladys") married a man by the name of Dowling. Little is known about Lorene Presley, the last-born of Elvis' aunts on his father's side.

On his mother's side, Elvis had eight aunts and uncles. The firstborn in that family, Effie Smith, died when one year old. Second-born Aunt Lillian worked as a secretary at Graceland, answering Elvis' fan mail. She had a son Bobby by Charlie Mann. Cousin Bobby became a hairdresser and took a famous photo at Elvis' funeral of Elvis in his coffin, which he sold to the *National Enquirer* for the reported sum of $78,000.

Third-born Aunt Levalle married Edward Smith (unrelated) and had two kids, Junior Smith and Gene Smith. Junior died of a convulsion in his 20s. Cousin Gene worked at Precision Tool with Elvis in the 1950s and went out on double dates with him; he was one of the Memphis Mafia until the late 1960s when he quarreled with Elvis. He some-times slept in Elvis' room at Graceland to keep Elvis from sleepwalking. Fourth-born Aunt Rhetha died in a house fire in Tupelo in 1940 or 1941. She had a son by the name of Harold Lloyd. Sixth-born (after Gladys) Uncle Travis, was sentenced to jail with Vernon for forgery and later worked as a gate guard at Graceland. He had two sons, Bobby Smith and Billy Smith. Billy, Elvis' closest cousin and one of the Memphis Mafia, lived in a trailer behind the main house at Graceland and helped take care of Elvis' wardrobe. Elvis played racquetball with Billy and his wife the day he died.

Seventh-born Uncle Tracy was a deaf-mute. He never married. Eighth-born Aunt Clettes married Vester Presley, the brother of Vernon, making her a double aunt. They had a daughter Patsy (mentioned earlier). Ninth-born Uncle John (Johnny) helped teach Elvis guitar and later worked as a gate guard at Graceland until his death in 1968. He never married.

Dodger: Grandma Minnie Mae

Elvis' maternal grandfather, Robert Lee Smith, died in 1932, and Octavia (Doll) Mansell, his maternal grandmother, died in 1935, so Elvis never knew them. Elvis' paternal grandfather and for a time the mayor of East Tupelo, Jessie D. McClowell Presley, did not get along with Vernon. In fact, Jessie refused to post Vernon's bail when he was arrested for forgery. Moreover, Jessie and Elvis' paternal grandmother, Minnie Mae Hood, were divorced in 1946, after 33 years of marriage, and Jessie remarried a schoolteacher by the name of Vera Pruitt. So, needless to say, Elvis wasn't very close to Jessie growing up. In 1956, after Elvis became successful, he spent some time with his grandfather in Louisville, Kentucky, and bought him a car. In 1971, Jessie went to an Elvis concert in Louisville. Yet they remained strangers.

So only one of Elvis' grandparents was important in his life and that was Minnie Mae. When Elvis was five years old, he threw a baseball during a temper tantrum, which she just managed to dodge. The story goes he nicknamed her "Dodger" at that time. Minnie Mae lodged with Vernon and Gladys in both Tupelo and Memphis and moved into Graceland with them. At Graceland, she was famous for wearing sunglasses around the clock and for using snuff. When Vernon traveled to Germany to be with his son, she went along.

Dodger died on May 8, 1980. Vernon had her buried in Meditation Garden next to her famous grandson.

Going for Gold

In 1958, Elvis' estranged paternal grandfather Jessie D. McClowell Presley—former husband of Minnie Mae and father of Vernon—released a seven-inch record as Grandpa Jessie Presley, trying to cash in on his grandson's fame. It is called *The Roots of Elvis* (Legacy Park 2000) and includes "The Billy Goat Song," "Swinging in the Orchard," and "Who's Kicking My Dog Around." Now there's a collectible for you!

Step-Stuff: Vernon's Second Marriage

Just to give you the complete picture of Elvis' immediate and extended family, I should mention that Vernon remarried not long after the death of Gladys in 1958. In 1959, while he was in West Germany with G.I. Elvis, Vernon met Davada (Dee) Elliot Stanley. Vernon and Dee (both marrying for the second time) were wed in 1960 at her brother's house in Huntsville, Alabama, in a private ceremony that Elvis did not attend. It's not surprising that, given the closeness of his ties to Gladys, the relationship between Elvis and Dee was never a warm one. Furthermore, Elvis thought Vernon was marrying too soon after Gladys' passing.

Dee Stanley had three sons by her first husband, Army Sergeant William Stanley (George S. Patton's former bodyguard)—William Job, Richard Earl, and David Edward (or Billy, Rick, and David) who grew up at or near Graceland and at one time or another were all part of the Memphis Mafia. David Stanley was on duty the day Elvis died. All have written books on Elvis. Dee Stanley Presley and Vernon were divorced in 1977. Vernon outlived his son by nearly two years, dying at age 63 of heart failure on June 26, 1979.

And what about Elvis' wife Priscilla and daughter Lisa Marie? You'll find out about them later (see Chapter 16).

How Great Thou Art, *1967, was one of Elvis' many gospel albums.*

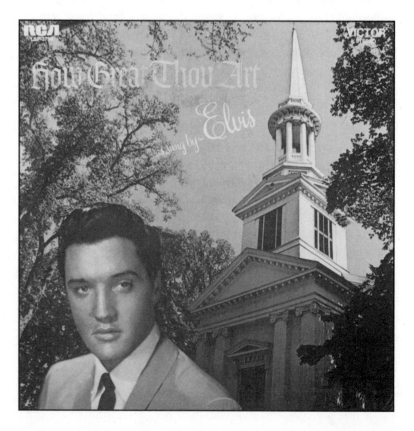

The Least You Need to Know

➤ Elvis' ancestors emigrated from the British Isles in the 1700s, settling first in North Carolina and gradually moving throughout the South.

➤ Both Vernon Presley and Gladys Smith, Elvis' father and mother, came from large, rural, destitute Mississippi families.

➤ Much of Elvis' extended family worked in his employ, usually for modest pay and with modest responsibilities.

Chapter 6

Poor Boy:
Growing Up Elvis

In This Chapter

➤ What was Elvis' boyhood like?

➤ What were Elvis' teen years like?

➤ How his early years shaped him as a man

In this chapter we'll discuss the forces that shaped Elvis in his formative years. In his song "Me and Bobby McGee," Kris Kristofferson could have been describing Elvis when he wrote, "Freedom's just another word for nothing left to lose." We'll see how some of the boldness Elvis exhibited in later years came precisely because he had "nothing to lose."

Boyhood Elvis: Let's go there. It's a rugged, impoverished place. But it's pure and innocent, too. And we get to see all their pieces coming together in the Little Prince who would be King.

Holy Alliance: Vernon and Gladys Get Married

On June 17, 1933, after a courtship of two months, Vernon and Gladys traveled to Pontotoc, 20 miles west of Tupelo, to be married. Gladys was 21, four years older than Vernon. They gave false ages on their marriage license, Vernon claiming to be 22 and Gladys 19.

The Word
The phrase **shotgun house** or **shotgun shack** is applied to the first home Elvis ever knew. But what does it mean? According to some, the term signifies a structure so small that a bullet could enter the front door and exit the back door without hitting a thing.

At first they lived with Vernon's parents on Saltillo Road, but, on discovering that Gladys was expecting, they set about making plans for their own home in East Tupelo, an adjoining town (annexed by Tupelo 13 years after Elvis' birth). By Tupelo's standards, East Tupelo was the other side of the tracks. Vernon and his brother Vester built a 15-by-30 foot, two-room, wood-frame and plank shotgun shack, on legs of concrete and brick, with a porch, three windows, and a pointed roof at 306 Old Saltillo Road.

Ramblin' Clan

The Presleys' poverty resulted in Elvis growing up in 14 homes (eight in Tupelo, six in Memphis) before he would buy his first place (on Audubon Drive in Memphis). Here are the eight residences in Tupelo (dates only supplied when known):

➤ 306 Old Saltillo Road (1935-1940): Shotgun shack built by Vernon and his brother Vester.

➤ Reese Street (1940-41): Vernon, Gladys, and Elvis moved in with Vester, Clettes, and Patsy.

➤ Kelly Street (1942): Rented apartment.

➤ Berry Street (August 8, 1945 to July 18, 1946): Vernon put $200 down on this house, but was forced to give it up when he couldn't make the payments. Grandma Minnie Mae lived here with Gladys, Vernon, and Elvis—and in every other home afterward.

➤ Commerce Street: Four-room house since destroyed to make room for a shopping mall.

➤ 510$^{1}/_{2}$ Maple Street: Located in South Tupelo, this is where Vernon, Gladys, and Elvis lived with Glady's cousin Frank Richards and his family.

➤ Mulberry Alley: Near the railroad tracks and Tupelo dump.

➤ 1010 North Green Street: Near the slaughterhouse.

A Moment in Time: The Birth of Elvis Aron Presley

The story goes that while she was pregnant, Gladys was certain she would have identical twins and that they would be boys. She had already chosen names—Jessie was Vernon's father's name (though Gladys, who didn't get along with Jessie, insisted that her son's name be spelled differently, Jesse) and Elvis was Vernon's middle name. The boys' full names were Jesse Garon and Elvis Aron, the middle names chosen following the Southern custom of rhyming twins' appellations.

The moment of Elvis' birth was full of anguish, yet it was full of joy. Twins were born, one dead and one alive. The living twin would change the world. The dead twin would live through his brother.

At 4:00 a.m. on the cold morning of January 8, 1935, Gladys Presley went into labor at home. Attended by Dr. William Robert Hunt, she gave birth to the first of twins. Tragically, the child was stillborn. Thirty-five minutes later, at 4:35 a.m, the second twin was born healthy.

Dr. Hunt later informed Gladys that she would be unable to bear any more children. The Presleys, Dr. Hunt noted in his record, were unable to pay the $15 fee. (It was eventually paid by the welfare office.) There are reports that Vernon was not present at the birth of his son.

The Word
The name **Elvis** is derived from the Old Norse word *alviss*, meaning "all wise." The name "Aron" or "Aaron" is from the Hebrew *Aaron*, meaning "exalted." Was Elvis an all-wise, exalted man? That works for me.

For the Record

Once and for all, is Elvis' middle name "Aron" or "Aaron"? On the birth certificate filled out by the attending physician, Dr. Hunt, it is "Aaron." On the birth certificate that Vernon filled out, it is "Aron." On Elvis' gravestone is found the spelling "Aaron," Elvis' preferred spelling and the one he formalized legally. In 1980, however, RCA released a record entitled *Elvis Aron Presley*. I prefer the "Aron" spelling because, intended or not, it is what Vernon wrote in his own hand.

Elvis' Mystical Twin Brother: Jesse Garon

The day after Elvis took his first breath, his brother Jesse Garon was buried. Jesse was buried in a makeshift coffin—a cardboard box—in an unmarked grave next to a tree at Priceville Cemetery outside of town.

For one who never knew a day on earth outside the womb, Jesse Garon has exerted a tremendous amount of influence on the living. It's assumed that one reason Gladys was

The King and I
"Many folks believe that when one twin dies, the other grows up with all the qualities of the other. If that did happen to me, then I'm lucky."

—Elvis

Return to Sender
It was assumed for years (a misconception not corrected by the Presleys) that Elvis was the firstborn twin. In 1980, Sara Potter, Dr. Hunt's daughter, discovered her father's notes on the 1,854 births he had attended. Those on the night of January 8, 1935 indicate that Jesse came first and Elvis second.

so protective of Elvis is that she had lost his twin and, in the process of the double birth, also lost the ability to have other children.

Jesse was a presence in the household and Gladys often referred to him in front of little Elvis. (In fact, Gladys kept a miniature casket in the living room as a somewhat macabre memorial.) She also often took Elvis to his brother's grave and taught Elvis that Jesse Garon was an angel with whom he could communicate by prayer. At age five, Elvis reportedly began to hear Jesse Garon's voice. Elvis later asserted he bore the sign of an identical twin on his body: Between the second and third toes of his right foot was extra skin, or webbing.

Toddler to Adolescent

The two dominant social forces in Elvis' formative years were poverty and religion. They influenced his mother Gladys and, through her, played a big part in Elvis' work ethic and his love of music.

As he grew up, his doting mother made certain Elvis had good manners. Gladys taught him to stand when adults entered the room, not to argue with or interrupt adults, and to respond to adults with "yes, sir" and "no, ma'am" when addressed.

What did Gladys and young Elvis do together? Gladys took him to church virtually every day from the time he was one month old. She also took him to camp revival meetings. Starting at age two, Elvis sang with gusto.

Meanwhile, Vernon worked a variety of jobs, struggling to make ends meet, including at various times as a milkman on a farm, truck driver, lumberyard man, and painter. Gladys worked as a sewing-machine operator for the Tupelo Garment Company and later at Reed's Department Store. The Presleys were about as poor as white people could be.

The year Elvis was two, 1937, was a rough one for the Presleys. Gladys' mother, Doll, died in June. Constantly in financial trouble, Vernon was indicted for forgery, along with a friend, Lether Gable, and Gladys' brother, Travis. (There is dispute about the amount of the forgery, some accounts claiming the three changed the $4 check to $14, others to

$40.) Vernon was imprisoned for some 30 months in legendary Parchman Farm State Penitentiary, a penal "farm" (think of the movie *Cool Hand Luke*) that featured chain-gang labor.

With Vernon gone, Elvis spent even more time just with Mama. Imagine how she clung to the child, the crown jewel in her bleak life. Gladys and three-year-old Elvis were evicted from their home for non-payment of their mortgage by Orville Bean, Vernon's boss and mortgage holder, and the man from whom he stole.

Elvis: Musical Prodigy?

Because of his church background, Elvis' first goal was to be in a gospel quartet. Later he learned country tunes from the radio (and memorized many by the age of nine), adding to his gospel repertoire.

Some accounts have Elvis making his first radio appearance when he was nine years old on WELO's "Black and White Jamboree." It was held at the Lee County Courthouse, accompanied by the local country performer Mississippi Slim.

When Elvis was ten years old, a teacher by the name of Mrs. J.C. Grimes asked the class whether anyone knew any prayers or hymns. The once and future king volunteered to sing "Old Shep." Mrs. Grimes asked Elvis to repeat the performance for the principal, Mr. J.D. Cole. Mr. Cole arranged for Elvis to appear in the talent show at the Mississippi/Alabama Fair and Dairy Show. He couldn't reach the microphone, so stood on a chair (or wooden box) and, unaccompanied, sang "Old Shep." Shirley Jones Gallentine won first place and the $25 war bond. Elvis won second prize (some accounts say fifth place)—no small potatoes: five bucks and free rides. We can imagine him on top of the world that night on the Ferris wheel. He was on the airwaves that night, too (for the first time), since local radio station WELO broadcast the talent show. Listen in, world—a star is in the making.

The King and I

"Since I was two years old all I knew was gospel music, and that music became such a part of my life that it was as natural as dancing. A way to escape from problems, and my way of release.... In church, I loved to hear the choir—my mother told me that when I was two years old, I would slide off her lap and stand there singing...."

—Elvis

Adolescent Elvis' Fantasy Life

Elvis had a fantasy world going in these years. He read comic books and adulated Superman, Batman, Captain Marvel, and, most of all, Captain Marvel, Jr. Unlike the sidekicks

The King and I
"When I was a boy I was the hero in comic books and movies. I grew up believing in a dream."

—Elvis

of other Superheroes (like Robin in Batman), Captain Marvel, Jr. was not totally subservient to his master and, in fact, had his own comic books and story lines. Around the age of 12, Elvis discovered Captain Marvel, Jr. and quickly became almost obsessed with him. Captain Marvel, Jr. was able to access his superpowers by invoking his father's name—it is probably not a stretch to theorize that Elvis, with a very weak father, would find appeal in the exact opposite.

On his 11th birthday, January 8, 1946, Elvis, who wanted a .22-caliber rifle (some versions have it a bicycle) for his birthday, was given a six-string guitar instead.

First Train to Memphis

Vernon was released from prison in October of 1940 (the amount of time he actually served is in dispute, ranging from nine to 30 months) and resumed his itinerant career, often living apart from the family, working in Memphis or on a WPA project in Como, Mississippi, 73 miles away. Elvis was seven years old and had to act the man while Vernon was away and accompany his mother to the hospital when she had a miscarriage. Gladys was hysterical and Elvis reportedly bawled his eyes out.

The King and I
"We were broke and we left Tupelo overnight. Dad packed all our belongings in boxes and put them on the top and in the trunk of a 1939 Plymouth…. We were poor, man. Things had to get better."

—Elvis

When Elvis was 10, Vernon became a deacon in the First Assembly of God church, thereby imparting some sense of respectability to the family. Elvis could feel proud about this accomplishment of his daddy's—finally something to feel proud about.

Then, on September 12, 1948, jobless and perhaps one step ahead of the law for moonshining, Vernon suddenly moved the family in their 1939 Plymouth to a tiny apartment in Memphis, Tennessee, where he hoped his luck would change.

More Rambling

Life wasn't easy in Memphis for the Presleys either; their first home, at 572 Poplar Ave., was a rooming house in which the Presleys shared a bathroom with 15 other families. Vernon found regular work hard to find, and by 1949 the family was receiving public assistance.

As in Tupelo, the Presleys lived in numerous Memphis locations. Here's a list of the Presleys' eight Memphis homes, including the two Elvis purchased after his talent changed their lives:

➤ 572 Poplar Avenue (September 12, 1948 to September 20, 1949): About a mile from the Mississippi River, this crowded boarding house held 15 other families.

➤ 185 Winchester Street (Lauderdale Courts), Apt. 328 (September 20, 1949 to January 7, 1953): A two-bedroom, ground-floor apartment in a 433-unit, federally funded housing project—monthly rent $35.

➤ 698 Saffarans Street (January 7, 1953 to April, 1953): Apartment house—rent $52.

➤ 462 Alabama Street (April 1953 to late 1954): Apartment building—rent $50.

➤ 2414 Lamar Avenue (late 1954 to mid-1955): Brick house, now the location of the Tiny Tot Nursery School.

➤ 1414 Getwell Street (mid-1955 to May 11, 1956): Frame house.

➤ 1034 Audubon Drive (May 11, 1956 to March 1957): The first home Elvis bought—price $40,000.

➤ And, finally, Graceland.

Young Elvis in Memphis

The day after arriving in Memphis, Elvis enrolled in the Christine School on Third Street as an eighth grader. This was not an easy time for young Elvis, an outsider in a new school and the object of ridicule because of his bad grammar and "backwoods" clothes. In addition, he was in a city now and school was harder, making it a challenge to pull off his customary Cs. Finally, with hormones raging, his voice started changing and he had to alter his singing, too. It was a difficult time, compounded by the family's worse-than-usual financial situation.

In September, 1949, Elvis entered Humes High School at 649 Manassas Street. Here, too, he was a gawky outsider. It didn't help matters when he failed to make the school glee club because of his unconventional singing style.

Teen Elvis' Fantasy Life

Elvis had graduated from comic books to movies in his fantasy world and drew on them more and more in creating his new self-image. He watched movies in all genres: dramas, romances, musicals, westerns, teen flicks—anything. The local movie houses were a place of escape with themes that seemed so much larger than his own life. Elvis was a boy who desperately needed to dream, and he took his own dreams seriously. The darkened Suzore movie theater showed young Elvis Presley there was so much more to be had from life; and, on his own, Elvis decided to grab for the brass ring.

Youth Gone Wild?

As the leader of a Youth Rebellion, Elvis must've been a wild teen himself, right? A real hellion?

Not really. In many ways Elvis wasn't much different from any other kid; and of course, the manners instilled in him by Gladys made him a quiet and unassuming young man. Still, he was a teenager, and he liked to have fun.

Like millions of other 1950s teens, Elvis was obsessed with automobiles. Cars represented freedom; they were a major part of the youth world sweeping the country (along with rock and roll), signaling to the culture at large that young people were doing their own thing, their own way. Elvis' first real independence from his family came with his first car: a 1942 Lincoln Zephr Coupe. Ironically, though it symbolized his independence, it was given to him by his parents, who bought it for $50.

Every boy's fancy eventually turns to one thing, and as he approached his teens, Elvis began thinking more and more about girls. He was a shy, quiet boy, and making contact with girls wasn't easy. Some of the names we know from Elvis' Tupelo years are Eloise Bedford, Caroline Ballard, and Magdalen Morgan.

As a 15-year-old in Memphis, he went steady with Betty McMahon. Another early girl-friend was Billie Wardlow. Elvis was by all accounts a flirt, showing real interest then suddenly turning his attention elsewhere. Doubtless, one reason for this habit (which lasted all of his life) would have been Gladys' reaction to Elvis having a regular girlfriend. He didn't talk about girls too much with Gladys; rejecting his mother was not a pleasant option for young Elvis to entertain. Still, to further his quest for young love, Elvis eventually asked his mama (politely no doubt) not to walk him all the way to school.

> **The King and I**
>
> "In school Elvis was real quiet. He wasn't one to just have people around him all the time, and he was different as far as his dress went, so some people just thought he was kinda' strange. But he always had two or three close friends."
>
> —Paul Dougher, Elvis' life-long friend

Like many teenage boys, he had a temper and got into some fights, but generally was considered reserved, even thoughtful. (But he definitely knew how to defend himself; young Elvis was not a wimp.) An outsider by nature and circumstance, he was often ridiculed and picked on, but he found a way to make friends—through music.

The second semester of his senior year, Elvis regularly skipped classes and even dropped out of school entirely for a time. But Gladys insisted he return to get his degree, and he graduated on time with his class in June. His grades were average, as was his score on his General Aptitude Test.

My Happiness: Gladys and Elvis

Burdened by years of poverty and heartbreak, Gladys had always found solace in religion and her surviving son, Elvis. (She had a miscarriage in 1942.) Much has been made of the unusual closeness between Elvis and his mother, but one thing is for certain: Gladys provided her son with a vision of a better life, instilling in him the idea that he could, indeed, be "somebody." It is doubtful that she (or her husband) had ever heard similar encouragement.

Gladys insisted her son learn good manners; this would be a hallmark of Elvis' behavior for the rest of his life, opening many doors that would have slammed shut early in his career, when his music and style put off a lot of people. Another interest Gladys brought to her son was music: She was a talented dancer who once pined for a professional career, and she sang and listened to church music all of her life.

There was, however, a problem: Gladys' drinking, which was beginning to become an embarrassment to Elvis. In fact, it is reported that in his late teens, after one of Gladys' drinking bouts, Elvis pledged that he himself would never drink—and for the rest of his life he rarely did.

For the Record

Elvis, like his mother, was a chronic sleepwalker. He was known to leave his mother's bed and walk out the front door. When he was six, she removed the doorknob from the shared bedroom to keep him from hurting himself.

Gladys was the wellspring of Elvis' sense of self-worth, but once the world discovered her son, she lost him. Which, of course, was inevitable; it is the way of the world. She had such a hold on him as a young man that he had to find a way to break away.

When Gladys died young—three years after he exploded nation-wide—Elvis was devastated. He knew his success had somehow not translated into contentment for Gladys. Simply put, he had not made his mother happy. Nor could he ever have. Through the controversial music that made him a star, Elvis was a rebel—against his mama.

Blue-Collar Elvis

In order to supplement the family's income, Elvis began working. In June 1951, Elvis began work at Precision Tools, helping make artillery shells for the U.S. Army at $30 a week, but he was fired after only a month because he had lied about his age.

Return to Sender
Some Memphis tours incorrectly point out the Loew's Palace Theater as the movie theater where Elvis worked, so they'll have an excuse to tell the anecdote about Elvis decking the snitch usher. The theater where Elvis really worked for a month was the Loew's *State* Theater—now long gone.

In April of the next year, he started a job as an usher at Loew's State Theater at 152 South Main Street—lousy pay, but he could see movies for free, and he liked the flashy uniform. This job also lasted only a month because he punched and knocked down a fellow usher who reported that Elvis accepted free candy from a female candy concessionaire.

The following August, he was employed by the Upholsters Specialties on West Georgia Avenue; once again he lied about his age. The next month he began work at Marl Metal Manufacturing Company at 208 Georgia Avenue, helping make dinette tables—the pay was a dollar an hour. He only lasted two months because Gladys made him quit when his teachers reported that he kept falling asleep in class.

Elvis' diploma. He was graduated from L.C. Humes High School on June 3, 1953.

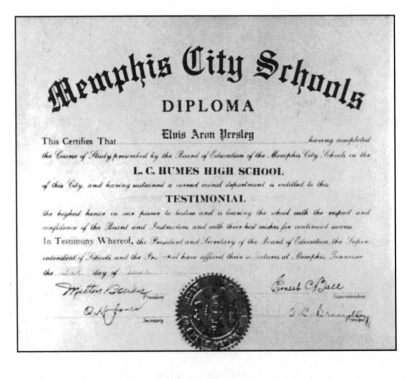

After graduation, Elvis tried Precision Tool again, but landed a full-time job as a truck driver for the Crown Electric Company (until fall of 1954 when his singing career was well underway)—at $1.25 an hour. He drove the company's Ford F-100 pickup truck or a blue panel truck, delivering supplies to the men on the job, or worked in the warehouse. His mama encouraged him to become an electrician, a higher-paying and more-respected job than driving a truck. He also moonlighted at the M.B. Parker Machinist Shop (quitting in September 1953).

Who's That Cat?

And where the hell did he come from? If Elvis was such a shy, polite boy—and a hick from the sticks, at that—where did he come up with the style, attitude, and guts to revolutionize the culture and redefine what *hip* was all about?

Gladys taught Elvis that he was different—he was *special*—giving him a burning self-confidence. The movies gave Elvis heroes to emulate and dreams to aspire to. He needed an *identity*, and he began to create one through his music, his clothing, and his hairstyle.

He was able to see and hear blues firsthand on Memphis' Beale Street, and he emulated black performers' moves, attitude, speech, and clothing. He began shopping where black people did, in particular at Lansky Brothers. They specialized in brightly colored clothing, including zoot suits and pegged trousers. He also wore white suede shoes. While other kids sported crewcuts, he wore his hair like the truck drivers who came through Memphis—long and greased with pomade in a *pompadour* style. In addition to guitar, he also taught himself piano. He learned to sing with his new "adult" voice. He bought his clothes with money from odd-jobs—he even reportedly sold his own blood occasionally.

There was a price to pay for his individuality, however. In 1950, for instance, he was kicked off the football team because he wouldn't cut his hair. He ended up working in the school library instead. He was *different!* In high school, where conformity is everything, being different wasn't all good—and remember, this was the 1950s.

The Word

Elvis began sporting a hairstyle he got from Tony Curtis called a **pompadour**, with the hair—*long* hair, for the time—brushed up and back from the forehead, with some kind of ointment, like pomade, to hold it. Elvis embellished his pompadour with a ducktail in back (also called a "DA" for "duck's ass").

The King and I

"Had pretty long hair for that time and I tell you it got pretty weird. They used to see me comin' down the street and they'd say, 'Hot dang, let's get him, he's a squirrel, he's a squirrel, get him, he just come down outta the trees.'"

—Elvis

I'm Gonna Be Famous Someday

In April 1953, one of Elvis' teachers, Mildred Scrivener, recommended that he perform in a school talent show—the Annual Minstrel. Elvis, surprised to be included, sang "Cold, Cold Icy Fingers." He was asked to do an encore and followed up with "'Till I Waltz With You Again." The students responded favorably, and Elvis later claimed that he was popular for his remaining time at school. Classmates took his stated intention to make it as a country singer seriously, and Elvis earned some respect as a result.

The next month, Elvis hitchhiked to the First Jimmie Rodgers Memorial Talent Show at the Lamar Hotel in Meridian, Mississippi. He sang "I'm Left, You're Right, She's Gone" and "Baby, Let's Play House" in both country and bluesy style. He didn't go over that well with the audience, but he won a guitar for second place.

With his confidence growing, Elvis played high school parties and at local clubs, sometimes for pay, sometimes not. He also participated in all-night gospel sings at the Ellis Auditorium in Memphis. More and more, Elvis was defining himself as a musician; this was his identity, his image to the world, expressed by his ever-present guitar, his wild clothing, and his radical hair style. For the first time in his life, Elvis was beginning to stand out from the crowd; instead of being ashamed of who he was and where he came from, he had the first glimmerings of what it felt like to be "somebody."

That summer—it's not known exactly when—Elvis made his first recording too. That one wouldn't launch his career, but his rocket was being fueled up.

Mythical Elvis

Fact or myth? There are so many conflicting reports when you dig deep into the life of Elvis. For example, how long did his father actually serve in prison? Did Elvis place second or fifth in the talent show when he was 10? Was his first radio performance at age 9 or 10? Did he want a bicycle or a .22 rifle for his 11th birthday when he was given a guitar instead?

Part of the problem is that his parents and relatives were nearly illiterate and few written records exist. Moreover, they were proud and purposely hid details of their background and poverty. (Vernon, for example, never talked about his incarceration). Another contributing factor is that stories get embellished by people seeking to make themselves more important.

Sometimes, the truth finally comes out—for instance, after Elvis' death, notes discovered by Dr. Hunt's daughter tell us that Elvis was the second, not the first twin born. But other times a writer/researcher can only weigh all the evidence and make the best guess. Sometimes the myth reveals at least as much truth as the facts. At the county fair, Elvis received an accolade, giving him motivation. Yet he didn't win, giving him motivation to work even harder. A second-place finish says it better than a fifth-place finish, doesn't it? Does it really matter if he wanted a bicycle or gun for his 11th birthday? The point is he got a guitar and the rest is history.

Rebel with a Cause

So you've learned some of the big events and influences in Elvis' childhood. How do we get to the heart of this man? How to best understand what he was and how it played a part in what he became?

The path he chose as an apparent rebel—long hair, outlandish clothing—gave him an identity, but it also kept him apart from the group. The truth is, Elvis was a good boy with good manners who was just a little rough around the edges. He was only superficially rebellious. He did not challenge society's values, he only wanted a share of the pie. And he wanted it bad.

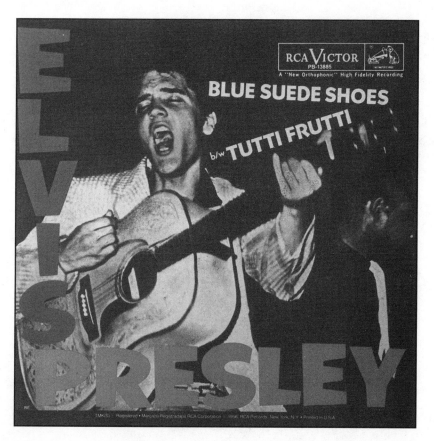

Single for "Blue Suede Shoes"/ "Tutti Frutti." Elvis rocking in 1956.

Elvis compensated for the obscurity and hopelessness around him with wild fashion statements, emulating black people, truck drivers, and movie idols. Elvis, overlooked and underappreciated (emotions common to teenagers, but in Elvis' case quite true: he *was* overlooked), did whatever he could to create an individual identity for himself. And it worked.

Somehow—improbably, given the influences around him—young Elvis Presley discovered something in himself that no one in his family ever had: ambition. And despite his upbringing, despite his deprivations—or perhaps because of them—Elvis took his enormous talent, fused it with his burning desire to succeed, and, against all odds, became somebody.

The Least You Need to Know

➤ Elvis spent his formative years in Tupelo and the rest of his life (primarily) in Memphis.

➤ As a child, Elvis always felt "different;" in his teenage years he went out of his way to emphasize his nonconformity.

➤ While in school, Elvis took many jobs, from usher to truck driver, to help his family stay afloat.

➤ Elvis was a rebel only in his cool appearance and his aggressive attitude when singing rock and roll.

Backbeat and Attitude: A Primer of Rock and Roll

In This Chapter

➤ The musical influences on Elvis

➤ Various musical genres defined

➤ How Elvis defined the rock and roll tradition

How do you measure musical influences on an individual who lived during a time—the age of radio—when so many styles and performers were being broadcast? (With Elvis at least, it was just radio—not MTV, too!) Even if you place Elvis in a cultural group (poor Southern whites who preferred hillbilly and country music), or in a church affiliation (where a white version of gospel music was sung), or in a neighborhood (as a teen, Elvis was known to visit Beale Street in Memphis, a home of the blues), you can't possibly nail down all the music he must have listened to.

Yet in interviews he identified some of his favorite artists. The songs he chose to perform further inform us of his tastes and influences. His extensive record collection also tells us a lot about his musical frame of reference.

This chapter will summarize the various types of music that are known to have played a part in Elvis' musical formation, citing some of the performers working in those styles. You'll also learn how those different styles came together around Elvis in the thing called rock and roll.

The Word
Hillbilly music (or mountain music) is an early American form of **folk music** (music sung by common folks) developed in the Appalachian Mountains in the 19th century, based on 18th-century English and Scottish ballads and African-American work songs.

Hillbilly and Proud of It

The music that has come to be known as *hillbilly music* was nurtured on the western frontier by European descendants, especially in the southern Appalachians, such as the Blue Ridge mountains. White settlers brought their traditional *folk* songs with them, especially Celtic ballads, as well as their instruments, the dulcimer and fiddle. They eventually discovered the banjo and the guitar. They were influenced by black work songs, brought to them by railroad work gangs beginning in the 1850s.

Hillbilly music or "mountain music" was a parent of country music.

Good Ol' Boys: Country Music

Country music, sometimes called country and western, is a fusion of hillbilly music, cowboy music, blues-style singing, and vocal-harmony church music.

The Carter Family, born out of the Appalachian tradition of hillbilly music, were the most important early influence on an entire generation of country singers, setting folk songs to string-band back-up. Their career together lasted from 1926 to 1943, and their greatest contribution was their recordings of the old songs known to everyone in that cultural community; the Carter Family created a recorded tradition that all who followed could take from. They celebrated the insulated, limited experience of small-town, rural Southern life.

The Word
Country music is a style of songwriting and singing popular especially in the South and West and drawing on hillbilly music, cowboy songs, blues-style singing, and the vocal harmonizing common to church music.

Jimmie Rodgers from Mississippi, a contemporary of the Carters, is considered "the Father of Modern Country Music." Rodgers, the first country superstar, left his home in Mississippi—literally hopping a train—and went out and experienced a world the Carters never saw. He combined hillbilly folk tunes with black blues and jazz (he played with Louis Armstrong) to create a new, more raucous country style. The Carters celebrated the status quo; they accepted the world as it was and made the best of it. Rodgers, whose recording career only lasted from 1927 until his death in 1933 at age 36, was an iconoclast who rebelled against the limits on Southern country life that the Carters extolled.

Another early form of country music, *bluegrass*, as played by Kentuckian Bill Monroe—the so-called "Father of Bluegrass"—has a lot of hillbilly in it. Bill Monroe himself played mandolin, but his bands typically also had guitar, banjo, fiddle, and bass, emphasizing speed and more instrumental sophistication. Elvis recorded Monroe's "Blue Moon of Kentucky" and "Little Cabin on the Hill." Monroe's performance and recording career began in the 1930s and lasted until his death in 1996.

Western Swing, out of Texas, with blues, big-band *jazz*, and polka influences—as popularized by Bob Wills and his group, the Texas Playboys—was another branch of country that became popular during that time. Although they popularized drums as part of country music, the Grand Ole Opry banned that instrument from their stage for years to come.

Nashville, Tennessee, became a center for country music, largely because of the Grand Ole Opry, originating on radio station WSM in 1925. There has always been a tension between traditionalists and modernizers in country music. By the late 1930s, the typical bluegrass string-band set-up was giving way to a pop-style, singer/back-up band configuration.

After World War II, the "honky-tonk" style, popularized especially by Hank Williams, who wrote intensely personal songs and sang with emotional directness, became the predominant country approach. Though all the different styles of country music share, to a larger or lesser degree, a common sensibility—a melancholy acceptance of the difficulty of life and the inevitability of death—Williams' view, unlike Jimmie Rodgers', was particularly bleak.

Going for Gold
Want to get inside Elvis' head with regard to musical influences? On your trip to Graceland, be sure to check out his large record collection—both LPs and 45s—many of which are on display in the TV room. You can get a sense of just how eclectic his tastes were—rhythm and blues, gospel, country, pop, jazz, and even classical and opera.

The Word
Bluegrass music is a form of country music popularized by Bill Monroe that combines country, jazz, gospel, and Celtic music, with an emphasis on traditional string instruments, such as guitar, banjo, mandolin, and fiddle.

The Word
Jazz is a form of music with a strong rhythmic understructure and solo and ensemble improvisation around the melody. Native to the United States, jazz has drawn heavily from the blues.

Elvis heard a lot of other different country performers growing up and early in his career who were known to have influenced him. Among them were Roy Acuff, Eddie Arnold, Jim Ed Brown, Ted Daffan, Jimmy Davis, Red Foley, Tennessee Ernie Ford, Johnny Horton, Jim Reeves, Marty Robbins, Hank Snow, Red Sovine, Ernest Tubb, Jimmy Wakely, and Slim Whitman.

An early musical influence on Elvis was a performer in Tupelo by the name of Mississippi Slim (Carvel Lee Ausborn), who broadcast live every Saturday from the local radio station WELO. He recorded country songs such as "Honky Tonk Woman," "I'm Through Crying Over You," and "Tired of Your Eyes." His younger brother James was Elvis' classmate. Some accounts of Elvis' life have Elvis' first radio appearance as being on Mississippi Slim's show on May 15, 1944.

Of all the country influences on Elvis, Jimmie Rodgers' rebellious, blues-oriented music had the most impact on the King's approach.

For the Record

You hear about Elvis on the Louisiana Hayride. What the heck was that? The Louisiana Hayride was a country music radio show broadcast live like the Grand Ole Opry (and sometimes referred to as the "Junior Grand Ole Opry"). Starting in 1948, it was broadcast Saturday nights from Shreveport's Municipal Auditorium on KWKH and carried by 190 CBS radio stations. Elvis first played the Louisiana Hayride in October 1954 and appeared regularly in 1955 and '56.

Inspiration from Above: Gospel Music

The term *gospel music* is thought to have first been used by Georgia blues singer Thomas A. Dorsey in the 1920s, who sang and composed spirituals in a popular style. Early black gospel typically used close harmonies. It evolved into a call and response form—with a soaring and impassioned lead singing over blues-based piano or organ, with shouted responses from the congregation.

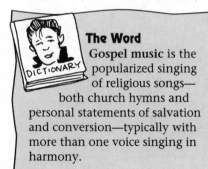

The Word

Gospel music is the popularized singing of religious songs—both church hymns and personal statements of salvation and conversion—typically with more than one voice singing in harmony.

Elvis heard black gospel on the radio and white gospel in church. He particularly admired the Golden Gate Quartet out of New York City, who also influenced his back-up group, the Jordanaires. During his career, Elvis covered many of their songs.

White gospel was based on the close harmonies of pre-World War II black gospel. Elvis also heard harmonized singing of spirituals on the radio. The Blackwood Brothers and Jake Hess and the Statesmen—gospel quartets out of Nashville—influenced and inspired Elvis.

But make no mistake, gospel or church music—particularly as experienced in Pentecostal churches like those the Presleys attended—was not peaceful or sweet. Rather, it was revival music that told of the coming Apocalypse. It was music meant to convince the sinners listening that they could escape their grimy world through the salvation offered by Jesus Christ. Gospel was intense and energetic, and young Elvis absorbed its power from the moment he was born. There's no denying this spiritual music's part in the physical power of rock and roll.

The King and I

"My first love is spiritual music—some of the old colored spirituals from way back. [I know] practically every religious song that's ever been written."

—Elvis

For the Record

The Blackwood Brothers were Gladys Presley's favorite gospel group. Elvis had them flown in to sing at her funeral in 1958. They sang "Rock of Ages" and "Precious Memories." Jake Hess and two members of the Statesmen sang "Known Only to Him" at Elvis' own funeral.

Blacks and the Blues

The *blues* evolved after the Civil War from the earlier music of slaves, emerging out of African-American field hollers, railroad work songs, church music, and rhythmic dance songs.

The five-note scale of African music was combined with the eight-note scale of European music by use of sliding notes, and a 12-bar chord progression provided structure. On top of the progression were personal and poetic lyrics. Early blues, performed typically on a guitar, was a "call-and-response," with the musician singing a line, then answering it with his guitar. Mississippi *Delta blues* is the earliest, acoustic style.

Blues music spread throughout the rural South and made its way to small towns and to big cities by way of traveling performers and the release of so-called *race records,* which were marketed to black people. Blues filtered into jazz. As early as the mid-1930s, T-Bone Walker was experimenting with early electric guitars. As blacks migrated north to Chicago in search of work, prosperity, and freedom from repression and racism in the South,

The Word

Blues is a musical form consisting of a 12-bar chord progression and lyrics typically dealing with the hardships of life and love. **Delta blues** refers to rural, acoustic blues typical of the southern Mississippi River region. **Chicago blues** refers to a more driving, electrified, urban blues.

electrified blues became increasingly popular and, in turn, influenced performers far and wide. Whereas acoustic guitars and harmonicas had been the predominant instruments, electric guitars and tenor saxophones now also wailed the blues.

Memphis was a regional center for the blues, and Elvis experienced the music firsthand. He went to the Handy Theater on Park Street (named after W.C. Handy, the "Father of the Blues"; Handy, like Elvis, is honored in Memphis with a statue). B.B. King, who remembers the young Elvis in various blues clubs, was a regular performer on Beale Street. In fact, his initials B.B. came from his local moniker—"Beale Street Blues Boy." He was also a DJ on the Memphis black radio station WDIC, which Elvis listened to. Some of the performers getting airplay in the late '40s and early '50s were Little Junior Parker, Willie Mae "Big Mama" Thornton, Joe Turner, Muddy Waters, and Howlin' Wolf. In Memphis, Elvis also heard Rufus Thomas (who was also a DJ), and Johnny Ace, who sang what his parents referred to as "sinful music"—and they weren't wrong; the music, whether overtly or not, was often about drinking, sex, and sin.

For the Record

There is some controversy over who deserves credit for the song "Hound Dog." "Big Mama" Thornton originally recorded it in 1952, in a slow, bluesy style, but she didn't write it. It was written by the (white) team of Jerry Leiber and Mike Stoller. Moreover, Elvis recorded the song—in a dramatically up-tempo fashion—only after hearing a Las Vegas lounge act (Freddie Bell and the Bellboys) perform it. (In fact, they added the famous line "you ain't never caught a rabbit.")

The same month that Elvis recorded it, July 1956, Stoller had to be rescued from the Italian liner *Andrea Doria,* which was rammed and caused to sink by the Swedish liner *Stockholm* off Nantucket. Stepping onto the dock in New York and greeted by Leiber, Stoller discovered his song was a huge hit. (Although "Hound Dog" was listed as the A-side of the 45, it only reached number two on the Top 100 chart. "Don't Be Cruel," the B-side, reached number one and stayed there seven weeks.)

Add Some More Rhythm to Those Blues: R&B

Rhythm and blues began as electrified blues with a stronger, more danceable beat. Early R&B was influence both by big-band jump blues and electrified Chicago blues. The term has come to be used for black or black-influenced music that breaks with the traditional blues 12-bar structure.

Elvis' early up-tempo songs, such as "That's All Right (Mama)," were rhythm and blues. That song was written by Arthur "Big Boy" Crudup, who Elvis cited as a major influence. Crudup also wrote "So Glad You're Mine" and "My Baby Left Me," also recorded by Elvis.

Other rhythm and blues performers known to have influenced Elvis were Big Joe Turner, who wrote "Shake, Rattle & Roll" and "Flip, Flop & Fly," both covered by Elvis. Roy Brown, who typically sang ballads, was a favorite of Elvis. In 1954, Elvis recorded Brown's atypical 1947 jump-blues song "Good Rocking Tonight." Bill Ward and the Dominoes (with lead singer Jackie Wilson) were another favorite. Jackie Wilson, during his subsequent solo career, became known as the "Black Elvis." Fats Domino of New Orleans was one of the most successful rhythm and blues performers of the late 1940s and the '50s. Elvis also cited him as an inspiration.

Three other performers who had success on the R&B charts and had an enormous influence on a generation of musicians were Chuck Berry, Bo Diddley, and Little Richard. Chuck Berry, from St. Louis, signed with Chicago-based Chess Records in 1955. His first Top 10 hit was "Maybellene." Mississippi-born Bo Diddley was signed by Chess Records in 1955 and soon had hits with "Bo Diddley" and "I'm a Man." Berry and Diddley's distinctive, trademark licks helped make electric guitar integral to rock and roll. Georgia-born Little Richard (born Richard Penniman), a singer and piano player, had his first hit with "Tutti Frutti," recorded in 1955 for Los Angeles-based Specialty Records.

The Word
Rhythm and blues is a broad term describing almost all black pop music. Essentially electrified blues with a danceable beat, R&B derived from swing jazz, blues vocals, and later big-band jump blues to become the direct link to rock and roll. Many of Elvis' earliest records were remakes of tunes originally done by popular R&B artists like Big Joe Turner.

The King and I
"The colored folks been singing and playing it just like I'm doing now, man, for more years than I know … Nobody paid it no mind until I goosed it up. I got it from them … I used to hear Arthur Crudup bang his box the way I do now, and I said if I ever got to the place where I could feel all old Arthur felt, I'd be a music man like nobody ever saw."

—Elvis

Pop Goes the Pelvis

Early Elvis is not associated with *pop* music—a term applied to songs backed up by big bands or orchestras with more emphasis on melody and less rhythm-driven—but crooner Dean Martin was known to have been one of his idols. Elvis also cited the lesser-known black crooners Billy Eckstine and Roy Hamilton, who also sang pop ballads. Bing Crosby and The Ink Spots also received national airplay during Elvis' formative years. Elvis expressed admiration for the Platters and their lead singer Tony Williams. During Elvis' later career, he sang more and more pop songs, crooning more and rocking less. He even became a good friend of Pat Boone—the clean-cut, straight-laced pop singer, Elvis' peer, and for a time, his competition.

The Word
The term **pop music** refers to musical arrangements of songs with an emphasis on melody, not rhythm, and orchestral accompaniment. Generally, pop avoids experimentation and stresses accessibility.

Radio Radio

As for music on the airwaves reaching young Elvis, radio station WHBQ aired out of Memphis and played country music and gospel music, catering to a white audience. Of course white pop music was also widely available. In 1948, the year Elvis arrived in Memphis, a new radio station came on the air—WDIA—with black DJs playing black musicians. B.B. King was a DJ in the early 1950s. But not just black people were listening. WHBQ caught on that a lot of whites were tuning into WDIA and launched a competitive Saturday night show called *Red Hot and Blue*, hosted by Dewey Phillips, which played black music.

For the Record

On July 7, 1954, Dewey Phillips first aired an Elvis Presley record, "That's All Right (Mama)," playing it 14 times. That same night, because of enthusiastic audience response, Phillips interviewed Elvis on the air—the King's first interview.

Just as many white people resisted black music, many black people resisted white music as well. The DJs at WDIA were instructed not to play any white artists. But Rufus Thomas, a musician as well as a DJ, liked Elvis' music so much, he played him regularly. So it can be said that Elvis helped music cross over in two markets; there was more to come later in his career when his songs climbed to the top on a number of different charts.

Shake, Rattle & Roll: The Birth of Rockabilly

Rockabilly is a brash, high-energy combination of blues and country. It features heavy, sharp lead guitar licks, boogie piano, slapping bass rhythm, and hard, fast drumming. Rockabilly was the first music in which the white boys tried to beat the black man at his own game: blistering, exciting, aggressive music. Rockabilly was by no means subtle, nor did it endure for long on its own, but rockabilly—as practiced at Sam Phillips' Sun Studios—became rock and roll in the hands of Elvis Presley.

In discussing the birth of rockabilly, you have to give a certain amount of credit to Bill Haley who started out as a country performer specializing in western swing, but who evolved to a rhythm and blues style as Bill Haley and the Comets. In 1952, he recorded the R&B song "Rock the Joint." His "Crazy Man Crazy" was the first rockabilly record to make the *Billboard* pop chart in 1953. He also had hits with "Rock Around the Clock" (considered by many to be the first official rock record) and Joe Turner's "Shake, Rattle & Roll."

Another rockabilly performer, who rocked with the piano the way Elvis did with the guitar, was of course Jerry Lee Lewis, who had a contract at Sun Records soon after Elvis went over to RCA. His first big hit was "Whole Lotta Shakin' Going On" in 1957, quickly followed by "Great Balls of Fire."

Carl Perkins, another Sun artist, was also part of the rockabilly tradition. He wrote and recorded "Blue Suede Shoes," a hit on country, pop, and R&B charts in late 1956. Elvis also recorded it that year and had a hit with it. Johnny Cash also signed with Sun and had a hit with "I Walk the Line" in 1956 before moving over to a much more pure country style.

Roy Orbison and Charlie Rich were two more performers who went on to national acclaim from early beginnings at Sun Studio. With its energy and strong guitar licks, rockabilly influenced—and continues to influence—many musicians and groups, including Creedence Clearwater Revival, Paul McCartney, The Stray Cats, and Elvis Costello, to name just a few.

For the Record

On December 4, 1956, Elvis, Johnny Cash, Jerry Lee Lewis, and Carl Perkins participated in an impromptu jam session in Sun Studios, beginning with the song "Blueberry Hill" and lasting for hours. Sam Phillips caught the session on tape, but because of legal complications due to Elvis' deal with RCA, results of the session—17 songs' worth—weren't released until 1980 as a bootleg album. In 1981, Sun, RCA, and the Elvis Presley Estate released an authorized version. In 1987, a second bootleg album was released, adding 22 songs to the original 17. The four individuals are referred to as the Million-Dollar Quartet.

The Birth of Rock

I'm getting into a sensitive area here. As you can see by the preceding discussions of the various types of music, rock and roll music—which has come to be called rock music—evolved out of a confluence of styles. Just as the evolution of blues into rhythm and blues is nebulous, so is that of rhythm and blues into rockabilly and rock and roll. The best way to state it, perhaps, is that the development of rock and roll was organic, with a lot of different styles coming together in the 1950s and then being embodied by one man: Elvis Presley.

Despite the contributions of various performers, it can be said that Elvis is the well-spring from which all rock and roll arrived. Why? First, he was the whole package, with a voice so huge and powerful and unique, he was able to incorporate disparate influences to-gether into a new sound. Second, he was such a brilliant performer that he was able to single-handedly embody this new fusion of musical styles and take it to people around the world.

Some might say that if Elvis hadn't happened along, someone else would have taken the mantle. Certainly it is true that there was a generation in the South that grew up with the same social, cultural, and religious influences, along with the phenomenon of radio, and they were all just waiting for the floodgates to open. However, Elvis Presley was the genius. His synthesis of styles, and his power and energy were uniquely his. No one could sing with his combination of intensity and natural ease. He took from many styles, but he copied no one. He was and is an American original.

The Least You Need to Know

➤ Elvis was influenced by many styles of music, in particular country, gospel, blues, rhythm and blues, and pop.

➤ Early Elvis can be defined as rockabilly; late Elvis, more as pop.

➤ Although there were many contributors to its development, it can safely be said that Elvis Presley is the key figure in the blending of musical styles to create rock and roll.

Part 3
Kingdom Coming:
The Rise of Elvis

Here we are on the cusp of history, as the rocket ship that was Elvis Presley gets ready to launch. How did this shy country boy magically (and almost instantly) transform himself from an inexperienced wannabe musician to a polished, supremely confident pro?

In Part 3, I'll tell you who helped him and what it was like to be there at the beginning of (rock) history. There are those remarkable first recording sessions for us to explore. We'll track the King's early performing triumphs—and a few rare bomb performances as well. I'll emphasize the importance of the mysterious "Colonel" Tom Parker, talk about his improbable past, and the controversy that swirls around him to this day.

Finally, I'll invite you discover an amazing series of "firsts" that Elvis experienced, from his first concerts to first TV appearance to his first Elvis Presley Day.

Chapter 8

Here Comes the
Sun (Records)

In This Chapter

➤ Who helped Elvis develop his talent?

➤ Elvis' first recording sessions

➤ The young performer comes into his own

We're at the dawn of history now. Young Elvis, like a shiny new hot rod, is at the starting line ready to blast off. Ready to meet his destiny. All the pieces were in place. He'd absorbed all the musical styles he needed. He'd created a hip, cool, outrageous fashion statement for himself. He felt special now. Cocky. Elvis was about to become the Man.

Yet he would attempt several launches before the rocket launched him into hyper-stardom.

In this chapter we'll meet the music professionals who were there at the beginning and were crucial to the development of Elvis' career. We'll talk about the first recording sessions. We'll talk about finding magic when you least expect it. We'll see an electrifying, magnificent, and improbable genius poised at the edge of greatness.

Meet Some Key Players

Four people in the music business, besides Elvis himself, played a huge part in Elvis breaking through as a recording artist. Let's meet them.

Sam's the Man

Producer Sam Phillips is credited with discovering Elvis, creating the Sun rockabilly sound, and then selling the rights to Elvis' music to RCA.

The first part of that sentence is only partially correct; perhaps more accurate is that Phillips deserves the *credit*, but his assistant, Marion Keisker, first recognized that Elvis was something special. In any case, Phillips was the pioneer of this new fusion between country music and rhythm and blues, and he helped create the rockabilly sound. He had a good ear for talent and recording, and was a master at using echo effects to enhance the sound. Phillips cared about this new music and respected the artists who were making it.

Sam Cornelius Phillips was born in Florence, Alabama, on January 5, 1923. In 1942, he was hired as a DJ by a Muscle Shoals, Alabama radio station—WLAY. He worked at a number of other stations before being hired by WREC in Memphis.

Sam Phillips' Memphis Recording Service, where Elvis first sang professionally.

In 1950, Phillips founded the Memphis Recording Service at 706 Union Avenue in Memphis, with the motto, "We record anything—anywhere—anytime." That Phillips did, recording various social functions around Memphis. He also charged the public four dollars to record one-sided acetates (the lowest quality record) in the studio. These earnings enabled him to invest in rhythm and blues artists, and he recorded a number of Memphis performers, such as B.B. King, Bobby Blue Bland, Howlin' Wolf, Little Junior Parker, and Little Walter (Walter Horton). Phillips sold some of these demos to record labels. His first attempt to have his own record label in 1950—Phillips Records—didn't work out. In February of 1952, he founded Sun Records, recording country as well as rhythm and blues. (Two years later, he established the music publishing company Hi-Lo Music.)

Sun Records' first release was "Drivin' Slow" by Johnny London. The first hit (and eighth release) for the fledgling label was "Bear Cat" by Rufus Thomas, an answer to Big Mama Thornton's R&B hit "Hound Dog." Elvis' first record, "That's All Right (Mama)," in 1954, prompted other rockabilly and country musicians to sign with Sun. In 1955, Phillips sold Elvis' contract to RCA Victor to invest in other artists, such as Carl Perkins. In the late 1950s, Phillips moved Sun Records to 639 Madison Avenue, from where he launched the Phillips International label. Shelby Singleton bought Sun Records from Phillips in 1969 and moved the company to Nashville. He later became the owner of WLVS in Memphis, its call letters referring to guess who.

The King and I
"Rock and roll and rhythm and blues tended not to be something you wanted to copy exactly. You wanted to feel it. We tried to get in the general bag of it and hope that it was successful. There were enough copyists."

—Sam Phillips

Sam Phillips was a country boy, unsophisticated in some ways, but he had vision, and a passion for music, especially the raw, new music emerging in the 1950s, and he had the insight and instincts to identify and nurture those who could make it. He had a deep love for the raw, traditional blues he had grown up hearing and wanted to give artists in that tradition, such as Howlin' Wolf, more exposure. A practical man, he also realized that if he could find someone to bring the power of black music to a white audience, he could change the world and get rich in the bargain. Sam Phillips, to use a writing analogy, was a gifted, brilliant editor who could bring out the best his artists had to give. Elvis Presley was fortunate indeed to meet him.

Will the Real Discoverer Please Stand Up?

Phillips' assistant manager, Marion Keisker, deserves some of the credit for "discovering" Elvis. She first met him, heard him, and had the sense to keep the first tape of him. She called him to the attention of her boss Sam Phillips more than once.

Marion Keisker, one of the first to champion young Elvis Presley.

The King and I
"Sam was always telling people he wished he could find a white boy who could sing like a black boy, so I kept trying to get Sam to listen to the tape I had made with the Presley kid, but it took months and months."

—Marion Keisker

Born in 1917, college-educated Marion Keisker started in radio in 1939. In the 1940s, she was known on the air as "Kitty Kelly." She later worked as an announcer with Memphis' WREC Radio, becoming known as "Miss Radio of Memphis." In early 1950, while Elvis was still in school, she went to work for Sam Phillips at Sun Records.

In 1955, Marion joined WHER, an all-woman Memphis radio station, while still working at Sun. In September 1957, Marion quit Sun to join the Air Force and worked as an assistant manager for the Armed Forces Television Network. Until her death in 1989, Marion Keisker remembered Elvis the way a grandmother recalls a favored child, "Here was a boy so pure, so sweet, so wonderful that he's unbelievable."

Take It, Scotty!

Scotty Moore was more than a guitar player with a great touch and a new style that combined chordal rhythms with single-note country and blues lines. He, like Sam Phillips and Marion Keisker, had a sense of what was out there and what would go over—namely, Elvis. Not that he knew it immediately. In fact, Scotty described the first cover songs Elvis sang as "no better than the originals."

Winfield Scott Moore III, from Gadsden, Tennessee and born in 1931, played guitar in a band while in the U.S. Navy. In 1954, he was part of Doug Poindexter's Starlight Wranglers along with bass player Bill Black. Scotty also worked as a hatter for his brother's dry-cleaning establishment to pay the bills. Sam Phillips used him from time to time as a session musician at Sun.

He became Elvis' first manager as well as his first lead-guitar player and was instrumental in defining not just Elvis' early sound but the sound of rock and roll. "Hound Dog," "Jailhouse Rock," "All Shook Up"—it's Scotty's guitar that you hear on all of Elvis' classic mid-'50s hits.

Moore parted company with Elvis on September 21, 1957; he was sick of the lousy wages, of getting no writing credit on the songs, and of making no royalties off his songs. He returned after two years, playing sessions with Elvis until 1968, including his legendary "Comeback Special." After leaving Elvis, Scotty continued his successful career as a musician and also became a studio owner in Nashville. Over the years, Moore was often kidded about giving up his contract as Elvis' first manager. He never regretted it however, saying, "I was interested in playing, not booking acts and not telling anybody how to sing."

Blackie the Bassist

Bill Black, known to his friends as Blackie, rounded out the sound of singer Elvis and guitarist Scotty Moore with his slapping bass. (He both plucked and slapped his upright instrument.) He also was an equal partner with Scotty as part of their trio and also deserves credit for developing the sound and the rhythm that won over the world.

Born in 1926, William Black grew up in Memphis. He and his two brothers, one of them also a musician, lived in the same apartment house at 462 Alabama Street as Elvis (whether they knew each other there or even possibly jammed together is unknown). Like Scotty Moore, Black played with Doug Poindexter's Starlight Wranglers. He had a laid-back country style, but for the up-tempo numbers he slapped his double bass to get a more lively rhythm going.

Like Scotty, Black quit working with Elvis in 1957—he and Scotty were still making a flat $200 a week while Elvis was already earning millions. Black later played in the Bill Black Combo and for a time owned a recording studio. He died in 1965.

For the Record

A famous bass player (and not a bad singer/songwriter either) by the name of Paul McCartney now owns the stand-up bass that Bill Black used for his recordings with Elvis; it still has the name "Bill" on it. He played it on the song "Baby's Request" on the Wings album *Back to the Egg* and proudly showed it off on his 1997 VH1 special plugging his *Flaming Pie* CD.

History in the Making: The First Recordings

Here's how the legend goes. Sometime in the summer of 1953, Elvis came to the Memphis Recording Service at 706 Union Avenue to record an acetate. Sam wasn't there but Marion was. Young, handsome, eager, polite, and somewhat cocky, Elvis stated that he wanted to record two songs for his mother's birthday. Now, since Gladys' birthday is in April, we can surmise one of four things: one, Elvis was really late on a gift; two, Elvis was really early on a gift; three, the "mom's birthday" part of the story is a myth; or four, Elvis was fibbing and he really just wanted to be discovered. I say four.

Here's the exchange between Marion and Elvis on that fateful day:

> **Marion:** "What kind of singer are you?"
> **Elvis:** "I sing all kinds."
> **Marion:** "Who do you sound like?"
> **Elvis:** "I don't sound like nobody."
> **Marion:** "Hillbilly?"
> **Elvis:** "Yeah, I sing hillbilly."
> **Marion:** "Who do you sound like in hillbilly?"
> **Elvis:** "I don't sound like nobody."

In any case, Elvis sang the rhythm and blues hits "My Happiness" and "That's When Your Heartache Begins." Marion, impressed by the voice, presence, and good looks of this 18-year-old, thought that maybe her boss would want to hear him—he always said he was looking for white talent who could sing like a black man—and slipped a tape in the Ampex tape machine while the acetate was being recorded, catching a good part of it. She wrote the note to go with the tape—"Elvis Presley. Good ballad singer"—plus Elvis' address and a neighbor's phone.

Sam listened to the tape and filed away the information, doing nothing. Gladys, though, whether it was a birthday gift or not, absolutely loved it and borrowed a record player to play it again and again.

For the Record

The acetate of "My Happiness" was found in the possession of a high school classmate in 1988 and is the first song on Elvis' *Complete 50's Masters* box set, on RCA. Another song, "I'll Never Stand in Your Way," apparently recorded at the same time, has recently been discovered and will be included on the four-CD set, *Elvis Presley Platinum: A Life in Music,* to be released in the summer of 1997.

On January 4, 1954, Elvis returned to the Sun recording studio. This time, Marion was out of the office and Sam Phillips was there. (The next day would be his birthday—a bit of trivia there.) Elvis spent four dollars again and recorded the country ballad "I'll Never Stand in Your Way" and "Casual Love Affair." Phillips wasn't blown away, but he again took Elvis' name and number just in case an opportunity arose. It did a few months later when a demo arrived from a Nashville publishing company for the song "Without You." The young black singer who had performed it could not be located. Marion reminded Sam of the "kid with the sideburns." Sam couldn't find the latest number, but remembered she had written down a neighbor's phone number and tracked Elvis down.

But Elvis didn't blow Sam away that session, either, and Sam gave up on the idea of using him on "Without You." Sam asked Elvis what else he could play and Elvis replied: "I can do anything." He performed parts of songs in a variety of styles, but especially heavy on Dean Martin's influence.

Elvis did not get a recording contract that day, but Sam Phillips was sufficiently impressed to think of Elvis as a long-term project. Sam and guitarist Scotty Moore often went to Miss Taylor's Restaurant down the block from the studio, and one day over coffee, Sam mentioned Elvis to Scotty as a talent possibly worth checking out.

These things don't happen overnight. Weeks went by. Months. Elvis' rise was still meteoric by any standards.

Return to Sender

Legend has it that Elvis was so excited about his first professional recording opportunity that he ran the 15 blocks to Union Avenue and arrived before Marion Keisker hung up the phone with him. You can believe that or not; but to Elvis, this moment was the breakthrough he had been dreaming of.

Practice Makes Perfect

A musician doesn't do his only work when playing before an audience or recording in a studio. In many ways, gigs are the pay-off—psychological as well as financial. The bulk of the work occurs in the practice sessions, and once Scotty Moore agreed to take Elvis on as a project, they spent many hours mastering a repertoire and crafting their sound.

The first day Elvis showed up at Scotty Moore's house to work with him and bassist Bill Black, he wore a pink suit and white shoes. No doubt he thought of this event as an audition. Bill and Scotty didn't quite get him, but they caught on that this kid had *something* and met with him again and again that summer in their spare time. They were still performing with Doug Poindexter's Starlight Wranglers, and the other Wranglers weren't too thrilled that Scotty and Bill had this other project going. But the kid probably wouldn't amount to much, right?

Meanwhile, Elvis was living and breathing music, taking in what the radio and Memphis clubs had to offer. He also played some gigs at the Eagle's Nest and the Bel Air Club, joining the Wranglers on some cuts and earning $10 for his efforts. With every appearance, however, his confidence and stage presence were growing.

In June 1954, Elvis went into the studio again to try to record "Rag Mop," a song by Johnny Lee Mills. To everyone's disappointment, the session did not produce anything Phillips deemed suitable for release. Back to the drawing board.

The Session

Finally, on July 5, 1954, the moment had arrived. Not that any of the parties involved knew that anything special would transpire. This was just one in a series of informal rehearsals, an attempt to make something happen. It was hot and humid—the temperature had broken the 100-degree mark that day. Elvis, Scotty, and Bill sweltered in the small studio, which didn't even have air-conditioning.

The first song they recorded, over several takes, was "Harbor Lights," by Jimmy Kennedy and Hugh Williams. The second was "I Love You Because" by Leon Payne. Uninspiring, Phillips thought, nothing special. Another bust of a session? Sam was beginning to wonder whether he'd made a mistake.

But then the magic moment occurred. Relaxing during a break, but no doubt feeling the tension of another wasted session, Elvis began horsing around, jumping all over and singing the old Arthur Crudup blues song "That's All Right (Mama)." Bill gave the jam session a driving R&B beat. Scotty played blues chords and country licks. Elvis attacked the song in his blues-influenced way.

Here's how Scotty Moore recalls it:

> *Elvis picked up his guitar and started banging on it and singing "That's All Right (Mama)." Jumping around the studio, just acting the fool. And Bill started beating on his bass and I joined in. Just making a bunch of racket, we thought. The door to the control room was open, and when we was halfway through the thing, Sam come running out and said, "What in the devil are you doing?" We said, "We don't know." He said, "Well, back up, try to find a place to start, and do it again."*

Going for Gold
The July 5, 1954, recording of "I Love You Because" (a splicing of take #3 and #5) was released in 1956 on the album *Elvis Presley*. Take #2 is on the 1976 album *Elvis—A Legendary Performer, Vol. One*. Check out those tracks to know what Sam Phillips heard just before he heard the sound he wanted.

Phillips was so impressed with the results, he asked them to repeat it so that he could tape it. They quickly worked out an arrangement—a count for the beginning, a certain number of verses, and an ending. The challenge was to sustain the "jamming" energy of the song. Phillips let the tape roll and caught what he had been searching for—a new sound where black meets white. Rockabilly, it came to be called; the recording still feels spontaneous and from the heart. Scotty Moore recalls that he liked what they'd done. "It was exciting, but what was it? It was just so completely different. We thought, 'Good God, they'll run us out of town!'" At that time, musical categories were still as segregated as restaurants in the deep South. What were people going to do with this crazy hybrid sound?

In the next week, in order to get two songs and release a single, Elvis, Scotty, and Bill recorded Bill Monroe's traditional bluegrass waltz, "Blue Moon of Kentucky." They souped it up in the new rockabilly style, and added a technique of Sam's called "slapback," whereby Sam would run the tape through a second machine, getting a strange echo effect.

"That's All Right (Mama)" would become the A-side and "Blue Moon of Kentucky" the B-side of Elvis' first commercial release. Within a week, before they had even pressed a master, Sun Studios had orders for 5,000 Elvis Presley records. By the end of the month, Elvis was a local sensation.

The ground was starting to shake: The Elvis phenomenon was beginning.

The Least You Need to Know

➤ Elvis' first recording sessions for Sam Phillips at Sun Studios were by no means a triumph.

➤ Marion Keisker, a savvy recording pro at Sun Studios, heard Elvis first and was the first recording professional to believe he had talent.

➤ Elvis' first hit recording was the result of a spontaneous jam session with guitarist Scotty Moore and bassist Bill Black.

➤ Sam Phillips, Elvis' first producer and already a music visionary who recorded many important Memphis blues artists, pioneered the rockabilly sound.

Chapter 9

Elvis Ascending

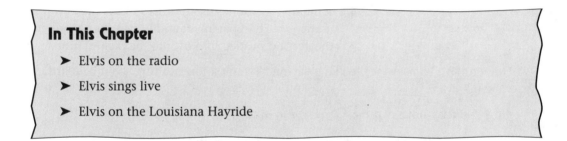

In This Chapter

➤ Elvis on the radio

➤ Elvis sings live

➤ Elvis on the Louisiana Hayride

Elvis no doubt felt he had paid his dues—musical and otherwise—and that it had been a long and winding road to this point in his life. (Though let's not forget that road was still only 19 years long.) But following the release of his first record—the 45 "That's All Right (Mama)" and "Blue Moon of Kentucky"—events happened incredibly fast.

Let's track that magical first summer and fall of 1954 and take the first of many high flying rides with the Hillbilly Cat. The world was about to change, lead by a sexy young kid thumping a guitar and singing his heart out.

Breaking the Sound Barrier: Elvis on the Radio

Radio had been as American as apple pie since the 1920s. By the 1950s, the vast majority of households had at least one. As a result, music was a part of most Americans' lives on a daily basis. Getting on the radio was essential for the promotion of a musician's career, and Elvis got on the radio fast. With the advent of tiny transistor radios in 1952 (by Sony), radio—and music—became portable. This meant that teenagers could listen to whatever music they wanted without their parents knowing about it. Good timing for Elvis.

By now you know Sam Phillips was a great producer who fostered Elvis' talent, right? Well, I bet you didn't know he was equally smart as a promoter. And he did it all without *payola*—the common practice of the time of bribing radio stations to play certain records.

The Word

Payola is the bribing of DJs (disc jockeys) and program directors to get artists airtime. Elvis is one of the few artists from his era (or any era) to hit the big time without using such disreputable methods.

Even before Elvis' first record was pressed, he sent an acetate to several Memphis radio stations, including WHBQ, WHHM, and WMPS. Dewey Phillips (no relation to Sam) had a Saturday-night show called *Red Hot and Blue* on WHBQ, which played black music. On July 7, 1954, shortly after 9:30 p.m., Phillips first aired "That's All Right (Mama)." He liked it so much and the response was so overwhelming that he played it 14 times. Dewey made some frantic phone calls trying to locate the new phenomenon. Elvis' parents found him at the Suzore movie theater and hustled him over to the radio station.

"Mr. Phillips," Dewey recalled Elvis saying, "I don't know nothing about bein' interviewed."

"Just don't say nothin' dirty," Dewey told him.

Elvis didn't. In the first of what would be countless interviews, Elvis was his usual shy and polite self. Pretending he was playing a record and they were just chatting, Dewey interviewed Elvis live on the air, making sure Elvis mentioned that he'd gone to Humes, a white high school.

Sam Phillips had assumed that WDIA, the all-black station, wouldn't play the record and hadn't given them an acetate the first night. But Rufus Thomas, the DJ/musician, wanted it and defied his program director's decision not to play it. Black people liked the song, too, and called to request it again and again. Most listeners actually thought Elvis was black.

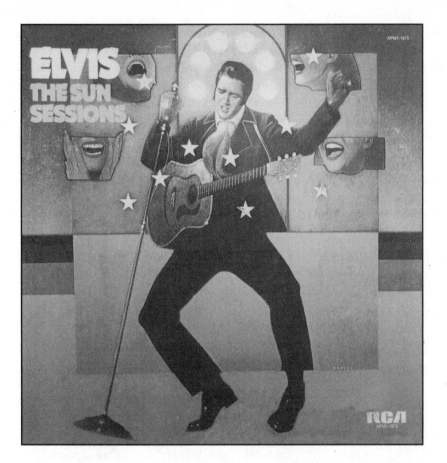

Elvis' Sun Sessions *album, released in 1975 (but recorded in 1954 and 1955) is my favorite Elvis record.*

The Blue Moon Boys: The Start of a Legend

After "That's All Right (Mama)" hit the record stores (and hit #3 on local charts), Elvis started doing nightclub gigs with Scotty Moore and Bill Black. But Elvis was still a truck driver; Sam Phillips hadn't given him an advance and there was no way in the world his parents would let him quit working. And although he had gotten some attention with his debut, he was by no means a sensation; he was too country for the black stations and too "black" for the country stations.

The remarkable thing about Elvis' early performing style is that it was created on the fly. Just like Elvis created his music almost completely by himself, so did he create his live act. When Elvis' first record was released he had never played a professional gig! Suddenly, the stage was waiting, so Elvis got up and started experimenting.

He was nervous, so he shook. The music and the rhythm were wild, and so were Elvis' moves. Even at his earliest shows, he could see and hear the excitement his moves created. So he got wilder, the wilder he got, the better the audiences liked it. It didn't take him long to shed his shy, mama's-boy image and reveal the playful prankster side of his personality. Bill Black was also a big part of the show, hooting, cutting up, slapping (and jumping on) his bass; Scotty was the anchor, with his driving electric rhythm guitar and stinging, country/blues leads.

In Bill's old Chevy, the three boys started roaming the South and Southwest, going as far as New Mexico. The venues were mostly country & western roadhouses, but the act was pure Elvis: wild, pelvis-jerking, out-and-out *rockin'*. Unfettered is exactly the right word, and up until then, the only places in America doing unfettered were black clubs with black patrons.

The roadhouses, informal by nature, were perfect. Not that the other performers were happy; Elvis, Scotty, and Bill made a lot of them furious with their "disgraceful displays." How would you like to follow Elvis onstage? In the blink of an eye, young Elvis Presley had re-created himself into something brand new—modern and original. And the audiences who heard him, especially the younger folks, went nuts. It didn't take long for Elvis' schedule to get full. Check out the summer and early fall of '54 as his career took off:

➤ On July 12, at Sam Phillips' urging, Elvis' parents sign a managerial contract on his behalf with guitarist Scotty Moore.

➤ On July 17, Elvis sits in with The Starlite Wranglers at the Bon Air Club.

➤ On July 19, 1954, the 45 record of "That's All Right (Mama)" and "Blue Moon of Kentucky" is officially released. At 9:00 in the morning, at Charles Records on Main Street in Memphis, the first Elvis record is ever bought—by one Eldene Beard. The floodgates are open. Fans begin asking him to sign their copies.

➤ On July 28, Elvis is interviewed by reporter Edwin Howard for the Memphis *Press-Scimitar*, his first print interview. (In a later review, the paper would call "That's All Right (Mama)" a "tremendous hit with teenagers.")

➤ On July 30, 1954, Elvis performs at the Overton Park Shell in Memphis at a concert featuring Slim Whitman.

➤ On August 7, Elvis, Scotty, and Bill play the Eagle's Nest in Memphis, billed as the Blue Moon Boys. That same day, the first *Billboard* review of an Elvis song appears. The magazine liked "That's All Right (Mama)" just fine, labeling Elvis, in its typical stilted fashion, "a potent new chanter who can sock over a tune for either the country or the R&B markets."

➤ On August 8, Elvis sings on Doug Poindexter's KWEM radio show.

➤ On August 10, the Blue Moon Boys play at the Overton Park Shell again.

➤ On August 18, the Blue Moon Boys play a baseball benefit show at Bellevue Park.

➤ On August 21, the Blue Moon Boys play in Gladewater, Texas.

➤ On August 22, the Blue Moon Boys play in Houston, Texas.

➤ On August 24 (or 27 or 29, depending on your sources), the Blue Moon Boys play a benefit at the Kennedy Veteran's Hospital.

➤ On September 9, the Blue Moon Boys play for the grand opening of the Katz Drug Store—he, Scotty, and Bill are set up on a flatbed truck. That same day, Marion Keisker organizes a fan club for the Blue Moon Boys.

➤ On September 10, Elvis, Scotty, and Bill record "Good Rockin' Tonight" by Roy Brown and "I Don't Care If the Sun Don't Shine" by Mack David. The single is released on September 25.

The King and I

"In the very early, early days, we were getting 25 to 50 bucks a night, maybe. I'm talking about short hops around Memphis. We just kept spreading out, and the further we went, the bigger the price. I mean, 50 or 60 dollars. And we were glad to get it, so we could buy gas to get home."

—Scotty Moore

For the Record

In 1949, Mack David wrote "I Don't Care If the Sun Don't Shine" for the Walt Disney movie *Cinderella*. But the song wasn't used. Patti Page released the song (Mercury 5296) in 1950, the year the movie came out without it. The next year, 1951, the Dean Martin-Jerry Lewis movie *Scared Stiff* came out, with Dean Martin singing the song. Dean Martin was one of Elvis' favorite singers, so it's no coincidence the King recorded it. In Elvis' 1954 version (Sun 210), there's an added verse written by—yes, Sun Records' own—Marion Keisker.

➤ On October 2, Elvis makes his only appearance ever on the most famous live country show in America, the Grand Ole Opry at the Ryman Auditorium, better known as the Opry House, in Nashville. On the Hank Snow segment of the show, he sings "Blue Moon of Kentucky" and "That's All Right (Mama)." He didn't go over well, most likely because he, Scotty, and Bill were messing with a bluegrass anthem, making the traditional "Blue Moon of Kentucky" rock instead of waltz. Elvis is devastated by the lack of response, and one report afterwards has it that he cried all the way home from Nashville. Jim Denny, the Opry's head of talent, makes dubious history that night when he suggests that Elvis go back to driving a truck.

Return to Sender
Although he scored big on the country charts, especially with "Blue Moon of Kentucky," he was never accepted by the Grand Old Opry. Elvis' showmanship and stage movements were too much; the reaction he got from teenage audiences, the controversy he sparked, and the commercial crisis that rock and roll threw country music into, led to his being thought of as part of the rock and roll tradition.

➤ On October 8, Elvis and the Blue Moon Boys (he was getting top billing now) play at the Silver Slipper in Atlanta, Georgia.

➤ On October 22, Elvis and the Blue Moon Boys possibly play a concert in New Orleans (no written evidence of this concert).

➤ In November, Elvis quits his truck-driving job with Crown Electric. He is now a full-time musician, with a one-year contract with the Louisiana Hayride radio show to appear every Saturday night for $18. His parents witness the contract signing. It is a bittersweet moment for his mother; she knows her boy is well on his way to success, but she also knows that success will take him away. Within a month, Gladys is suffering depression about Elvis' long absences.

The Hillbilly Cat Takes a Louisiana Hayride

Elvis, Scotty, and Bill were no longer known as the Blue Moon Boys. Elvis was already too big for that. Now he was known as the Hillbilly Cat, and not only did he perform concerts all over the South, he made a deal with the Louisiana Hayride to appear as a regular. A regular drummer on the Louisiana Hayride radio program, D.J. Fontana, performed with Scotty and Bill and became a full-time member of the band in the fall of 1955.

The King and I
"He was purty hot in the area anyway and he tore the house down (on his first performance). He was the kingpin. Horace Logan was program director for the station and when Horace heard Elvis that first time, he did 14 back flips."

—D. J. Fontana

The Louisiana Hayride, created in 1948, was a live-radio Saturday night country music show in Shreveport, Louisiana, broadcast live on KWKH from the packed Shreveport Municipal Auditorium. The Louisiana Hayride has been referred to as the "Junior Grand Ole Opry." It was also nicknamed "the Cradle to the Stars." Many country artists, like Webb Pierce, Kitty Wells, Faron Young, and even Hank Williams, got their first big break on the Hayride.

Portions of the show were syndicated via CBS to 190 radio stations throughout the South and Texas.

Elvis first played on the Louisiana Hayride on October 16, 1954, then again the next Saturday. He appeared on the Lucky Strike-sponsored part of the show, which introduced new talent. On November 6, he signed a contract for regular appearances on the show. Elvis' initial salary was $18 a performance; Scotty and Bill each earned $12.

For the Record

On November 6, 1954, Elvis (with Scotty and Bill) made the only commercial of his career. The spot, for Southern Made Doughnuts, was aired on the Louisiana Hayride. Elvis' pitch for the donuts went like this: "You can get 'em piping hot after four p.m., you can get 'em piping hot. Southern Made Doughnuts hit the spot, you can get 'em piping hot after four p.m."

When Elvis renewed his contract with the Louisiana Hayride a year later, his pay was increased to $200 a night. But there was a clause in his contract stating that he would have to pay $400 for every missed performance, which happened more and more with his growing success and other demands. In 1954, Elvis played the Louisiana Hayride nine times, 33 times in 1955, and eight times in 1956.

Elvis' final Hayride concert was on December 15, 1956, a benefit for the Shreveport YMCA at the Louisiana Fairgrounds. Nine thousand screaming fans showed up. At that time, the album *Elvis* was number one on the *Billboard* Chart and *Love Me Tender* was the hottest movie.

Even Bigger Things to Come

By the end of 1954, Elvis had played concerts in Tennessee, Louisiana, Texas, Arkansas, and Georgia. With the schedule heating up in 1955, he, Scotty, and Bill rode all over the South with Bill's bass strapped to the top of the car, playing nightclubs, road houses, high school auditoriums, and fairgrounds. They would return to Memphis for other concerts and for recording sessions at Sun records, and head down to Shreveport for radio broadcasts.

Exposure from the Louisiana Hayride and his other concerts led to Elvis' growing popularity and increasing controversy. His stage antics were absurd to many people, offensive to others—the phrase "Elvis the Pelvis" was heard more and more. As early as May 13, 1955, at a concert in Jacksonville, Florida, his presence incited a riot of adulation and excitement.

As Elvis' career progressed, more and more people joined the bandwagon (more like a surging locomotive). Among them were three managers, the third and final being Colonel Tom Parker, who would manage Elvis until the end. We'll meet the advisers who helped Elvis shape his remarkable career in Chapter 10.

The Least You Need to Know

➤ Durng the summer his first record was released—1954—Elvis achieved instant success on local Memphis radio.

➤ With one big exception—a lukewarm reception at the most famous country radio show in the country, the Grand Ole Opry, resulting in his not being asked back—Elvis' success was meteoric.

➤ Elvis became a regional hit by playing numerous concerts throughout the South and by appearing on the popular live-radio show the Louisiana Hayride.

Chapter 10

Join the Circus: Colonel Tom Parker and Other Ringleaders

In This Chapter

➤ Meet Scotty Moore, first manager

➤ Meet Bob Neal, second manager

➤ Meet Colonel Tom Parker, third and last manager

Elvis was an individualist who carved his own special place in music and entertainment. But he was also used to having a person obsessing over him—his mother—so the idea of having a manager wasn't completely new. After a temporary arrangement with Scotty Moore, then a brief go-round with a real, if small-time, manager, Bob Neal, Elvis ended up signing with Colonel Tom Parker. The Colonel played the father figure for Elvis, usurping some of whatever influence Vernon had in the Presleys' affairs.

The enigmatic, Svengali-like Parker would become entwined with Elvis the singer, the actor, and ultimately the person. Their relationship would be one of the most controversial and debated of Elvis' life.

Scotty at the Helm

After the wild response to Elvis' first being played on the radio in the summer of 1954, producer Sam Phillips and guitar player Scotty Moore—whom we came to know in Chapter 9—thought they had better protect him and themselves from people who might take financial advantage. They encouraged Elvis to sign a contract with Scotty as his *manager*.

The Word

In popular music, a **manager** oversees and coordinates the affairs of a group or artist. He may also be the **promoter** of certain events; a **booking agent**, who gets jobs; or a **press agent**, who handles the media. A manager is confidante, mentor, masseuse, bodyguard, sycophant, lawyer, accountant, or any combination.

On July 12, 1954, Elvis and his parents—remember he was still just a kid, only 19—signed a one-year contract with Scotty. The guitarist would receive 10 percent of all Elvis' earnings.

Gladys loved that her son was getting so much attention, and she had been enthralled to hear him on the radio, but she also was nervous that this music career would take her little boy away from her. She did what she could to stay in the middle of his affairs, calling Sam Phillips again and again. Both Sam and Marion Keisker had to be diplomatic and find new and better ways to tell Mama that it was really "all right."

Ukulele Bob

On January 1, 1955, Scotty Moore let Elvis out of the managerial contract so he could sign with a real manager—Robert Neal Hopgood, known professionally as Bob Neal. Neal had been a DJ during the 1940s with his own show, *The Bob Neal Farm Show* on WMPS, on which he played ukulele and told jokes. He also hosted a show called *The High Noon Roundup*, featuring local country singers. Neal also owned the Bob Neal Record Shop on Main Street in Memphis. In 1952, he started the Memphis Promotions Agency at 160 Union Avenue. He managed Elvis for 15 percent of his earnings with an additional 10 percent going to promotion. Scotty Moore, Bill Black, and D.J. Fontana would henceforth be paid salaries.

In February 1955, Colonel Thomas Parker helped Bob Neal book Elvis at a concert in Carlsbad, New Mexico. He also became friends with Elvis' parents. Soon enough, Bob Neal would be on the outs as well.

The Colonel Takes Command

Colonel Tom Parker officially signed on as Elvis' manager/agent on March 15, 1956. Elvis had first met the Colonel and two of his aides on February 6, 1955, at Palumbo's Cafe located at 85 Poplar in Memphis. At that time, Parker arranged for young Elvis to appear on the same bill as Hank Snow, whom Parker also managed. On August 15, 1955, Elvis had signed a contract with Parker for other concert appearances, although he remained under contract with Neal for another seven months.

Colonel Tom Parker with Elvis.

The Colonel handled some big acts (Hank Snow at the time and formerly Eddy Arnold—both country stars) and had connections to better-paying gigs. For a time, Elvis paid Neal his 15 percent and the Colonel an additional 25 percent. The March 15, 1956, contract, officially making Parker his only representation, kept Parker's share at 25 percent. Parker would later up his percentage to 50 percent. When it comes to Elvis, there's plenty to go around, right?

Illegal Alien, Carny, and Dogcatcher Supreme

Colonel Parker remains one of the most mysterious figures in the Elvis saga. He claimed to have been born in Huntington, West Virginia with the name Thomas Andrew Parker, but now the truth about him has been revealed.

Colonel Parker, alias Andreas Cornelius van Kujik, was a young man with big aspirations when he illegally immigrated to the United States from Holland in 1929. In 1929 or 1930 he enlisted in the U.S. Army at Fort McPherson in Atlanta, serving until 1932. He met Marie Mott Ross in Tampa, Florida, marrying her his final year in the military; they did not have children.

Parker returned to Holland on one occasion with presents for everyone in his large family. He headed back to the U.S. several months later. He wrote his family that he had joined the army, signing all letters now as Tom Parker. But the letters stopped arriving in 1932 and the family heard nothing for three decades. In 1961, however, one of Parker's brothers saw a picture of one Tom Parker with Elvis Presley. He knew right away this dead ringer for Andreas Kujik was his brother. This brother, Ad van Kujik, actually went to the United States and met Parker; for the rest of his life he refused to discuss the meeting.

Return to Sender

"Colonel Tom Parker" was born Andreas Cornelius van Kujik in Breda, Holland, on June 26, 1909, one of nine children. His father had worked with horses as a soldier, and his French mother had traveled with a carnival. Colonel Parker never officially became a U.S. citizen and until his death was an illegal alien.

But it wasn't convenient at the time for Tom Parker to reveal his true identity—at least not for another two decades when he was in legal contention with the Elvis Presley Estate, which accused Parker of gross mismanagement and, well, greed. How could a man be sued in U.S. courts, Parker asked in his defense, if he weren't really an American citizen? It was a lovely bit of sleight of hand and, although control of the estate was transferred out of the Colonel's sticky fingers, he did receive a $2 million settlement. It wasn't the last time the Colonel laughed all the way to the bank.

Return to Sender

Now come on, was Colonel Parker a real colonel? Not even close. The military title was honorary, bestowed upon him by Louisiana Governor Jimmie Davis in 1948 (kind of like Colonel Sanders). Parker used it to further his image as a man in control. Interestingly, Elvis called him "Admiral." Gee, why not?

Parker became a carny (a person who works at a carnival, not Art Carney the actor) like his mother, promoting a number of shows at carnivals, fairs, and circuses. Among those shows the carnival barker barked about were the Great Parker Pony Circus and Colonel Parker and His Dancing Chickens. How do you make chickens dance to music? Why, make the bottom of their cage a hot plate, but cover the hot plate with sawdust, so the audience won't see it. Parker obviously had some sort of grudge against animals, because at age 32 he became the dog-catcher of Tampa.

It wasn't a big leap from the carny circuit to the traveling hillbilly shows of that time in the South; the shows followed each other from town to town, often using the same venues. It was all just entertainment to the local folks. Parker adapted his promotional talents to music and, by the early 1950s, a number of prominent singers were rotating through his stable, including Eddy Arnold, Gene Austin, Tommy Sands, and Hank Snow. Though not exclusively, most of his clients were country musicians and Parker handled them competently, if not spectacularly. (He did have a falling out with Arnold, who fired him summarily when he became suspicious, fairly or not, of Parker's financial dealings.)

So Why the Colonel?

Think about it. All Elvis really wanted to do was play music, make money, and have fun. From the age of 19 he was a singer; he never had to develop the practical skills most people do, and consequently remained a teenager in many ways. He didn't have business acumen. Nor did his parents or anyone else in his family. The Colonel opened up a world to them that, despite Elvis' sudden success, they really didn't feel they could conquer without him.

Colonel Parker *was* good at what he did—a clever promoter and ruthless negotiator. He made things happen. He got Elvis some good gigs early and got him top-dollar paydays consistently—much better pay than his peers were getting. He got Elvis national exposure. Didn't he deserve a big piece of the pie?

Greed Is the Word

Throughout Elvis and the Colonel's career together, there are many examples of the Colonel looking out for himself first and Elvis second. On January 2, 1967, Parker managed to convince the King (get a load of this one!) to pay him 50 percent of every penny he earned (industry standards range from 15 to 25 percent). The new contract lasted until January 22, 1976. A 50 percent commission is, in all likelihood, the highest management contract in show business history.

In the mid-1960s, Vernon, who was in over his head with the Colonel (make that *way* over), threatened to fire him. Parker quickly produced an itemized bill for $5 million owed him by Elvis, and Vernon backed down.

In 1973, Parker advised Elvis to sell his catalog of singles and albums to RCA for $6 million, half of which would go to the Colonel. Elvis complied. The colonel had investments; Elvis did not. Guess who made out tax-wise?

During Elvis' Vegas period, the Colonel was famous for his heavy and very public gambling (craps and roulette—by no means the games with the best odds). He lost about a million a year.

The day after Elvis' death, Parker had Vernon sign documents giving his company Factors Etc., Inc., the rights to market all Elvis-related products. In 1980, Parker made a deal with Warner Brothers for the rights to a film on Elvis; Parker and the Elvis Presley Estate each got $200,000. Parker's employees and associates got $350,000, much of which also probably ended up in the Colonel's pockets.

In May 1980, a probate court appointed Memphis entertainment attory Blanchard L. Tual as legal guardian of Elvis' daughter Lisa Marie, giving him powers to investigate the financial relationship of Elvis and Parker. Tual's finding: Parker had "violated his duty." All payments were to cease and charges were brought against Parker. He settled out-of-court, divesting himself of all Elvis-related assets and agreeing not to use Elvis' name in any endeavor. After 25 years, the King was posthumously free of his puppet strings.

The bottom line is that Elvis thought he needed Parker. He probably liked him, too. Parker made him money. (It's important to remember that poor-boy Elvis didn't make big money until he hooked up with the Colonel.) He took over where Gladys and Vernon left off, tending to the details of Elvis' life beyond the home. When he was with Elvis, he fussed over him the way Gladys always did. He had a kind of magnetism that enabled him to sell people just about anything—including dancing chickens.

The Colonel always called Elvis "my boy"—as in, "Can you do my boy a favor?" There's probably a hint in there about the nature of their relationship.

What Might Have Been?

No matter how much money Parker took from him, Elvis was certainly comfortable. There was a greater downside to the relationship. Despite the phenomenal commercial success that Elvis enjoyed for over 20 years, Colonel Parker stood in the way of much more that Elvis could have accomplished artistically. Elvis was a brilliant interpreter of songs. He showed true talent and potential as an actor as well. A manager with better musical and creative sense would have been concerned with Elvis' place in history and provided him with opportunities to demonstrate and expand these talents.

The Colonel, who screened song submissions, acted as a music critic and no doubt prevented Elvis from hearing and recording lots of good material. He also drove away many talented songwriters by insisting on outrageous terms—Hill and Range, the publishing company he oversaw, which controlled all of Elvis' music, insisted on half the publishing rights and half the writer's share. This

Going for Gold
To probe more deeply into the relationship between Elvis and Tom Parker, read *Elvis and the Colonel* by Dirk Vallenga and Mick Farren, published by Dell in 1988. It is well-researched and entertainingly written. An earlier book of the same title, written by Mike Mann and published by Drake Books, is an "authorized" and less investigative biography.

penny-wise, pound-foolish approach didn't change until 1968, when producer Felton Jarvis left RCA to oversee Elvis' recording career.

The Colonel could also have helped Elvis be selective in choosing movie scripts. Elvis had real acting talent, but the Colonel insisted he sing in all his movies. There were times when Parker turned down roles in Elvis' name because the money wasn't big enough. Some of these, such as *Thunder Road* (1958) and *A Star is Born* (1976), were quality films. Some were wonderful films, like *West Side Story,* in which Elvis was offered the role of Tony opposite Natalie Wood, and *Midnight Cowboy*, in which he was offered the title role that eventually went to Jon Voight.

Parker was a detriment to Elvis' international success as well: The only foreign country Elvis ever played was Canada—three gigs before he met Parker. It's assumed that the reason Parker discouraged Elvis from playing internationally was because he was afraid his own illegal alien status would be found out. Elvis never, for example, toured England, Germany, or Japan although his popularity in those countries was enormous.

The King and I

"Anybody who'll pay my boy a million dollars can make any kind of picture he wants."

—Colonel Tom Parker

Finally, Elvis might have benefited more from a manager who cared about his welfare and warned him of the pitfalls of excess. Parker, save for his voracious gambling and eating, lived a moderate lifestyle and could have served as a true mentor to Elvis. Instead, he kept his eyes glued on the financial road and kept their personal relationship distant. Instead of warning Elvis of the pitfalls of his lifestyle, particularly drug use, Parker, by all accounts, ignored the problem completely. For this, if nothing else, he deserves condemnation. Maybe he just didn't care, or maybe having Elvis fat, drugged, and happy served his purposes.

The King and I

"I never interfere in Elvis' personal life. What goes on with him away from business, I don't know. I never mix into it."

—Colonel Tom Parker

Two Men Buried with the Truth

Andreas Cornelius van Kujik, a.k.a. Thomas Andrew Parker, a.k.a. the Colonel, died a rich man in Las Vegas of complications of a stroke on January 21, 1997, at the age of 87. He missed the 20th anniversary of the King's death by a mere six months. Parker died as he had lived, an enigma. He never admitted the true facts of his life. He was a shrewd businessman who needlessly paid exorbitant taxes and gambled away millions. He wasn't a drinker or a drug user, yet never said a word about Elvis' excesses. He helped make Elvis rich beyond his wildest dreams, but also helped stultify his creative side. He never wrote his autobiography, despite huge offers from publishers; in fact, he rarely was even interviewed. Some people feel he was a self-created genius, an American hero. Others think he was a vastly overrated, greedy buffoon.

The Colonel once said: "I never talk about myself." But other people sure talked *about* him. Opinions about him, even among knowledgeable sources, vary wildly. For me, writer Dave Marsh (author of this book's Foreword) has it right when he describes Parker as "in the running for the most overrated person in show business history."

Colonel Tom Parker had a vice-grip on Elvis Presley, and of course Elvis bears the responsibility for allowing himself to be controlled so completely. Why did he? Was he happy, or was he the Colonel's biggest sucker? The inside story of their relationship is one of the great untold tales in show business. Throughout this book, Parker's name will come up again and again. Despite his recent death, the Colonel—like Elvis—lives on in myth, controversy, and confusion.

The Least You Need to Know

➤ Elvis had two other managers before Colonel Tom Parker: Scotty Moore and Bob Neal.

➤ A mysterious man, Colonel Parker wasn't a Colonel but rather an illegal Dutch immigrant who worked for years in circuses and carnivals.

➤ Colonel Parker made Elvis an enormous amount of money, but he charged Elvis exorbitant fees and ignored his personal problems.

➤ Elvis died not knowing that Parker didn't have a passport—the reason the King never played overseas.

Chapter 11

Elvis the Pelvis

In This Chapter

➤ Elvis firsts

➤ Elvis strikes gold in concert and in studio

➤ Elvis controversies

➤ Elvis is crowned King

By 1955, Elvis had gone from a local to a regional phenomenon. But there was no middle-ground when it came to Elvis: critics loved or hated him; audiences went berserk when he performed. Older people generally resented him; teens, especially the girls, went ga-ga.

Controversy also began to swirl around him. Why? Because Elvis wiggled his hips, thrust his pelvis, leered seductively, and danced on-stage without inhibition. He was overtly *sexy* and *dangerous*—and he enjoyed teasing his audience, especially the girls.

A Series of Firsts

Elvis kept up his relentless schedule of concerts and recording sessions in 1955 and 1956, and his reputation grew nationally. Colonel Tom Parker took over his management full-time and got Elvis more and more exposure.

By the end of 1956, Elvis had become a regular on national television, and his first movie had been released. He was a household name, well on his way to conquering the world.

The years 1955 and 1956 saw a series of firsts for Elvis as his career accelerated. I'll lay them out for you here, then go into some of them in greater detail in the next few chapters.

Northern Exposure

In January 1955, Elvis got his first radio air-time up North. DJ Bill Randle of WERE in Cleveland, Ohio, played one of his records.

Cleveland was also the site of Elvis' first concert in the North. Then-manager Bob Neal traveled with the boys on this jaunt because they were opening up a new frontier. Since Sun Records had no distribution, they carried records to sell in the trunk. On February 26, Elvis played the Circle Theater Jamboree. DJ Bill Randle was impressed and set up a television audition for Arthur Godfrey's New York-based show *Talent Scouts*.

Randle also played an Elvis record soon after that in New York City.

Return to Sender
Everything seemed to come easy for Elvis, but let's not forget the rejections he suffered on his climb: He bombed at the Grand Ole Opry and flunked his first TV audition for Arthur Godfrey's show. Elvis also had constant attacks from parents and religious leaders. I'm not suggesting we bring out the violins, but Elvis paid his dues.

First Television Appearance

On March 5, 1955, Elvis made his television debut on the Louisiana Hayride, telecast by the Shreveport station KWKH-TV. Introduced by Horace Logan, he reportedly sang "Uncle Pen" by Bill Monroe, although no footage exists to confirm this.

First National TV Audition

In March 1955, Elvis, Scotty, and Bill flew to New York City to audition for Arthur Godfrey's show *Talent Scouts*. They didn't get the job. They didn't even meet Godfrey. But it marked Elvis' first trip to New York City and his first trip on an airplane.

First Riot

On May 13, 1955, Elvis played a concert at Gator Bowl Baseball Park in Jacksonville, Florida, the last day of a five-day swing through the state. 14,000 fans attended. At the end of the show, Elvis, in his charming, somewhat naughty way said, "I'll see you all backstage, girls." Unfortunately, many took him at his word and rushed the dressing room, many climbing through an open window. Teenage girls ripped clothes off Elvis, taking his coat, shirt, and boots. When he made it to his Lincoln Continental, they began writing their names, numbers, and love messages all over it in lipstick.

First Record to Chart

In July 1955, "Baby Let's Play House" reached number 10 on the *Billboard* Country Best-Seller chart and number five on the Country Disc Jockey chart. It was Elvis' first record to appear on national best-seller charts. "Baby Let's Play House" was his most successful record for Sun—and his sexiest.

For The Record

Elvis had a lifelong thing for pink Cadillacs. Shortly after buying his first pink Caddy, Elvis recorded "Baby" and added the lines: "You may have a pink Cadillac/But don'tcha be nobody's fool." The song, which had been a 1955 hit on the black charts by composer Arthur Gunter, is about a boy trying to talk a girl into having sex; the words "pink Cadillac"—especially when sung by Elvis—were clearly a double entendre, referring to both a car and the physical core of womanhood. Happily for Elvis, most of his audience didn't get the reference. Imagine the public outcry if they had?

Let's Make a Deal: First Big Contract

On November 20, 1955, RCA, at Parker's behest, purchased Elvis' contract from Sun Records for $35,000. Hill and Range Music bought Sam Phillips' Hi-Lo Music publishing company for $15,000. For his part, Elvis received a $15,000 bonus to cover possible future royalties for his Sun releases. Why would Sam Phillips do such a seemingly crazy thing? He needed the money and Parker knew it.

On January 10, 1956, Elvis went to Nashville and recorded "I Got a Woman" by Ray Charles and "Heartbreak Hotel" by Tommy Durden and Mae Axton. In this session, Elvis was joined by Scotty, Bill, and D.J. Fontana, plus Nashville regulars Chet Atkins on guitar and Floyd Cramer on piano. Gordon Stoker, Ben Speer, and Brock Speer provided back-up vocals.

The next day, Elvis recorded "I Was the One" (written by Aaron Schroeder, Claude DeMetrius, Hal Blair, and Bill Pepper), which became the B side of "Heartbreak Hotel."

Heartbreak Hotel Goes First-Class

On January 17, 1956, RCA released "Heartbreak Hotel" with "I Was the One" as the B-side. In April, "Heartbreak Hotel" reached number one on the Top 100 chart. It also was number one on the Country Best-Seller chart, the Country Juke Box chart, and the Country Disc Jockey chart, and reached number five on the Rhythm and Blues chart (his first record to reach the R&B chart). Moreover, it was Elvis' first million-seller.

For the Record

Here's an odd bit of trivia: "Heartbreak Hotel" was written by a school-teacher and former music publicist named Mae Boren Axton. She also happened to be country singing star Hoyt Axton's mother.

Look, Mama, I'm on TV

On January 28, 1956, Elvis made his national television debut on Tommy and Jimmy Dorsey's *Stage Show* and sang "Flip, Flip & Fly." Elvis was a natural on television: The camera loved his heavy-lidded good looks, and his performance generated the most mail in the show's history. (He would appear five more times—February 4, 11, 18, and March 17 and 24.) Other TV shows would follow, including *The Milton Berle Show* and *The Ed Sullivan Show*.

For The Record

The producer of the Dorsey Brothers *Stage Show* was none other than Jackie Gleason, who was no Elvis fan but a good businessman who saw that the audience wanted him. "If I booked only the people I like," Gleason said at the time, "I'd have nothing but trumpet players on my show. It was and is our opinion that Elvis would appeal to the majority of the people." Incidentally, *Stage Show* was the lead-in for Gleason's own legendary show, *The Honeymooners*.

Elvis' First Long-Player

On March 13, the album *Elvis Presley*, with its classic pink-and-green lettering and iconic photo of the singing Hillbilly Cat, was released by RCA. The album consisted of five tracks recorded at Sun records and seven at RCA (Side 1: "Blue Suede Shoes," "I'm Counting on You," "I Got A Woman," "One-Sided Love Affair," "I Love You Because," and "Just Because"; Side 2: "Tutti Frutti," "Tryin' to Get to You," "I'm Gonna Sit Right Down and Cry (Over You)," "I'll Never Let You Go (Little Darlin')," "Blue Moon," and "Money Honey"). Every track is a gem—tightly arranged and fresh-sounding.

First Screen Test and First Movie Deal

On April 1, 1956, Elvis auditioned for a part in *The Rainmaker*. He didn't get the role. (Earl Holliman got the role Elvis would have played.) Five days later, Elvis signed a seven-year, three-movie contract with Paramount Pictures. Elvis' contract was for $100,000 for the first film, $150,000 for the second, and $200,000 for the third.

Elvis Craps Out in Vegas

On April 23, 1956, Elvis opened the New Frontier Hotel in Las Vegas, Nevada. He was paid $8,500 a week and shared the bill with comedian Shecky Greene and the Freddie Martin Band.

The older, middle-American audience couldn't have been more different from his teenage fans. They just didn't get Elvis. Within days, outside on the hotel's marquee, Elvis' name, which had been on top, was moved beneath Greene and Freddie Martin. He didn't go over well, and the booking was canceled halfway through the scheduled four weeks. (But Elvis would return triumphantly 13 years later and rule the town until his death, as you'll find out in later chapters.)

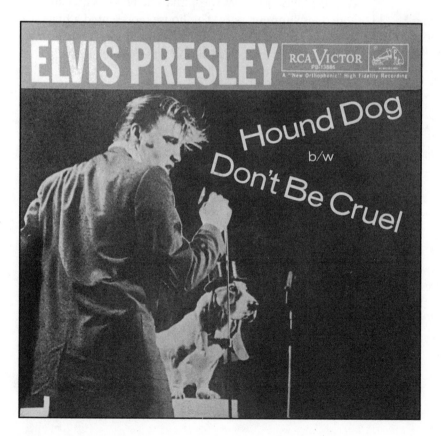

The cover for the single "Hound Dog"/ "Don't Be Cruel." Vintage 1956 Elvis.

For the Record

Within days of Elvis' Las Vegas opening, his name, which had been listed first, was dropped below that of Shecky Green and the Freddie Martin band. This was hard on Elvis, but history has a way of sorting things out. Freddie Martin is hardly a household name.

Happy Homeowner

On May 11, 1956, the Presleys moved into 1034 Audubon Drive in a fashionable section of Memphis. Elvis had bought it for $40,000 the month before. The Fifties-modern, one-story house had three bedrooms, a game room, a double carport; Elvis' bedroom was pink. The Presleys quickly added a swimming pool. The house represented a huge sea of change in the Presley family fortunes; for the first time in any of their lives, desperation was no longer a daily spectre.

The King and I
"It's [the house on Audubon Drive] something my mother always wanted but never talked about. It was as if she didn't want to let anyone know about her dreams. But I knew. I wanted to get my mama a home."

—Elvis

First Movie

On August 23, 1956, the movie *Love Me Tender* began filming. Elvis did not play the lead in this movie, which was originally going to be called *The Reno Brothers*. Richard Egan played the lead, Elvis played the younger brother, Clint Reno, who dies. (Oops, just gave away the end of the movie!) It was released on November 15.

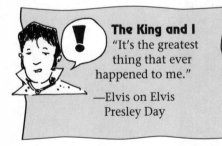

The King and I
"It's the greatest thing that ever happened to me."

—Elvis on Elvis Presley Day

It's Elvis Presley Day!

On September 26, 1956, Tupelo, Mississippi, gave Elvis a heart-shaped key to the city and declared it Elvis Presley Day. This was the first in a series of Elvis Presley Days, proclaimed by various states. Elvis performed at Tupelo's Mississippi-Alabama Fair and Dairy Show before a near-hysterical crowd of over 20,000 fans. (He wore a blue velvet shirt, sewn by Gladys, and blue suede shoes.) Admission price to a see the King?: $2.00.

Sold Out

In 1954, 1955, and 1956, Elvis played nearly 400 gigs. In addition to Tennessee, Louisiana, Texas, Arkansas, and Georgia, other states were added to the list: in 1955, he played his first concerts in Mississippi, Missouri, Alabama, New Mexico, Ohio, Florida, North Carolina, Virginia, Oklahoma, Indiana, and Kentucky; in 1956, he played his first concerts in South Carolina, Washington D.C., California, Colorado, Nevada, Minnesota, Wisconsin, Kansas, Nebraska, Iowa, Michigan, and Arizona. He also went to New York to record TV performances.

In early 1955, he was selling out high school auditoriums. By that spring, he was filling civic auditoriums. By 1956 he was selling out stadiums. In Dallas' Cotton Bowl, for example, Elvis played to a crowd of over 26,000 screaming fans on October 11, 1956. The performance began with the spotlight catching Elvis sitting in a Cadillac convertible as it headed for the stage. The audience went nuts, Elvis laughed, and the fans went even crazier. Mass hysteria, the first in rock history, was getting to be commonplace whenever Elvis played.

People were paying their hard-earned money to see someone who audiences once thought of as the Hillbilly Cat, then as Elvis Presley, and then as Elvis. The posters trumpeting his shows had it right: The Nation's New Singing Sensation! Varying his pace between rockers like "Long Tall Sally" and ballads like "Love Me Tender," young Elvis Presley, all of 21 years of age, was in complete control.

The King and I

"Touring is the roughest part. It's really rough. You're in a town, you do a show, you come off, you ride in a car, you go on to the next town. I get all keyed up after a show. It's hard to relax."

—Elvis

Top of the Pops

As Elvis' name spread and popularity grew, he sold more and more records. In July 1955, "Baby, Let's Play House" hit number 10 on the *Billboard* Country Best-Seller chart. Soon after, "I Forgot to Remember to Forget" and "Mystery Train" both began climbing the charts as a Sun release. By February 1956, having been released on a record by RCA as well, both songs hit number one on the Country Chart. The list of accomplishments is staggering, even by today's standards:

➤ Most of Elvis' 1956 RCA releases charted. Moreover, the following singles were gold records: "Heartbreak Hotel," "I Was the One," "I Want You, I Need You, I Love You," "Don't Be Cruel," "Hound Dog," "Any Way You Want Me," and "Love Me Tender."

➤ These 1956 songs were Top 10 hits: "Heartbreak Hotel," "I Want You, I Need You, I Love You," "Hound Dog," "Don't Be Cruel," and "Love Me Tender."

➤ And these 1956 songs were number-one singles on the *Billboard* Top 100 Chart: "Heartbreak Hotel" and "Don't Be Cruel."

➤ The RCA album *Elvis Presley*, released on March 13, 1956, was the first in history to sell a million copies. His second album, *Elvis*, released on October 19, 1956, reached number one on the *Billboard* Top Ten chart.

Going for Gold
Remember "Old Shep," the song Elvis sang to win second prize at the Mississippi/Alabama Fair and Dairy Show? On September 2, 1956, Elvis recorded several takes of the song, singing and playing piano. A radio-only release was used to promote the album *Elvis*. That single is extremely rare. Moreover, some early copies of the album (with a "17 S" after the RCA LPM-1382) have the song on them and are worth a lot as well. "Old Shep" can be heard on other not so rare albums as well.

To me, this, and the Sun sessions, were the golden period of Elvis' recording career. He had all his creative juices flowing and was breaking new ground with his rockabilly arrangements and vocal expressiveness. Moreover, the selected material was much of the best of rhythm and blues. Check out Elvis' brilliant, breathtaking version of Junior Parker's "Mystery Train"—his last Sun single, recorded on July 11, 1955. You'll never hear better music. Elvis' versions set a new standard for the type of music that was coming to be called more and more "rock and roll."

Elvis continued to sell records and bust the charts for years to come. It's not that he was the only performer making hit records during these years; it's the number of hits and the length of his career that make him unique. The popularity of other performers would fade, while his would keep growing exponentially.

Girls Fainting and Parents Panicking

As you've read, Elvis caused his first riot in Jacksonville, Florida, on May 13, 1955. Now more and more, he drew crowds wherever he went—autograph seekers and worse (clothing seekers). The *bobby-soxers* were going bananas over him.

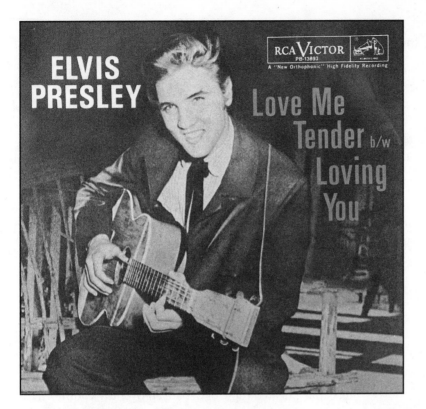

The cover for the 1956 single "Love Me Tender"/ "Loving You." Elvis again goes for the girls with a couple of ballads.

Meanwhile, he was getting more negative reviews and angry responses from parents, educators, and religious leaders. Fundamentalist Christians regularly denounced him—somewhat ironic, given his First Assembly of God background and his love of gospel music. On June 2, 1955, in Amarillo, Texas, educators and parents demonstrated against him before a concert at the City Auditorium. Elvis' first song to chart, "Baby, Let's Play House," didn't help douse the fires. The lyrics were interpreted to mean "let's play unmarried sex"—which is, well, exactly what the song was saying.

The Word
Teenage girls in the 1940s and early '50s were known as **bobby-soxers** because they wore short white ankle socks. Elvis wasn't the first to wow the bobby-soxers; first came Frank Sinatra and later Eddie Fisher. Early in his career, some writers referred to Elvis' fans as **country bobby-soxers**.

> ### For the Record
>
> The film *Blackboard Jungle*, released in 1955, was the first movie to feature a rock and roll song—Bill Haley and the Comets' "(We're Gonna) Rock Around the Clock" plays over the opening credits. The movie, starring Glenn Ford and an up-and-coming Sidney Poitier, is about teenage behavior in a New York City school system and helped make America associate rock and roll music with juvenile delinquency.

At some concerts, the music could barely be heard because of screaming fans. Even at a traditional venue, such as the Louisiana Hayride, he was causing a ruckus. On January 21, 1956, he had to be rushed from the premises when the teenage girls in the crowd began to crowd the stage.

In early 1956, it became a custom at Elvis concerts for an announcer to proclaim, "Elvis has left the building." The intent was to discourage fans from rushing backstage, although of course, the fans stopped believing it after a while.

The controversy that Elvis stirred up started as a local matter, generated around local response before and after his concert appearances. But when he started showing up on television and in the movies in 1956, Elvis' "negative influence" on American youth became a heated topic of debate all over the country. The phrase "devil's music" was used in reference to rock and roll and Elvis' songs. In some communities, he was even subject to restraining orders—a police officer or magistrate would watch an afternoon show to see if an evening show would be allowed or not. Sometimes, a ridiculous compromise would be reached—no wiggling on stage.

The King and I
"He [Elvis] is the most obscene, vulgar influence on America today."

—Hedda Hopper

The King and I
"That ["Elvis the Pelvis"] is about the stupidest thing I've ever heard from a so-called intelligent adult."

—Elvis

The vulgarity debate puzzled Elvis ("It's just music and singing," Elvis said. "That's all.") and vastly irritated his mother Gladys who said, "My boy wouldn't do anything bad, no such thing. He's a good boy, a boy who has never forgotten his church upbringing."

A June 1956 issue of *Time* magazine referred to Elvis as "the Pelvis," and suddenly the phrase "Elvis the Pelvis" (which Elvis disliked) had permanently entered the American lexicon. That same month an issue of *Look* had an article entitled "The Great Rock 'n' Roll Controversy." Who was it primarily about? Who else?

"King of the Whole Wide World"

In October 1956, *Variety* magazine referred to Elvis as "The King of Rock 'n' Roll." There wasn't a formal crowning of course, but it was now official.

So what does a King make? Why this label for Elvis? Record sales and ticket sales that beat the competition count. Musical influence over other performers also counts. But, most of all, from that period of Elvis' life on, when people heard his name they thought of rock and roll; and when they heard the phrase rock and roll, they thought of Elvis Presley.

The Least You Need to Know

➤ 1955 and 1956 were Elvis' prime years, during which he went from regional to national stature.

➤ By 1956, Elvis had conquered radio, TV, film, recordings, and stage.

➤ Like every other legendary performer, Elvis paid his dues and had his share of early failures.

➤ Elvis was attacked as obscene by many factions, particularly by religious leaders.

Part 4
Top of the World, Mama: The Reign of Elvis

In Part 4, I'll tell you about Elvis at his peak, when his talent and power were at a maximum (before the pressures began to impact his art and his personality). For this reason, it's one of my favorite sections of this book: There was an innocence to him then, a joy in the discovery of new experiences and new heights. The world was his for the taking—and he lapped it all up.

We'll learn about his remarkable first television appearances and, very shortly thereafter, his blitzkrieg assault on Hollywood. (Hey, nobody ever said Hollywood producers were dumb: They took one look at young Presley and saw a star they knew would light up the Big Screen the same way he did the little box.)

We'll also see him uncomplainingly join the Army and take few special privileges along the way. But Elvis ended up being rewarded: His tour of duty removed the public perception of him as being a wild, untamed rock and roller.

Lastly, we'll look at the people in his life: his loves and his closest buddies, the Memphis Mafia. So hop on board. The last train to Memphis is ready to roll.

Elvis in TV Land

Elvis and television were made for one another. The young medium was searching for stars, especially those who would appeal to teens and the huge Baby Boomer generation which, by the mid-1950s, was just beginning to exercise its financial might. Elvis was perfect for the camera. It loved him, and he was a natural—relaxed and thoroughly unintimidated by the unblinking eye.

In Elvis Presley, television found a new star who, by the end of 1956, had exploded into the national consciousness. The fact that America's teenagers seemed to have lost their sanity en masse over Elvis made the controversy grow exponentially. Without the tube, Elvis would, of course, have been a star; with it, he became a national phenomenon, and by 1957 he was a millionaire.

Hayriders on the Storm

As I informed you in Chapter 11, in the list of Elvis' "firsts,"-on March 5, 1955, Elvis—with Scotty Moore and Bill Black—made his television debut on the Louisiana Hayride. The show was telecast by Shreveport's KWKH-TV. He was introduced by emcee Horace Logan and reportedly sang "Uncle Pen" by Bill Monroe. Alas, poor Elvis mavens, no tape of the show exists to confirm this.

Though the television version of Louisiana Hayride was just a local broadcast, the radio broadcast was national and definitely the big-time. The six-year old Hayride, broadcast on Saturday nights on a 50,000 watt clear-channel signal, reached over half the country and was serious competition for the reigning country music behemoth, the Grand Ole Opry. Stars like Hank Williams, Webb Pierce, Slim Whitman, and Jim Reeves had gotten their start on the three-hour long Hayride, now being touted as the "Cradle of the Stars."

Being number two, the Hayride attempted to be a little more adventuresome in its choice of musical guests, and Elvis certainly represented a risk, particularly after doing so poorly on his Opry debut. But the Hayride audience was younger and hipper, and they "got" Elvis immediately. The Hayride quickly signed Elvis as a regular and he and the boys began making the weekly 16-hour round trip to Shreveport in Scotty's beat-up Chevy. The Hayride had an important secondary effect as well—regular performing gigs in clubs and other venues from the Hayride exposure.

Knowing how far his career went—you may think the event seems small; but imagine what a big deal it was at the time—this recent technology called *television*, broadcast live right into people's homes. (Although invented and developed before World War II, television did not have cultural clout untl the late 1940s and early 1950s. By 1955, 67 percent of American households had television sets. And here was the Hillbilly Cat appearing on them.

And remember folks, less than a year before, Elvis didn't even have a record out. Now he was a regular on a national radio show and had even appeared on a local TV show. Radio was the foundation of Elvis' success, but this first, albeit modest, television appearance, was a harbinger of great things to come—and come soon.

Closer to the Promised Land: Arthur Godfrey

In March 1955, Bob Neal took Elvis, Scotty, and Bill and flew to New York City to audition for Arthur Godfrey's CBS-TV show *Talent Scouts*. Then the country's most important amateur and young professional talent showcase, the weekly, primetime *Talent Scouts* had given stars like Pat Boone, The McGuire Sisters, and Shari Lewis their first national exposure. Talk about hitting the big time. Not only that, this marked the first time Elvis flew on an airplane, and it was his first visit to the Big Apple. (New York was cold, expensive, and frenetic: Elvis didn't like it one bit.)

But Elvis wasn't quite "talented" enough, at least not by the standards of Godfrey's people. The audition didn't get him a spot on the show, and he didn't even meet Arthur Godfrey. Was it that Elvis wasn't *good* enough in their minds? Or was it that he was too controversial? Of course, the Godfrey people didn't have to explain or justify their thinking. They just said in so many words: "Thanks but no thanks." Hey, Arthur's loss.

For the Record

About the time Elvis auditioned for *Talent Scouts*, so did Pat Boone. Pat Boone got the job, Elvis didn't. Not surprising. Elvis was a bad boy; Pat was the clean-cut, religious, great-great-great-grandson of old "Daniel" Boone— and, of course, he wore white buck shoes. Despite their chart rivalry, the two singers became good friends. Elvis collected Boone's records and, in a 1957 interview, said Boone was "undoubtedly the finest voice out now, especially on slow songs." In 1964, Boone recorded an album of Elvis' material, *Pat Boone Sings…Guess Who?*

The trip to New York City wasn't a complete waste, however. Elvis and the boys got to go to Harlem's legendary Apollo Theater and catch Bo Diddley, one of his favorites and another of the founding fathers of rock and roll.

Elvis was depressed on the flight home. He was going back to Memphis. Back to earth. Back to the reality of 100-mile drives to yet another one night stand. *Talent Scouts* was Elvis' first grab at the brass ring. He missed.

To the Moon, Elvis, to the Moon!—Jackie Gleason

In 1956, Jackie Gleason, "the Great One," produced the Dorsey Brothers' *Stage Show* on CBS, broadcast out of New York. The variety show was struggling in the ratings and Gleason, who personally supervised the broadcasts, decided to give Elvis a spot, though he made it clear he was not a fan. (That same spring, Gleason gave Bobby Darin—who later worked with Elvis in recording sessions—his national TV debut; he sang "Rock Island Line.")

On January 28, 1956, Elvis made his first national TV appearance on *Stage Show*. Elvis ran out, launched into "Shake, Rattle & Roll," gyrated wildly during Scotty's solo, switched to "Flip, Flop & Fly" in the middle (both were Big Joe Turner songs), almost fell down at the end, took a hair-waving bow, and was gone! Make no mistake: This was a rock and roll night.

The King and I
"If I booked only the people I like, I'd have nothing but trumpet players on my show."

—Jackie Gleason

In the following weeks, Elvis appeared five more times on the Dorsey show: February 4, 11, and 18, and March 17 and 24. On the February 4 show, Elvis sang "Baby, Let's Play House" and Little Richard's signature song, "Tutti Frutti." The first song outraged conservatives because it hinted at sex out of wedlock. "Tutti Frutti" also had sexual connotations (as Little Richard himself later admitted). In later appearances, Elvis performed a wide range of material, including country and gospel. On February 11, he sang "Heartbreak Hotel," his first number-one song, for the first time on national TV.

The cover of the 1956 single "Heartbreak Hotel" and "Jailhouse Rock."

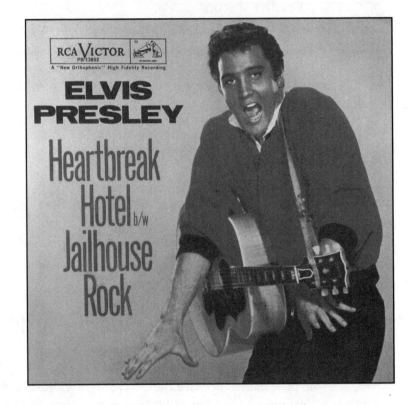

Elvis managed to pull in a very respectable 18.4 percent of the TV audience, but Perry Como, singing "Hot-Diggity, Dog-Diggity" over on NBC, won 34.6 percent of viewers. Ratings were consistently around 20 percent for all Elvis' appearances.

Anchors Away: Milton Berle

On April 3, 1956, Elvis played NBC-TV's popular, but waning, *Milton Berle Show*. "Uncle Miltie," one of television's first superstars, had been on the tube continously since 1948, and had just moved his show from New York to Hollywood. (It didn't help the ratings and the show was cancelled in June of 1956.)

One of the first color variety shows, Berle broadcast his April 3 show from the deck of the USS *Hancock*, anchored at San Diego. Elvis sang "Shake, Rattle & Roll," "Blue Suede Shoes," and "Heartbreak Hotel." The sailors and girls just loved him. So did girls at home. The ratings were 30 percent and climbing. Berle, who paid Elvis $5,000, also did an embarrassingly corny skit with Elvis playing "Elvin" Presley and Berle playing his twin brother, Melvin Presley. Gladys must have felt a little weird about that, having lost Elvis' twin, Jesse Garon, during childbirth. For some time after the show, members of Elvis' inner circle jokingly called him Elvin.

Elvis moved around the stage so much during rehearsals that he was missing his mark—a chalk line—and was often off camera. Milton Berle, a perfectionist with a huge ego, reportedly admonished "Elvin," telling him that the camera was going to miss one of them and it wasn't going to be Uncle Miltie.

On June 5, 1956, Elvis again appeared on *The Milton Berle Show*, broadcast from Los Angeles. On the show he sang "Hound Dog," a Jerry Lieber/Mike Stoller number, for the first time on TV and shocked America. What a dirty song! Why, it implies all sorts of things! Not to mention the slow, bluesy, bump'n'grind ending that Elvis and the boys tacked on—that, my fellow Americans, was the last straw!

Jack Gould of the *New York Times* wrote: "Mr. Presley has no discernible singing ability." John Crosby of the *New York Herald Tribune* called Elvis "unspeakably untalented and vulgar." There was plenty of irony in criticizing Elvis' "vulgarity," since Milton Berle specialized in cross-dressing humor and breast jokes.

Again, Elvis took in over 30 percent of the TV audience. He also sang "I Want You, I Need You, I Love You." How disgusting! Think of a young man daring to express such thoughts! The Berle show may have been the first example of what would become a huge issue later in the 1960s: the Generation Gap. America's teenagers *understood* Elvis. Adults didn't.

The King and I

"As a rule most of the adults are real nice... (they) say, 'I don't personally like your kinda music but my children like it.' Well I ain't got any kick about it, 'cause when I was young I liked the Charleston."

—Elvis

Doggin' It: Steve Allen

On July 1, 1956, Elvis appeared on NBC-TV's *Steve Allen Show*, broadcast from New York. (Allen would later turn his local late-night talk show into a network version—and *The Tonight Show*, with Allen as its first host, was born. To show America he wasn't such a bad boy, Steve Allen decided to dude him up in a tuxedo and sing the controversial "Hound Dog"—yep—to a basset hound sitting on a stool.

It was a goofy and unfathomable setting for Elvis. Steve Allen, who was a talented but conventional musician as well as a comedian, seemed bent on having fun at Elvis' expense. Elvis showed he was a good sport, but humiliation hung in the air. To see the perfect image of youthful defiance trussed up like a Christmas turkey was simply unseemly. Some critics noticed the misuse of the young rocker, assailing Allen for "fouling" Elvis. Fans picketed the studio the next day.

Elvis would have the last laugh, however, because Ed Sullivan—whose top-rated television show was beaten that night by the fledgling Allen show by an astounding 55 to 15 percent—decided he *had* to have Elvis. History was about to be made.

Yes, It Was a Really Big Shew: Ed Sullivan

Ed Sullivan, whose so-called *Toast of the Town* show would, at 23 years, eventually be the longest-running variety show in television history, had resisted the notion of putting "Elvis the Pelvis" on his show. "Old Stone Face" was a conservative, cautious man who abhorred risks. He was also a businessman, who had given Bob Hope his East Coast television debut, and had hosted everybody from Irving Berlin and Walt Disney to Albert Schweitzer and of course, later, The Beatles. When his competitor, Steve Allen, tromped him in the ratings with Elvis, Ed got nervous. He too would capitalize on Elvis. He telephoned Colonel Parker to talk deal. Parker, whom Sullivan had repeatedly ignored, knew he was in the driver's seat and negotiated the most astounding deal in television history: $50,000 for three appearances.

It worked. The broadcast of *The Ed Sullivan Show* on September 9, 1956 got 82.6 percent of the TV audience—an estimated 53 million people—the largest television audience in history and a record that stood until The Beatles appeared on Sullivan's show in 1964. But Ed missed all the fun because he was involved in an auto accident in Connecticut. (Convenient, because he didn't have to publicly eat crow for his earlier words, "I wouldn't have Presley on my show at any time.") That first Sullivan show was broadcast from Los Angeles with distinguished British stage and film actor Charles Laughton as the unlikely host. Elvis sang "Don't Be Cruel," "Hound Dog," "Ready Teddy," and "Love Me Tender."

Elvis' second appearance on *The Ed Sullivan Show*, on October 28, 1956, this time out of New York, was as successful as the first. This time, Ed himself got to introduce the King. Elvis sang "Don't Be Cruel," "Love Me Tender,"

Going for Gold

Want a tour of Elvis' early TV career? Go to the Ed Sullivan Theater, 1697 Broadway between 53rd and 54th Streets. This is *not* where Elvis appeared on *The Ed Sullivan Show,* but where he appeared on *Stage Show* when it was CBS Studio 50. Continuing chronologically, head to Hudson Theater, 44th Street near Broadway, where Elvis appeared on *The Steve Allen Show*. Then march over to the Maxine Elliot Theater, 39th Street near Broadway—where Elvis appeared on *The Ed Sullivan Show.*

"Love Me," and "Hound Dog." Elvis brought in 57 percent of viewers that night. Ed helped make Elvis more famous, but then, Elvis helped make Ed more famous, too.

Not everyone was happy, however. In particular, Jack Gould of the *New York Times*, who hated young Elvis, suggesting that "selfish exploitation and commercialized overstimulation of youth's physical impulses is certainly a gross national disservice." (Talk about overheated—old Jack needed a chill pill.)

For his third and final appearance, Elvis was faced with a backlash. Middle America thought Elvis' moves were dirty, and Ed Sullivan and the CBS censors got nervous. So for his January 6, 1957, appearance on *The Ed Sullivan Show*, Elvis was filmed from the waist up.

There's gratitude for you. Imagine. After all the viewers Elvis had brought in, the network cut half of his act: America didn't get to see him shake those famous hips. Ed (and CBS studio executives) had wimped out. The music was great, though: Elvis sang his heart out on "Hound Dog," "Love Me Tender," "Heartbreak Hotel," "Don't Be Cruel," "Too Much," "When My Blue Moon Turns to Gold," and "Peace in the Valley." At the end of the show, Sullivan announced, "I wanted to say to Elvis Presley and the country that this is a real decent, fine boy."

After a rollercoaster year, this would be Elvis' last regular TV appearance. In the remaining 20 years of his career, he would make only three more special TV appearances: Frank Sinatra's "Welcome Home, Elvis" special, the 1968 "Elvis" comeback special, and the legendary "Elvis: Aloha via Satellite" special in 1973. Finally, in 1977 after Elvis' death, the "Elvis In Concert" special aired, featuring performances from what proved to be his final concert tour.

Return to Sender

Everyone knows Ed Sullivan cut Elvis off at the waist when he performed on his show, right? Actually, not until the third show did Sullivan bow to the censors. Elvis' first two appearances on *The Ed Sullivan Show* generated so much excitement and controversy that Sullivan wimped out for the third show, which is what everyone remembers.

But Mom, I Love Him!

Imagine the scenes taking place in households all over '50s America while Elvis rocked their TV sets. Up to now, parents may not have caught on to rock and roll. Now the whole family was tuned in together. Remember, kids didn't have TVs in their bedrooms then. TV was a shared, living room experience. Parents could now see the Pelvis in motion and make their own assessment. Some secretly dug it. Some laughed it off. Others hit the roof. Outrage! Vulgarity! Sex! Sin!

The King and I
"After his famous first appearance on the *Ed Sullivan Show* in 1956, my aunt told me how foolish I was to sit screaming with joy at the spectacle of that vulgar singer on TV. It was then I knew that she and I lived in different worlds, and it was then that kids' bedroom doors slammed all over America."

—Maureen Orth, writing in *Newsweek* after Elvis' death in 1977

The King and I
"If those kids want to pay their money to come out and scream and yell, it's their business. They'll grow up someday and grow out of that. While they're young, let them have their fun. Don't let some old man that's so old he can't get around call them a bunch of idiots."

—Elvis, 1956

Not only were their daughters influenced, some of them screaming and swooning, their sons loved it, too. Males all over the country started imitating Elvis, slicking their hair back, growing sideburns, and souping up their wardrobe. Now when kids rebelled against their parents—some of them even joining gangs—parents blamed it, if not on Marlon Brando in *The Wild One* with his black leather jacket, then on Elvis and that thing called rock and roll.

Many in show business who worked with Elvis, however, came to respect his professionalism and his good nature. Ed Sullivan announced to his audience that Elvis was "a real decent, fine boy," and went on to say that he had "never had a pleasanter experience ... with a big name."

Elvis' television triumph represents the larger triumph of Elvis and the younger generation over the snobbery of the New York media establishment—the "cultural elite" of the time. Much of their distaste for Elvis wasn't based on his "vulgarity" or "immorality"; that was just a cover for regional, class, and racial prejudices. To them, Elvis was a Southerner and a redneck, playing a mix of hillbilly and black music—four strikes against him. His music was distasteful, tacky, moronic, and, most of all, low class. Resorting to moral judgment was just the establishment's way of arousing public disapproval—even among people they were prejudiced against.

Of course, that's not the whole story: What the *kids* responded to was the fun, energy, and physical freedom of Elvis' music and stage presence—which did seem improper, if not immoral, to the older generation.

The Least You Need to Know

➤ Television stars like Jackie Gleason, Steve Allen, and Milton Berle, may not have liked Elvis' music, but they loved the ratings he got.

➤ History was made when 53 million people watched Elvis on *The Ed Sullivan Show*.

➤ Controversy erupted between adults and teens when Elvis burst into America's living rooms on the tube.

Chapter 13

Hooray for Hollywood: Elvis in the Movies

In This Chapter

➤ Elvis' movies: roles, fellow actors, music

➤ Elvis' life in Los Angeles

➤ Elvis' unrealized potential as an actor

Elvis' film career spanned 13 years—his movies were the bridge between Early Elvis and Late Elvis. His first films helped him reach the peak as an entertainer; his late movies might be called the low point of his career, after which he had to look deep inside himself and reinvent himself as a performer.

The movies Elvis starred in range from the good to the silly. Although nobody will ever single out an Elvis film as great cinematic art, they are as a whole the highest-earning series of musicals ever, grossing almost $150,000,000. They are important as film history, social history, and, more to the point, *Elvis* history. Besides, the flicks are fun: Who can resist seeing Elvis cast as a champion race-car driver or singing and dancing around at a clambake?

What Might Have Been: Actor vs. Star

Elvis knew quality when he saw it. He was inspired by James Dean in *Rebel Without a Cause* and Marlon Brando in *The Wild One*. Movies had been a big part of his fantasy life as a young boy. Yet he didn't take hold of his movie career and shape it effectively.

The Colonel played a big part in Elvis' choices, because all deals went through him. Probably the decision that had the greatest impact on Elvis' acting was to sing or not to sing. Parker had control of his music career and wanted to keep it tied in with Elvis' film career. Elvis the serious actor meant a more independent Elvis, and the Colonel couldn't have that. Elvis was reportedly offered a part in *Thunder Road* (1958), a quality film about moonshining, but the Colonel asked for too much money. Parker also nixed *The Defiant Ones* (1958), simply because there was no singing. The role (and lauds) went to Tony Curtis.

> ### For the Record
>
> Elvis was later given the chance to play an aging rock star opposite Barbra Streisand in *A Star is Born*, released in 1976. It would have been a meaningful role for Elvis and a fascinating comeback to the silver screen for the rest of us. Colonel Parker squelched the deal—again—by asking for too much money. Kris Kristofferson ended up with the role.

The scripts Parker okayed for Elvis only got worse. The Colonel reportedly didn't even read them; Elvis didn't pay much attention either until it was time to memorize the lines. Money was at the heart of Elvis' film career and content came to mean less and less.

When Elvis went to Hollywood, he befriended several of the late James Dean's crowd. Natalie Wood, whom Elvis dated and we'll discuss later, was one of these. Another was actor Nick Adams, who would later land a role as Johnny Yuma in the Western TV series *The Rebel*.

The King and I
"I think that if he'd ever done a serious role and been directed properly, he could have been quite marvelous."

—Dennis Hopper

Colonel Parker was threatened by Elvis' new friends because he thought Elvis might find a new independence (personal, leading to financial) from him. He put Nick Adams on a secret retainer to act as a spy and report back to the Colonel if Elvis was talking deals to anyone.

The sad part of Elvis' movie career is that the star did have genuine acting talent. He fared remarkably well in his early movies, despite his limited experience. There's a terrific scene in *Jailhouse Rock* when he kisses Judy Tyler until she's breathless, then, when she protests, growls "That's just the beast in me." Even in the later, weaker movies, he carried them with insouciant charm.

Lighting Up the Screen

On April 1, 1956, during a trip to Los Angeles for *The Milton Berle Show*, Elvis auditioned at Paramount Studios. He was asked to act various emotions, sing a song ("Blue Suede Shoes"), and perform a scene from a film in pre-production, *The Rainmaker,* with an actor by the name of Frank Faylen. Elvis was trying out for the role of Jimmy Curry. Unhappy with his performance, Elvis asked for a second chance and the next day acted a scene with actress Cynthia Baxter.

Elvis thought he'd done well enough during the two *Rainmaker* screen tests to announce that he had "a movie coming out in June with Miss Katherine Hepburn and Mr. Burt Lancaster. It's a dream come true." He went on to say that he "wouldn't care about singing in the movies." The only movie Elvis made in which he didn't sing was *Charro!*—and that had one of his songs over the closing credits. His dream of becoming a "serious" actor never materialized.

Part of the responsibility for that missed opportunity must rest with Elvis. But Tom Parker—listed as a "technical adviser" on Elvis' films—deserves more of the blame. He dangled money in front of Elvis— which Elvis, always the poor boy in his heart, gladly took—and didn't give a damn about the quality of the projects. For Parker, first, second, and last, it was always the money. As Fats Domino, another great rocker once said, ain't that a shame?

Although he didn't land the role in *The Rainmaker* (it went to Earl Holliman), seven days after the screen test, on April 6, 1956, Elvis signed a movie contract with Paramount Pictures—a seven-year, three movie contract. Paramount later contracted him out to other studios as well, and he ended up making the most movies for MGM. Other film production companies he worked for were Allied Artists, National General Pictures, Twentieth Century-Fox, United Artists, and Universal.

Going for Gold
Here's a tip for you TV trivia buffs. Does the name Frank Faylen ring a bell? He was Dobie's dad on the show *The Many Loves of Dobie Gillis*. Look for him on Nick at Nite!

Return to Sender
Some sources state Elvis had only one screen test (for *The Rainmaker*), but Hal B. Wallis, who produced nine of Elvis' movies, had him test for the role of a construction worker for *Girls of Summer*, from a play by Ralph Nash. Natalie Wood read with him. It was irrelevant, because Colonel Tom Parker would not agree to Elvis appearing in a movie without singing.

Elvis on Celluloid

In the sections that follow, I've laid out Elvis' film career to help you follow the peaks and valleys. As you settle down with your popcorn, don't forget he went from being a boy of 21 to a man of 34.

The Golden Age of Elvis Movies

Elvis made four movies before going in the U.S. Army: *Love Me Tender*, *Loving You*, *Jailhouse Rock*, and *King Creole*. Two of these, *Love Me Tender* and *Jailhouse Rock*, were black and white, and rank among the more interesting Elvis movies. At the time, he still aspired to be a serious dramatic actor and he really tried to accomplish something. Although they were made on a frenetic schedule (Elvis began filming *Love Me Tender* on August 23, 1956, and the movie was released on November 15), the writers, directors, and producers were going for something special too.

The King and I
"I have a lot that I'd like to accomplish in time. I'd like to improve in a lot of ways. For one thing, the acting thing, but it'll take time. You can't overstep your bounds."

—Elvis

His first movie, *Love Me Tender*, is, interestingly, a western, although not a particularly authentic one (case in point, Elvis' swivel hips). Elvis plays Clint Reno, an ex-Confederate soldier who falls in love with his brother's fiancee after his brother is thought dead in the Civil War.

Loving You, released in July 1957, tells the story of Deke Rivers, a guitar-playing delivery-truck driver who is discovered by a country-and-western promoter and made a star; obviously, the film has some autobiographical elements. It was directed by Hal Kanter and Elvis played opposite Lizabeth Scott and Wendell Corey.

In *Jailhouse Rock*, released in October 1957, Elvis plays Vince Everett, a not particularly likable character who goes to jail for manslaughter—and, upon release, is discovered by a rock and roll promoter and made a star (seeing a common thread yet?). Another interesting note: The title song was Elvis' favorite production number, and Elvis choreographed it.

King Creole, released in July 1958, traces a musician's rise to stardom, this time a New Orleans nightclub singer; like *Loving You*, this has some "autobiographical" elements. Based on Harold Robbins' novel, *A Stone for Danny Fisher*, the film was directed by Michael Curtiz, the Hungarian born filmmaker most famous for the classic, *Casablanca*. Elvis' performance as singer Danny Fisher is solid if not brilliant.

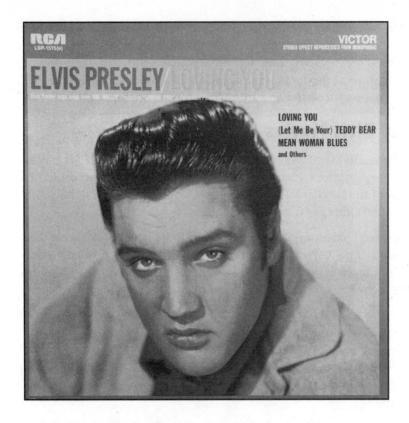

The cover of the soundtrack for Loving You (1957), Elvis' second movie.

The Silver Age of Elvis Movies

After Elvis was discharged from the Army, it made perfect economic sense to capitalize on the world's fascination with GI Elvis. Hence we have *G.I. Blues*, released in November 1960, and directed by the veteran Norman Taurog, best known for *Boy's Town,* starring Spencer Tracy and Mickey Rooney. Elvis plays Tulsa McLean, a footloose soldier in Germany who falls for a local dancer played by Juliet Prowse. *G.I. Blues* was black and white, Elvis' last non-color movie.

Flaming Star was released a month later, another Western, but with Elvis playing Pacer Burton, a part Kiowa-Indian rancher. He sang only two songs. Directed by the able Don Siegel, who filmed the acclaimed science fiction masterpiece *Invasion of the Body Snatchers* and the highly praised John Wayne Western, *The Shootist*, the film is downbeat, unusual, and represents some of Elvis' very best acting.

Wild in the Country followed in early summer of 1961. Directed by Phillip Dunne (*The Ghost and Mrs. Muir*), it's the most literary of Elvis' movies. The Clifford Odets script has him playing struggling writer Glenn Tyler opposite Hope Lange and Tuesday Weld.

141

Blue Hawaii, released in November 1961 has Elvis as Chad Gates, a tour guide and singer who must kow-tow to a powerful mother played by Angela Lansbury. The film established a new tone for Elvis movies—an exotic setting, a boy-gets-in-trouble-but-gets-girl-in-the-end plot, and big musical production numbers. *Blue Hawaii*, the movie and the soundtrack album, was highly successful and led to later similar attempts.

The Bronze Age of Elvis Movies

Follow That Dream, released in May 1962, about Florida homesteaders, and *Kid Galahad*, released the following August, about a boxer, were to a certain extent throwbacks to Elvis' first movies. A re-make of the excellent 1937 Humphrey Bogart/Edward G. Robinson film (directed by Michael Curtiz), this *Kid Galahad* could use a nap. A long one.

Follow That Dream, directed by Gordon Douglas (who two years later would direct the last "Rat Pack" movie, *Robin and the Seven Hoods*) is a comedy with precious few laughs and forgettable songs, including the corny "On Top of Old Smokey." Colonel Tom Parker is, per usual, listed as the technical adviser—alas, he obviously didn't do much advising on this turkey.

Girls! Girls! Girls!, released the following November, had a sailing theme and, once again, a Hawaii setting, indicating more of the same to follow. *Girls!...*, with Norman Taurog once again directing, is about as thin as it gets, with silly songs like "Song of the Shrimp." Elvis does manage to hold our attention when he sings *Return to Sender*, one of the film's very few good moments.

Of the releases the next two years, 1963 and 1964—*It Happened at the World's Fair*, *Fun in Acapulco*, *Kissin' Cousins*, *Viva Las Vegas*, and *Roustabout*—the most interesting is *Viva Las Vegas*. The setting, as would become evident by the 1970s, fit the King. Elvis plays a race driver opposite Ann-Margret and their chemistry is obvious. Directed by George Sidney, who helmed the successful musical *Bye Bye Birdie* (based on the Broadway musical about a young singer very much like Elvis Presley), it features some excellent songs, including "The Yellow Rose of Texas" and "Come On, Everybody"—and of course, the immortal title track.

The Stone Age of Elvis Movies

By this point in Elvis' film career, it becomes apparent that all involved, including Elvis, are just going through the motions. The quality of the scripts deteriorates and the quality of the music declines, as do the general production values. The movies have different costumes, different exotic locales, and different babes, but the plots—and Elvis' characters—are interchangeable. The movies are fun to watch for trivia and occasional energized moments, but one is pretty much as good as another—which is to say they're not particularly good. And Elvis knew it.

The cover of the soundtrack for Girls! Girls! Girls! (1962). This strikes me as the perfect title for an Elvis movie.

1965 offered *Girl Happy*, *Tickle Me*, and *Harum Scarum*. Directed by Boris Sagal, who later filmed the acclaimed television mini-series *Rich Man, Poor Man*, *Girl Happy* has Elvis, of all people, chaperoning a group of college girls. One of the young babes is Shelly Fabares, and she may be the only thing worth looking at in this thoroughly forgettable Elvis vehicle. *Tickle Me* (good Lord, couldn't they have come up with better titles?) has Elvis working at an all-girl dude ranch and singing unmemorable songs. Elvis is kidnapped in the Arab-themed *Harum Scarum*—maybe the print should have been.

In 1966, it was *Frankie and Johnny*; *Paradise, Hawaiian Style*; and *Spinout*. Directed by Freddie de Cordova (who went on to fame as Johnny Carson's *Tonight Show* producer), *Frankie and Johnny* is set on a riverboat and has Elvis as a singer who likes to gamble. The film features good music, including

The King and I

"Who is that fast-talking, hillbilly son of a bitch that nobody can understand? One day he's singing to a dog, then to a car, then to a cow. They are all the damn same movie with that Southerner just singing to something different."

—Elvis

"When The Saints Go Marching In," and "Down By The Riverside," as well as plenty of pretty girls and a nice turn by Harry Morgan as a piano-playing songwriter.

Paradise, Hawaiian Style has Elvis as a pilot returning to the islands to run a helicopter service; it's a very familiar movie because it's a lot like *Blue Hawaii*. Not nearly as good as *Frankie and Johnny*, and with songs like "Scratch My Back (I'll Scratch Yours)" not much to listen to either.

Spinout, another Norman Taurog feature, has Elvis playing a race-car driver and represents the 10th anniversary of Elvis' film career. As Mike McCoy, Elvis must choose between three beautiful women, Shelley Fabares, Diane McBain, or Deborah Walley; instead of making a decision, Elvis marries them all off and keeps his beloved freedom. The film reunited Fabares with Carl Betz, playing her father, who also played her dad on *The Donna Reed Show* from 1958 to 1963.

In 1967 came *Easy Come, Easy Go*; *Double Trouble*; and *Clambake*. *Easy Come, Easy Go* should have went. Elvis plays a frogman and sings dumb songs like "Yoga Is As Yoga Does"— a duet, amazingly, with Elsa Lanchester, the actress who played *The Bride of Frankenstein*. The duet is almost as scary.

The last Elvis film from that year, *Clambake*, is also one of his weakest. Elvis plays a millionaire's son, a tough thing for this Elvis fan to believe, who ends up winning a big powerboat race. Weak songs and another odd duet, this time with a lip-synching Will Hutchins doing "Who Needs Money." A good supporting cast featuring Bill Bixby, Gary Merrill, James Gregory, and Shelley Fabares can't save this clam; one of Elvis' weakest efforts, I'm afraid. One highlight: Shelley Fabares loses her bikini top while swimming.

In 1968, we got *Stay Away, Joe*; *Speedway*; *Live a Little, Love a Little*; and *Charro! Stay Away, Joe*, directed by Peter Tewksbury, is disappointing because of its stereotypical portrayal of Native Americans (remember, Elvis had Indian blood)—the exact mistake the very good *Flaming Star* managed to avoid. Elvis, as Joe Lightcloud, does look Indian, but gosh, Burgess Meredith? I don't think so.

Thankfully, *Speedway*, though by no means wonderful, is much better and solidly entertaining. Elvis plays a stock car driver with Nancy Sinatra as the love interest. Watching the sparks fly between Elvis and Nancy, it's easy to see why Priscilla was jealous of their relationship. Lots of real drivers show up, including legends Cale Yarborough and Richard Petty.

Charro!, a bonafide Spaghetti Western, stars Elvis—sporting a beard—as a reformed outlaw framed for a crime. The supporting cast is weak and Elvis, attempting to play his role straight, is trapped in what can only be called a bomb.

The end is near, however. In 1969 came *The Trouble with Girls (and How To Get Into It)* and *Change of Habit*. Set in a traveling medicine and educational show the 1920s (the flavor of which is well captured), *The Trouble with Girls* has good music ("Swing Down, Sweet Chariot") and a good performance by Elvis as the show's manager. There's an excellent supporting cast—one of his best—with Vincent Price, Dabney Coleman, John Carradine, Joyce Van Patten, and Marilyn Mason, making her screen debut. Look for Memphis Mafia member-in-good-standing Jerry Schilling doing a quick turn. A fun movie—but, again, what a drippy title.

Change of Habit asks us to buy Elvis as a doctor. Directed by William Graham, Elvis is a physician working in the ghetto who learns about life from some wise nuns, one of whom is played by a deliciously young Mary Tyler Moore. In his last dramatic role, Elvis is at least attempting to do better material, but the mix—songs and melodrama—just doesn't work.

Documentary Elvis

In addition to Elvis' 31 feature films, he appears in two documentaries of his concert career in the '70s:

➤ *Elvis, That's the Way It Is*, released in 1970, revolves around Elvis' appearance at the International Hotel in Las Vegas.

➤ *Elvis On Tour*, released in 1972, shows Elvis on a 15-city tour.

These two documentaries are the only real record of Elvis' decline over the course of the 1970s. Though they are sometimes a sad portrayal of arrogance and even self-parody, they also evidence flashes of Elvis' remaining brilliance, and of his fans enduring adoration. Yes, they show the King in decline, but they also reveal the magnetic, awesome talent that remained.

A third documentary, *This Is Elvis* (1981), which features terrific early TV and concert footage, can't exactly be considered an "Elvis documentary" because it features dramatic reenactments and voice-over narration from an Elvis sound-alike. However, *This Is Elvis*, from Executive Producer David Wolper (who has won over 30 Emmys; *Roots* is one of his many credits), is a worthy, even indispensable, view of the King and, despite some errors and flaws (those reenactments are a bit schlocky), I recommend it highly.

Return to Sender

Not all of Elvis' late movies were critical flops. *Elvis On Tour* won a Golden Globe by the Hollywood Foreign Press for best documentary of 1972. It's quality filmmaking to go along with quality performing and singing by the King.

Sharin' the Spotlight: Elvis' Co-Stars

Imagine acting with the King. What was it like? First we'll look at the beautiful actresses who starred opposite him. Then we'll find out about some of the notable actors who appeared in films with him.

Elvis' Leading Ladies

America was tuned into the choice for Elvis' female co-stars. Imagine playing opposite him and smooching on the screen? At least, the boys who had to endure their girlfriends' crushes on Elvis had someone to fantasize about too—they were generally All-American, girl-next-door types.

The King and I
"Elvis is a young man with an enormous capacity of love....but I don't think he has found his happiness yet."

—Dolores Hart, 1957

In a few cases, a particularly charismatic female co-star—Ann-Margret, Nancy Sinatra, Shelley Fabares—seems to energize Elvis. Not surprisingly, Elvis was frequently romantically linked off-screen with his co-stars. "People think I'm a sex maniac," he once joked about the public's perception of him, "but I'm just natural."

It's impossible to know which stars had affairs with Elvis while making his movies. (Mary Tyler Moore once joked that she was the only co-star Elvis hadn't slept with—but she *was* joking.) One thing we can say with certainty, he wasn't lonely.

Here are some of Elvis' on-screen loves, listed by movie:

➤ *Loving You*—Dolores Hart. A popular starlet in the '50s and '60s, Dolores Hart made a decidedly un-starlet choice when she entered a convent; she eventually became Sister Dolores.

➤ *King Creole*—Carolyn Jones. For hard-core TV junkies, Carolyn Jones will be forever remembered as Morticia in the series *The Addams Family*.

➤ *G.I. Blues*—Juliet Prowse. The attention Elvis paid to Juliet Prowse during the filming of *G.I. Blues* caused a rift with her steady guy, Frank Sinatra (to whom she was later engaged).

➤ *Flaming Star*—Barbara Eden. After *Flaming Star*, Barbara Eden went on to a successful TV career, her most notable role being Jeannie in *I Dream of Jeannie*.

➤ *Wild in the Country*—Tuesday Weld and Millie Perkins. Stunning starlet Tuesday Weld's real name is Susan and she was born on a...Thursday. Fans of Matthew Sweet know her face from the cover of his *Girlfriend* album. Millie Perkins' first film was *The Diary of Anne Frank,* for which she won an Oscar for Best Supporting Actress.

➤ *Girls! Girls! Girls!*—Stella Stevens. A former *Playboy* centerfold, the gorgeous Stevens was born in the town of Hot Coffee, Mississippi, endearing her forever to your loyal author.

➤ *Viva Las Vegas*—Ann-Margret. One of the stars Elvis was closest to, and one of the few to attend his funeral, Ann-Margret (Olsson) has starred in such diverse films as *Carnal Knowledge* and *Grumpy Old Men.*

➤ *Roustabout*—Barbara Stanwyck. Born Ruby Stevens in Brooklyn, N.Y., the veteran Barbara Stanwyck had made her fame, and garnered four Oscar nominations, as a tough, no-nonsense, yet thoroughly feminine star in such films as *Double Indemnity* and *Stella Dallas*. Throughout the filming, Elvis addressed her only as "Miss Stanwyck" and she loved him for it.

➤ *Girl Happy*—Shelley Fabares. Now the co-star of TV's *Coach* with Craig T. Nelson, Shelley was also in *Spinout* and *Clambake.*

For the Record

Of all Elvis' female co-stars, Shelley Fabares, who acted in *Girl Happy*, *Spinout*, and *Clambake*, was reportedly Elvis' favorite. Her three Elvis co-starring roles are the most of any actress. Fabares had her own number-one hit with 1962's "Johnny Angel," which was replaced at number one by Elvis' "Good Luck Charm."

➤ *Harum Scarum*—Mary Ann Mobley. A former Miss America, Mary Ann Mobley also made *Girl Happy* with Elvis in 1965.

➤ *Frankie and Johnny*—Donna Douglas. Donna Douglas will be forever remembered by hormone-driven teenage boys for her role as the fully-blossomed Elly May Clampett in the TV series *The Beverly Hillbillies*, one of television's most successful "rural" comedies.

➤ *Speedway*—Nancy Sinatra. And where, you ask, did Elvis meet Nancy Sinatra? When he stepped off the airplane at McGuire Air Force Base in New Jersey after returning from his tour of duty in Germany—Nancy was the Army's official greeter.

➤ *Change of Habit*—Mary Tyler Moore. For her role as nun Sister Michelle Gallagher, Moore was awarded a Golden Turkey Award.

Notable Actors in Elvis' Movies

Here's a list of some actors you might have heard of who appeared alongside Elvis:

➤ *Kissin' Cousins, Roustabout*—Jack Albertson. I once had the great pleasure to spend time with Albertson, a former Vaudeville performer who moved to Broadway, feature films, and television. He won an Academy Award for his wonderful performance in the poignant *The Subject Was Roses*.

➤ *Kid Galahad, Change of Habit*—Ed Asner. Former president of the Screen Actor's Guild, Ed Asner is probably best known for his role as Lou Grant in *The Mary Tyler Moore Show* and *Roots,* for which he won a total of six Emmys. He made his film debut in *Kid Galahad.*

➤ *Clambake, Speedway*—Bill Bixby. Every child of the '70s remembers Bill Bixby—first as Eddie's father in *The Courtship of Eddie's Father* ("People let me tell ya 'bout my best friend..."), and later as Dr. David Banner, a.k.a. *The Incredible Hulk.*

➤ *Kid Galahad*—Charles Bronson. Most famous for his series of *Death Wish* films, Bronson—a former coal miner of Lithuanian descent—made 15 films with his late wife, actress Jill Ireland.

➤ *The Trouble With Girls*—John Carradine. A gifted Shakespearean actor, Carradine made over 250 films of various genres, but may best be known for his roles in numerous horror movies, including three Dracula pictures.

➤ *The Trouble With Girls*—Dabney Coleman. A gifted comic actor best known for the film *9 to 5. The Trouble With Girls* was Coleman's second film.

➤ *Loving You*—Wendell Corey. Like Elvis and Lizabeth Scott, his co-stars in *Loving You*, Corey, a versatile, solid actor, was signed by producer Hal Wallis (who made nine Elvis films).

➤ *King Creole*—Dean Jagger. Upright character actor Dean Jagger was probably miscast as Elvis' weak, world-weary father in *King Creole,* but he was a gifted actor who won an Academy Award for Best Supporting Actor in the World War II flying drama *Twelve O'Clock High.*

➤ *King Creole*—Walter Matthau. Quick, bet you can't spell Academy Award winner actor Matthau's real first name. (Answer: Matuschanskayasky.)

➤ *Stay Away, Joe*—Burgess Meredith. Gifted actor Burgess Meredith pushed Sylvester Stallone to be his best in *Rocky,* for which he was nominated for Best Supporting Actor in 1976. (He received his first supporting actor nomination for *The Day of the Locust* in 1975.)

➤ *King Creole*—Vic Morrow. Rugged star of the 1960s television series *Combat*, Vic Morrow was killed, along with two Vietnamese children, in a helicopter accident while filming John Landis' *Twilight Zone-The Movie*.

➤ *The Trouble With Girls*—Vincent Price. One of the greatest horror film stars of all time, the mellifluous-voiced Price was a gifted stage actor as well.

➤ *It Happened at the World's Fair*—Kurt Russell (as a boy who kicks Elvis). Russell, now a major movie star whose credits include *Executive Decision*, played Elvis very effectively in the 1979 ABC-TV film *Elvis*, produced by Dick Clark Productions.

➤ *Live a Little, Love a Little*—Rudy Vallee. In the 1920s, Rudy Vallee was one of the first pop singers to engender mass female swooning with songs like "The Vagabond Lover" (which also was his nickname).

With a Little Help From My Friends

Elvis' family, friends, and musicians appeared in a number of his movies. It was a way for Elvis, who was never completely comfortable with the Hollywood set, to keep the people who meant the most to him nearby. And employed. Elvis has received more than his share of criticism for this practice and, I for one, don't think it's warranted. He was a poor kid who was busily making it and his instinct was to share with those closest to him. What's wrong with that?

Not to be outdone, Colonel Parker made sure to be employed himself—always room for another paycheck, right?—as a technical advisor on the set of many Elvis movies.

Family:

➤ Vernon Presley—*Loving You; Live a Little, Love a Little*

➤ Gladys Presley—*Loving You*

Friends:

➤ Joe Esposito (Memphis Mafia)—*It Happened at the World Fair; Kissin' Cousins; Spinout; Clambake; Stay Away, Joe; The Trouble With Girls*

➤ Charlie Hodge (Memphis Mafia)—*Clambake, Speedway, Charro!*

➤ George Klein (childhood friend and Memphis DJ)—*Frankie and Johnny, Double Trouble*

➤ Jerry Schilling (Memphis Mafia)—*The Trouble With Girls*

➤ Sonny West (Memphis Mafia)—*Kid Galahad; Stay Away, Joe*

➤ Red West (Memphis Mafia)—*Flaming Star; Wild in the Country; Follow That Dream; Girls! Girls! Girls!; It happened at the World Fair; Fun in Acapulco; Viva Las Vegas; Roustabout; Girl Happy; Tickle Me; Harum Scarum; Paradise, Hawaiian Style; Spinout; Live a Little, Love a Little.* Red West holds the record for most appearances in Elvis films—14.

The Word
A technical adviser for a film is an expert who advises on the set. For a movie with a military theme, a technical adviser might help make the firearms authentic. In the case of Colonel Parker, all his title meant was that he received an extra fee because he managed Elvis Presley.

Musicians:

➤ Scotty Moore (guitar player)—*Loving You, Jailhouse Rock, G.I. Blues*

➤ Bill Black (bass player)—*Loving You, Jailhouse Rock, G.I. Blues*

➤ D.J. Fontana (drummer)—*Loving You, Jailhouse Rock, G.I. Blues*

➤ Mike Stoller (piano player and songwriter)—*Jailhouse Rock*

➤ The Jordanaires (vocal group)—*Loving You* (plus credits for vocal accompaniment in 18 other movies)

Movie Musicology

In Elvis' early movies, a lot of attention was given to the songs. One of Elvis' biggest hits, "Love Me Tender," was the featured song of his first movie. For the movie *Jailhouse Rock*, rock and roll composers extraordinaire Jerry Lieber and Mike Stoller (remember "Hound Dog" from last chapter?) were hired to write the title song.

For the Record

The Reno Brothers was the original title of *Love Me Tender,* but when the song became a huge success, the producers decided that the movie should carry the same name. Good move.

But in the 1960s, the music quality degenerated along with the movie quality. The songs were created to fit the plots and suffered from the same overt "cuteness." They might as well be called novelty songs: "Rock-a-Hula Baby," "Harem Holiday," "Adam and Evil," and "Yoga Is As Yoga Does" are examples of the shallow cleverness that infected the movie songwriting. They were a far cry from the heartfelt rhythm-and-blues classics that catapulted Elvis to the top. Yet, through them all—no matter how bad the material—his voice shines through. Yes, that boy could sing.

For the Record

Dolores Fuller, the ex-wife of legendarily awful film director Ed Wood (*Plan 9 From Outer Space*, 1959) co-wrote a number of Elvis tunes, including "Do The Clam" for *Girl Happy* and "Beyond the Bend" for *It Happened at the World's Fair*. This may well be a commentary on the quality of material Elvis was getting for his films. (Colonel Tom Parker's methods and cheapness drove most songwriters away.)

One interesting aspect of Elvis' movie music is the duet singing. This is not something he did much of in his recording and stage careers. So the movies give us another side of his talent—working with other vocalists.

Elvis sang duets in the following movies:

➤ *King Creole*—"Crawfish" with Kitty White.

➤ *Wild in the Country*—"Husky Dusky Day" with Hope Lange.

➤ *It Happened at the World's Fair*—"How Would You Like to Be" with Vicki Tiu; "Happy Ending" with Joan O'Brien.

➤ *Girls! Girls! Girls!*—"Earth Boy" with Ginny and Elizabeth Tiu.

➤ *Fun in Acapulco*—"Mexico" with Larry Domasin.

➤ *Viva Las Vegas*—"The Lady Loves Me" with Ann-Margret.

➤ *Frankie and Johnny*—"Petunia, the Gardener's Daughter" with Donna Douglas (dubbed by Eileen Wilson).

➤ *Paradise, Hawaiian Style*—"Scratch My Back, Then I'll Scratch Yours" with Marianna Hill; "Queenie Wahine's Papaya" and "Datin'" with Donna Butterworth.

➤ *Easy Come, Easy Go*—"Yoga is As Yoga Does" with Elsa Lanchester.

➤ *Clambake*—"Who Needs Money" with Will Hutchins (dubbed by the Jordanaires' Ray Walker).

➤ *The Trouble With Girls*—"Signs of the Zodiac" with Marilyn Mason.

➤ *Speedway*—"There Ain't Nothing Like a Song" with Nancy Sinatra.

California Dreamin': Mansions and Movie Stars

During the late 1950s and 1960s, Elvis lived in Southern California much of the time. During his lengthy stays in the City of Angels, Elvis met stars of screen, television, and music, some of whom became "real" friends. Among the latter were singers Rick Nelson and Pat Boone, actors Max Baer, Jr. (from *The Beverly Hillbillies*), Gary Lockwood (*2001: A Space Odyssey*), and Dennis Crosby (son of Bing).

The Beatles, who absolutely adored Elvis, along with their manager, Brian Epstein, spent an evening at Elvis' house in Bel Air. The meeting between Elvis and The Beatles began uncomfortably—largely in silence—until Elvis suggested he get out some guitars. At that point, the night turned into a rhythm and blues jam session, and doubtless, had there been a tape recorder, would have yielded the best-selling bootleg album in history.

Elvis had homes at the following California addresses:

➤ Knickerbocker Hotel, Ivar Avenue—guest (1957).

➤ Beverly Wilshire Hotel, Wilshire Boulevard—guest (late 1950s).

➤ Regent Beverly Wilshire, Wilshire Boulevard—guest (late 1950s).

➤ 565 Perugia Way, Bel-Air—rental (1960-63 and 1963-65).

➤ 1059 Bellagio Road, Bel-Air—rental (1963 and 1965).

➤ 10550 Rocco Place, Bel-Air (Stone Canyon)—rental (1965-67).

➤ 1174 Hillcrest, Trousdale Estates near Los Angeles—purchased by Elvis for $400,000 (May 1967).

➤ 144 Monvale, Los Angeles (Holmby Hills)—purchased by Elvis for $400,000 (late 1967).

➤ 845 Chino Canyon Road, Palm Springs—ordered built by Elvis for $85,000 (1965).

➤ 1350 Leadera Circle, Palm Springs—rental (1970).

One reason he lived in so many houses was marital problems with Priscilla—Elvis and Memphis Mafia members lived at 1174 Hillcrest after his divorce while Priscilla and Lisa Marie stayed at 144 Monvale.

He Did It His Way?

As we've seen in this chapter, Elvis' movie career can be fairly characterized as one in which he performed adequately in a succession of formulaic movies. Which is certainly not to say that they are not enjoyable to watch, because they can be. So what do we make of this part of his career?

The heart of the matter is money. Elvis was once advised by writer Lloyd Shearer to delay jumping into films and instead go to college. Writing about the incident 20 years later, Shearer remembered that Elvis "looked at me with amazement. 'I don't 'spect you ever been poor. We Presleys—we been poor as far back as I can remember.'"

And there you have it—as pure and simple as a guitar riff. Elvis took the money and accepted his fate. As convicts often advise one another, "If you can't do the time, don't do the crime." Elvis could do the time. When he was making movies he was on the clock. Doing a job.

The sad aspect is that Elvis did have real acting talent. He did remarkably well in his early movies, despite almost no experience. Even in the later, weaker films, he carried them off with insouciant charm.

Bottom line? His movies, when not judged too harshly—when viewed, say, on a relaxed Saturday afternoon, perhaps with some friends and an adult beverage or two—are perfectly pleasant entertainment. So Elvis isn't Brando. So what? Did you ever hear Marlon sing in *Guys and Dolls*?

Go to the bank on this: Elvis was a better actor than Brando was a singer.

The Least You Need to Know

➤ Elvis' movies weren't especially good, but they made lots of money.

➤ Despite Elvis' ambitions to become a serious actor, he never made a movie in which he didn't sing.

➤ In films, Elvis starred opposite many beautiful leading ladies and several actors who were famous or became known later on.

➤ The music in Elvis' films is contagiously fun, but generally doesn't have the soulful rock of Elvis' early recordings.

Soldier Boy: Elvis in the Army

On December 19, 1957, one Milton Bowers, the Memphis draft-board chairman, hand-delivered Elvis' draft notice to Graceland. Elvis was to enter the U.S. Army on January 20, 1958. Fortunately, he received a 60-day deferment so he could finish filming *King Creole.*

As with most things involving Elvis, enormous controversy surrounded his potential service. Elvis fans, of course, didn't want him drafted at all. Many veterans, particularly the American Legionnaires, detested everything he stood for—youth and freedom among them—and wanted him taught a lesson. Poor Milton Bowers was caught in the middle, taking grief from all sides. "I eat, sleep, and drink Elvis," Bowers said. "With all due respect to Elvis, who's a nice boy, we've drafted people who are far, far more important than he is. After all, when you take him out of the entertainment business, what have you got left? A truck driver."

Obviously, Bowers' grasp of good public relations was tentative. Elvis' fans howled even louder. It did not a whit of good.

The Word
Despite every attempt to continue business as usual with a draftee like Elvis Presley, the Army had to take special measures. They drew up plans for **Operation Elvis** to handle fans at every stage of his service—and deliver the tons of mail to him (500 to 1,000 a day in West Germany).

The King and I
"All I want is to be treated as a regular GI. I want to do my duty and I'm mighty proud to be given the opportunity to serve my country."

—Elvis

The King and I
"When he was in basic training, Elvis looked great. The dye had grown off his hair—his real hair was light brown. He couldn't wear the lifts in his shoes. He had a nice tan. He was so handsome and down-to-earth. That was the time when he was really himself. It's what I would have loved for him to be like all the time, but that could not be."

—Anita Wood, Elvis' girlfriend

On March 24, 1958, Elvis Presley was inducted into the U.S. Army. (To his credit, Elvis refused sweetheart deals offered by both the Marines and the Navy in exchange for joining their branches.) The next day, his hair was buzzed off at Fort Chaffee in Arkansas by a James Peterson. (And then it was burned to discourage souvenir hunters.) Two days after that, he was given medical inoculations for typhoid, tetanus, and the Asian flu. On March 28, 1958, Elvis and his fellow recruits were bused to Fort Hood, Texas, for basic training. Elvis' every move was captured by legions of photographers.

So intense was the attention from the media and the fans, the Army initiated *Operation Elvis*. The operation consisted of specially assigned personnel, the Army equivalent of PR reps, who followed the dictates of an enormous Elvis file filled with policy and logistical guidelines for dealing with every interaction Elvis had with the press and his fans. America had a celebrity soldier boy!

Back to Basics

Elvis the soldier was made-to-order for the media. As a GI, he could now be classified as a "good boy." The media could run stories without controversy or backlash. Everything about Elvis' Army hitch was newsworthy. For example, the last woman to kiss Elvis before he boarded the USS *General Randall*—model Lillian Portnoy—became nationally known (for 15 minutes). So did the boxed cheesecake she gave him. Elvis' comings and goings were covered faithfully.

All reports indicate that Elvis did everything he could to fit in with the other trainees, that he applied himself diligently, and that he treated his officers with respect. He never mentioned the money he was losing. (His pay was $78 a month, some $100,000 less per month than he had been earning making movies and records!)

In late May, Elvis, on leave after completing basic training, attended the Memphis preview of *King Creole*, which was greeted warmly by the critics—not always Elvis' biggest fans.

When Colonel Tom Parker found out that a soldier could live off-base if he had dependents living nearby, he arranged for Gladys and Vernon—who desperately missed their only child—to move nearby. Since Elvis supported his parents, he qualified to live off-base and rented a four-bedroom house at 906 Oak Hill Drive in Killeen, Texas, for three months while he was in advanced training.

Farewell, Gladys

In late July 1958, while living in Killeen, Gladys, only 46 years old (though she claimed to be 42), became ill. Elvis drove her to a doctor in Temple, Texas. Gladys was overweight, and her years of unhealthy eating habits—which included fatty foods, diet pills, and excessive drinking—had taken their toll. With her health declining, Vernon took her by train back to Memphis, where she was admitted to Methodist Hospital.

On August 7, Elvis, on emergency ("compassionate") leave, flew from Waco, Texas, to visit her at Methodist. Her doctors felt that Elvis' presence would brighten her spirits, but Gladys was too far gone. She died on August 14 from a heart attack, partly due to complications from hepatitis. (Ironically, the father of Elvis' closest friend, Red West, died eight hours after Gladys.) Elvis was beyond distraught.

Gladys' lavish, $20,000 funeral took place at Graceland on August 16, pastored by Reverend James E. Hammill at the First Assembly of God Church. She was buried at Forest Hill Cemetery (later to be re-interred at Graceland). When the coffin was lowered into the ground, Elvis held on desperately to the coffin. It took several men to pry him off. He was crying, close to hysteria. On Gladys' tombstone, installed several weeks later, were the words, "She was the sunshine of our home."

A devastated Elvis locked himself in his room at Graceland for eight days. Elvis finally returned to boot camp on August 24. His hurt and pain over his mother's death probably never left him. Gladys' eldest sister, Lillian, said that after Gladys' died, Elvis changed "completely," and "never seemed like Elvis ever again." He had lost his anchor, the person he was most like in the world, and who most loved him. That Gladys did not live long enough to fully enjoy his success was a theme that Elvis would frequently return to. "She was more than a mother," Elvis said after her death. "She was a friend who would let me

The King and I
"Elvis stayed at the cemetery while they lowered the coffin. It was the most heart-wrenching. God! Elvis tried to jump in the ground with his mother. They were holding him back and screaming. It was really just the worst thing I had ever seen."

—Barbara Pittman, singer and family friend

The King and I
"Oh God, everything I have is gone."

—Elvis

talk to her any hours of the day or night if I had a problem…. I found out that she was right about almost everything."

Innocent Abroad

When Tom Parker learned that Elvis was being assigned to Germany, he hustled Elvis into RCA's Nashville studios to stockpile as many songs for future release as possible. Many Presley doubters predicted that, with the King out of action for two years, his popularity would wane. Parker made sure that wouldn't happen. In fact, during his time in the Army, Elvis had eight top-ten hits, including "Wear My Ring Around Your Neck," "Hard-Headed Woman," "A Fool Such As I," and "Big Hunk O' Love."

On September 19, 1958, Elvis traveled with his unit from Fort Hood to Brooklyn, New York, where he was greeted by a huge crowd. Three days later, the unit boarded the USS *General Randall* for departure. The ship arrived at the port of Bremerhaven in northern West Germany, on October 1, 1958. When "Der Elvis" arrived, thousands of people were waiting. Girls were shouting "Elvis! Elvis! Elvis!" For the King, it was a reassuringly familiar scene.

Soldier Elvis, 1958.

Elvis, toting a duffel bag, waved to the crowd and then boarded a troop train along with his 800-man battalion and rolled to a dreary U.S. Army base just outside Friedburg, an hour due north of the city of Frankfurt.

The first four days, the press was on the Army base with Elvis. The military was most understanding with the media. (It had a point to prove; that it was treating Elvis like any other soldier boy.) But the reporters milling around got in the way of the daily grind and they were told their time was up.

About five days after Elvis arrived in West Germany, Vernon, Elvis' grandmother Minnie Mae (on her first flight), Red West, and too-fat-to-fight Lamar Fike flew from New York to Frankfurt, then on to Ritter's Park Hotel at the town of Bad Homburg near the Army base. Elvis moved in with his family and friends and stayed with them during the remainder of his hitch (except while on maneuvers or leave).

For the Record

If Elvis' Memphis Mafia was so dedicated to their King, how come none of them signed up with Elvis? As it happens, Lamar Fike did at least try to enlist. The Army took one look at the 270-some-odd pounder and said thanks, but no thanks. The King was on his own...sort of.

The group soon moved to the Hilberts Park Hotel in Bad Nauheim, another neighboring town, then to the Gruenwald Hotel, also in Bad Nauheim. But the group was asked to leave here because of shenanigans—Elvis and Red West not only had water-gun and shaving-cream fights, they also started a fire. Then the Presleys rented a five-bedroom, white stucco house at 14 Goethestrasse in Bad Nauheim, West Germany, from October 1958 to the end of 1959.

On October 5, the Army banned all fans and reporters from the base in order to get on with business. When Elvis pulled guard duty, however, his radar-like fans would some-how find him. One night there were so many fans surrounding him that Elvis had to be rescued by a couple of platoons of soldiers. It was the last guard duty Elvis ever pulled.

Gunner Presley: Name, Rank, and Serial Number, Please

Elvis was Private 53310761, Company D, 1st Medium Tank Battalion, 32nd Armor, 3rd Army Division. His primary duty was as scout jeep driver to Platoon Sergeant Ira Jones. As such, he had to monitor the condition of the roads.

The Army went out of its way to appear that it was giving Elvis no special treatment. Yet generals and lesser officers wanted to meet him and did their best to make sure nothing happened to the King during their watch. To make sure all went well with Private Presley, they followed the guidelines of Operation Elvis to deal with their famous draftee.

One thing that did not happen was an Elvis performance. Despite repeated attempts by the Army brass, Colonel Parker rebuffed all such requests. Unlike other popular singers before him, like Eddie Fisher and Vic Damone, Elvis, at Parker's insistence, refused to join the Special Services branch which, in effect, would have made him a singer who happened to be wearing a uniform. Parker, quite rightly, was making sure to promote Elvis as a loyal, god-fearing American, not a wild-eyed, rock-and-rolling bad boy.

As usual, Parker was thinking about Elvis' image, and this time he was on the money. Elvis' Army career did much to alleviate the vitriol that had been leveled at him prior to his Army service. Parker had deftly reshaped Elvis' image, positioning him to make his next career step—from Rocker to Entertainer. Many would not be happy with the change. John Lennon spoke for many when he observed that after the Army, Elvis was creatively diminished.

On November 27, 1958, Elvis was promoted to private, first class. Shortly thereafter, Elvis bought his first foreign car, a white BMW roadster (immediately dubbed by the German press "Der Elviswagen"). On June 1, 1959, Elvis was promoted to specialist fourth class and, on January 20, 1960, Elvis was promoted to sergeant. The King had been recognized as a fine soldier. Meanwhile, Russian leaders were blasting Elvis as "public enemy number one." (Imagine how apocalyptic they would've become if they'd known Elvis was taking karate lessons—which began the King's lifelong interest in martial arts.)

The King and I

"If I had to rate Elvis as a soldier, I'd rate him very high—the highest. He really knew the basics, and they say he'd done well in basic training at Fort Hood—caught on fast. He was good with vehicles. Even though there were a lot of guys who tried to help him, he maintained that vehicle very well by himself."

—Ira Jones, master sergeant

Return to Sender

It's assumed that Elvis took stimulants as a soldier in West Germany—Dexedrine to keep him up at night while on duty. But what is not generally known is that Elvis probably began this habit when touring the South, playing one-night stands, then driving, then playing again. His mother's weight problems might have been his first source of drugs—speed-based diet pills.

Deutschland Days, Fräulein Nights

Elvis had an active love life while in the Army. (You'll meet some of the women he dated there in Chapter 15.) He also managed to take in some music, catching Bill Haley and the Comets twice in October 1958 (and even posing with him for photos in Haley's dressing room). He also took leaves to German cities and to Paris. Elvis frequented the Folies-Bergere, the Carousel, the Moulin Rouge, the Cafe de Paris, and the 4 O'Clock Club. Alas, there is no record of Elvis meeting Brigitte Bardot, the reigning French sex goddess, which he had lightheartedly cited as one of his goals upon embarking for Europe.

While in West Germany in September 1959, Elvis met a 14-year-old Air Force brat by the name of Priscilla Ann Beaulieu. You'll find out quite a lot about this would-be queen in Chapter 15.

GI Blues: Sickness and Homesickness

Elvis often spoke of homesickness as well as missing his mother. His first Christmas without her was especially tough on him. Even his normally ebullient grandmother, Minnie Mae, the "family" chef, was in a funk and couldn't bring herself to cook a Christmas dinner. Elvis, with Red West and Lamar Fike, went to the base commissary and had a GI turkey meal.

During this time, Elvis, while dating exotic Europeans, also corresponded regularly with his steady girl, Anita Wood. He complained of loneliness and worried about the effect his absence would have on his career. Elvis shared these same concerns with Lamar Fike and Red West.

On June 3, 1959, Elvis was hospitalized for a week with tonsillitis at the Frankfurt Military Hospital. He was hospitalized again in late October with the same condition. Earlier that month, while on maneuvers in Wildflecken, Elvis nearly died of carbon monoxide poisoning while running his jeep's heater for warmth.

His only other injury while in the Army was a broken finger, suffered while playing a football game with fellow GIs.

For the Record

On January 1, 1959, German newspapers reported that Elvis Presley had died in a car crash. A '50s-style media frenzy erupted, complete with sobbing teens. It turned out that it was Vernon who had flipped Elvis' black Mercedes on the autobahn while returning from the Army PX in Frankfurt with Elvis' secretary, Elisabeth Stefaniak. Elvis raced his own BMW to the crash scene at high speed. So prevalent were the rumors of his demise that Elvis was compelled to make a public appearance.

Home Sweet Home

On March 2, 1960, having done his patriotic duty, Elvis flew from West Germany to the U.S. After a stopover at Prestwick Airport in Scotland, he arrived, in the midst of a blizzard, at McGuire Air Force Base in New Jersey. The crowds came out to greet him, of course. So did Nancy Sinatra, as the Army's "official greeter." His return to the U.S. was front-page news all over the country and the world. The Colonel, knowing Elvis' dislike of flying, rented a private railroad car for the 48-hour rail trip to Memphis' Union Station. A jubilant mob met him and a police escort took him home to Graceland.

> ## For the Record
>
> Vernon Presley remarried on July 3, 1960 (after Elvis' Army hitch) to Davada (Dee) Stanley in Huntsville, Alabama, former wife of Army sergeant William Stanley, whom Vernon had met in West Germany. Elvis, unhappy that Vernon was marrying so soon after Gladys' death, did not attend the ceremony. With the marriage, he gained three step-brothers, Billy, Rick, and David, who would become his bodyguards. However, the relationship between Dee and Elvis was never more than barely cordial.

The King and I
"His kind of music is deplorable, a rancid-smelling aphrodisiac."

—Frank Sinatra, 1957

The King and I
"He was a tremendous asset to the music business."

—Frank Sinatra, upon Elvis' death in 1977.

Welcomed by Old Blue Eyes

On March 26, 1960, three weeks after returning home, Elvis taped "The Frank Sinatra-Timex Special: 'Welcome Home Elvis'" at the Fountainebleau Hotel in Miami. It was shown on ABC-TV on May 12, 1960. Ironically, Elvis actually sang with Old Blue Eyes himself—a duet of Elvis' "Love Me Tender"—who more than once had put down the new music when Elvis was an up-and-coming rock and roller.

Rat Packers Peter Lawford, Joey Bishop, Sammy Davis, Jr., and daughter Nancy Sinatra also appeared on the show. No doubt the 45-year-old Sinatra, whose career was in a trough, was feeling competition from young Elvis, who was driving girls wild just as Sinatra had done 20 years before. The show aired the following May 12 and most of America watched.

Back to Babylon

Meanwhile, back in Hollywood, Elvis began filming *G.I. Blues* on May 2, 1960, playing a soldier by the name of Tulsa McLean opposite Juliet Prowse—who was dating Frank Sinatra. The film was shot on Paramount's lot in Los Angeles in eleven weeks and marked the first of nine Elvis films that Norman Taurog would direct. *G.I. Blues* was released on November 23, 1960, and was the 14th highest ranked film of the year. The soundtrack of the film quickly reached 1 million records sold.

No doubt about it, Sgt. Elvis Presley hit the streets running upon his return from Germany. In five months he appeared on a huge television special (and earned a remarkable $125,000 for singing two songs), made a movie, and recorded a soundtrack. The juggernaut had picked up where it had left off.

> **Going for Gold**
> Elvis filmed all of his scenes for *G.I. Blues* on the Paramount lot in Hollywood beginning in May 1960. Yet, before Elvis had signed on to the project, producer Hal B. Wallis sent a second unit to scout locations in Idstein, Germany. We don't see Elvis in West Germany in the movie, but we see where he was posted just months before.

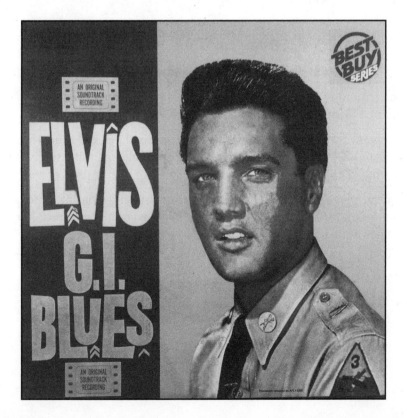

After his honorable discharge from the Army, Elvis' first movie was G.I. Blues *in 1960. This is the cover from the original soundtrack recording.*

Sleeping Through the '60s

A long, lost weekend beckoned, however. On February 25, 1961, Elvis performed at Ellis Auditorium in Memphis. A month later, on March 25, he gave a benefit concert for the USS *Arizona* Memorial Fund in Honolulu. These would be his last live performances until 1968.

After Elvis' Army hitch, Elvis focused almost exclusively on his movie career, spending more and more time in Hollywood and Beverly Hills, acquiring vast wealth, and making films and music of steadily deteriorating quality. He created an insulated world of friends, family, and courtiers, partying the years away in the confines of Graceland and a series of Hollywood residences. He recorded some great singles during the '60s, but stopped performing live entirely, and eventually saw his viability as a rock and roller beginning to slip away.

With the arrival of The Beatles, The Rolling Stones, and a new crop of bands inspired by Elvis and rock and roll's first generation—not to mention the cultural upheavals that drew the lines between youth, rock and roll, and the old-guard American values to which Elvis adhered—Elvis began to seem out of touch, and out of date. Did Elvis still matter? Did Elvis still care?

The Least You Need to Know

➤ Elvis did nothing to dodge the draft and became a solid, above-average soldier.

➤ During his advance training in Texas, Elvis' mother Gladys became ill and died shortly thereafter in a Memphis hospital. Her only son was devastated.

➤ While serving in the Army in Germany, Elvis was besieged by fans, had numerous romances, made a number of media appearances, and even released some songs, but did not publicly sing.

➤ After his release from the Army, Elvis returned to mainstream show business, no longer the rockin', rollin', Hillbilly Cat. Focusing on his movies, he performed live only two more times until 1968.

Chapter 15

Love Me Tender: Young Love and Family Life

In This Chapter

➤ Elvis plays the dating game

➤ Elvis and Priscilla

➤ Elvis as husband and father

Elvis was an active hound dog, so to speak. From the beginning, he was a red-blooded American male who was linked romantically with many women. He was married only once, however, to Priscilla Beaulieu (although other women have made preposterous claims that he married them). Priscilla would also give birth to the only child proven to have been his. (There have also been several unsubstantiated claims that Elvis fathered other kids, but if that's so, Elvis himself is alive, too!)

It would take an entire book to describe the King's entire love life. One thing's for sure, Elvis didn't lack for company! In this chapter you'll find the real dish on Elvis' romantic involvements—balanced with the so-called "purity" of his relationship with Priscilla.

For the Love of Elvis

Here's a chronological list of some of the women in Elvis' life in the pre-Priscilla years and their connection to him—with some carry-over to while they were together. When you are, arguably, the most desired man on the planet, it's hard to say no. Besides, Elvis was a true gentleman, and gentleman don't say no when asked by a lady. If you want the scoop on the major loves of Elvis' later life in the late 1960s and '70, relax...be patient. We'll get there in Chapter 18.

➤ **Caroline Ballard** was an early girlfriend in Tupelo when Elvis was nine. Her father was a minister at the Presley's church.

➤ **Eloise Bedford**—Elvis' girlfriend in the fifth grade at East Tupelo Consolidated School.

➤ **Magdalen Morgan**—Another Tupelo girlfriend.

➤ **Betty McMann**—Dated Elvis in Memphis in 1950-51. She claims she taught him to dance.

➤ **Billie Wardlaw**—Dated Elvis in Memphis in 1951.

➤ **Tammy Young**—Dated Elvis in high school.

➤ **Dixie Locke** —Elvis' steady date during high school and beyond.

For the Record

Ah, young love! Elvis and Dixie Locke met at a roller rink in 1953 and were an item until 1955. They went to football games, double-dated, and attended her prom in 1954. Elvis has said that he wanted to marry Dixie, but she turned him down because he was beginning to spend too much time on the road with his band. The pair broke up but remained close, and Dixie was active in Elvis' first fan club.

➤ **Regis (Wilson) Vaughan**—Elvis' senior-prom date in 1953. She was a 14-year-old freshman at the time. They went together during most of that spring.

➤ **Anita Carter**—Member of the singing Carter Family who dated Elvis in 1955 while touring on the same bill with him.

➤ **Barbara Pittman**—Singer who recorded for Sun Records and dated Elvis in the mid-1950s.

➤ **Sharon Wiley**—Woman who dated Elvis in the mid-1950s.

➤ **June Juanico**—Receptionist Elvis met at a concert in Biloxi, Mississippi and dated in 1955-56.

➤ **Marilyn Evans**—Las Vegas showgirl who dated Elvis in 1956 and was present at the Million-Dollar-Quartet session at Sun Records. (Remember from Chapter 5... We're talking about Elvis, Johnny Cash, Jerry Lee Lewis, and Carl Perkins.)

➤ **Diana Dors**—British actress/bombshell (England's attempted answer to Marilyn Monroe) who met Elvis at a Hollywood party in 1956. The buxom platinum blonde claimed to have had an affair with the King, including a vacation in Mexico, while she was married.

➤ **Natalie Wood**—Hollywood actress who had romantic relations with Elvis, but later the two became just friends. Interestingly, it was Wood, just 18 but already a veteran of 14 films, who was worldly wise and Elvis, the 21-year-old rock and roller, the square. "He didn't drink," Wood said later. "He didn't swear. He didn't even smoke!" The differences were ultimately so great that their "Motorcycle Romance"— so dubbed because they bought Harleys together in Memphis—didn't ever really rev up. As Wood said, "We were too young." (Natalie Wood, who married actor Robert Wagner twice, died tragically in a boating accident in 1981 at age 43.)

For the Record

What man *wasn't* attracted to Natalie Wood, the beautiful star of *Rebel Without a Cause* and *West Side Story*? Elvis certainly was. The two were introduced by a mutual friend, actor Nick Adams. (Elvis, a big James Dean fan, couldn't have missed her in *Rebel*.) They were an item for a short time in 1956. She spent some time in Memphis and created a national stir by cruising around with Elvis on his Harley. They had a real affection for each other but, for reasons that had more to do with their careers than love, things didn't work out. Over the years they remained in touch and continued to speak highly of each other.

➤ **Kitty Dolan**—Singer at the Tropicana who dated Elvis in 1956.

➤ **Yvonne Lime**—Actress who dated Elvis in 1956-57 during the filming of *Loving You*.

➤ **Anita Wood**—Nineteen-year-old Memphis disc jockey and host of the TV show, *Top Ten Dance Party*. She attracted Elvis' attention in July 1957 and they went out seriously for over four years before Anita reportedly broke the relationship off by announcing to Elvis and Vernon that they "weren't going anywhere." Wood went on to a modest recording career, which included two Elvis novelty songs, "I'll Wait Forever" and "Memories of You," as well as other light pop songs in the 1960s.

Return to Sender

Was Elvis engaged to Anita Wood? According to Colonel Parker, the answer is a big NO. Wood was one of Elvis' first serious romances, and many insiders thought Elvis should marry her. In fact, Elvis did give her a diamond ring. But the idea was quickly squashed by Colonel Parker, who didn't want his boy tied up with any one woman. While in Germany, Elvis met Priscilla, which effectively ended his relationship with Wood. Wood went on to become a beauty-pageant winner and record several songs.

The King and I
"He [Elvis] had really pretty lips, and he was very handsome. Elvis was my first love. You never forget that. I had never even gone steady with anyone, so when I was 19 years old and met Elvis, I immediately fell in love with him. He made a big impression on my life."

—Anita Wood

➤ **Rita Moreno**—Award-winning actress of stage, screen, and television who dated Elvis in 1957, while he was filming *Loving You*. The Puerto Rican-born actress won an Oscar as best supporting actress for the 1961 film *West Side Story*, which happened to star Natalie Wood.

➤ **Mamie Van Doren**—Known as the poor man's Marilyn Monroe, the famously buxom actress dated Elvis in 1957 while she was married to musician Ray Anthony.

➤ **Tempest Storm**—Stripper who dated Elvis in 1957 in a relationship the press dubbed the "seven day whirl."

➤ **Dottie Harmony**—Vegas showgirl who dated Elvis in 1957 and accompanied him to his pre-induction Army physical.

➤ **Barbara Hearn**—Actress who dated Elvis in the late 1950s and early 60s. He met her in 1957 while filming *Loving You*, in which she had a bit part.

➤ **Dolores Hart**—Actress who dated Elvis in 1958 and played opposite him in *Loving You* and *King Creole*. She later became a nun, Sister Dolores.

➤ **Carol Connors** (born Annette Kleinbard)—Lead singer of the Teddy Bears who dated Elvis for 10 months in 1958. Elvis had asked to meet her after he heard her sing the hit "To Know Him Is To Love Him."

➤ **Bobbie Gentry**—Well-known singer who dated Elvis in the late 1950s. She had the first and biggest hit of her career in 1967 with "Ode to Billy Joe."

➤ **Vera Tschechowa**—German actress who dated Elvis intermittently in West Germany in 1958-60.

➤ **Margrit Buergin**—Woman who dated Elvis in West Germany. A German national, she worked as a stenographer. Elvis called her "Little Puppy." He reportedly broke it off because she didn't speak English—those language barriers can certainly be pesky to true love.

➤ **Anjelika Zehetbauer**—Nightclub dancer who dated Elvis in West Germany. He called her his "German Fräulein."

➤ **Jane Clarke**—Dancer Elvis met at the Lido club in Paris, while he was on leave there in 1959. They met again in 1963 when she was performing at the Tropicana Hotel in Las Vegas.

➤ **Patti Parry**—A teenager Elvis met in a chance encounter in 1960, Patti Parry, who described herself as a "nice Jewish girl," was a fledgling hairdresser who became an unofficial member (and only woman) of the Memphis Mafia. Elvis adopted her as a little sister and she stayed in his life off and on until nearly the end.

➤ **Nancy Sharp**—A wardrobe assistant who dated Elvis in 1960 during the filming of *Flaming Star*.

➤ **Sharon Hugueny**—Actress who dated Elvis in 1963 while young Priscilla lived at Graceland.

➤ **Shelley Fabares**—Actress who appeared with Elvis in three of his films and who was the favorite of all his female co-stars. She dated him in 1965-67. As a singer, she had a million-selling record, "Johnny Angel," which reached number one in 1962.

Going for Gold

How does one get picked up by a famous star? Try the direct approach, like Patti Parry did. She met Elvis when she and a girlfriend were driving down Santa Monica Boulevard in Los Angeles. While stopped at a red light, she rolled down a window and said, "You look familiar. Don't I know you?" He asked her over to his house in Bel Air. Alas, the romance turned platonic. They stayed friends over the years, like brother and sister.

➤ **Jackie Deshannon**—Well-known singer/songwriter (one of her biggest hits was "What the World Needs Now Is Love") who dated Elvis in the mid-1960s.

➤ **Ann-Margret**—Voluptuous screen actress who met Elvis in 1964 while starring opposite him in *Viva Las Vegas*. The two were romantically linked, but the relationship developed into a powerful friendship that lasted through the end of Elvis' life. Originally, she was billed as a sex kitten—who in some ways resembled a female counterpart to Elvis: vibrant, sexy, and unrestrained.

For the Record

Want a fun read? Try Ann-Margret's autobiography, *Ann-Margret: My Story*. In it, she circumspectly describes what is obviously a strong connection between her and Elvis; clearly, they were more than merely friends. She and husband Roger Smith attended Elvis' funeral and spent time at Graceland with the family. And there should be no doubt about the affair or its intensity; Linda Thompson, Elvis' last great love, has said, "I know that Elvis loved Ann-Margret...he used to talk about how he would have married her but circumstances just got kind of convoluted." The circumstances? In all likelihood, Ann-Margret's insistence on maintaining her career.

As you can see, Elvis' love life was busy and remarkably varied. The reality seems to be that Elvis was destined to have a life-long series of brief, often one-night, affairs with an enormous number of beautiful women. Clearly, he genuinely enjoyed the company of the opposite sex; he was repeatedly described by his various mates as "sweet" and "polite"—rarely were there (at least publicly) recriminations at the brevity of the affairs. Not hard to believe, considering the significance of his relationship with one particular woman: his mother, Gladys. It's really quite simple: Elvis liked women, and they liked him back.

The Word

If you really want to be recognized as a true Elvis authority— and who doesn't?—you'll need to know Elvis' nickname for Priscilla. He called his one and only wife **Cilla**. Now you can show off your newfound knowledge!

So how and why did he segue into marriage with Priscilla? In large part, because he had promised to. Remember, despite everything, Elvis was, to use Natalie Wood's word, "conventional." He made a promise to a young girl and he kept it.

Priscilla the Princess

Although Elvis had many loves—or at least love interests—in his life, the one we associate with him is Priscilla Ann Beaulieu Presley. She was the young princess who came to Graceland and later married the King.

The King's Child Bride

So how does a King choose his Queen? At a grand ball? Not exactly…

Elvis met Priscilla Ann Beaulieu in November 1959 while stationed in West Germany. Elvis was 24 at the time, Priscilla 14. Priscilla's stepfather, Air Force Captain Joseph Paul Beaulieu, was stationed at Weisbaden along with Elvis. (Her real father, Lt. James Wagner, was a dashing Navy pilot who died in a crash in 1945 on the way back to see his wife and daughter, who had been born in Brooklyn five months before, on May 24, 1945.)

Currie Grant, an airman assigned to Special Services (and therefore used to catering to celebrities as part of his job) was stationed near Weisbaden during Elvis' tour of duty. In August 1959, he introduced Elvis and Priscilla. Currie and his wife Carole escorted Priscilla to Elvis' rented house at 15 Goethestrasse in Bad Neuheim. Priscilla was wearing a blue-and-white sailor dress and white socks. Elvis reportedly was immediately bowled over by the 5'3", 14 year old—who, in Elvis' defense, looked much older—declaring, "She looks like an angel." For the rest of Elvis' time in Germany—some six months—Elvis and Priscilla saw one another regularly. When Elvis left Germany, he told the distraught schoolgirl that he loved her.

In March of 1960, Elvis returned to the United States, but he kept thinking about young Priscilla Beaulieu. They spoke on the phone from time to time. Finally, Elvis took action, convincing Priscilla's mother and step-father, in a series of calls, to allow her to visit him for two weeks at Graceland for the 1960 Christmas holidays. It was by all accounts a magical time, with Priscilla impressing everyone, including the male-bonded Memphis Mafia, with her poise, intelligence, and maturity.

Elvis' pursuit of Priscilla continued until he convinced her parents to let Priscilla move to Memphis in October 1962, with Elvis paying for her education. A Catholic, Priscilla enrolled and graduated from Immaculate Conception High School in Memphis on June 14, 1963. Later she went on to a finishing school.

Return to Sender
Airman Currie Grant has reported that Priscilla pursued Elvis. But Priscilla claims Elvis had Currie approach her. Why would Priscilla lie? Any teenage girl would want to meet the famous Elvis Presley—thousands did. But for Currie to admit he was hustling up an underage girl for Superstar Elvis—that wouldn't make him look so good.

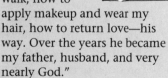

The King and I
"He taught me everything; how to dress, how to walk, how to apply makeup and wear my hair, how to return love—his way. Over the years he became my father, husband, and very nearly God."

—Priscilla Presley

Elvis and Priscilla,
1967.

Over the next years, Priscilla and Elvis lived together at Graceland, basically as man and wife. He showered her with gifts, including cars and jewelry. Elvis continued to date other women, being uncharacteristically discreet to protect Priscilla's feelings. Whatever the nature of their relationship, it is clear that, certainly in the beginning, Elvis held Priscilla in the highest regard and outwardly treated her with respect. Priscilla had almost everything a girl could want: money, an extravagant lifestyle, and the sexiest man on the planet.

Wedding Bells

On May 1, 1967, Elvis and Priscilla were married at a suite in the Aladdin Hotel in Las Vegas. It was a private ceremony—so private that even most of the Memphis Mafia were excluded (causing friction and resentment that would last for years). The ceremony, presided over by Nevada Supreme Court Justice David Zenoff, was held in the hotel owner's private suite. Michelle Beaulieu, Priscilla's 13-year old sister, was the maid of honor. Joe Esposito and Marty Lacker were co-best men.

So who *were* the lucky guests? Honored attendees included: Vernon Presley and his second wife, Dee; Ann and Paul Beaulieu (Priscilla's mother and step-father); Donald Beaulieu (Priscilla's brother); Patsy Presley Gambill (Elvis' cousin) and her husband Gee Gee (Elvis' chauffeur); Colonel Tom Parker; George Klein (Memphis DJ and Elvis' childhood friend) and his wife, Barbara Little; and Harry Levitch (Memphis jeweler who had delivered the ring) and his wife Francis.

The Presleys' wedding breakfast consisted of fried chicken, suckling pig, oysters Rockefeller, and champagne. The six-tier, seven-foot-high wedding cake was decorated with hearts, silver bells, and roses. The band played "Love Me Tender." On May 29, Elvis held a second wedding ceremony and reception at Graceland for family, friends, and employees.

The King and I
"Elvis and Priscilla spent their honeymoon at the Circle G Ranch—yes in a house trailer! Let's face it, Elvis was not a normal human being. He liked unusual things, and staying in a trailer was exciting to him."

—Joe Esposito, friend and employee

Marriage Certificate

BOOK 248   405254

State of Nevada |
County of Clark. | ss.   No. A 175632

This is to Certify that the undersigned JUSTICE DAVID ZENOFF
did on the ___1st___ day of ___May___ A.D. 1967 join in lawful
Wedlock ELVIS ARON PRESLEY
of MEMPHIS   State of TENNESSEE
and PRISCILLA ANN BEAULIEU
of SHELBY   State of TENNESSEE
with their mutual consent, in the presence of Joe Esposito
and Marty Jacker who were witnesses.
Recorded at the Request of David Zenoff
Date MAY 5 1967
In Book of Marriages, Clark County, Nevada.
Records, Paul E. Horn, Recorder
Fee $1.00 indexed ___ Deputy.   JUSTICE, SUPREME COURT OF NEVADA
                                        (Sign this in official capacity.)

Elvis and Priscilla's Marriage Certificate, May 1, 1967.

Elvis and Domestic Life

It was a stormy relationship. Although Elvis loved Priscilla, he continued to have many affairs. As intelligent as Priscilla was, it didn't take her long to figure out that her husband was stepping out. They had lived together for five years; she now was 21, and he was 32.

Going for Gold

In February 1967, Elvis bought Twinkletown Farm 10 miles south of Graceland—in DeSoto County, Mississippi—for $300,000. He changed the name to Circle G (for Graceland; it then became the Flying Circle G since there was already a Circle G in Texas) and raised horses and cattle, and vacationed there. You can still visit: the Flying Circle G is off Route 301 near Walls, Mississippi, (601) 781-1411.

There were, of course, many good times. Elvis liked to have lots of people around, on his terms, and Priscilla was a good sport about sharing her husband with others. Some of the Memphis Mafia resented Priscilla, blaming her for their not being invited to the wedding. Actually, she had nothing to do with it. Colonel Tom Parker orchestrated the wedding, and Elvis vetoed few if any of the arrangements. (Even Red West, Elvis' close friend for so many years, was invited only to the reception after the service.)

Further complicating the relationship between the newlyweds was that Elvis' career was in a down period. He hadn't performed live in years, and his movies had become limp star vehicles. His spending continued unabated. Elvis was frustrated and bored. And he took it out on his wife. They were both using Dexedrine from time to time, and drug-influenced fights—including physical ones—were not uncommon. Elvis even suggested that they separate. But Priscilla was pregnant, and a separation would have looked terrible in the press. And Elvis, for all his philandering, genuinely looked forward to being a father.

Fatherhood: Their Daughter, Lisa Marie

Lisa Marie Presley was born on February 1, 1968, nine months to the day after Elvis' and Priscilla's wedding. Elvis was nervous. An entourage of friends and police helped him get through it. Elvis was too nervous to announce the birth to the press, and had Vernon do it for him.

For the Record

Lisa Marie Presley was born at 5:01 p.m. on February 1, 1968, on the fifth floor of the east wing of Baptist Memorial Hospital in Memphis. She was delivered by Dr. T.A. Turman. She weighed six pounds, 15 ounces, and was 20 inches long. Her middle name, Marie, was given to her in honor of Colonel Tom Parker's wife. Nancy Sinatra, who acted with Elvis in the movie *Speedway*, and with whom Elvis had been romantically linked, gave the baby shower.

Lisa Marie grew up mostly at Graceland. Priscilla did what she could to keep Lisa Marie out of the spotlight and create a normal reality for the child. By and large, she succeeded, against great odds.

Meanwhile, Elvis—well, he was a busy man. He was an affectionate father and certainly a good provider, lavishing Lisa Marie with extravagant gifts; but he was also an absentee dad much of the time. Elvis had begun a enormously successful comeback in 1968, and he began spending more time on the road. And more time in Vegas. Priscilla and Lisa Marie traveled primarily between Los Angeles and Memphis. Their lives, gradually, began to move apart.

The Word

Just as Elvis had an affectionate name for his mother ("Baby" and "Satinin"), for his grandmother ("Dodger"), and for his wife ("Cilla"), he had pet names for Lisa Marie too—**"Buttonhead"** and **"Yisa."**

Even with a wife in the nest, Elvis was a man who still very much loved women. In Part 5, we'll meet some other ladies in his life and see how and why his marriage to Priscilla dissolved.

The Least You Need to Know

➤ Elvis started dating girls from when he was a little boy and had a slew of sweethearts before he became famous.

➤ Once he became famous, Elvis dated many women in show business, including Ann-Margret, Rita Moreno, and Natalie Wood.

➤ Elvis' only wife was Priscilla Beaulieu, whom he first met in Germany when she was 14 years old.

➤ Elvis' only child, Lisa Marie, was born on February 1, 1968.

➤ Elvis was largely an absentee husband and father.

Meet the Memphis Mafia

Like royalty of ancient times, the King of Rock and Roll needed a court—trusted and loyal companions who could be counted on to provide not only essential services, but simple friendship as well. The men who made up what came to be called the Memphis Mafia were that and more. The circle that surrounded Elvis was a buffer, a wall of protection from the realities of celebrity and the pressures of fame. They served the King for reasons that went far beyond a job.

Bodyguards, road companions, concert technicians, valets, bookkeepers, drivers, pranksters, jesters, protectors, and players, Elvis' boys were always up for a little touch football, a late-night trip to the movies or the roller rink, a good practical joke, a couple of games of pool, or a ride around the grounds on the golf carts. They were on constant call; whenever Elvis was ready to roll, they were, too. They carried guns and studied martial arts, just in case (and because Elvis happened to like both as hobbies). They were also a party waiting to happen, with a never-ending supply of beautiful women at their beck and call.

Goodfellas, One and All

When you think Mafia, what comes to mind? Cement shoes? Bodies in automobile trunks? Bugsy Siegal in Vegas? Movies like *Goodfellas* and *The Godfather*? Marlon Brando and Robert DeNiro?

No, the Memphis Mafia wasn't a crime organization, but you might say there are some similarities between the authentic Mafia and the Memphis Mafia. The Italian Mafia has a notorious (and often romanticized) reputation. But members of the Mafia share a definite bond: They are inseparably linked and would risk life and limb to protect each other. The Godfather makes all rules and final decisions in the Italian Mafia, and all must respect and honor him: He is, in effect, royalty, and must be treated and protected as such.

The Word
The phrase **Memphis Mafia** referred to the tight-knit group of friends, relatives, employees, and others who catered to Elvis' every whim and attempted to keep him out of harm's way.

In Elvis' case, the *Memphis Mafia* consisted of friends, relatives, co-workers, and general hangers-on whom Elvis happened to like and trust. Just like in the Italian Mafia, these men would do anything their Godfather, Elvis, wanted—even if it meant fostering bad habits that would lead to Elvis' demise.

Let's Have a Party!

Elvis' entourage were hired and fired and fired and hired, but somehow they were always around. It was hard on their own personal lives, but there were perks. There was the lifestyle, the travel, the limelight—and the girls. Nice work, if you can get it!

The King and I
"They [the Memphis Mafia] are the feel of where he came from. They are old friends and base roots. Elvis is very comfortable because he keeps himself surrounded by pieces of his past."

—Bill Bixby, Elvis' costar in *Clambake* and *Speedway*

Once you were in the Memphis Mafia, Elvis treated you like family. You could count on him for your livelihood. And he could be exceedingly generous above and beyond your salary if you were on his good side. He was always good for a loan or a down payment on a house. He gave his boys money, jewelry, cars, and clothes—plus a sense of belonging to something big. For over 20 years, the Memphis Mafia shared the candy store with the King.

Elvis' reason for sharing this never-ending party with these guys? Elvis loved his Southern roots and truly enjoyed the company of his Memphis brethren. They grew up listening to the same music, eating the same foods, eyeing the same hot cars, ogling the same gorgeous out-of-reach women (who were now very much within reach), playing the same sports, watching the same movies, and so on. They were lusty, good-ol' Memphis boys who liked to have fun. And, just like Elvis, most of them knew what it was like to be poor.

Yet there was also a downside to all of this partying. One had to beware of Elvis' temper, which was often ignited by the stresses of performing and celebrity status. And Elvis didn't like to hear the truth about how his partying ways might negatively affect his judgment and/or endanger his health. Members of the Memphis Mafia had to walk on glass with Elvis. One day he might be a buddy playing touch football, the next he'd throw you out of Graceland because of an offhanded remark.

All in all, the Memphis Mafia got a wild, exhilarating ride on the Elvis express. Only in the final few years (which we'll get to) did things start to sour.

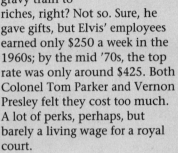

Return to Sender
Working for the biggest entertainer in America was a gravy train to riches, right? Not so. Sure, he gave gifts, but Elvis' employees earned only $250 a week in the 1960s; by the mid '70s, the top rate was only around $425. Both Colonel Tom Parker and Vernon Presley felt they cost too much. A lot of perks, perhaps, but barely a living wage for a royal court.

Roll Call: The Inner Circle

Here's where you'll find out everything you need to know about those who were privy to Elvis' most secret moments. You'll find a wide range of characters, from the most devoted, to the betrayers, to those who simply liked to have a good time. All of them shared at least one thing: They made their living off of Elvis.

Joe Esposito: The Memphis Don

Joe Esposito, a lifelong friend of Elvis until the end, was often referred to as the "Don" of the Memphis Mafia. And he was actually Italian—second generation, to be precise.

Esposito, the only "Yankee" in the Memphis Mafia, met Elvis while they were stationed in West Germany. Over the years he took on a wide range of chores for the Elvis machine—*road manager*, *bodyguard*, and part-time bookkeeper, among others. "Diamond Joe" or "the Lion," as Elvis called him, was the man Elvis relied on to "meet" female fans.

The Word
In the music business, a **road manager** oversees all details of touring, traveling, lodging, as well as coordinating with the local folks providing the concert site. Much of the work takes place before the arrival of the musician or musicians to the concert location.

Elvis considered him family, and he and Marty Lacker (who we'll soon learn about) stood up with Elvis when he married Priscilla. Joe's wife, Joan, was Matron of Honor. Elvis' loyalty to Joe never faltered, even when he was sued by him and his partner, "Dr. Nick" Nichopoulos (we'll find out about him in Chapter 20) in 1977, when their racquetball business, Presley Center Courts, went down after huge financial losses. Esposito, like Red West (details about Red are coming up—don't worry), did bits in many of Elvis' films. It was Esposito who called Priscilla in Los Angeles to tell her that Elvis had died.

Joe Esposito today, the Memphis Mafia member Elvis depended on more than any other.

Esposito's memoir of his 20 years with Elvis, *Good Rockin' Tonight*, was called by Colonel Tom Parker "the most honest and truthful book ever written about Elvis." In the last line of that memoir, Esposito succinctly describes Elvis as "the most extraordinary ordinary man."

After Elvis' death, Esposito went on to manage concert tours for The Bee Gees, Karen Carpenter, Wayne Newton, and Michael Jackson, among others.

Lamar Fike: (Hefty) Comic Relief

Lamar Fike, nicknamed "Buddha" and "the Great Speckled Bird" by Elvis, was an over-weight, music-entranced young man who, as a teenager, began hanging out at various recording studios around town. Some stories have it that Fike literally hung around outside the gates of Graceland for so long that Elvis finally took pity on him and invited him in. Fike contends that he was in the studio of Sun Records one day in 1955 talking with Sam Phillips, owner of Sun Records, when Elvis walked in wearing one of his wild outfits, and the two hit it off. Either way, Fike was a member in good standing of the Memphis Mafia until the end.

Fike saw something special in Elvis and the unlikely duo became friends. By 1957, he was a charter member of the Memphis Mafia and a key player on the team. Fike was Elvis' right-hand man, taking care of all of the nitty-gritty details. He handled travel details and supervised the technical aspects of mounting the shows on the road. At 300 or so pounds, Fike is blessed with a strong sense of humor and a willingness to take a joke.

The King and I
"He liked his clothes to be different from everybody else's. He used them to attract attention and make himself different from the other young guys.... I wouidn't have dressed like that but I knew right away what he was doing and I liked it."

—Lamar Fike

Elvis enjoyed poking fun at Fike, but his loyalty was unquestioned: When Elvis needed him he was always there. As mentioned in Chapter 14, when Elvis was drafted, Fike tried to enlist but was turned down because of his weight. He did, however, go to Germany and live with Elvis and his family during his tour of duty.

Fike also turned out to have a good ear for material that suited Elvis. He discovered several hits for Elvis, including "Kentucky Rain," "It's Midnight," and "T-R-O-U-B-L-E." Though repeatedly fired and re-hired in his various loosely defined jobs (which included concert lighting and transportation), Fike remained with Elvis, for whom he was the butt of increasingly pointed jokes, until he quit to manage the singer Brenda Lee in 1962. Fike returned to the fold several years later and served as one of the pallbearers at Elvis' funeral.

The King and I
"You wouldn't last very long with Elvis if you didn't have a sense of humor. He would just eat you up and spit you out. But as long as you could give as good as you got you'd be fine."

—Lamar Fike

Over the years with Elvis, Fike developed a network of contacts in the music business and later went on to a successful career in music publishing. Today he is also a personal manager, producer, and talent scout. Lamar Fike is a highly controversial figure for many Elvis fans, since he was one of the main sources (and co-copyright holder) used by Albert Goldman in his terribly mean-spirited biography *Elvis* (for more on *that* dubious work, check out the Bibliography, Appendix C).

Alan Fortas: The Muscle Behind Elvis

Alan Fortas was a Memphis high-school football star (and nephew of Supreme Court Justice Abe Fortas) who received a full scholarship to Vanderbilt University. Fortas was a long-timer in the Memphis Mafia, on the team as a bodyguard and assistant from 1958 to about 1969. One of Elvis' closest comrades and confidants, Fortas arranged travel between concerts. He would occasionally join Elvis on stage, playing tambourine. Today he is a Memphis businessman.

For the Record

Alan Fortas always said that Elvis had a heart of gold. The King proved it when Fortas' dying father was hospitalized and Elvis told Alan to go back to Memphis and tend to his father. "You stay in Memphis," Elvis said, "and if it's two years, you pick up your paycheck every week, and if you come back, you're fired." That Christmas, Elvis visited Fortas' father in the hospital and presented him with a gold pocket watch. It was a typical act of kindness, according to Fortas, and a side of Elvis that his friends saw regularly.

Larry Geller: Some Spirituality with Your Haircut?

After giving Elvis a particularly good haircut in April of 1964, Larry Geller left his job at Jay Sebring's salon in Beverly Hills to become the King's personal hair stylist. (A few years later, Sebring, along with actress Sharon Tate and others, was murdered by Charles Manson and followers.)

Geller's fascination with religion and the occult intrigued Elvis, and soon Geller, nicknamed "Guru" by the King, was stocking Elvis' Beverly Hills house with books on all aspects of the weird and strange. The two would talk for hours about religion, parapsychology, the supernatural, and the mystical world. To show his appreciation, Elvis gave Geller a Cadillac (a typical Elvis gift).

Colonel Parker was threatened by the increasing influence of Geller on Elvis and in 1967 succeeded in getting rid of him. But Geller's aura remained. For the rest of his life, Elvis continued to dabble in the occult and read about the supernatural aspects of religion, developing a particular fascination with contacting his brother Jesse, who died at birth. He also continued to speak and meet with Geller.

Geller has written or participated in several personal accounts of his life with Elvis, including his own book, *If I Can Dream: Elvis' Own Story*. Geller gave Elvis *The Scientific Search for the Face of Jesus*, the book he is thought to have been reading when he died (see Chapter 20 on the King's death). For a selected Elvis bibliography see Appendix C.

The King and I
"Don't forget, Larry, angels fly because they take themselves so lightly."

—Elvis (to Larry Geller, 1977)

Charlie Hodge: Ol' "Slewfoot"

"Slewfoot" Charlie Hodge, a gifted guitarist and gospel singer from Decatur, Alabama, was with Elvis almost at the beginning and at the end. For more than 17 years, he lived at Graceland and took care of personal business for the King. On the road he was always there to hand Elvis the trademark scarves he tossed out to the audience during a show.

Hodge, the butt of many jokes because of his height (5'3"), met Presley during a television show in 1956 and the two singers hit it off from the start. They joined the Army at the same time, did basic training together at Fort Hood, shared the same troop ship to Europe, and were stationed together in Germany. Hodge, with Elvis and Red West, wrote the song "You'll Be Gone," which Elvis recorded in 1965. To see Charlie in action, check out Elvis' "Comeback Special," where Slewfoot is playing guitar, singing harmony, and generally having one heckuva a good time. Of all the Memphis Mafia, Charlie Hodge was the only professional musician. His songs have been recorded by Pat Boone, Ricky Nelson, and Elvis. A good and loyal friend who genuinely cared for Elvis, Charlie Hodge is one of the few Memphis Mafiosi whose reputation has never been tarnished.

The Word
Ever hear the name **El's Angels**? No, not the biker gang. Maybe you've heard the name **Elvis Presley's Boys**. These were the two original names used to describe Elvis' friends, bodyguards, and hangers-on who guarded the King from the outside world.

Marty Lacker: High-School Chum

Marty Lacker, a New Yorker who moved to Memphis at age 15 and had known Elvis since high school at Humes, joined the Memphis Mafia around 1960 and worked for Elvis until 1967 when an argument over money between him and Vernon resulted in his dismissal. The real force behind his firing may have been Tom Parker, who detested the fact that

Lacker, a sensitive and independent man, was one of the few Mafia members not to kow-tow to the Colonel at the drop of a hat.

Like other members of the crew, Lacker was many things to Elvis, including personal secretary and bookkeeper. He was best man at Elvis' wedding—along with Joe Esposito—shortly before he was fired in 1967. Lacker lived at Graceland with his wife and three children—and was introduced to drugs there. Elvis gave him several automobiles and quite a bit of jewelry over the years, though Lacker was not the sort of man who graded friendship based on gifts. His wife, Patsy, feels that Elvis himself helped bring about Lacker's own drug abuse problem, from which he has recovered. In *Elvis: Portrait of a Friend*, a candid 1979 book he wrote with his wife, Lacker was honest about Elvis' (and his own) drug problems.

Jerry Schilling—a.k.a. "Cougar"

Elvis met Jerry Schilling on a Memphis basketball court, soon after he recorded his first song, "That's All Right (Mama)." Called "Cougar" by Elvis, the handsome Schilling became a full-time Memphis Mafioso in 1964, quitting Arkansas State University in his senior year. He remained with Elvis as a personal aide until 1976.

A gifted athlete, Schilling often organized Elvis' touch-football games and studied martial arts with the King. Schilling, with Red West, accompanied Elvis on his famous visit to meet Richard Nixon at the White House. He left Graceland to become a film editor at Paramount, eventually going into music management and film production. Schilling married the stunning Myrna Smith, one of the Sweet Inspirations, Elvis' female backup group, and was a trusted adviser to Priscilla Presley in running the Elvis Presley Estate.

The King's Cousins

William "Billy" Smith and Elvis were family, maternal cousins who grew up together and never grew apart. Elvis went to great lengths to include Billy in his world. Billy was never far away, living in a trailer behind Graceland with his wife, Jo. Billy and Jo played rac-quetball with Elvis on the day he died.

Gene Smith was a cousin of Elvis' (and of Billy Smith's) and one of the earliest members of the Memphis Mafiosi. He and Elvis were childhood friends; they worked odd jobs together, double dated, and remained extremely close. Gene lived at Graceland and was responsible for wardrobe. He and several others left in 1969 over a payroll disagreement with Vernon.

The Step-Stanley Boys

The Stanley brothers moved into Graceland in 1960 when their mother, Dee, married Vernon. The relationship between Elvis and the Stanley boys wasn't brotherly (they were not part of his will), but all three worked for him at various times and they shared good times with him—and some very bad times at the end.

William "Billy" Stanley, born in January of 1953, is the oldest of the Stanley boys and spent the least time with Elvis. Called "Charlie Manson" by Elvis because of his sinister look, Elvis used Billy as yet another bodyguard. He has authored or contributed to several books on Elvis; in one he claimed that Elvis had an affair with his 18-year-old-bride. Today, he's a Nashville based, semi-professional race-car driver.

Rick Stanley was also born in 1953. Like his younger brother, David, Rick was on Elvis' payroll as an aide and personal bodyguard. Also like David, he developed a drug problem and was arrested in 1975 for trying to pass a forged prescription for amphetamines at a local hospital. He has been said to be a source of drugs for Elvis. He was fired after an argument with Linda Thompson, one of Elvis' mid-'70s girlfriends, but came back after Linda and Elvis broke up. Rick Stanley underwent treatment for drug abuse, entered the ministry in the late 1970s, and continues to preach today.

> **The King and I**
>
> "Rickey and I would have died if Elvis hadn't died first."
>
> —David Stanley (on drug problems)

For the Record

In 1974, Elvis was doing a show in Las Vegas when David Stanley spotted members of the band Led Zeppelin in the audience. A huge Zeppelin fan, Stanley cajoled Elvis into inviting them up to his suite. The star-struck band were in awe and barely managed to speak. Elvis, who called the band "Lead Zipper" and wasn't impressed with their image, entertained them briefly then escorted them to the door. As they were leaving, Robert Plant, Led Zep's lead singer, turned and began a dead-on impersonation of Elvis singing "Love Me." Elvis blinked, then grinned broadly and joined in. They finished the song walking down the hall, sounding for all the world like Elvis doing a duet with himself.

Born in 1955, David Stanley, against his mother's wishes, started working for Elvis as a teenager. He began as personal security on concert tours and at Graceland, eventually quitting high school to become a full-time employee and member of the Memphis Mafia. He was on duty at Graceland the day Elvis died. David Stanley was close enough to Elvis to know the extent of his drug addiction, and he has recovered from his own serious drug problem. He has been involved with several Elvis-related projects over the years, and lives with his second wife, Ginny, in Dayton, Ohio.

Wild, Wild Wests: Sonny and Red

Delbert (Sonny) West, also known as "Mr. Eagle," was introduced to Elvis by his cousin, Red West (see below). As a member of the Mafia, he was a tough and determined body-guard who was also responsible for the care and maintenance of Elvis' fleet of automo-biles, motorcycles, snowmobiles, golf carts, vans, and anything else that was motorized.

Delbert lived on the grounds at Graceland with his wife Judy. His love of cars luckily coincided with Elvis' taste in gifts, and over the years Elvis awarded him with numerous Cadillacs, Harleys, and pickup trucks. A good-looking man, Delbert did bits in several films and toured with Elvis until 1976 when he, Sonny, and Dave Hebler were fired after a fight with Vernon over, as usual, money. This was more than a pattern with Vernon, it was an obsession. Probably a legacy of his destitute background, Vernon resented paying anybody anything.

Robert (Red) Gene West was born and bred in Memphis. Red knew Elvis longer than anyone else in the Memphis Mafia, with the possible exception of Elvis' cousin Gene Smith. Elvis and Red met at Humes High, where Red was a gifted football player and boxer. West liked Elvis and stuck up for him in several schoolyard battles.

The two men became fast friends and, when Elvis started hitting the road with the Blue Moon Boys in 1955, Red went along as the driver. He joined the Marines in 1956 and hooked up again with Elvis in 1960 after Elvis returned from his hitch in the army. Red was a tough guy, aggressive and strong, perfectly capable of taking care of business and not afraid of a fight. The combo of Sonny and Red were not noted for their light touch, but they could certainly keep trouble away from the King.

For the Record

Elvis liked nothing more than a good practical joke. A death threat was once made on Elvis in Las Vegas (unfortunately, not uncommon), and as a joke, he called his backup gospel group, J.D. Sumner and the Stamps, and asked if they would accompany him to his hotel suite, acting as a human shield. Meanwhile, Elvis had Red West and other Mafia boys hide in the suite with blank guns. When Elvis and the unsuspecting Stamps hit the suite, Red and company burst out, guns "firing." Elvis screamed, clutched his chest, and crashed onto a coffee table. A horrified Sumner leapt onto Elvis, putting his body between the "killers" and Elvis. Elvis laughed hysterically. Sumner, a deeply religious man, erupted with a stream of profanities; Elvis couldn't have asked for a better response.

As his bodyguard, Red accompanied Elvis to Hollywood and began a film, television, and commercial career of his own, appearing in many of Elvis' films (see Chapter 13) and doing bits in many other films and television series as an actor and stuntman. West was also a singer and songwriter, and composed or co-wrote at least eight songs that Elvis recorded, including: "You'll Be Gone," "Separate Ways," "Holly Leaves and Christmas Trees."

Red West's relationship with Elvis was unique because Red, a no-nonsense sort of man, spoke more frankly to Elvis than anyone else dared. In that sense, he served as Elvis' conscience; when he was fired there was no one—save perhaps Joe Esposito—who even tried to tell Elvis he was living an unhealthy and dangerous lifestyle.

For the Record

By the 1970s, Red West was increasingly troubled by Elvis' use of drugs. When he, his cousin Sonny, and Dave Hebler were fired by Vernon in 1976, they collaborated on a book, *Elvis: What Happened?*, to get a man they loved to "take care of business"—and clean up his drug use. Instead, it threw Elvis into a deep depression from which he never recovered: The King died 15 days later. With its almost prophetic title and eerie timing, the book became a best seller.

The More the Merrier: The Outer Circle

OK, we've covered the starting line-up, as it were; now I'll tell you about the guys you might call the "bench" players. They were connected to Elvis and certainly knew more inside stuff than the average fan, but they weren't as privileged as the so-called Mafia.

Names you might like to know:

➤ **Richard Davis**—Elvis' personal valet. Davis was an active Memphis Mafioso for almost eight years, and he played a tough game of touch football. He was fired in the 1969 coup (one of many) by Vernon, who was unhappy with the influence of the Mafia (and the money he had to pay them) on his son; he was replaced by the King's step-brother Rick Stanley.

➤ **Cliff Gleaves**—Gleaves was a rockabilly singer, an old Elvis friend from Memphis, and an early member of the Mafia in the 1950s. Gleaves went to Hollywood with Elvis for the filming of *Love Me Tender*; was in the studio for the Million-Dollar-Quartet session with Jerry Lee Lewis, Johnny Cash, and Carl Perkins in 1956;

accompanied Elvis in for his draft physical in 1957; and was in Europe during the Army days. He remained in Elvis' circle for several years and became a Memphis disk jockey.

➤ **David Hebler**—A karate champion, Hebler was a late addition to the Memphis Mafia, first meeting the King in 1972 when Elvis came to work out at his studio in California. He joined the crew in 1974 as a bodyguard and lasted two years before he was fired along with Red and Sonny West.

➤ **George Klein**—A popular Memphis disk jockey, Klein graduated in the same class at Elvis from Humes High, where he was class president. Klein started working in a Memphis radio station about the time Elvis began recording; in fact, Klein even cut his own record with Sam Phillips' Sun Records. Klein introduced Elvis to one of his first girlfriends, Anita Wood, and his last, Ginger Alden—and countless others in between. When Klein married Barbara Little, Elvis not only was best man, he paid for the wedding, which was held in his suite at the Last Vegas Hilton. Though Klein was close to Elvis throughout his life, he cannot be considered a member of Elvis' inner circle because he had his own career and didn't travel with Elvis, or count on him for his livelihood.

For the Record

George Klein and Elvis shared more than music as a career choice; they also shared a plastic surgeon. According to Joe Esposito, Elvis, who had decided to have cosmetic surgery on his nose, began to get cold feet as the operation approached. So he "enlisted" George Klein to go with him, saying, "If you can do it, then it's okay for me to do it." Klein signed up and Dr. Morry Parks, Hollywood's doctor to the stars, altered both of their noses. (Take a look at Elvis' bridge, early and late, and you'll see the subtle effects of the surgery.)

➤ **T.G. Sheppard**—Country singer who was skating at the Rainbow Rollerdome in Memphis when he was pushed to the floor during one of Elvis' rowdier skating parties. He and Elvis became friends, and he attained a limited Mafia status. He hung out with the crowd, attending events and parties. T.G. invited Linda Thompson to a private night at the movies in the early 1970s and introduced her to Elvis. Elvis asked her out and they began a relationship that lasted until shortly before he died.

➤ **Sam Thompson**—At the suggestion of his younger sister, Linda Thompson, Sam, a college graduate and former Memphis sheriff's deputy, was hired to serve as a bodyguard for Elvis on and off in the mid-70s. Although he wasn't personally close to Elvis, Thompson, an articulate and thoughtful man, was considered a friend of the family and a trusted member of Elvis' entourage. Just 29 when Elvis died, he went on to law school and to serve as a judge in a Memphis juvenile court.

The King and I

"This is my corporation which travels with me all the time. More than that, all these members of my corporation are my friends."

—Elvis

The Least You Need to Know

➤ The Memphis Mafia consisted of Elvis' closest friends, relatives, and employees. They acted as his confidantes, bodyguards, and personal assistants, serving his every need and whim.

➤ There were many perks to working for Elvis, but also several downsides, such as low wages.

➤ With only a few notable exceptions, members of the Memphis Mafia ended up quitting or getting fired.

Part 5
Free-Fallin':
The Decline of Elvis

After almost a decade of no live performances, with his career in a downturn, Elvis Presley reinvented himself in a place where he had failed years before: Las Vegas. Today there remains some disagreement over the artistic merit of Elvis' Vegas years. Yet there is no debate over his commercial success: Elvis became even more of a larger-than-life icon as a result.

But there was a price to pay, as well. The pressures of performing and living up to his image were too much for Elvis. He became increasingly lonely, despite many women; he began to use prescription drugs excessively; and he constantly rewarded himself with unhealthy food and excessive spending habits.

Looking back, it's obvious that Elvis was in trouble. But he kept performing, kept thrilling and rewarding his audiences, and kept working at a terrible and dangerous pace. Finally, the inevitable occurred. At age 42, Elvis Presley died. Don't worry! We'll get to all the gory details, including the attempt to cover up the cause of Elvis' death and reactions to it from family, friends, and the culture at large.

Chapter 17

King of the Desert: Star of Vegas, Hitmaker Supreme

In This Chapter

➤ Elvis' famous "Comeback Special" on TV

➤ The King triumphantly returns to Vegas

➤ Elvis' grueling concert tours

1968. Remember that year? Big changes. The Tet offensive in Vietnam confirmed the vulnerability of U.S. forces. Martin Luther King, Jr. was assassinated in Memphis. Around the world students took to the streets to protest the Vietnam war and other issues. Bobby Kennedy was killed in California. Police battled citizens at the Democratic National Convention in Chicago. Soviet tanks invaded Czechoslovakia. Richard Nixon was elected president. Astronauts orbited the moon for the first time (on Apollo 8). LSD was the drug of choice.

And Elvis? The year was a high point in Elvis' personal life, but it began at a low point in his career. Lisa Marie was born, but he was unfulfilled as an artist. He was still a commercial success, but critics decried his succession of mediocre films and their mediocre soundtracks. Elvis himself was bored, saying, "You can't go on doing the same thing year after year." Was his reign about to end?

The answer is no. Elvis looked deep within himself and came up with a solution to resurrect his career. He knew he had to convince the Colonel that he'd made up his mind. He wanted to play live again.

Black Leather: The Legendary Comeback Special

On June 21, 1968, Elvis had his final dress rehearsals for a show to be aired on NBC—"Elvis." On June 27, Elvis began taping in Burbank, California, performing two one-hour sessions in front of a live audience, dressed completely in black leather and looking as cool as ever. In truth, he was nervous about his first live concert in almost 10 years. The stakes were high, and for one of the few times since his career took off, Elvis had to give everything he had.

The show, produced and directed by Steve Binder, aired on the night of December 3, 1968. It had great ratings, with a 32 audience rating and a 42 share—but don't bother to figure out what those numbers mean. The important thing is that "Elvis" was the highest-rated show for the week. Reviews were enthusiastic. The King was back.

The King and I
"The credits flashed, the camera focused on Elvis, and to our utter disbelief there he was, attired in black leather, his skin glistening, his hair long and greasy, his look forever young and callow. I don't know if I can convey how transcendent, how thrilling a moment it was."

—Peter Guralnick, *Lost Highway*

The King and I
"This show is a matter of video history significance… Presley is one in a lifetime…. In his area, Presley is the champ."

—"Elvis" producer Steve Binder, 1968

Elvis never looked better. He got in shape for this performance and was a lean, rockin' machine, with his dyed, jet-black hair matching his black leather. Aside from being in superb physical condition, there was almost a glow about Elvis that night, which director Binder's cameras caught by staying close on him the entire show. For my money, no one has ever looked better on stage than Elvis Presley did the night of December 3, 1968. As a case in point, more women between the age of 18 and 49 watched Elvis than any other show on television in 1968.

Creatively, the show was a brilliant success. It was "unplugged" long before the word ever came into our vocabulary through MTV. Elvis' nervousness, both at the immediate prospect of playing live again and the long-term effects this show would have on his career, fueled his performance with an intensity he hadn't displayed in years—and seldom would again. His voice, deeper and more mature than it had been 14 years before in the Sun studio, no longer reached those high notes without effort, but the effort gave his voice a thrilling, raw edge no one could have expected. From the climax of "Guitar Man," the opening number, to the soulful conclusion of "If I Can Dream," the gospel-tinged closer, Elvis almost roars with an awesome power.

Everyone has a favorite moment from this special. To me, the masterpiece was his playing the old blues tune "Lawdy Miss Clawdy" along with his old musician buddies Scotty Moore, Charlie Hodge, and drummer D.J. Fontana. (Remember, Bill Black passed away in 1965.)

But there were lots of highlights. Elvis sang 18 songs that evening including "Trouble" and "Guitar Man" (the opening numbers); "Baby, What You Want Me To Do?"; a medley of "Hound Dog," Heartbreak Hotel," and "All Shook Up"; "Jailhouse Rock"; "Love Me Tender"; "Are You Lonesome Tonight?"; "Blue Christmas"; "One Night With You"; and the finale, "If I Can Dream," written especially for the show.

The appearance marked the beginning of almost continuous touring for the next nine years. He still had commitments in Hollywood, but the next phase of his life was about to begin. Although simply called "Elvis" at the time, this concert has come to be known as the "Comeback Special."

The King and I
"It gave me new life. I was human again."

—Elvis, 1969

On New Year's Eve Elvis broke the news to Colonel Tom Parker that he wanted to get out of the movie business and tour again. And take one guess where he played…

Viva Las Vegas!

In 1968, Las Vegas meant crap tables (and buffet tables), showgirls, Liberace, Englebert Humperdink, and Frank Sinatra's Rat Pack. By the end of 1969, Vegas became almost synonymous with Elvis. The King had invaded a new country and, in blitzkrieg fashion, had made it his own.

On July 31, 1969, Elvis opened before a celebrity-rich crowd at the brand-new International Hotel in Las Vegas. He again looked trim and fit, energized, and in complete control. Dressed in a black, karate-like outfit (designed by Bill Belew, who did the costumes for the "Comeback Special"—that leather suit looked great, but was it ever *hot!*), he opened with "Blue Suede Shoes," and sang, among others, such diverse hits as "Heartbreak Hotel," "All Shook Up," "Don't Be Cruel," "In The Ghetto," "Suspicious Minds," "Yesterday," "Hey Jude," and "Johnny B. Goode."

The King and I
"When I work with a live audience, I can see and hear their response and I feel more like myself."

—Elvis

195

Having failed in Vegas 13 years earlier, Elvis was understandably nervous. But he had no reason for concern. He sang great, and the fan response was overwhelming. The series of concerts through August 28 broke house records, drawing more than 100,000 people and grossing 1.5 million dollars. He earned a reported $100,000 per week.

For The Record

The historic deal for Elvis' return to Las Vegas was negotiated by Colonel Tom Parker and Alex Shoofey, president of the International Hotel, owned by Kirk Kerkorian. The Colonel took notes on the tablecloth as they hammered out the deal, including a proviso that if Shoofey left the hotel, the contract could be renegotiated. In 1971, Kerkorian sold the hotel to Baron Hilton, whereupon Shoofey retired and veteran hotel executive Henry Lewin took over. Soon after, Lewin—a legendarily tough negotiator himself—was visited by the Colonel, toting the old tablecloth with, among other things, the scribbled contract renegotiation clause. Suffice it to say, Lewin made a new deal.

Elvis returned to Las Vegas in 1970, playing from January 31 to August 28. Then he did Houston, at the Astrodome, from February 27 to March 1. Then he came back to Vegas from August 10 to September 7.

The cover of Elvis: That's the Way It Is. *Elvis at one his many peaks, this time in 1970.*

Elvis would play all over the country in the 1970s, but it was Las Vegas that would forever become associated with this period of his life. The common pattern was to play Vegas for a series of concerts every January, often returning later in the year for another engagement, and visit other cities all over the country in between.

All That Glittered Was Gold: Elvis' Stage Magic

The new live shows were not just about the music and the Pelvis. They were about Elvis the King—pomp and circumstance. In other words, they were about glitter and glitz as well as musicianship and sexuality. They were choreographed around his image—his arrival on the stage was dramatized, as was his departure. Elvis worked each crowd as if it would be his last. No longer the supercharged Hillbilly Cat, Elvis was now a consummate professional: smooth, powerful, and passionate, already seeming more myth than man.

Elvis had an intuitive feeling for what his audience wanted to hear. The order of the songs was strictly Elvis' choice, though he welcomed suggestions from his musicians. There were surprisingly few special effects, and little emphasis on production values. Elvis was the show: The audience knew it, the hotel executives knew it, and Elvis knew it. Extra adornment (outside costuming, which I'll get to) was unnecessary.

Elvis' shows presented the full range of his singing talents—pop ballads, country standards, gospel hymns, and rocking R&B. His touring band, organized at the beginning of 1970—the TCB Band—was powerful and polished. Like to know the musicians he worked with? Well, here they are:

➤ James Burton on lead guitar

➤ John Wilkenson and Jerry Scheff on rhythm guitar

➤ Glen D. Hardin on piano

➤ Joe Osborne on bass

➤ Ronnie Tutt and Hal Blaine on drums

➤ Pat Houston on trumpet

➤ Marty Harrell on trombone

In addition to his TCB band, Elvis had a backup female vocal group, The Sweet Inspirations, who played with him on both concert dates and in studio sessions. The Grammy award-winning foursome backed up Aretha Franklin before moving over to Elvis. The group's members:

➤ Cissy Houston (mother of Whitney Houston)

➤ Estelle Brown

➤ Sylvia Shemwell

➤ Myrna Smith (who became Jerry Schilling's wife)

And what was Elvis' goal when he left the stage? Like any great performer, "I like to leave them wanting more," he once said.

Liberace, Move Over: Costume Changes

Liberace wasn't the only flamboyant dresser in Vegas. Elvis was pretty creative, too. He helped design an expensive series of white jumpsuits for his second string of engagements in Las Vegas. He based them on 19th-century Victorian fashions he'd seen in a book. He liked the flashy image, but he also liked the comfort, mobility, and the fact that they concealed weight fluctuations. They were a big hit with his fans, and soon became as much a trademark in the 1970s as the satin jackets were earlier in his career. He had two of most of the styles, in case one got damaged. By also adorning these with scarves and jewelry, Elvis was attempting to exude his image as the King as much as possible.

For the Record

Elvis first met Liberace in Las Vegas at the Riviera Hotel in 1956, when he asked for Liberace's autograph to give to his mother. At the meeting, as documented in photos, Elvis held a candelabra and sang "Blue Suede Shoes" while Liberace posed with a guitar, pretending to play. Liberace's elaborate costumes influenced Elvis to enhance his own image—which culminated in Vegas Elvis. Elvis was known to show his respect by sending guitar-shaped flower arrangements for Liberace's openings.

The scarves led to another Elvis tradition: He would anoint them with his sweat (and Elvis perspired heavily during his highly active performances) and toss them to the audience at the end of a concert. Elvis had boxes of them, and one of his crew, usually Charlie Hodge, would always be ready to give him more to throw. Audience members would move toward the stage near the end of concerts in hopes of getting the saturated prize. Imagine, owning Elvis' body oils! What a treasure for some lucky fan!

Sometimes, Elvis would actually even throw jewelry—and then the crowds would really start to get wild.

Takin' Care of Business: Elvis' Work Ethic

Touring became an obsession for Elvis. To quench his need to perform, and to keep the money rolling in to support his gilded life-style, he could no longer indulge his fear of flying. He criss-crossed the country, playing hundreds of gigs, like his old days in the South. The work load was tremendous. For example, in 1970 Elvis played over 135 live dates. In 1973, over 165. It was a brutal pace.

Travel was often a nightmare for Elvis, and he took steps to alleviate his burden. In 1975, he purchased a Convair 880, built by General Dynamics of San Diego, California, for $250,000. (This was long before private jets were common; in fact, the first one Elvis had ever seen was Kirk Kerkorian's, owner of the Las Vegas Hilton, which he used to fly from Vegas to Houston in 1970.) He spent an additional $800,000 for customization. Elvis' master bedroom on the jet had a queen-size bed and a bathroom with golden fixtures. Elvis named the plane *Lisa Marie* (yes, after his daughter). He also referred to it as "Hound Dog One" and "Flying Graceland." It sat 28 people. That same year, Elvis purchased a JetStar, built by Lockheed of Georgia. Elvis nicknamed this craft "Hound Dog Two." This smaller jet sat 10 people.

Return to Sender

Think life on the road is glamorous? The realities are quite different. The hours are long, the pressure intense, and the fans demanding in their expectations. Touring takes stamina, patience, and a high tolerance for long hours. Despite the fact that Elvis was not taking proper care of himself, he hated missing shows due to illness, and rarely canceled dates until the very end of his life.

For the Record

Elvis first heard the phrase **Taking Care of Business** on an NBC special featuring Diana Ross and the Supremes and the Temptations. Elvis decided to make "TCB" his motto and had jewelry designed by jeweler Lee Ableseron of Los Angeles. The letters were mounted over a lightning bolt, probably based on the lightning symbol on the comic-book character Captain Marvel, Jr.'s costume. All members of the Memphis Mafia were given ID bracelets with the logo and their nicknames. Elvis' backup band in the '70s was called the TCB Band. He also gave jewelry to women with the lettering TLC and the lightning bolt, for "Tender Loving Care." Elvis was buried wearing a diamond TCB ring.

Aloha!—Satellite Elvis

On January 14, 1973, Elvis played the world—or at least a big chunk of it. His live concert, "Elvis: Aloha from Hawaii," at the Honolulu International Convention Center, was beamed worldwide via an Intelsat IV communications satellite. This marked the first time that a program was telecast around the world by satellite. A record one billion people in 40 different countries (including people in Communist China!) watched the King.

On January 9, Elvis arrived in Hawaii for this novel event; he was booked into the Hawaiian Village Hotel in Honolulu. The next two days, he rehearsed, with a third day for a dress rehearsal before a live audience. He rested the next day—January 13—which was hailed Elvis Presley Day in Hawaii. Then, on January 14 at 12:30 a.m. Honolulu time (to catch prime time in Japan), he performed the concert itself in front of 5,500 fans.

The King and I
"I appreciate their wanting to see me and their loyalty. I intend to continue to perform as long as I am able and for as long as they want me. I really love singing for my fans. It's my life. I want them to be excited and to go away saying, 'Man! Wow!'"

—Elvis

Return to Sender
It is a misnomer to describe Elvis' Hawaiian concert as "live." Certainly it was performed live, but only the Far East actually saw it as it was performed. Europe saw it the next day. But "Elvis: Aloha From Hawaii" wasn't seen live in the U.S. at all, but broadcast on tape some two-and-a-half months later.

The ratings were phenomenal: for example in the Philippines, 92 percent of the audience watching television that night were watching Elvis; in Japan, an almost unbelievable 98 percent of the audience tuned in to Elvis. More people would eventually watch the broadcast than had watched the astronauts of Apollo 11 walk on the moon.

What an extravaganza! Elvis had special guest performers in concert with him, including The Sweet Inspirations, Kathy Westmoreland, and J.D. Sumner & the Stamps, all backed by The Joe Guercia Orchestra. Elvis wore a cape over a white two-piece jumpsuit decorated with an American eagle and stars. In addition to tossing scarves to the audience, Elvis gave forth his cape. Bruce Spinks, a sportswriter for the *Honolulu Advisor*, was the lucky individual who caught it.

On January 15, the show was rebroadcast in 28 European countries (why leave Europe out?). Then, on April 4, an expanded 90-minute version was aired as a TV special on NBC. It was the top show of the week, garnering a 33.8 rating and a 51 share.

According to producer Marty Passeta, at $2.5 million, "Aloha from Hawaii" was "the most expensive entertainment special ever done." Elvis made $1 million dollars himself. The Kui Lee Cancer Fund received $85,000 in charity, some $60,000 more dollars than expected when the show was planned.

From the instant Elvis strode on stage, he was in complete control. "It's like the old days," he said. And indeed it was. Elvis sang 23 songs during the concert, finishing with "I Can't Help Falling in Love with You." Highlights of the highlighted-packed night included "C.C. Rider," "Steamroller Blues," "Johnny B. Goode," "Blue Suede Shoes," "Suspicious Minds," and the "Hawaiian Wedding Song." Elvis, who rarely admitted to nervousness, had openly talked about how tense he was before the concert, saying, "This certainly gets your attention." There wasn't any need for concern. The King, once again, was a master.

Gambling with His Body

Elvis pushed himself and pushed himself some more. He was happiest when performing and took what drugs he had to in order to get up for the shows and then in order to sleep afterwards. (You'll find out more than you want to know about Elvis and drugs in Chapter 19.) He battled bouts of tonsillitis (as in his Army days) and laryngitis. When his voice or his body gave out, he would rest, often in Palm Springs. Then he'd set out on the road again.

It was a dangerous and, of course, unhealthy lifestyle; one that more than one performer has succumbed to. But Elvis, as usual, was different. He pushed harder and played harder than most. He had an iron constitution and an ingrained work ethic. (He also had a greedy manager with huge personal gambling debts, and his own, shall we say, excessive lifestyle.) The image of Elvis as lazy is erroneous and offensive.

Only at the very end of his life—those disastrous last months—did Elvis lose control. Before that, he was working; in fact it can be said that he was literally working himself to death.

Going for Gold

The original broadcast of "Elvis: Aloha from Hawaii" benefited the Kui Lee Cancer Fund (and opened up Asian markets for Elvis). The American broadcast of the show was sponsored by the Chicken-Of-The-Sea Tuna Company. A double album, *Elvis—Aloha from Hawaii Via Satellite*, was released by RCA on February 14. The few albums with the Chicken-of-the-Sea logo are now collector's items. Look for them.

The cover of the 1971 album C'Mon Everybody. *A classic Vegas Elvis pose.*

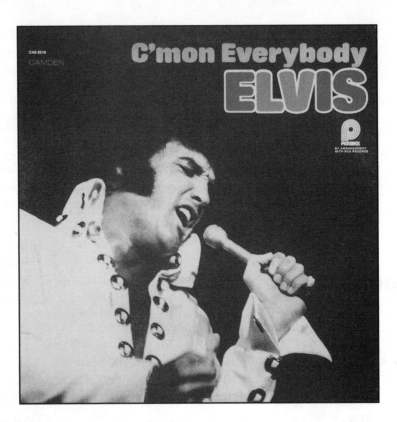

Meanwhile, the Records

Earlier in Elvis' recording career with RCA, country guitarist and performer Chet Atkins produced many of Elvis' songs. Moving more and more into management in the 1960s, Atkins did not tend to Elvis' music as much and it suffered. In 1966, Felton Jarvis became Elvis' producer at RCA. Then in 1970, he left RCA to devote himself full-time to Elvis' career. In a brief period of time, he helped revitalize it.

A major reason for the pre-Jarvis decline in the quality of Elvis' music—in addition to the factory-like atmosphere of making his movies and their soundtracks—was that Colonel Tom Parker established two publishing companies, Elvis Presley Music and Gladys Music, which took high percentages of songwriters' royalties. It was difficult, if not impossible, to attract top writing talent with such penurious terms. Once again, the Colonel's greed impacted negatively on Elvis. Which is not to say that Elvis didn't continue to produce hits in the 1970s; in fact he had 19 top-40 hits on the Billboard Charts from 1970-1977. The hits just kept coming.

Mac Davis wrote two songs that Elvis made hits in 1969: "Don't Cry, Daddy," which reached number 6 on Billboard's Hot 100 and "In the Ghetto," which reached number three on the *Billboard* Top 100 chart. On November 1, 1969, Mark James' "Suspicious Minds," released the September before, reached number one on the Top 100 chart, the last Elvis song to do so. Elvis had another hit with Baker Knight's lovely ballad, "The Wonder of You," which was released in 1970 and hit number 9 on *Billboard's* Top 100 (and number 1 in Great Britain). Another song that fit the King perfectly was Eddie Rabbit and Dick Heard's "Kentucky Rain," released in February 1971; it hit number 16 on the Hot 100 chart. Dennis Linde's "Burning Love," released in August 1972, reached number two on the Hot 100 chart.

These songs were more pop-rock than R&B, but they had a driving sound and emotional vocals that were 100% Elvis.

Going for Gold

Elvis' version of "My Way," (originally a French song written by Gilles Thibault, Claude Francois and Jacques Revaux; English lyrics were written by Paul Anka) and, of course, also sung by Frank Sinatra, is a pop treatment. But Elvis delivers a personal rendition some consider superior to Old Blue Eyes'—and his version charted higher.

The Least You Need to Know

➤ Elvis made a triumphant comeback to live performing beginning in 1968 with a TV special titled "Elvis."

➤ Elvis grossed huge amounts of money during his Vegas performances and has become a symbol of that city's glitz and glamour.

➤ From 1969 through the end of his life, Elvis maintained a tortuously demanding concert schedule. The taxing labor and pressure caused him great physical and emotional harm.

➤ Elvis' comeback also included the first rock concert broadcast by satellite—which reached a record one billion people worldwide—as well as unforgettable hits such as "In The Ghetto" and "Suspicious Minds."

Graceland at dusk.

The howl of the Hillbilly Cat: Elvis Presley's first full-length album for RCA.

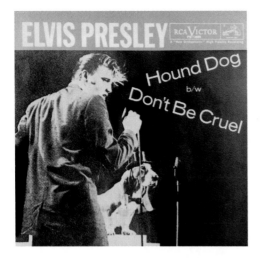

"Hound Dog," gold record single, 1956.

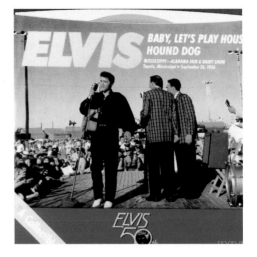

The sleeve for a recording of Elvis performing at the Mississippi-Alabama Fair and Dairy Show on Elvis Presley Day (September 26, 1956) in his hometown of Tupelo, MS.

The boy who would be King.

In his 1956 Elvis album, the King looks serene and beatific.

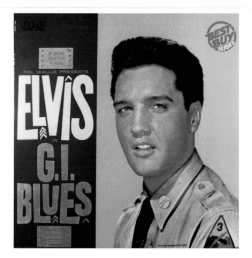

The most famous GI in America, Private Elvis Aron Presley.

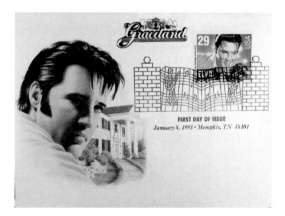

The album cover for A Date With Elvis. *What father wouldn't be proud to have such a fine escort for his daughter?*

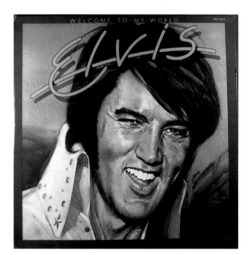

A beautiful portrait of Elvis adorned his 1977 Elvis: Welcome To My World *album.*

A first day issue, in Memphis, of the best-selling "Young Elvis" stamp.

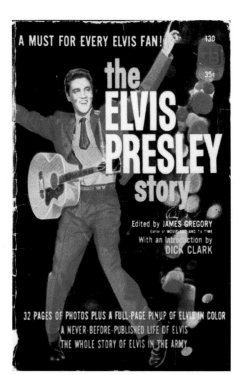

The Elvis Presley Story, *the first book ever written about Elvis. There would be quite a few others.*

The famous pink Cadillac Elvis gave his mother.

Many people feel King Creole *was Elvis' best film. This is the cover to the soundtrack.*

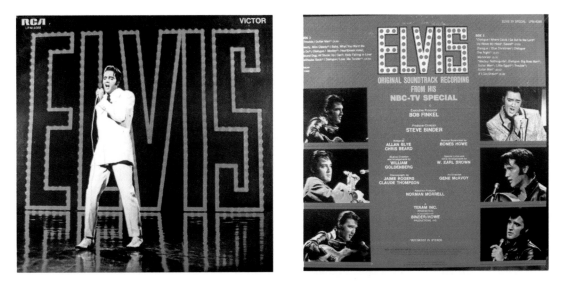

The album cover from Elvis, *the soundtrack of the King's "Comeback Special," showing him performing "If I Can Dream" at the show's conclusion, and in the famous black-leather suit.*

This portrait of a young Elvis adorns the stairway in Graceland.

The elaborate statue of Jesus in the Meditation Gardens on the grounds at Graceland.

Souvenir menu from 1971.

Elvis' home in the sky, named for his daughter, the Lisa Marie.

The statue of Elvis at the west end of Beale Street in Memphis.

Elvis' gravesite is alwys covered with flowers and messages from his fans.

Chapter 18

It Hurts Me: The Women in Elvis' Later Years

In This Chapter

➤ Elvis' marriage ends

➤ Linda Thompson and other lovers

➤ Priscilla and Lisa Marie during and after the break-up

It did not take long for Priscilla to realize her marriage wasn't working out. She was consistently left behind while Elvis further pursued his career. She heard reports of affairs. Even when he was with her, he was never far from his ever-present Mafia buddies. From Priscilla's point of view, Elvis did not return the affection she gave him. After the birth of Lisa Marie, Priscilla felt abandoned sexually as well as psychologically, in more ways than one she was alone.

Elvis went through a succession of lovers, some significant, most simply casual affairs. (The one-night-stand women were dubbed "Queen for a Day" by the Memphis Mafia, who did most of the picking and choosing for Elvis.) Of course, in the politically incorrect world of rock groupies of the early 1970s, there were always women ready, willing, and able to serve the King. Only a few lucky ones were recognized by Elvis and the Mafia as a real "girlfriend."

Your Cheatin' Heart

The King and I
"I didn't want to change Elvis, but I did have the romantic delusion that once we were married, I could change his lifestyle."

—Priscilla Presley, *Elvis and Me*

The King and I
"Marriage and fatherhood hadn't altered (Elvis') behavior with other women in the slightest. He had continued to have his many affairs and one-night stands, juggling three or more women at a time."

—Joe Esposito,
Good Rockin' Tonight

Return to Sender
Many women claim to have dated, married, or had children by the King. Some perhaps are telling the truth; others, no doubt, just want publicity or money. One Hollywood waitress, Patricia Ann Parker, even brought a paternity suit against him in August 1970. She dropped her suit after Elvis passed a lie detector test and a blood test proved that her son was not his.

While Elvis was on the movie set making the same film over and over again, Priscilla was at home with the baby. When he was able to stop the films, you think he went home to wife and baby? Nope. He went on tour again, seemingly oblivious as to how the time away—and his philandering—would affect his family.

Priscilla Presley had her hands full with Elvis, no question, but don't get the idea that she was a helpless little princess. In her autobiography, *Elvis and Me*, Priscilla describes an incident in Los Angeles when a female Elvis fan followed her car. When Priscilla confronted the woman, she called Priscilla a "whore." Whereupon Priscilla Beaulieu Presley, that perfect Southern belle, dropped the name-caller with a lovely uppercut to the mug.

But Priscilla was powerless when it came to controlling the Elvis lifestyle, which included not just women, but more and more drug use.

You'll remember in Chapter 15 I briefly went through the women in Elvis' early life. He reportedly had affairs with a young actress named Cybill Shepherd (you know her today as the star of her own TV show) for a time in 1966 and later in 1970. He also had a relationship with Frank Sinatra's daughter, Nancy, in 1968, who was acting in *Speedway* with him. (Oddly, Nancy Sinatra threw Priscilla's baby shower, and the two women reportedly got along pretty well.) More seriously—before either of them—there had been Ann-Margret, with whom Elvis had made *Viva Las Vegas* in 1964. The boy just couldn't help himself.

Even when there was no truth to stories of romance, the press linked him with his leading ladies anyway, as was the case with *Change of Habit* costar Mary Tyler Moore. Elvis was also linked with Susan Henning in 1968, a former Miss USA, who had a bit part in *Live a Little, Love a Little* (which he was apparently doing in real life). There were literally scores of others. Many have become public with the plethora of books about Elvis. You have to wonder how many went unreported.

Separate Ways

By the end of 1971, Elvis was balancing his heavy touring schedule with an increasingly strained home life. More and more, Elvis would spend time away, especially in Las Vegas, where in the words of Joe Esposito, "they always had a good time." Priscilla was unhappy about spending so much time alone at Graceland, but Elvis, for reasons that were becoming more obvious by the day, would not allow her to accompany him on tour. Or even to Vegas, except for opening and closing nights. Things reached a head during the Christmas holidays of 1971, with little cheer to go around.

Some years before, Priscilla had had an affair with a Los Angeles dance-studio owner. Now Priscilla found someone more significant: a handsome, expert karate instructor named Mike Stone who was teaching her more than just a few karate moves. Elvis had first met him briefly at a karate tournament in Hawaii, then again at the Las Vegas Hilton. Ironically, it was he who suggested Stone become Priscilla's instructor. Elvis was furious when he found out about the affair and there are a number of reports that Elvis wanted to kill Stone himself or at least have him killed.

Finally, the inevitable happened: Elvis and Priscilla separated on February 23, 1972. Priscilla and Lisa Marie moved out of Graceland and into 144 Monovale Street in the exclusive section of Holmby Hills, Los Angeles.

Elvis filed for a divorce from Priscilla in Santa Monica, California on August 18, 1972; the divorce was eventually finalized on October 9, 1973. Along with custody of Lisa Marie, Priscilla received a lump sum of $2 million, $6,000 a month alimony for 10 years, $4,200 a month alimony for one year, $4,000 a month child support, $25,000 from the sale of their Los Angeles home, and five percent of two of Elvis' music publishing companies. (The original proposal was a lump sum of $100,000, $1,000 a month in alimony, and $5,000 a month in child support. Tsk, tsk, Elvis! Maybe she went off with the karate instructor, but you weren't exactly Mr. Chaste yourself!)

> **The King and I**
> "I'm leaving. I don't feel as if we're married. It's over."
>
> —Priscilla Presley

> **Going for Gold**
> In his "Elvis: Aloha From Hawaii" broadcast, Elvis enthralled his fans (and perhaps, somewhere down deep, Priscilla too) when he sang "Always on My Mind." The poignant lyrics made us all think of his break-up with Priscilla. Rent the video and see for yourself how you have to fight back the tears.

The title of Elvis' last studio album, 1977's Moody Blue, *is, unfortunately, an accurate description of Elvis late in life.*

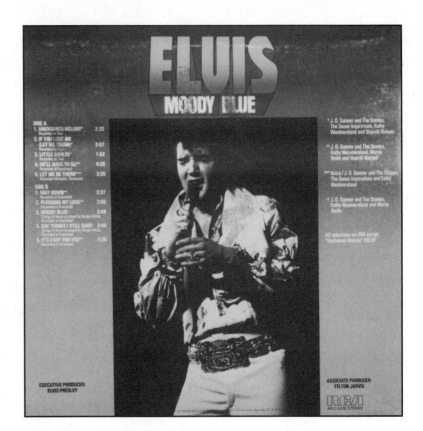

Elvis was heartbroken. Was it because Priscilla was his one true love? Or because he couldn't possess and control her anymore? Or because she had, in effect, left him for a "nobody"?

For the Record

When word of Elvis' separation, then his divorce, filtered out to his fans, thousands of them responded with sympathy cards, flowers, teddy bears, and, of course love letters. In many of these notes, female fans offered themselves up to the King. Sure, these expressions of love helped him get through a rough period, but he was disconsolate that he had lost Priscilla.

I've Lost You: Post-Elvis Priscilla

Although there was constant tension in their relationship, Priscilla and Elvis remained in close contact to facilitate the comings and goings of Lisa Marie and to protect her interests.

Mike Stone, the karate teacher, moved in with Priscilla at her two-bedroom apartment in Huntington Beach, California. Stone's wife (yes, he had a cheatin' heart too), meanwhile, sued him for a divorce in 1972 and won custody of their two children. Priscilla and Stone were an item until 1975. Stone moved back to Las Vegas, where he found work as a dealer. Priscilla also had a long and stormy affair with Michael Edwards, a male model who, predictably, wrote a book so bad I won't even mention the title.

Priscilla Presley went on to a successful film and TV career. She was a regular on the TV show *Dallas* and co-host of *Those Amazing Animals*. In addition, she demonstrated a wonderful comedic side in the three successful *Naked Gun* films, opposite Leslie Nielsen. Priscilla was also the executive producer of the movie of the week, *Elvis and Me*, based on her book.

As executor of the Elvis Presley Estate, she has a controlling interest in the running of Graceland. A savvy businessperson, she has turned a close-to-bankrupt estate into an asset worth more than a $100 million.

Today she lives with businessman Marco Garibaldi, with whom she has a son, Navarone, who was born on March 1, 1987. So Lisa Marie has a younger brother after all.

"Don't Cry, Daddy": Lisa Marie after the Breakup

Lisa Marie was only four years old when her parents separated. With the divorce, Priscilla had full custody of their daughter; Elvis had visitation rights. When she came to Graceland, he did his best to make her stays memorable.

Nine-year-old Lisa Marie was visiting her dad at Graceland at the time of his death. With the death of Vernon and Minnie Mae, she became the sole heir of Elvis' will, with Priscilla as the executor of the estate.

In 1978, Priscilla sent Lisa Marie to school at the Church of Scientology in Los Angeles, but she dropped out in 1980. Like many teens in the second half of this century, Lisa Marie has had to wrestle with drugs, alcohol, and personal problems. Her troubled life and famous lineage continue to fascinate the media—especially the tabloids. It shouldn't

The King and I

"I'm not concerned anymore about the fans. They're wise enough to see through any lies. But what about Lisa? What is she going to think about her daddy when she grows up?"

—Elvis

come as a surprise: The plot twists and turns seem more like a soap opera than something that could happen to a real person.

On October 3, 1988, when she was 20, Lisa Marie married Danny Keough (a studio bass player whom she had met in 1984) at the Celebrity Center International of the Church of Scientology in Hollywood, California. Priscilla was there with eight other relatives and friends. That fall, Priscilla and Lisa appeared in television commercials for the Oldsmobile Cutlass Calais.

On May 29, 1989, Lisa Marie herself became a parent, giving birth to a seven-pound, two-ounce girl—Danielle Riley Keough. She had another child with Keough, a boy named Benjamin Storm, born October 21, 1992. The marriage to Keough ended in divorce, the date not made public.

In February 1993, Lisa Marie, now age 25, decided to leave the management of the Elvis Presley Estate, including Graceland, to Jack Soden, head of Elvis Presley Enterprises, Inc., for at least five more years. Until that time it had been in trust.

On May 26, 1994, in a secret ceremony at the home of Judge Hugo Alvarez in the Dominican Republic, Lisa Marie Presley married internationally famous pop singer Michael Jackson. (Say *what?!*) Perhaps the marriage was just a way to get positive press for both of them. Jackson had recently settled out of court on lurid child-molestation charges. Lisa Marie who so startlingly resembles her father, was seeking her own identity and a fresh, drug-free start.

It's easy to see how Jackson's image could benefit from the marriage, but Lisa Marie's? Aside from the more serious child-molestation charges, and in spite of his still-prodigious talents, Jackson has become one of music's strangest eccentrics, an androgynous, asexual, surgically altered man-boy. The bizarre scenario of *Elvis Presley's daughter* marrying him was almost a tabloid writer's fantasy. *Why would she do it?* In any case, they sure seemed cozy together when interviewed by Barbara Walters on the ABC-TV show *20/20*.

But America didn't seem to buy it and thought it was just a matter of time before they broke up. The only surprise was how little time it took. Michael has gone on to father a child by his former nurse. And Lisa Marie, with her singing career having gone nowhere, is still seeking her own identity. The real story behind the marriage may never be told. We can certainly wish the best for Lisa Marie as she comes to terms, unfortunately in public, with her role as the heir to the King of Rock and Roll.

My Baby Left Me: Linda Thompson

In 1972, George Klein introduced the stunning Linda Thompson, an English major and reigning Tennessee beauty queen, to Elvis. Thompson, a native of Memphis, has said they liked one another instantly, that they "just clicked." They began to date and Linda moved into Graceland the same year. She stayed for four years, during which time she was Elvis' constant companion, friend, lover, and confidante. Unlike his former girl-friends and even his former wife, Linda accompanied him on tour and stayed with him in Vegas. Elvis spent hundreds of thousands of dollars on clothes and jewelry for her, and took care of all her financial needs.

As Elvis' drug abuse worsened and his condition deteriorated, it became more and more difficult to live with him, and Linda finally left in 1976. The reports on her are mixed: A few accuse her of gold-digging and taking advantage of him towards the end, but most people close to the situation are convinced that she loved Elvis and that he loved her. For example, hairdresser/spiritual guru Larry Geller thought that "Linda was fabulous for Elvis, just fabulous."

Certainly, Linda Thompson was involved with Elvis when he was in serious decline, abusing drugs and people close to him, heading inevitably for an early death. A bright and vivacious woman in an impossible situation, she did everything she could for as long as she could. And then, like almost everyone who was close to Elvis, she left.

It can safely be said Thompson made it on her own. And to her credit, it can be said she did it without writing a tell-all book. She went on to work in television, appearing on the country show *Hee-Haw* and doing commercials. She is now married to Grammy award-winning producer David Foster and lives in California.

"His Latest Flame": Ginger Alden

Ginger Alden was Elvis' last "regular" girl friend. A local beauty queen from Memphis (Miss Traffic Safety, Miss Mid-South, and runner-up Miss Tennessee University), "Gingerbread" (Elvis' nickname for her) was the last person to see the King alive. Although impossible to verify, Alden claims that Elvis proposed marriage in

The King and I

"There were times when it was like living a fairy tale, and Elvis truly was Prince Charming. He was the kindest, most sensitive, the funniest, most talented, most gorgeous and sexiest. He was all the wonderful things that only Elvis could be, and yet there were times when he was very, very difficult. His life was very difficult."

—Linda Thompson

The King and I

"She [Linda Thompson] was good for him. She did the best she could and hung in there as long as possible. It just got real hard near the end."

—David Stanley, Elvis' stepbrother

The King and I

"Oh, we're getting married. We're going to an-nounce our engagement at Christmas."

—Ginger Alden

The King and I
"(Ginger's) beautiful and nice, but I'm not about to get married."

—Elvis

Going for Gold
Look for Ginger in two low-budget films, the fictionalized bio-pic *Living Legend* (1980), and an even more obscure film the next year, *Lady Grey*. Trust me, neither one received an Academy Award.

Going for Gold
Many women who claimed romantic escapades with Elvis have written books. A congressional aide named Joyce Bova wrote a book called *Don't Ask Forever* about her affair with Elvis. A dancer named Lucy de Barbin wrote the kiss-and-tell *Are You Lonesome Tonight?*, in which she claims that Elvis fathered her daughter. What's interesting about both women is that, like Linda Thompson, they looked a lot like Priscilla.

January 1977. (Most insiders, including Joe Esposito, do not support Alden's contention.) What we do know is that he showered her with gifts, including cars and expensive jewelry.

Twenty years younger than the King, Alden, who looked somewhat like Priscilla with dark hair and blues eyes, was a quiet, passive girl in awe of Elvis. This certainly was not a relationship of equals.

She went on to a brief recording career in the early 1980s and has made TV commercials. She has also acted in at least one film and has sold stories to various newspapers about her life with Elvis. In an ironic postscript to her relationship with Elvis, Alden's mother sued the Presley estate, claiming that Elvis had promised to pay off a $40,000 mortgage on her house.

Lovers and Other Strangers

Wait! Don't turn the page! I'm not finished yet! Believe it or not (and I'm sure you will), during his marriage to Priscilla and four-year relationship with Linda Thompson, Elvis also had affairs with other women, in particular, Barbara Leigh and Sheila Ryan.

Elvis met the stunning Leigh, a Southern-born starlet, in 1971 when she was 23 and dating Jim Aubrey, a far older man (and legendary ladies man) who was then president of MGM. They immediately began an affair that lasted for a year-and-a-half, during which time Elvis gave her, among other things, a Mercedes and a special gun collection.

During the time she was with Elvis, Leigh was also dating actor Steve McQueen. When Elvis found out about the relationship, he was annoyed and began pulling away from the relationship—especially when Leigh didn't respond to his calls. The relationship cooled, and Leigh left him a few months before Priscilla and Elvis broke up.

Joe Esposito introduced the beautiful, 19-year-old Sheila Ryan to Elvis while they were in Las Vegas in 1972. Ryan overlapped with Linda Thompson—which Linda seemed to be able to deal with. Elvis gave Ryan the customary car—this time a Camaro—and even a diamond ring, which she was wearing when he introduced her to a Las Vegas audience as his girlfriend (with Priscilla in the audience!).

The King and I

"(Elvis) was a good lover.... Above all he was a great kisser."

—Barbara Leigh

Ryan was with Elvis in the period when he began to gain a great deal of weight and ingest more and more drugs. She was frustrated by her inability to help him lose weight or curb his drug use. Finally, after a year-and-a-half of increasing frustration, Ryan left Elvis for a weekend with her parents—and never returned.

Sheila Ryan later married actor James Caan, with whom she had a child.

The King and I

"Elvis wasn't about sex for me. He was about innocence and being a kid."

—Sheila Ryan

He Couldn't Help Falling in Love

Attention, seekers of the Elvis truth: It's hard to be of one mind about Elvis. On the one hand, he obviously was a cad and a cheat and should have been a better husband and father. But on the other hand, his life and career since his late teens revolved around being a sex symbol. He was a man who loved music and had to tour away from home to bring it to people. He was a man who loved women and beautiful women threw themselves at him. Could he have been stronger? Yes. Would he have been Elvis then? No. So, let's just appreciate him for what he was, not what he should have been. In Chapter 19, we'll get to know more about Elvis' interests and inner life.

The Least You Need to Know

➤ Elvis' marriage to Priscilla Presley was troubled and ultimately doomed.

➤ Despite a rocky start with post-Elvis relationships, Priscilla Presley has since gained tremendous public respect, having made Graceland a hugely profitable empire and delivering some fine performances on TV and in films.

➤ Like her father, Lisa Marie has also had substance-abuse problems and stormy relationships, most notably her marriage to the King of Pop, Michael Jackson.

➤ Elvis dated and loved many women, though it seems his relationship with Linda Thompson was the closest he came to real love following Priscilla.

Chapter 19

Heartbreak Hotel: Secret Elvis

In This Chapter

➤ Elvis in his private life

➤ Elvis' toys and hobbies

➤ Elvis and drugs

Describing the psyche of any celebrity is no easy task. With Elvis Presley—a complex individual who has had so many conflicting things said about him—the task is even more challenging.

As a young man, he was vain, seeking attention through his flamboyant clothes and his desire to sing; but he was also humble, respectful of adults, and almost as shy of the spotlight as he was desperate for it. The paradoxical sides of Elvis created a constant conflict between an outgoing public person and a lonely private man; between brilliant artist and self-parodying clown; between megalomania and generosity; between super-lover and family man; and between responsible citizen and outlaw.

In this chapter, we'll try to find out what Elvis was really like. We'll never get all of the answers, but until he shows up at your local mall, alive and ready to answer all your questions, we'll have to make do with the facts we have.

Night Owl

All of Elvis' life—the early touring grind, his life in the Army, his time as an actor, his late touring grind—he never had a regular schedule. He came to be a night owl. He had to fill up his nights with people and activities. And drugs: uppers to stay awake, downers to sleep. He would take long, lonely drives to pass the time. He had a 24-hour kitchen and ordered up meals from his cook in the middle of the night.

Because of his erratic sleep patterns, Elvis was at times almost in a daze when awake. In his early years, his sparkling eyes would fix on you. Now they looked past you. Yet despite his chronic fatigue, Elvis always managed to call up energy and focus when on stage.

Bingeing, American Style: The Elvis Diet

One taste many of us share with Elvis is a love of junk food. He couldn't resist carbohydrates, fried foods, and sweets. In other words, fat, cholesterol, and sugar. I'm getting chest pains just thinking about it.

So you might say Elvis' taste buds were pretty satisfied with life on the road. Cheeseburgers were a regular order. (His cook was nicknamed "Hamburger James.") His favorite sweets were banana splits and jelly doughnuts. When at home, he usually ordered up the grease, such as fried peanut-butter-and-banana sandwiches (no lie!), fried chicken, pork chops, bacon (he liked it burned), and corn bread in buttermilk. Probably the healthiest (okay, *nothing* he ate was truly healthy) of his favorite foods were beefsteak tomatoes, mashed potatoes, and sauerkraut. His favorite drink is reported to have been Pepsi. He also drank Nesbitt's Orange Soda and Diet Shasta.

Elvis certainly went overboard in his eating habits, but as you can see from the above, his tastes stemmed from his Memphis roots. He simply *loved* Southern cuisine and ate it wherever he went.

Searching for Some Soul

In Part 1, I discussed Elvis' religious upbringing. You'll recall he was part of the First Assembly of God Church and that, as a musician, he expressed his spirituality through gospel music. After his mother's death, Elvis began reading the Bible regularly. For a time in the 1960s, Elvis held Bible readings in his home.

As he advanced in years, Elvis sought other philosophies. His interest in karate (discussed a little later on) led him to Eastern teachings. He read about Buddhism, Hinduism, and Taoism. Elvis wore a *Chai* Hebrew life symbol around his neck along with a Christian crucifix and a Star of David. When asked why, he responded, "I don't want to miss out on heaven because of a technicality."

Elvis had several gurus help guide him on his spiritual quests. As I mentioned earlier, California hair stylist Larry Geller acted as a spiritual mentor. For a time, Elvis studied under Yogi Paramahansa Yogananda, author of *Autobiography of a Yogi*, at the Self-Realization Fellowship Center in Los Angeles. Later he went under the tutelage of the Yogi's successor, Sri Daya Mata, author of *Only Love*.

Elvis was not exactly what you'd call a voracious reader—he loved comic books as a child, especially *Captain Marvel*—but those books he did read usually had some spiritual angle. Some books reported to be regular reading late in Elvis' life include the Bible; *The Face of Jesus,* by Frank O. Adams; *The Impersonal Life,* by Joseph Berner; *The Infinite Way,* by Joel Goldsmith; *The Prophet,* by Kahlil Gibran; *The Secret Doctrine,* by Helena P. Blavatsky; *The Secret Teachings of All Ages,* by Manly P. Hall; and *The Shroud of Turin,* by Ian Wilson.

The Word
Chai or **chi** is both a Hebrew letter and word; it is a symbol of life itself. Elvis wore the symbol around his neck along with a Christian crucifix and a Star of David.

Movie Addict

Elvis was a movie maven who watched thousands of movies in his lifetime. As a young boy, they were a big part of his fantasy life. It's easy to see why his ambitions as an actor overrode his musical endeavors for a time.

After he became too famous to go to the movies like you or me, he often rented movie theaters to watch flicks all night long. (He and his pals were known to drive their motorcycles right into the lobby and park them there.) He also had a movie projector at Graceland and a film collection.

Going for Gold
Here's a tip! Hold an "Elvis picks" night. Elvis had some pretty good taste in movies; rent any two (or three, if you have a long night ahead): *Rebel Without a Cause, The Wild One, Patton, Dr. Strangelove, Monty Python and the Holy Grail, The Party, The Pink Panther, Dirty Harry, The Wild Bunch, Across 110th Street, One Flew Over the Cuckoo's Nest,* and *A Streetcar Named Desire.*

Elvis the Athlete

Elvis was blessed with an enviable male physique, and could hold his own in whatever sport he played. The Army certainly helped get him in top shape and, for what it's worth, he did play a boxer convincingly in *Kid Galahad*.

Elvis' favorite sport was football. As mentioned in Chapter 16 on the Memphis Mafia, he loved getting together with the boys to play a pick-up game of touch football. It all started when he was stationed in West Germany and played with the GIs. When he returned to Graceland, the games continued at home. Guess what position Elvis played? You guessed it—quarterback.

For the Record

Elvis was a whiz at pro-football trivia. He boasted in a 1962 interview that he could name every NFL football player in the game. Elvis rooted for the Cleveland Browns—Cleveland was the site where Elvis played his first northern gig in 1955. In 1968, he sponsored a Memphis team called the Elvis Presley Enterprises; sometimes he even played with them.

In the 1950s, Elvis frequented the Rainbow Rollerdome with friends to watch the Amazonian women beat each other up in the roller derby. He also would rent it for the whole night to roller skate with friends. He and his buddies were known to play rough games they called "War" and "Crack the Whip," their personal variations of roller derby games.

Return to Sender

Elvis the eighth-degree black belt? His rank was in effect honorary because he was, after all, Elvis Presley. Sparring partners would let him win; teachers would let him advance to the next level. Watch Elvis use karate in *G.I. Blues* or other movies. Watch him in his later concerts when he used karate moves. He's okay, but he's no master. Chuck Norris would have kicked his you-know-what.

In the 1960s and 1970s, Elvis' chosen form of exercise was karate, which he first studied while in the Army. He took lessons from a number of instructors in both *tae kwon do* and *kempo*. He reached the level of black belt in 1960 and went on to eighth-degree (although insiders say his teachers promoted him not for his skill-level but because he was Elvis). He used karate moves in movies and onstage. Tiger or Tiger Man was Elvis' karate name. He loved his hobby and even named the speedboat he drove on McKeller Lake *Karate*.

Elvis also was a skilled racquetball player and, as I previously mentioned, he built a racquetball court at Graceland. The day he died he played racquetball with Ginger Alden, his cousin Billy Smith, and Billy's wife, Jo.

Consumer Elvis: A Boy and His Toys

Elvis was an impulsive and compulsive shopper. He filled his life with toys—cars and guns were his favorite purchases. With all that money, why not?

Cars, Cars, Cars

Elvis owned many cars in his lifetime, most of which he sold, traded, or gave away. You can still see many of them at Graceland today, however: the pink 1957 Cadillac Fleetwood 250, known as his mother's (although she didn't drive or even have a license); a purple 1956 Cadillac El Dorado convertible; 1971 and 1973 Stutz Blackhawks; a white 956 Continental Mark II; a white 1971 Mercedes Benz 280 SL Roadster; and a black 1975 Dino Ferrari 308 GTT4 Coupe. A 1957 and 1976 Harley-Davidson are also on display.

Have Gun, Will Travel

Elvis had a fascination with guns. At the time of his death, he had a collection of 37 firearms, including rifles, shotguns, machine guns, and pistols. He often packed a piece—on the road and even at Graceland. In the 1970s, he was known to have a two-shot derringer strapped to his ankle during concerts. He bought many of his guns at Kerr's Sporting Goods in Beverly Hills—in December 1970, he spent $38,000 there, buying Christmas gifts for himself and Memphis Mafia members. Many of these were customized with the TCB lightning flash. One of his favorite pistols—now on display at Graceland—has an "E" engraved on one side of the turquoise handle and a "P" on the other.

Many gun-related anecdotes have come forth involving Elvis and his *compadres*. His temper grew with time—drug jags don't help—and so did his proclivity for blowing away TV sets. Elvis would lose his cool and fire away at the tube whenever a talking head said something obnoxious. He'd also fire at a car that wouldn't start, at a restaurant ceiling if the service was poor, or at hotel chandeliers because they were there. Elvis was also known to stand on his balcony and use Lisa Marie's swing set as a target.

For the Record

Sometimes guns came at Elvis. Jerry Lee Lewis (aptly named "the Killer") was jealous of Elvis' fame. He felt he deserved at least an equal place (and equal pay) in the pantheon of rockabilly stars. In the wee hours one Memphis night, Jerry Lee, known for his drunken temper, showed up at Graceland's gate, waving his gun around and demanding to see Elvis. On the phone from his bedroom, Elvis told the guard to call the cops.

Santa Elvis: Generous to a Fault

Elvis was known for his generosity. He showered gifts upon those close to him, again especially cars, guns, and jewelry. He also gave cars away to strangers—favorite models were Cadillacs, Lincolns, Mercedes, Porsches, Corvettes, and Grand Prix. In September 1974, for example, Elvis bought every Lincoln Continental Mark IV in stock at Shilling Lincoln-Mercury in Memphis and gave them all away. Christmas in September!

Elvis also gave away $100,000 every Christmas to charities, and donated money during the rest of the year too. Between 1957 and 1967, he is known to have given more than $1 million away.

The King and I
"Elvis wanted to be an example to young people. Some say that because he used drugs, he couldn't. But they overlooked the fact that he never used illegal drugs. The drugs were always prescribed by his physician. He was a very sincere and decent man."

—Richard Nixon

Return to Sender
One of the more enduring post-death Elvis hoaxes is that he wanted to pursue his dream of being a government agent and faked his own death to go underground. Anyone who knows Elvis knows that his true love was singing, and he wouldn't disappear for a secret-agent fantasy. But, if you see a guy with black sideburns carrying a badge, salute him—just in case.

Special Agent Presley

As Elvis' popularity grew, so did the need for law enforcement and security around him. Elvis was always respectful of police and security people assigned to guard him and assure the safety of fans. In return, they would offer him honorary badges and uniforms and induct him into their fraternities. As early as 1957, he posed in full uniform with Mississippi state troopers. His collection quickly grew and so did his fascination with law enforcement.

On December 20, 1970, Elvis flew to Washington, D.C.—under the cover name of Jon Burrows—with Memphis Mafia pals Sonny West and Jerry Schilling. Staying in Room 506 at the Washington Hotel, he managed to get a handwritten letter and a resume to President Richard Nixon by way of Senator George Murphy. In it, he expressed his love of country and his desire to help in the war against drugs, and asked for federal credentials. He also offered congratulations that Nixon had been chosen one of the Top Ten Outstanding Men of America and pointed out that he was on this list too. He sent Nixon his number at the hotel and six private phone numbers in Memphis, Beverly Hills, and Palm Springs, along with the Colonel's. He also stated that he would stay in D.C. as long as it took to get what he wanted and that he had a gift for the President.

After a long wait in a White House lobby, Nixon finally received Elvis the next day. Elvis, reports have it, was "mellow," due to pharmaceuticals. Finally, upon being led in, the King shook hands with the President. Elvis presented the President with a commemorative World War II Colt .45 pistol (a la General Patton) in a wooden box. In return, Elvis got what he wanted—a Narcotics Bureau Badge.

And make no mistake, Elvis wanted to use his badge. When he got back to Memphis that day, he called David Stanley upstairs and announced that he was "deputizing" him so that he could uncover drug users at Humes High, where Stanley was going to school. It was, obviously, a bizarre concept, but for weeks Elvis questioned Stanley each day when he returned from school about the drug use he might have seen. Ironic, given that all the Stanley boys became drug addicts under Elvis' influence.

What Music Did Elvis Listen To?

As a young man, Elvis was open to all kinds of music. He learned from musicians he saw and complimented them often—for example, he would wax poetic about singer Roy Orbison's ("Pretty Woman," "Ooby Dooby"—you know, the legend) voice. His record collection at Graceland, for the most part, reflects his eclectic tastes when he was young, especially rhythm and blues, country, and gospel.

During the Hollywood years, Elvis lost touch with the contemporary music scene. After his resurrection as a performing artist, he stayed to a certain extent in his own world, except when choosing songs. He was threatened by the *British Invasion*; Memphis Mafiosi have reported, for example, that he didn't even know who guitar great Eric Clapton was.

In 1964, during the British Invasion, The Beatles appeared on *The Ed Sullivan Show* for the first time. They broke Elvis' long-standing record in terms of TV audience. Elvis resented the Fab Four—how could he not when girls were carrying signs saying "Elvis is Dead, Long Live Ringo?"—but sent a telegram congratulating them anyway.

Other favorites included Nat King Cole and Tom Jones. Elvis hated talented singer Robert Goulet and went out of his way to criticize him. Elvis complained that Goulet had an incredible voice but put no soul into it—the ultimate sin from Elvis' point of view. He once even shot out a TV on which Goulet was singing.

The Word
The term *British Invasion* refers to the period in the 1960s when a lot of the hits on the American charts were by British bands. The Beatles were the vanguard. Other prominent bands included The Animals, The Dave Clark Five, Herman's Hermits, The Rolling Stones, and The Zombies.

The King and I
"Once Elvis really got going, he didn't listen to much other music. He definitely wasn't up on what was going on. That was odd to some folks, and Elvis knew that reaction, but he once told me, 'If I listen to everybody else, it'll take the edge off of me.'"

—Lamar Fike

Love of Animals

Aside from singing, Elvis shared something else in common with Michael Jackson—the performer who (briefly) was the King's son-in-law: love of animals. Here are some pets Elvis owned:

➤ **Dogs:** Baba, a Collie (while in Hollywood in the 1960s); Boy, a mutt (first dog during his childhood); Edmund, a Pomeranian (with Elvis when he died); Foxhugh, a Maltese terrier (a gift for Linda Thompson); Getlo, a chow; Honey, a puppy (a gift for Priscilla at Christmas 1962); Muffin, a great Pyrenees; Sherlock, a basset hound; Snoopy, a Great Dane; Stuff, a poodle; Sweetpea (a gift for his mother by Elvis in 1956); and Teddy Bear of Zixi Pom-Pom, a poodle (given to Elvis in Germany).

➤ **Cats:** Fluff (a gift from Elvis to Lisa Marie); Puff (another cat for Lisa Marie).

➤ **Horses:** Bear, a Tennessee walking horse; Domino, a quarter horse; Rising Sun, a palomino; plus 18 other horses.

➤ **Miscellaneous:** Scatter, a chimpanzee; peacocks; a mynah bird known to say, "Elvis, go to hell!"

For the Record

Scatter, a three-foot, 40-pound chimpanzee, had been a TV star on a Memphis show before coming to live with Elvis at Graceland and in Los Angeles. As Elvis' pet, he became a drinker, favoring scotch and bourbon. He also became violent and spent his final days in a cage behind Graceland. Sadly, he died prematurely of cirrhosis of the liver.

A Fool Such as I: Drugged Elvis

Finally, and without question most seriously, was Elvis' now well-known dependence on various pharmaceuticals. Elvis might have used drugs to help him tour in 1955-57. He reportedly used drugs to stay awake as a GI in West Germany. He was also known to use amphetamines in order to lose weight before shooting a movie. He came to depend on a number of drugs to perform, to sleep, to fight nausea, to fight headaches, to fight depression—the whole spectrum of poly-drug abuse.

But remember—and this is important to understanding Elvis' mentality—these were *prescription* drugs. Doctors had prescribed them for him, so for that reason he probably didn't see an ethical or moral dilemma. And why should he? The drugs were legal! He didn't take them purely for "recreation." Interestingly, he rarely drank or dabbled in illegal drugs—although numerous sources have him smoking marijuana on occasion. His avoidance of alcohol probably had a lot to do with witnessing Gladys' own alcohol problems, which were severe enough to cause cirrhosis of the liver, one of the causes of her early death.

In previous chapters I've mentioned one Dr. George Constantine Nichopoulos ("Dr. Nick") of Memphis. You may even have heard about him on the news at one time or another and been unsure of his connection to the King. To put it simply, Dr. Nick was Elvis' personal doctor; he provided the prescriptions for the various "medicines" Elvis took on a regular basis. Tish Henley, a nurse, lived in a trailer at Graceland and dispensed drugs on Dr. Nichopoulos' orders. When in Las Vegas, Elvis saw Dr. Elias Ghanem, a Lebanese-born doctor with a celebrity practice. Over one seven-month period, pharmacist Jack Kirsch at the Prescription House in Memphis prepared 5,684 pills for Elvis.

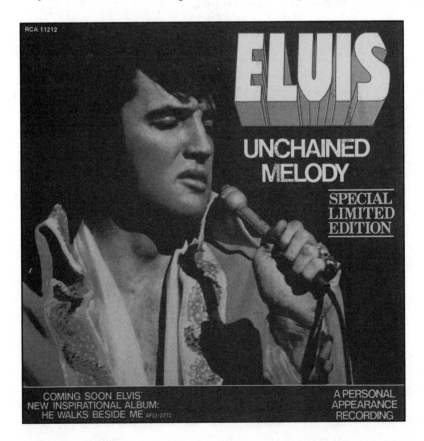

The cover of a 1978 disc jockey promotional 45 Elvis: Unchained Melody. *Elvis often was in psychological pain in his later years and this 1977 picture captures that emotion.*

In video clips of Elvis late in life, onstage and off, it's painfully clear how stoned he is—the glazed eyes, the rambling speech, the slurred words. If there was any doubt, his dependency on drugs was confirmed at the time of his autopsy. In his stomach were found the following: Amytal, codeine, Demerol, morphine, Nembutal, Placidyl, Methaqualone (Quaaludes), Sinutab, Valium, and Valmid.

Elvis was prepared for his daily regime wherever he happened to be. His *kit*, containing his prescription drugs, was always close by.

The truth of his drug use has come out in great detail since Elvis' death. Dr. Nichopoulos drew up documents, referred to as "Protocols," which laid out what drugs Elvis was to receive daily while on tour:

➤ **Stage 1** (at 3:00 p.m., when Elvis typically awoke): A "voice shot," consisting of vitamins and herbs, medication for dizziness, a laxative, three appetite suppressants, and testosterone.

➤ **Stage 2** (one hour before going on stage): A second "voice shot," medication for vertigo, a decongestant with codeine, an amphetamine, and sometimes Dilaudid (synthetic heroin).

➤ **Stage 3** (following the performance): A pill for lowering blood pressure, an antihistamine, a sedative or tranquilizer, and Demerol.

➤ **Stage 4** (at bedtime): A Quaalude (Methaqualone), Placidyl, a laxative, a blood-pressure pill, and three sedatives.

➤ **Stage 5** (if Elvis could not sleep): more Quaaludes and Amytal.

Elvis, by the way, was knowledgeable about the effects of the drugs he took; he kept *The Physicians' Desk Reference*—the definitive text on prescription drugs and their interaction—close at hand and constantly referred to it. Like many drug abusers, Elvis knew what he was doing to himself—and kept doing it anyway.

Rite of Passage

In the summer of 1977, Elvis' lifestyle—his diet, his drug use, his touring, and the pressures of his fame—caught up with him. The world was shocked and saddened by the sudden death, at only 42 years old, of the King of Rock and Roll. In the rest of Part 5, we'll look at the events surrounding his death and his "cultural reincarnation." If you missed it or have never read about it, this may be a catharsis for you—a rite of (sad) passage—as it was for so many of us at the time.

The Least You Need to Know

> ➤ Unhealthy eating habits, prescription drug use, and irregular hours all played a part in Elvis' decline.

> ➤ Elvis was a deeply religious man and explored many different religious philosophies.

> ➤ Elvis' hobbies included sports (watching and playing), guns, buying gifts for people, cars, and, of course, music.

> ➤ Elvis met with President Richard Nixon and was awarded a Narcotics Bureau Badge.

> ➤ Elvis loved animals and kept many at Graceland.

Elvis Has Left the Building

The last eight months of Elvis' life were characterized by increased prescription drug use. For the first time in his performing career, Elvis was regularly missing dates due to "illness." Other times, when he did perform, he forgot lyrics, slurred his words, stumbled on stage—in short, the King was no longer able to hide the fact that he was a drug addict in deep personal trouble.

Before, whenever he had been presented with a challenge, Elvis rose to meet it. Now, in 1977, he was running on empty—disinterested in life, depressed, obese, and in desperate straits. His death at only 42 years of age was a deep tragedy but, in retrospect two decades later, inevitable. For those who worshipped Elvis from the beginning—anyone who had a passing interest in rock and roll—these were sad times indeed.

Elvis' early death has been referred to throughout this book. It's finally time to deal with it. Be prepared for the grim and the tragic. Elvis was so dynamic and charismatic, it's hard to believe he ceased to exist. But to quote Neil Young on dying rock stars, "It's better to burn out than fade away."

At the End of Lonely Street

As you learned in earlier chapters, Elvis' prescription-drug use started early. Doctors provided him with amphetamines to keep him awake on the road and to get him "up" for a performance. Inevitably, the amphetamine (or Dexedrine) would create a need for a downer: something to help Elvis—a lifelong insomniac even without drugs—to get to sleep. The downers Elvis favored were codeine, Demerol, Quaalude, Dilaudid, and Placidyl. These were powerful, dangerous drugs. And very easy to abuse.

At the end of his life, every night, always after midnight, Elvis would be given a packet of drugs by someone from his inner circle. The combination included various medications, including ample Demerol. If the first packet didn't get Elvis to sleep, he'd take another packet, and sometimes a third. Because Elvis often ate right before he took his drugs and went to bed, he was constantly choking on his food. On a regular basis, friends and bodyguards had to save him from choking to death.

Elvis didn't use drugs recreationally like most other rock stars. In other words, he didn't use them to "get high," but to escape from reality, to shut himself down. From a psychological point of view, Elvis was self-medicating himself. He was, of course, ashamed and embarrassed about his behavior, but unable or unwilling to address the problem head on. Remember, this was before the Betty Ford Clinic, before other big names were admitting to drug and alcohol problems, being publicly praised for their admission, and seeking out help. Elvis was scared to death that he'd be "found out." From his point of view, he felt he'd already been skewered by the press and public. And in 1977, he may have been right. (Or, tragically, he might have been embraced by the public for his courage—the first celebrity to go public with drug problems—and leadership. We'll never know.)

The King and I
"I'd rather be unconscious than be miserable."

—Elvis

It has been reported that John O'Grady, a friend of Elvis' and an ex-FBI agent, and Ed Hookstratten, Elvis' Los Angeles lawyer, attempted an "intervention" (a confrontation designed to force someone to recognize a drug or alcohol dependency) with Elvis. They were completely rebuffed.

At the end, Elvis was on a slippery road downhill. He was depressed and trapped. (When greeted with a "Good morning," Elvis would snarl back, "What's good about it?") He was grossly overweight and some 80 pounds heavier than he should have been. Puffy and bloated, he looked (and, doubtless, felt) terrible.

A case can be made that Elvis was trying to kill himself, even if that impulse was purely subconscious. Obviously he didn't care about living. Ultimately, it doesn't matter. Elvis was ingesting lethal amounts of prescription drugs from a number of physicians. The result was inevitable. No one could have continued to consume the quantities of medications that Elvis was taking and live for long.

In the springtime of 1977, starting on April 1, Elvis interrupted his hectic touring schedule to spend six days in Baptist Memorial Hospital in Memphis. The press release said he suffered from fatigue and intestinal flu. There was truth in this, but the underlying cause was his dependency on amphetamines and barbiturates.

He returned to Graceland and remained there until April 18th. On the 21st, he performed again—in Greensboro, North Carolina. His pattern was that he would perform some concerts, then cancel others, returning to Memphis to recuperate. But he always rescheduled the canceled concerts, not wanting to disappoint fans.

On June 19 and 21, the beginning of summer 1977, Elvis filmed performances in Nebraska and South Dakota for the upcoming TV special, "Elvis in Concert," which didn't air until two months after his death, October 3, 1977, on CBS-TV. Vernon Presley ended the one-hour show with some brief remarks. Scenes from this special included in the film *This Is Elvis* show a sick, tired, overweight, and groggy Elvis going through the motions of his performance. It's a disturbing, almost eerie portrait of a man self-destructing in slow motion. It's hard to believe he let himself be filmed in that state—or that the fans, clamoring for his scarves, are still so obviously worshipful. It's even harder to believe that this is actually *Elvis Presley*. Watching it today, the end seems frighteningly near.

For the Record

On June 26, Elvis performed publicly for the final time—at Market Square Arena in Indianapolis, Indiana. (Uncharacteristically, some might even say prophetically, Elvis brought Vernon up on stage, which he rarely did, and introduced him to the audience.)

Elvis spent a lot of the summer at Graceland in bed. He sometimes rallied to see visitors, other times not. Suffering from chronic constipation (a side effect of his heavy drug use), he spent many hours in the bathroom, reading. The only activity that seemed to give him any pleasure was playing gospel music on the piano in the music room. Meanwhile, during that summer, worried fans congregated outside Graceland.

The Bellhop's Tears Keep Flowin'

On August 1, the book *Elvis: What Happened?* hit the stands. Written by Memphis Mafiosi Red West, Sonny West, and Dave Hebler, with Steve Dunleavy, it revealed to the world Elvis' private life—his dependency on drugs, sexual escapades, gun-play, and paranoid, obsessive behavior. Elvis was both hurt and furious. His secrets were out. He had been betrayed. The Colonel told him by phone not to worry—in effect, that any publicity is good publicity.

But Elvis was obsessed by *Elvis: What Happened?* and couldn't get it out of his mind. How could three of his Memphis Mafia—his closest allies and protectors—betray him? According to the Wests and Hebler, they were doing what they thought was right to scare Elvis and bring back the King they knew and loved. Others saw it as revenge for having been fired by Vernon Presley a few months before—and as a way to gain profit at Elvis' expense.

For the Record

Before the publication of *Elvis: What Happened?,* Elvis managed to get copies of the book's galleys. David Stanley remembers being called into Elvis' bedroom at Graceland to find Elvis sitting in the middle of his bed, "crying, really crying," with the galley pages spread all around him. "It's the loneliest thing I ever saw," Stanley wrote later. "My life is over," Elvis said, "I'm a dead man... How could Red and Sonny do this to me, we were in school together, we were friends. I love those guys." It was the beginning of the end for Elvis. His closest friends were exposing his secrets. "With them gone," David Stanley observed, "and all his secrets out, it was like a wing came off a 747. Elvis just went straight down."

Lisa Marie came to town in August, which perked Elvis up. On the night of August 8—from 1:15 a.m. until dawn—he rented Libertyland amusement park for her. (Libertyland was the renamed old Fairgrounds amusement park, which Elvis had so often rented in far happier times.) But he could barely keep himself together, and others had to escort Lisa Marie on most of the rides. Still, Elvis had not completely given up; for example, in an attempt to prepare for his upcoming 12-date East Coast tour, he began a diet on August 10.

On August 15, the last full day of his life, Elvis awoke at four in the afternoon, about typical for him, had breakfast and then played with Lisa Marie, who was busily driving her go-cart around the grounds. There are reports that he later rode around Memphis on his Harley with Ginger.

At Graceland that evening, he played with Lisa Marie and put her to bed about 9:30. (Even at the end, drugged virtually night and day, Elvis managed time with his daughter every day.) He played some songs at the piano with his cousin Billy Smith and his wife Jo. He also spent part of the day trying to get a print of the hot new movie *Star Wars* for Lisa Marie to see.

That evening, after 11:00, Elvis left Graceland in his black Stutz Bearcat with Ginger Alden, Billy Smith, and Charlie Hodge to have a cavity filled at Dr. Lester Hofman's dental office in Memphis. Ginger also had work done. Who else but Elvis would have dental work at such an ungodly hour?

The Desk Clerk's Dressed in Black

Monday became Tuesday, August 16, 1977. By this point in his life, Elvis' sleep patterns were askew. When most of the Western Hemisphere slept, he battled the nighttime demons. Everything in Elvis' world was upside down. When the last day of his life began, at midnight, Elvis was in the midst of his busy schedule.

He returned to Graceland from the dentist at about 12:30 a.m. Larry Geller, his hair-dresser/friend who was in Memphis preparing to leave on the tour later that day, remembers being shocked at Elvis' appearance. "I'd seen him in bad shape before," Geller wrote later, "but nothing like this."

At about 2:00 a.m., Elvis called downstairs and instructed Sam Thompson (his ex-girlfriend's brother and today a Memphis judge) to take Lisa Marie back to California that day, return her to Priscilla, and then jump back on a plane and join the tour in Portland. He also phoned his chief of security, Dick Grob, with some additional instructions about the song list for the upcoming tour.

Sometime around 2:30 (yes, in the morning!), Elvis and Ginger played racquetball with cousin Billy Smith and his wife Jo. After they finished playing sometime around 4:00, Elvis rode a stationary bicycle for a short while. There was even an impromptu sing-along at the grand piano in the music room. Elvis and Ginger then went upstairs. They were joined by Billy Smith, who washed Elvis' hair.

At this point, the sequence of events is difficult to know exactly. Some reports have step-brother Ricky Stanley, who was on duty that night, delivering three packets of the customary nightly medication to Elvis, either all at once, or, more likely, in separate visits. (In any case, the packets were absolutely standard operating procedure; Elvis took them, in varying amounts, every night.) By dawn, Elvis was reading in bed, and Ginger had fallen asleep.

Sometime between 8:00 and 9:00 the next morning, Elvis' aunt, Delta Mae Briggs, brought him a glass of water, the morning newspaper, and further medication, supplied by Elvis' physician, Dr. Nichopoulos, whose office Elvis called for a further prescription. They chatted briefly.

Ginger Alden woke up about 9:00 and Elvis told her he couldn't sleep and was going into the bathroom to read. "Okay," Ginger reports she said, "Don't fall asleep." Elvis responded with his last words, "I won't."

Around 2:15 in the afternoon, Ginger awakened and knocked on the bathroom door. When she didn't get a response, she walked in and found Elvis face-down on the red-shag bathroom carpeting, green pajama bottoms at his ankles, a book in hand: *The Scientific Search for the Face of Jesus*. Despite numerous different versions about who first found Elvis and who came next, it has now been established that Ginger Alden first saw his body (though she didn't know he was dead) and called downstairs for help.

Bodyguard/valet Al Strada showed up first, immediately realized the severity of the situation and called for the senior staff member, Joe Esposito, who came upstairs immediately. Esposito examined Elvis, immediately recognized the symptoms of rigor mortis and concluded that Elvis was dead; nevertheless, he began pressing down on his chest over and over in a futile attempt to give him life.

By this time, as you might imagine, all hell broke loose at Graceland. Lisa Marie was crying. Vernon Presley arrived in the bathroom and collapsed next to his son. Charlie Hodge was hysterical. Elvis' primary physician, Dr. Nichopoulos, was called; so was the Fire Department. (Meanwhile, someone cleaned up Elvis' drug paraphernalia—David Stanley has claimed responsibility—and the room was "clean" when the paramedics arrived.)

The King and I
"My daddy's dead! My daddy's dead!"
—Lisa Marie Presley

The King and I
"I have something terrible to tell you. Elvis is dead."
—Joe Esposito to Colonel Tom Parker

The Memphis fire department's Unit No. 6 arrived shortly after 2:30 p.m. on August 16, 1977, and took the body to Baptist Memorial Hospital seven miles away. Doctors tried to revive him with cardiopulmonary resuscitation for some 30 minutes.

At 3:30 p.m., Elvis Aron Presley, 42 years of age, weighing 258 pounds, was pronounced clinically dead by Dr. Nichopoulos. At 3:32 p.m., Memphis radio stations were broadcasting the news. The first wave of fans descended on Graceland along with the media. Many more would follow as word spread.

He'll Never, Never Be Back

At Vernon Presley's request, an autopsy was performed by Dr. Jerry Francisco, the chief medical examiner of Shelby County.

The autopsy was conducted on the night of August 16 by Dr. Francisco and a number of Baptist Hospital pathologists, including Dr. Eric Muirhead (the hospital's chief of pathology), Dr. Harold Sexton, Dr. George Bale, Dr. Thomas Chesney, Dr. Raul Lamin, Dr. James Hoolbert, Dr. J.A. Pitcock, Dr. Roger Haggit, and Dr. Noel Florendo. Also present were Dr. Nichopoulos, Dan Warlick, the medical examiner's chief investigator, Issac Henderson, a pathologist's assistant, two hospital security officers, and three policeman.

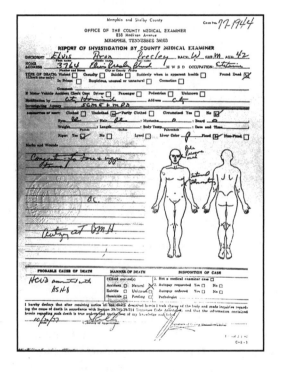

The two-page report on Elvis' death from the Shelby County Medical Examiner.

At a press conference that night, Dr. Francisco announced to the world that Elvis Aron Presley had died of natural causes, stating, "The results of the autopsy are that the cause of death is cardiac arrhythmia due to undetermined heartbeat."

Not all the doctors who had worked on the autopsy agreed. Even in death (and some might say *especially* in death), Elvis Presley would prove to be controversial.

Dr. Nichopoulos agreed with the finding. The alleged cause of death—cardiac arrhythmia—was formally announced by Maurice Eliot, a spokesperson for the hospital. There was no mention of drugs in Elvis' system.

The Royal Funeral

Elvis' body was moved to the Memphis Funeral Home at 1177 Union Avenue in preparation for his funeral.

Because of the number of fans flocking to Memphis, Vernon Presley decided to hold a private funeral at Graceland and a modest ceremony at Forest Hills Cemetery (hundreds of policemen would control the growing crush of mourners). During the wake, with Elvis lying in state nearby, Colonel Parker had Vernon sign papers giving him control of merchandising Elvis-related products. Talk about bad taste!

For the Record

At Elvis' funeral, Colonel Tom Parker wore a bright blue shirt, no tie, and a baseball cap. It seemed odd to many that the Colonel would show so little respect for the man he had spent so much of his life serving. Was it just another business day for him? Or, as with everything else Elvis, was it simply a weird postscript to a life that had gone from the sublime to the ridiculous?

Return to Sender

The "final photo" of Elvis shows the King in his coffin at the funeral. It was secretly taken by his cousin Bobby Mann, who sold the photo to the *National Enquirer* for a reported $78,000; the magazine printed it on the front page. This issue sold 6.5 million copies; however, the photo's authenticity has been questioned, since it shows a much younger, thinner Elvis.

The funeral, coordinated by Joe Esposito, who had taken care of so many of the practical details of Elvis' life, took place at Graceland on Thursday, August 18, 1977 at 3:00 p.m. on a typically warm Memphis summer day. The eight pallbearers were: Dr. George Nichopoulos, Esposito, Lamar Fike, Charlie Hodge, Jerry Schilling, Billy Smith, Gene Smith, and George Klein. (Elvis' music producer Felton Jarvis, formerly of RCA, was to have been included, but he could not attend.)

Also in attendance were: Priscilla, Lisa Marie, Vernon, Minnie Mae Hood Presley, and other family members; Colonel Tom Parker; Jerry Schilling; Ginger Alden; Linda Thompson; Ann-Margret; Roger Smith (Ann-Margret's husband); Tennessee Governor Raymond Blanton; Chet Atkins; James Brown; Sammy Davis, Jr.; and Caroline Kennedy (covering the event for *Rolling Stone* magazine).

Reverend C.W. Bradley, pastor of the Woodvale Church of Christ in Memphis, was the officiating minister. The evangelist Rex Humbard of the Cathedral of Tomorrow in Akron, Ohio, also said some words. Jackie Kahane, a comedian who frequently opened for Elvis gave a eulogy (he didn't try to be funny); Jake Hess and the Statesmen sang "Known Only to Him"; James Blackwood performed "How Great Thou Art"; The Stamps sang "Sweet, Sweet Spirit" and "His Hand in Mine"; Bill Baize of The Stamps soloed on "When It's My Turn"; and Kathy Westmoreland sang "My Heavenly Father Watches Over Me."

For the Record

The Reverend C.W. Bradley, the main eulogizer, gave a frank portrait of Elvis. After pointing out Elvis' good qualities, including his love of family, and briefly touching on his remarkable career, he went on to discuss touchier subjects: "Elvis was a frail human being. And he would be the first to admit his weaknesses. Perhaps because of his rapid rise to fame and fortune, he was thrown into temptations that some never experience. Elvis would not want anyone to think that he had no flaws or faults. But now that he's gone, I find it more helpful to remember his good qualities, and I hope you do, too."

After the funeral, Trent Webb drove the hearse carrying Elvis' body to Forest Hill Cemetery. Accompanying it were 14 (some reports state 11, others 15) white Cadillacs with motorcycles alongside. The eight pallbearers carried Elvis to the gravesite, where he was laid to rest in a mausoleum next to Gladys. Even in death, Elvis is inseparably close to his Mama.

All state flags in Tennessee were flown half-mast that day. Elvis' music echoed on radio stations all over the country.

Cover-Up! Conspiracy in the Air

The rumors about Elvis' death ran rampant—a persistent one was that he had faked his death as a publicity stunt or to elude fans until he was well. People did not want to believe that the King was dead.

For the Record

There were at least two precedents for the confusion over whether a rock and roll star was dead or not. First was the case of the "Paul Is Dead!" hoax, in which false rumors were spread that The Beatles' famous composer/singer/bassist was dead when he was very much alive.

The other rumor regarded Doors' singer and poet Jim Morrison, who had often kidded about faking his death and skipping to Africa before he actually did die in Paris on July 3, 1971 (under strange circumstances). Jim and Elvis may be together— but it's in Rock and Roll Heaven, not in Africa, Hawaii, or anywhere else.

There did turn out to be a cover-up, but the truth brought no good news. It began at Graceland when Memphis Mafiosi removed all drugs and drug paraphernalia from Elvis' bedroom and bathroom. It continued through the autopsy findings when Dr. Francisco and Dr. Nichopoulos did not tell it like it really was. Throughout Elvis Presley's life those close to him protected his image at all costs. Why would it be any different at his death?

For The Record

At a press conference on the day of Elvis' funeral, Joe Esposito told a roomful of reporters, "Elvis didn't take drugs," and that there were "absolutely no drugs whatsoever." Of course, Esposito knew better than anyone that the exact opposite was true. But he had been covering up for Elvis for so long, it was as if he were on automatic pilot. To his credit, in his book about Elvis, *Good Rockin' Tonight*, he forthrightly admits the cover-up, writing, "The habit of rote denial would die slow and hard."

But the truth came out and, little by little, the public began to receive it. On August 19, a spokesperson at the hospital stated that Elvis "had the arteries of an 80-year-old man. His body was just worn-out. His arteries and veins were terribly corroded."

Original reports had it that Elvis died of a heart attack—which certainly makes sense, considering Elvis' obesity (caused primarily by his cholesterol-rich diet), drug use, cortisone injections (for allergic reactions), and family history. (When Elvis died, Vernon was recovering from a serious heart attack.) Dr. Jerry Francisco has never fully backed away from his original finding of arrhythmia.

Hospital officials present at the autopsy later admitted that Elvis died from polypharmacy—multiple drug ingestion. Evidently, he had a virtual medicine cabinet in his belly. It was revealed that traces of the following drugs were in Elvis' stomach at the time of death: Amytal, codeine, Demerol, morphine, Nembutal, Placidyl, Quaaludes, Sinutab, Valium, and Valmid. All of these were prescribed to him by Dr. Nick and others. Unfortunately, autopsy reports, notes, and photographs all mysteriously disappeared by August 19. Moreover, the contents of Elvis' stomach were thrown out.

Other examinations of the evidence have yielded other plausible causes of Elvis' death, including: a phenomenon called the Valsalva maneuver (essentially straining on the toilet leading to heart stoppage—plausible because Elvis suffered severe constipation, a common reaction to drug use); anaphylactic shock (caused by either an extreme allergic reaction or reaction to potent—i.e., street—drugs); even suffocation (after blacking out) on the thick carpeting of his bathroom.

All sorts of theories also made the rounds. Graceland's chief of security, Dick Grob, floated a theory, altogether bogus, that Elvis died of bone cancer. Another rumor said he asphyxiated.

David Stanley, Elvis' step-brother, even collaborated with Albert Goldman, author of the bitter biography *Elvis*, on an article for *Life* magazine in which he claims that Elvis committed suicide. Elvis Presley *did not* kill himself. In fact, he was having a fairly pleasant day, seemed upbeat, had enjoyed his daughter's visit, and was looking forward to the beginning of his East Coast tour the next night.

Not long after the Goldman/Stanley article, Dr. Nichopoulos, in a book proposal, made the outlandish claim that Elvis was murdered, even implying that the killer was David Stanley, a skilled karate expert. There was virtually no evidence to support this view, which was roundly dismissed.

It would take years to determine the actual cause of Elvis' death. One journalist in particular, Beth Tamke, who covered the medical beat for Memphis' morning newspaper, the *Commercial Appeal*, wouldn't accept Dr. Francisco's heart diagnosis. Eventually, Tamke would get a copy of Elvis' death

Going for Gold

The best book, by far, concerning Elvis' death and the cover-up that followed, is *The Death of Elvis* by Charles C. Thompson II and James P. Cole (Delacorte Press, 1991). It is a thorough, uncompromising, and finally sobering look at the death (and life) of the King of Rock and Roll.

The King and I

"The king is always killed by his courtiers. He is overfed, overindulged, over-drunk to keep him tied to his throne. Most people in the position never wake up."

—John Lennon

certificate, which did not mention drugs; the death certificate was the key to a series of doors that Tamke would open, eventually leading to the true cause of Elvis' death. A television producer, Charles Thompson, then of ABC's *20/20,* also made important contributions in the search for truth.

So reader, you should at least now know the following:

1. Elvis is, in fact, dead.

2. He died due to causes stemming from his prescription drug addiction.

3. There were conspiracies involved in Elvis' death, but these related primarily to the Memphis Mafia's attempts to conceal Elvis' addictions.

4. Any other rumors or stories you hear are most likely fiction. Got it?

Dr. Nick Indicted

In September 1979, Dr. George Nichopoulos was charged with 20 counts of "willingly and feloniously" overprescribing drugs to Elvis—19,000 doses in the final $31\frac{1}{2}$ months of Elvis' life—by the State of Tennessee's Board of Medical Examiners. His medical license was suspended for three months in January 1980. On May 16, 1980, a Shelby Country grand jury charged the doctor with "unlawfully, willfully and feloniously dispensing" 10 controlled substances.

For the Record

In a special episode of *20/20* on ABC, host Geraldo Rivera discussed Elvis' death, Dr. Jerry Francisco's autopsy, and Dr. George Nichopoulos' treatment of Elvis. On December 27, 1979, *20/20* aired a second program devoted to Elvis' death. Both programs were critical of Drs. Francisco and Nichopoulos, and helped to reveal the truth: that Elvis' multiple-drug use caused his death.

Dr. Nichopoulos was cleared on all counts—not guilty of over-prescribing addictive drugs to 10 patients, nor of malpractice, nor of unethical conduct.

The Day the Music Died

The news of Elvis death spread like a firestorm. Thousands of people descended on Graceland. But it was more than just the congregation at Graceland that were plunged into deep mourning. Throughout America—throughout the world—people were forced to begin adjusting to a world without Elvis.

But Elvis endured. What is immortality anyway? It's not about eternity; even the sun will one day burn out. It's about influence from beyond the grave. And Elvis is at the top of the list of mortals with enduring influence, musically and culturally. In the remaining chapters we'll examine this influence—both the expected and the unexpected. Elvis may have physically gotten off the bus, but the bus is still rocking and rolling.

The King and I
"Elvis, we came by to see you, but you were gone. You left on tour with our Lord, we know. Here within our hearts always and ever we love only you, your smile, the sparkle in your eyes, how can we forget? We didn't come to say goodbye, until we climb these golden stairs, let's just say until we meet again."

—Anonymous message on a Graceland wall

The Least You Need to Know

➤ At the end of his life, Elvis was physically and spiritually sick and barely functioning.

➤ Elvis Presley died from polypharmacy—multiple drug ingestion. All of the drugs were prescribed by his physicians.

➤ The cause of Elvis' death was covered up by the Memphis Mafia. Many people have since come up with other ridiculous and unsubstantiated theories and conspiracies.

Chapter 21

The Day After the Music Died

1935 - 1977

In This Chapter

➤ The fate of other Presley family members

➤ Celebrating Elvis in death

➤ Elvis' post-mortem business

A number of other events after Elvis' death kept him in the news. Some of these were commercial endeavors intended to keep the Elvis gravy train rolling—or at least the Memphis Mafia and the Presley clan's gravy train rolling. Others were serendipitous, serving to further the mythical aspect of the Once and Future King. Either way, some very strange things happened in the Elvis world, so it's no wonder many believe Elvis had some connection to metaphysical forces.

Invasion of the Body Snatchers

Going for Gold
If you're serious in your devotion to Elvis, you should memorize the words at Graceland's eternal flame:

To Elvis in Memoriam. You gave yourself to each of us in some manner. You were wrapped in thoughtfulness and tied with love. May this flame reflect our never-ending respect and love for you. May it serve as a constant reminder to each of us of your eternal presence.

On August 29, less than two weeks after the King's death, three men—Ronnie Lee Adkins, Raymond Green, and Bruce Nelson—paid a visit to Forest Hills Cemetery at night. They wore dark jumpsuits and bulletproof vests, and carried a rifle, pistols, and grenades. They were caught, arrested, and charged with trespassing. Rumor had it that a mysterious party had offered them $120,000 for the delivery of Elvis' body. But, on October 5, charges were dismissed. The court bought their defense. They didn't want to steal Elvis' body, they claimed. They wanted to prove that his body wasn't in the mausoleum and that Elvis was still alive.

Vernon didn't wait for the verdict. He realized his son's body would not survive the ages undisturbed at Forest Hills. On October 2, he had Elvis and Gladys' bodies re-interred in Graceland's Meditation Garden.

Just a Little Bizarre: First Anniversary

On the first anniversary of the King's death, the city of Memphis decided to do something special, and events were scheduled without certainty as to their drawing power. The Memphian movie theater, which Elvis used to rent for all-night-screenings, for example, held festival of his films. At the Brooks Memorial Art Gallery, Andy Warhol presented his painting *Elvis Forty-Nine Times*. Not far away in northern Mississippi, at the Circle G Ranch, a sunset memorial service was held at the base of the concrete cross Elvis had erected.

The King and I
"Which will seem more absurd to students of our time, the nationwide flap in the 1950s that kept Elvis Presley's gyrating hips from being televised or the hysteria with which his fans this week commemorated the first anniversary of his death?"

—*The New York Times, 1978*

Not so strange, you say, except perhaps Warhol's white hair. But wait. The event was destined to turn bizarro. A big fire drew most of Memphis' fire department. The police also had an issue with their contracts and went on strike. Authorities had events canceled, imposed a curfew, and called in the National Guard to handle the unexpected. Is that all? you ask. No, an employee at the electric company hit the bottle a little too hard and knocked out power in most of the city. Some of the thousands of fans who showed up spoke of a "visitation of Elvis' ghost." The media fed on it all.

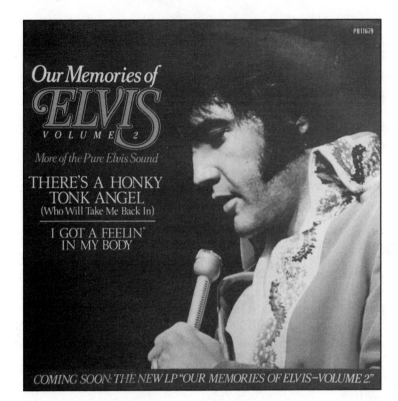

P811679

Our Memories of

ELVIS
VOLUME 2

More of the Pure Elvis Sound

THERE'S A HONKY
TONK ANGEL
(Who Will Take Me Back In)

I GOT A FEELIN'
IN MY BODY

COMING SOON: THE NEW LP "OUR MEMORIES OF ELVIS—VOLUME 2."

The title of the 1979 promotional album Our Memories of Elvis *describes what much of the business of post-mortem Elvis was (and is) all about.*

A certain tone was set for Elvis coverage in the future. It was no longer just about Elvis, Superstar. Elvis, Supernatural became a cultural icon that day.

Cast in Bronze

In September 1978, Las Vegas furthered the Dead Elvis phenomenon with its own special events. On September 1–10, the first annual Elvis Presley Convention was held at the Hilton Hotel, once Elvis' home away from home. Impersonators performed and voted on who impersonated the King the best. (We'll take a good hard look at impersonators in Chapter 22.)

This was related to the "Always Elvis" festival, promoted by Colonel Tom Parker (who still had his

Return to Sender

In the weeks before Elvis died, at least two psychics—Jacqueline Eastland on a Los Angeles TV show and Mark Salem in a Philadelphia newspaper—predicted that Elvis would die soon. Nothing psychic about that—Elvis had looked like death for some time. *After* his death, psychic David Behr alleged to have contacted Elvis and sold the taped conversation with the King for a mere $9.95.

mouth under the Elvis money faucet) and Vernon Presley (unfortunately, still a second banana to the Colonel in financial matters), with a multimedia production and memorabilia display. On September 8, the Hilton unveiled a life-size bronze Elvis statue (life-size in height if not in weight—the statue weighed 400 pounds) by sculptor Carl Romanelli. Priscilla, looking absolutely ravishing, was on hand. Representatives of RCA also presented Vernon with 15 gold and platinum records in recognition of Elvis' massive posthumous record sales. Meanwhile, at the Las Vegas International Airport, Elvis' Convair 880 jet, the *Lisa Marie*, was on display.

"Always Elvis," however, was savaged by the press as tasteless and exploitative. Attendance the first day was good, but soon after Presley fans shunned the display, far preferring Graceland as the place where Elvis should be remembered.

Goodbye, Vernon

After Elvis' death, Vernon Presley got on with his life. On November 15, 1977, he and his second wife, Dee Stanley, threw in the towel on their 17-year marriage, which had been floundering for years. (In fact, Vernon brought his girlfriend, Sandy Miller, to Elvis' funeral, not Dee.) They traveled to the Dominican Republic, where quick and inexpensive divorces provided a steady revenue stream for the impoverished island. Ever the penny pincher, Vernon was, if nothing else, consistent.

Vernon died of heart failure on June 26, 1979, the second anniversary of his son's last live performance. (He had suffered a heart attack four years before, on February 5, 1975.) He was 63 years old and was buried next to Gladys and his son.

Vernon's will sagely called for Priscilla to be the executrix of the Presley estate. It was one of the few astute business decisions Vernon ever made. He left his own personal estate primarily to Sandy Miller, who had three children to care for.

The bottom line on Vernon Presley? He was a man from the lowest socioeconomic strata of society, with little education and few breaks, who lived in abject poverty until his son hit it big. For Vernon, money, or rather the fear of losing it, was everything. Still, if you're an Elvis fan like I am, it's hard not to resent Vernon for failing to understand his own limitations and for not reaching out for the astute business advice his son so desperately needed.

The King and I
"Well Sandy, I'm going."

—Vernon Presley's last words, to his girlfriend, Sandy Miller

The King and I
"The pitiful part of it was, Elvis left all his personal business up to Vernon, and Vernon had a third-grade education.... Vernon was terrible as a business person, but unfortunately Elvis relied on him."

—Marty Lacker

But Elvis, ever the good and devoted son, loved his Daddy unequivocally and wanted only that he be happy; he did his level best to make that happen. By and large, he succeeded. In that success, and in their warm relationship, there is a great deal to be proud of for both father and son.

Tupelo Too

As I told you earlier, when Elvis was asked what kind of monument, if any, he would want built in his honor in Tupelo, he answered "a chapel for my fans to meditate in." He got his wish with a groundbreaking in Elvis Presley Park in Tupelo on January 8, 1979, and a dedication of the $80,000 Elvis Presley Chapel on August 17.

Goodbye, Minnie

Grandmother Minnie Mae Hood Presley died on May 8, 1980, at the age of 86, and was buried in Graceland's Meditation Garden with Elvis, Vernon, and Gladys.

Elvis always said that Minnie Mae would outlive them all, and he was right. She was nearly as tall as her grandson, thin as a rail, enjoyed snuff, cooked good "Southern" food, and said what she wanted

The King and I
"How could he die before me? I'm the old one. I'm supposed to be gone."

—Minnie Mae Presley, the day Elvis died

when she wanted. "Dodger," as Elvis often called her, had a sharp sense of humor and could take a joke as well as she gave one. Elvis doted on her, visited with her daily, and showered her with presents.

The Empire Strikes Back

In May 1980, a probate court appointed Memphis entertainment attorney Blanchard L. Tual as Lisa Marie's legal guardian, giving him powers to investigate the financial relationship between Elvis and Colonel Parker. Tual discovered, among other things, that Parker had made many deals in which he made more than Elvis, that he had suffered enormous gambling losses at the International Hotel in Las Vegas where he booked Elvis (clearly a conflict of interest), and he was getting 50 percent commission even after Elvis' death. Since Parker had "violated his duty," the court ordered the Elvis Presley estate to sue. All payments were to cease and charges were brought against Parker. He settled out of court in early 1983, divesting himself of all Elvis-related assets—he made a final $2 million by selling his interest to RCA—and agreeing not to use Elvis' name in any endeavor.

Colonel Parker was 87 in February 1997 when he died in Las Vegas of complications from a stroke. His death got some attention in the press, but not much considering his central role in Elvis' career. There will be no memorial gatherings for Parker in Las Vegas every February as there are for Elvis every August in Memphis.

On June 7, 1982, Priscilla Presley opened Graceland as a museum. It annually grosses about $7 million. In 1984, the State of Tennessee ruled that the Elvis Presley Estate has unqualified right to control all use of Elvis' name and likeness. So if a company wants to get in the business of marketing Elvis, it has to strike a royalty deal with the estate and its marketing branch, *Elvis Presley Enterprises*, of which Graceland is a subsidiary. Priscilla Presley receives a management fee from the estate, estimated at between 2.5 and 5 percent.

The Word
Elvis Presley Enterprises, formerly a company established by Colonel Tom Parker, is now the marketing entity of the Elvis Presley Estate. It directs the running of Graceland as well as the licensing of Elvis products. Record royalties go directly to the Elvis Presley Estate, however.

More Tube and Theater Time

Elvis in the words of songwriter Kris Kristofferson was "partly truth and partly fiction." TV specials have continued to honor him, and movies, both feature and television, have tried to capture his essence.

TV Specials Devoted to Elvis

The following TV shows have honored the King since his death:

➤ "Elvis in Concert" (first aired October 3, 1977)—This was the one-concert footage filmed in June. It became a one-hour special on CBS. It told us what we already knew: that Elvis had been really sick and that, even so, he could still manage to sing effectively. At the end of the program, Vernon Presley spoke to the world of his son.

➤ "Memories of Elvis" (first aired November 20, 1977)—NBC three-hour special hosted by Ann-Margret with footage from the 1968 "Comeback Special" and "Elvis: Aloha from Hawaii" special.

➤ "Nashville Remembers Elvis on His Birthday" (first aired January 8, 1978)—NBC one-and-one-half-hour tribute special, hosted by Jimmy Dean, with recollections by Hollywood personalities and musical tributes by country performers. It was later broadcast in a one-hour format as "Elvis Remembered: Nashville to Hollywood."

➤ "Mondo Elvis" (1984)—Syndicated special showing Elvis-mania. Also called "Disciples of Rock."

➤ "Elvis: One Night With You" (first aired January 5, 1985)—Parts of the 1968 NBC "Comeback Special," telecast on HBO.

➤ "Elvis Presley's Graceland" (first aired January 8, 1985)—A tour of Graceland, hosted by Priscilla Presley (much like Jackie showed us the Kennedy White House); on Showtime.

➤ "Elvis '56" (August 16, 1987)—Special with early home movies, photographs, and TV footage of Elvis; telecast on Cinemax.

➤ "The Elvis Files" (August 14, 1991)—A special based on the book of the same name, suggesting that Elvis faked his own death after working for the FBI to convict a mobster, narrated by Bill Bixby.

➤ "Elvis: The Great Performances" (April 1992)—two-hour special, hosted by Priscilla, with concert footage and home movies.

Movie Matters

In the years since Elvis' death, he has proven a surprisingly fertile topic for movies depicting different episodes in his life—or fictional events that never happened.

In 1979 the TV movie *Elvis* aired, with Kurt Russell playing the young King (through his first comeback concert in Las Vegas in 1969). A singer by the name of Ronnie McDowell recorded the songs that Russell mouths convincingly. John Carpenter directed.

In 1981 a movie called *Elvis and the Beauty Queen*—about Elvis' affair with Linda Thompson—aired on NBC. Don Johnson gained 40 pounds to play Elvis late in life.

In February 1988, ABC broadcast a two-night miniseries, *Elvis and Me*, based on Priscilla's 1985 book. Dale Midkiff played Elvis, and Susan Walters played Priscilla.

One 1988 feature film, *Heartbreak Hotel*, directed by Chris Columbus, is the story of a boy and his friends who kidnap Elvis (played by David Keith) in 1972 for the sake of the boy's mother, an avid Elvis fan (played by Tuesday Weld, Elvis' co-star in *Wild in the Country*).

Elvis and the Colonel was a 1993 TV movie with Beau Bridges playing Colonel Tom Parker.

Elvis is often referenced in many non-Elvis movies, sometimes in theme (1989's very fine *Mystery Train*, directed by Jim Jarmusch); sometimes in dialogue (*Baby, The Rain Must Fall*, 1965); sometimes through his music (*Diner*); sometimes by a prop, such as a photo (*Grease*, 1978); sometimes through impersonators (*Honeymoon in Vegas*, 1992); and sometimes as a ghost (*True Romance*, 1993).

The Music, First and Foremost

Let us not forget that Elvis started with the music and the music is now and forevermore the bottom line. Any Elvis-related event leads to an increase in airplay for Elvis' songs. All the hoopla surrounding his death and subsequent events served to boost record sales. (In fact, RCA reported a remarkable 8 million Elvis records were sold in the week after his death.) Elvis records are sought after as collectibles, and re-issues of his music on tapes and CDs are strong sellers. Since Elvis has died, it is estimated that earnings from his music are at least 10 times what he earned when he was alive (which was $100 million). In 1979 it was learned that Colonel Parker never made Elvis a member of BMI, Broadcast Music, Inc., the organization that collects musicians' royalties, thus losing Presley millions of dollars. Over 50 Elvis albums and boxed sets have been released since his death, with plenty more coming.

One of my favorites is RCA's 1993 boxed set, *Elvis From Nashville to Memphis—The Essential 60's Masters I,* which includes 130 digitally remastered tracks. Another one I recommend for your collection is *The Beginning Years*, a 1985 Louisiana Hayride release featuring Hayride performances from the 1950s, as well as an Elvis interview with Hayride host Horace Logan.

Then there's RCA's *The Complete Sun Sessions*, a wonderful two-disc set that includes 16 master recordings, 12 alternate takes, and six more outtakes.

To experience Elvis' love of gospel music, check out *Elvis Gospel 1957-1971, Known Only to Him,* which RCA released in 1989. You can't go wrong with *Elvis Presley—The Number One Hits*, released by RCA in 1988, or *Elvis Presley, The Great Performances*, released by RCA in 1990, for a great overview of his studio and live performance hits.

But these are just one man's choices and there are so many choices. My advice is to head for your local record emporium and check out the full range of what's available; my favorites are the older hits, but whatever you choose, you won't be making a mistake.

Elvis Ad Infinitum

Although there is never a shortage of Elvis references day in and day out (Elvis is everywhere!), two times a year he receives extra attention: his birth date, January 8, and his death date, August 16. The latter has become the more emphasized event because of the tradition of devotees gathering at Graceland. People tend to think in round numbers, so the 10th anniversary was huge. But, with Elvis, patterns are broken. The 11th was even bigger, and it doesn't seem to matter how the numbers fall anymore. Now nearly a quarter of a million people flock to Graceland each Elvis Week (usually August 9-17)—and the number grows significantly each year.

Memphis belongs to Elvis once again, as does Tupelo and the Circle G Ranch. Events such as concerts, video shows, lectures, art exhibitions, art contests, tours, and benefit memorial runs and dinners for various charities are held. The biggest moment of the Tribute Week is the Candlelight Service at Graceland—a vigil when thousands of fans with lighted candles walk from Elvis Presley Boulevard through Graceland's gates to the gravesite and back. Graceland also holds a special luncheon for fan-club officers.

Going for Gold
Should you want to visit Graceland on or around the 20th anniversary of the King's death, reservations are a must. You can contact Graceland by dialing 1-800-238-2000.

For the Record

In November 1991, the National Park Service listed Graceland on its National Register of Historic Places because of its "exceptional significance." The dedication of the fans and their desire to see Elvis' dream home made this happen very quickly.

In Part 6, we'll see how Elvis keeps popping up all over our culture: he's impersonated, he's sighted (even on Mars), he's reincarnated, he's represented in art, he's referenced by politicians, he's studied in the classroom, and he's worshipped almost as a religious figure. We'll take a look at how he's collected, too.

The Least You Need to Know

➤ Each anniversary of Elvis' death is a huge public event in Memphis.

➤ Since Elvis' death, strange things have occurred that some people have interpreted as involving supernatural forces.

➤ In death, the marketing of Elvis has become ever more profitable.

➤ Elvis' estate, guided by his ex-wife Priscilla Presley, is a money-making industry whose profits increase yearly.

The King and I
"When they celebrated the 10th anniversary of Elvis Presley's death, it was more like a canonization. People lined up to visit Graceland. Middle-age women—and yes, men, too—with tears in their eyes. I couldn't believe one woman saying, 'Elvis' death meant more to me than a death in my own family.'"

—actor Kirk Douglas

Part 6
All the King's Things

There has never been another celebrity who, after death, became as popular as Elvis. Sure, there is often nostalgia when a famous person passes away, but with Elvis Presley something completely different happened: He got bigger—making more money, attracting more attention. The interest in Elvis post-death, is unprecedented.

His personal possessions are probably the most popular and expensive collectibles in history. His original records and sheet music are worth big bucks. Licensed Elvis products are everywhere. In this part I'll give you some tips on what's worth collecting, what's not, and how to avoid being ripped off. I'll even suggest a visit to his home, Graceland, as well as a few important sites along the way.

Elvis is supposed to be about joy, and the joy of collecting and keeping a piece of Elvis for yourself is what Part 6 is all about. So…enjoy. Elvis lives forever.

Chapter 22

Elvis: Cult or Culture?

In This Chapter

➤ Elvis impersonators

➤ Elvis and American culture

➤ The Elvis cult

Dead Elvis lives on and on. He fills a need in many people. For some it's simply his music. Others see their youth in all that was Elvis. Others imitate him as a ritual form of empowerment. Still others have deified him, obsessively tracking anything to do with Elvis. And there are those who refuse to believe that he is really dead.

For the rest of us, the Elvis phenomenon is a strange and inexplicable experience. Yet we can't help but watch it with both amusement and fascination.

Some of the manifestations that are Dead Elvis result from pure capitalism—riding the Elvis gravy train, so to speak. Others result from a sincere quest by individuals for something beyond their own lives—and Elvis is certainly "beyond" us.

Elvis Wannabes: Impersonators 'Round the World

Hey, I admit it. As a kid, after seeing Elvis on *The Ed Sullivan Show*, I stood in front of a mirror more than once and mimicked my newly discovered hero. I dropped out of the running pretty quickly, but many other fans kept going, honing their impersonation skills. Even while he was alive, Elvis impersonators were all over the place, some doing the Early Elvis thing, some the Late. Some, with true vocal talent, tried to sound like him; others had to settle for looking like him. Halloween brought out many closet imitators.

One ersatz Elvis even performed alongside the King. On May 6, 1976, at Lake Tahoe, Nevada, one Douglas Roy from Canada was lucky enough to be invited on stage by Elvis. Elvis smiled as Roy convincingly sang "Hound Dog."

After Elvis' death, Elvis impersonation got a nod from Elvis' people in September 1978 with the first annual Elvis Presley Convention in Las Vegas—Vernon and Colonel Parker were on hand. Since that time, the Elvis impersonation business has become a cottage industry, with hundreds of practitioners—one estimate is 3,000. Many work in Las Vegas, but you can find them all over North America in both the U.S. and Canada, and in other countries as well, especially England and Japan. Impersonators play concert halls, nightclubs, bars, cruise ships, fairs, carnivals, weddings, parties, charity bazaars, nursing homes, hospitals, record stores, and so on (all the places that bands perform). Some impersonate Elvis full-time; others moonlight.

There is no such thing as an authorized Elvis imitator—the Elvis Presley Estate has given up trying to regulate them, but they certainly don't approve of them. Most fan clubs no longer endorse particular impersonators. Some Elvis imitators have gone so far as to change their names legally to Elvis Presley; others, to Elvis' movie characters.

The Elvis Presley Impersonators International Association Convention (708-297-1234) sponsors gatherings of impersonators at various locations. They held their first convention in Chicago in June 1989.

The King and I
"I think Elvis Presley will never be solved."

—Nick Tosches, rock critic

The King and I
"We're called Elvis impersonators—that's what we are. The guys who try to be Elvis 24 hours a day become head-cases. Most of us are just trying to imitate him and his style—not fill his shoes."

—Will Reeb, Elvis impersonator

Going for Gold
A good place to catch a number of Elvis impersonation acts is—where else?—Las Vegas. Try Vegas World at 2000 Las Vegas Boulevard (702-383-5264); or the Imperial Palace at 3535 Las Vegas Boulevard (800-634-6441).

A talent directory entitled *I Am Elvis*, first published in 1991, lists more than 200 Elvis impersonators. The book *Return to Sender: The First Complete Discography of Elvis Tribute & Novelty Records, 1956-1986* by Howard F. Banney (Pierian Press, 1987) lists songs and albums released by impersonators.

Here are some noteworthy impersonators:

➤ **Herbert Baer**, a foundry worker in Manitowoc, Wisconsin who became the first impersonator to change his name legally to Elvis Presley.

➤ **Julian and Angelo Campo**, a father and son team who work out of Chicago. They favor satin suits.

➤ **Rusty Dee**, a part Native American and part Irish imitator from St. Petersburg, Florida. Dee brings his Native American qualities to bear when he imitates Elvis. His Indian name is Little Eagle and he wears an eagle necklace, which he designed. Let's not forget that Elvis also had some Indian blood.

➤ **Jimmy Ellis**, an Elvis impersonator on recordings, not onstage. Shelby Singleton, who bought Sun Records from Sam Phillips in 1969, released records with Ellis singing during the 1970s in an effort to trick record buyers into thinking it was really Elvis. Then, after Elvis' death, he recorded under the name Orion Eckely Darnell, a fictional character created by Gail Brewer-Giorgio in her novel *Orion* about a rock star who fakes his death. To this day, some (way-out) folks actually still insist Ellis a.k.a Orion is indeed Elvis.

➤ **El Vez**, the stage name of one Robert Lopez. He started out as the curator of a Los Angeles art gallery and came up with the idea of a Latino Elvis during a 1988 exhibition surrounding Elvis themes. He has toured with the "Memphis Mariachi Band" and back-up singers, the "Elvettes." When El Vez sings, "Blue Suede Shoes" becomes "Huaraches Azul"; "In the Ghetto" becomes "In the Barrio"; and "Viva Las Vegas" becomes "Viva La Raza."

➤ **The Flying Elvi**, Elvis impersonators who actually jump from airplanes. They started out as skydivers who found work in the 1992 film *Honeymoon In Vegas*.

The King and I

"I see myself stepping into this outline. I turn my mind's eye inward and create a mental picture of Elvis—of course, I keep my physical eye turned outward so I don't fall off the stage—and then I invite listeners into my realm."

—Doug Church, Elvis impersonator

The King and I

"I eat Elvis, live Elvis, work Elvis, but most of all I pray with Elvis."

—Julian Campo, Elvis impersonator

The concept of Elvis-clad skydivers worked so well in the movie that they've stayed together to work air shows.

➤ **Clarence Giddens,** one of the few African-Americans known to work full-time as an Elvis impersonator. He works out of Nassawadox, Virginia.

➤ **Raymond Michael** (Hebel) is a Los Angeles-based singer who has been impersonating Elvis since he was a college freshman in 1972; in a 1996 World Wide Web poll he was voted the number one Elvis "illusionist" in the world.

➤ **Ross Henderson,** imitator who works out of Brisbane, Australia. Henderson has six back-up musicians, three female vocalists, an assistant to hand him water and scarves (a la Elvis), 13 jumpsuits, and $80,000 worth of sound and lighting equipment.

➤ **Kiyoshi Ito,** Japanese Elvis imitator. You read it right! Elvis has a loyal Japanese following. If you're in Tokyo, make sure to catch his act.

➤ **Andy Kaufman,** well-known, now-deceased comedian (*Taxi* and, occasionally, *Saturday Night Live*) who performed Elvis in the 1970s while Elvis was alive. In his comedy routine, Kaufman convincingly incorporated the rockabilly and the Vegas Elvis.

➤ **Janice Kucera,** female Elvis impersonator. In 1966, at the age of 16, she traveled to Memphis and met Elvis. She also saw him perform in Las Vegas. One year after his death, she began working as a professional impersonator and is one of the few women who has had a successful career doing so. Her hometown is Exeter, Nebraska.

For the Record

John Lennon an Elvis imitator? Yes, the intellectual Beatle did a damn good Elvis. While playing in Hamburg, Germany, in the early days of the Beatles, he often launched into his Elvis impression. On Lennon's *Live in New York City* album, he covers "Hound Dog."

Paul McCartney (or should we say "Sir Paul" now that he's been knighted?) also worships the King and over the years has covered several Elvis tunes. On the Beatles' *Live at the BBC*, you can hear him doing an admirable "That's All Right (Mama)." McCartney often sang in Elvis' style on a few of his own compositions, such as "Name and Address" (on the 1978 Wings album, *London Town*).

➤ **Little Enis,** deceased early Elvis imitator who chose his name based on the phrase "Elvis the Pelvis." You can imagine what that makes Enis.

➤ **Ronnie McDowell.** What do you say when an Elvis fan gets his own fan club? Such is the case of Ronnie McDowell, one of the most famous impersonators of all, and one of the very best. (McDowell sang all the Elvis songs in *Elvis* [1979], which starred Kurt Russell, and *Elvis and the Beauty Queen* [1981] which starred Don Johnson as Elvis and Stephanie Zimbalist as Linda Thompson.)

➤ **Alan Meyer**, former NASA engineer now working out of Las Vegas. He's one of the highest-paid Elvis impersonators, making up to $50,000 a week for his shows.

➤ **Miguel Quintana**, the youngest of all Elvis imitators. Born July 19, 1986, "Little Elvis" started imitating Elvis professionally at the age of three. He works out of Englewood, Colorado.

➤ Not to be left out is the band **Dread Zeppelin**, which performs reggae versions of Led Zeppelin tunes with lead vocals by gigantic Elvis impersonator Tortelvis. Now that you're an Elvis expert, check out their first album, *Un-Led-Ed*, and see how many of the inside Elvis references you can catch. Example: The man who hands Tortelvis his water and towels onstage is named Charlie Haj.

> **The King and I**
> "There's never going to be another King. We are just knights in his shining armor."
> —Tony Roma, Elvis impersonator

Elvis impersonation has even made it to Broadway. *Elvis Lives* was a musical with an Elvis look-alike impersonator—Larry Seth. The play won an *Evening Standard* Award for Best Musical in 1977.

More than 50 Elvis impersonators found work in April 1992—for the U.S. Postal Service. They were hired to remind people to vote for which stamp they favored, Early or Late Elvis. (Out of just over 1 million votes cast, Early Elvis garnered 851,000 votes.) It is estimated that more than 1,200 impersonators performed through the U.S. on January 8, 1993 (Elvis' birthday) when the stamp was released.

For the Record

So you still don't think America and the world has recognized the Elvis impersonation phenomenon? At the 1984 Olympic games in Los Angeles, Elvis impersonators were part of the extravaganza. They were even at the Seoul Olympics in 1988. At the 1986 centennial and restoration celebration of the Statue of Liberty—one of the most prevalent American symbols—another American symbol was honored. Two hundred Elvises were part of the variety show staged on Liberty Island in conjunction with a fireworks display.

Oh, by the way, there's an Elvis Impersonator Hall of Fame. The organization holds annual meetings in Las Vegas to induct new members. And, you should know, there are even Priscilla impersonators out there. One reportedly married an Elvis impersonator! There is, after all, some order in the universe.

Is He Alive or Is He Risen?—Elvis Sightings

The first recorded Elvis sighting took place in 1988 at Felpausch's Supermarket in Vicksburg, Michigan, when Louise Willing reported she saw Elvis in the checkout line. The supermarket tabloid *Weekly World News* picked up the story, publishing it in May 1988, with the headline "Elvis Is Alive!" The article also reported that Elvis had been spotted eating a Whopper and drinking a milkshake at a Burger King in nearby Kalamazoo. Good for business (both newspaper and fast-food business, that is).

Since that time there have been numerous sightings: Elvis in Las Vegas; Elvis at Graceland; as a New York City policeman under the name Alvis Lishkowitz; Elvis at Chernobyl after the meltdown; Elvis at the Oscars; maybe in your living room!

One piece of evidence often used to "prove" that Elvis is alive is that an anagram of his name is L-I-V-E-S. Makes you think, doesn't it?

Remember that Jon Burrows was one of Elvis' code names? Well, someone assumed it—along with Elvis' social security number—and lived the fantasy that he was reincarnated Elvis. Whoever lived this fantasy through December 1991 has never been identified. In any case, this mystery helped further the notion that Elvis had faked his own death, leading to such unapologetically loony (and I'm being nice here) books as Gail Brewer-Giorgio's *Is Elvis Alive?* (Tudor, 1988), which was sold with a cassette allegedly containing an answering machine message of Elvis after his death.

The Word

I Saw Elvis. Powerful words. In World War II, GIs were known to write "Kilroy Was Here" on walls in both Europe and Asia as a way of asserting the American presence. During the Persian Gulf War, the chosen inscription was "I Saw Elvis." Thinking about Elvis evidently helped them get through the hard times.

The former Atlanta Falcons head coach, Jerry Glanville, is an Elvis nut who used to hold a pair of tickets for Atlanta home games in Elvis' name at the box office. Trouble is, Elvis reportedly rooted for the Cleveland Browns. Maybe now that they've moved to Baltimore, he'll reconsider.

An "Elvis Tour '88" sweatshirt has a list of sightings on the back. A clever idea, but it's long past time to update it!

Way Out There in Elvisland

Elvis has come to symbolize America to the rest of the world. But to America, he's coming to symbolize the otherworldly. There's no end to the weirdness surrounding the Kid with the Sideburns. Here's a sampling of some more strange encounters in popular culture.

Elvis Redux

Elvis reincarnate? If you can prove your child is the reincarnation of Elvis Presley, you're going to make a lot of money. You don't even have to prove it, just claim it. That's what a woman by the name of Deborah Patterson did with regard to her son Baby Aaron, born in 1978. For $20, you too can get a membership card for the Baby Elvis Fan Club plus a T-shirt and newsletter.

Elvis Phone Home

Move over ET. Elvis as an alien? Or at least aboard an alien craft? Close encounters have been described in tabloids more than once in which an alien sings Elvis or Elvis peers out of a UFO window. It makes some sense—doesn't it? Elvis claimed to have seen two UFOs himself—one in Memphis and one in Los Angeles, over his Bel Air home. Maybe the little green men were checking him out. And remember: Mulder, the character from the show *The X-Files*, is an Elvis fan. Who knows?

Along this line of an extraterrestrial connection, it has been theorized that Elvis was— I mean "is"—a cosmic entity with different incarnations on different planets. In one photograph of the planet Mars, taken by the Mariner Orbiter in the late '80s, the ridges and shadows of a mountain make it look like a human face—guess whose.

For The Record

Speaking of Mars, that grand old tabloid the *Sun* sported the following headline in its September 20, 1988 issue: "Statue of Elvis Found on Mars." The newspaper went on to breathlessly report that "stunned scientists are trying to make sense of the most extraordinary discovery in space exploration"—i.e., the statue (beamed back to earth, via satellite). The *Sun* theorized that the aliens, who apparently erected the statue, thought that Elvis was a lord or a King. At least they got the King part right.

The Word
I am and I was.
Elvis reportedly
spoke this enig-
matic phrase under
his breath at concerts during his
final concerts in 1977. Only
people in the very front rows
caught it. It has been interpreted
in a number of ways—by some
to confirm his faking his own
death, and by others to confirm
a divine purpose. Maybe he was
just mixing up Popeye's "I yam
what I yam."

The King and I
"Brief were my
days among you,
and briefer were the
words I have spoken.
But should my voice fade from
your ears, and my love vanish
in your memory, then I will
come again."

—from *The Prophet* by
Khalil Gibran, one of Elvis'
favorite books

The King and I
"I'd like to
resurrect Elvis. But
I'd be so scared of
him I don't know
whether I could do it."

—John Lennon

The Elvis Psychic Hotline

Then of course there are the psychics. Who better to contact beyond the grave than Elvis? In 1987, for instance, at the Berkeley Psychic Institute (also known as the Church of the Divine Man), a psychic by the name of Bill Falcone claimed to be regularly channeling Elvis. Falcone's story had *some* legs (bear with me here, I know we're treading on thin ice) because he interpreted Elvis in terms of Elvis and his twin, Jesse. According to Falcone, the two spirits struggled over the one surviving body: Elvis, the good spirit, who was deeply religious; and Jesse, the bad spirit who was a rebel and evolved into a bully, drug abuser, and gun nut. Why not the other way around?

Elvis is as American as apple pie—a better metaphor would be as American as hamburger. Or Elvis as fast food? One pretty gross story has it that Elvis' body was removed before the burial and replaced with a dummy, then ground up and sold by the ounce to be eaten as hamburger meat. The market for Elvis burgers? Why, the decadent rich and famous of rock and roll, who would want a piece of the King's magic.

If numerology happens to be your thing, perhaps you can find meaning in the following: Elvis used Richard Strauss' composition "Also Sprach Zarathustra" as part of his stage performance in the 1970s—you know, the momentous piece of music used in the opening sequence of the movie *2001: A Space Odyssey*. So what, you say? Well, add the month Elvis died (8) with the day he died (16) and the year he died (1977). What do you get? 2001. Not satisfied? Well, we've got other ways to get to 2001. Add the day Elvis was born (8), with the day he died (16), the age he died (42) and the year he was born (1935) and you've got… 2001! Watch out! If Elvis hasn't come back already, he may be paying us a visit with the new millennium!

Elvis in Academia

Attention, class! Professors now teach their students about Elvis. It is estimated that some 300 college courses on the King—music and sociology—are offered around the country (and abroad, too). He comes up in courses on 20th century popular music and on sociology. For example, the sociology department of the University of Mississippi offers the course "Leisure & Pop Culture" with Elvis a prominent part.

On August 6–11 in 1995, at the University of Mississippi's Oxford campus (45 miles west of Tupelo), academics held an International Conference on Elvis Presley. During this six-day festival of learning, which drew people from all over the world, the various aspects of the Elvis phenomenon were discussed. The book *In Search of Elvis: Music, Race, Art, Religion,* edited by Vernon Chadwick (Westview, 1997) has essays touching upon some of the themes discussed at the conference, which has become an annual event *Elvis after Elvis: The Posthumous Career of a Living Legend* by Gilbert B. Rodman (Routledge, 1996) is another scholarly look at the Elvis phenomenon.

Then there are the writers Greil Marcus and Peter Guralnick, who, in my opinion, have produced the best stuff ever written about Elvis. You'll read more about them in Appendix C. In particular, Marcus' collection of essays, *Dead Elvis,* explores the phenomenon of Elvis, his fans, and his critics, in the years since his death, including a withering dismissal of one of Elvis' harshest biographers, Albert Goldman.

Elvis in Art

Elvis images and references continue to show up in both folk art and fine art. We've already discussed Andy Warhol—but there's much more. In 1991, for example, the Chicago Art Association held the first annual All-Elvis Art Show with paintings, silkscreens, and sculptures relating to Elvis.

One artist—Joni Mabe—has concentrated on Elvis themes. One work is entitled *Love Letter to Elvis*, a painting with images and lettering. She is highly successful abroad with a traveling exhibition that she calls *The Traveling Panoramic Encyclopedia of Everything Elvis.*

A folk artist by the name of Reverend Howard Finster, has also received international attention. Finster grew up in the hills of west Georgia and only received schooling through the sixth grade. He has created a substantial body of Elvis-related artwork in mixed media, as well as album-cover artwork used by such bands as R.E.M. and Talking Heads.

> **Going for Gold**
> Jim Jarmusch's 1992 film *Mystery Train* examines the impact of Elvis on the lives of strange people staying in a ratty hotel in downtown Memphis (with singer Screaming Jay Hawkins as the night clerk). The Japanese tourists in search of something, *anything* Elvis-related are a particular joy.

This poster trumpets an anniversary celebration of Elvis's death. Dead Elvis XVI? We are not amused.

Presidents and Kings: Elvis in Politics, Too

It has been theorized that Bill Clinton was elected President of the United States because he reminded people of Elvis—the twang in his voice, his eyes when he smiles, the hint of a sneer. Clinton certainly made the most of any connection to the King (what's a president next to a king?), referencing his adoration of Elvis and his music on numerous occasions and lobbying for the Young Elvis stamp the winter and spring before. He even proudly bore the political nickname "Elvis." An accomplished amateur musician (saxophone), Bill Clinton knows the Elvis catalog well, and even sang an impromptu, passably good version of "Don't Be Cruel" during an interview with Charlie Rose on PBS during the 1992 campaign.

On August 20, 1992, when President George Bush accepted the Republican nomination for a second term, he mentioned Elvis twice. And, to cap off the competition for the King's blessing, Early Elvis and Late Elvis imitators attended Clinton's inaugural celebration.

Define the Elvis Obsession?—Don't Even Bother

So how does one define this obsession with Elvis? Is it a cult or simply culture? Of course, it's a culture unto itself now; whatever your bag is, Elvis is there, in music, books, art, movies, memorabilia, impersonations, sightings, and conspiracy theories. If you pay attention, you see how ubiquitous Elvis Aron Presley is as a cultural reference and realize the impact he still has on people's lives. Much of it is pure commercialization. Wild theories about Elvis always sell tabloids.

But is it a cult? You can say Elvis has *cult status*, but there's hardly an organized cult surrounding him. Deification and comparisons to Jesus by some does not a cult make. You cannot call an annual candle-light vigil an organized religion. For some impersonators, their act is a kind of religious revival, but for others it's a way to make music and make a living.

Famous peoples' deaths generate a special kind of interest. The Kennedy assassination will forever be a debated subject. Marilyn Monroe's death has been looked at again and again. Some fans still reach conspiratorial and/or mystical conclusions about the deaths of Jim Morrison and John Lennon. Morrison's gravesite outside Paris is often visited as is John Belushi's on Martha's Vineyard in Massachusetts. But the Elvis post-death phenomenon—all things considered—is in a league by itself.

> **Going for Gold**
> A book that attempts to define the cult aspect of the Elvis phenomenon is former BBC religious correspondent Ted Harrison's *Elvis People: The Cult of the King* (HarperCollins, 1992). He makes the case that the Dead Elvis phenomenon in all its manifestations might very well be "a religion in embryo."

Having Fun Yet?

One of Elvis' favorite expressions to friends and family was "Y'all havin' fun?" Let us never forget the joy that was Elvis. He started with joyful music and he has continued to bring people joy, even after his death.

> **Going for Gold**
>
> Here's an Elvis exercise. Start writing down every Elvis reference you come across in popular culture—on TV and in movies, in newspapers and magazines, in conversation, wherever. The list will get long pretty fast.

He had many names, nicknames, sobriquets, and code names in the course of his career. However you think of him—as "the Kid with the Sideburns," "the Hillbilly Cat," "the Memphis Flash," "the King of Western Bop," "the Atomic-Powered Singer," "the King of Rock and Roll," "the King," "Jon Burrows," "Elvis Aron Presley," "Elvis Aaron Presley," or simply "Elvis"—remember, despite the hardship and suffering he endured, especially early and late in life, he was—and still is—most about joy.

The Least You Need to Know

➤ Elvis impersonators are, like Elvis himself, everywhere.

➤ Some people believe strange forces are at work with Elvis. Among the bizarre theories at work: he's still alive; he's been reincarnated; and he was (or is) an alien.

➤ The culture's obsession with Elvis has, improbably, grown ever larger with each passing year.

➤ No matter how peculiar the Elvis phenomenon seems at times, it's important to remember that he merely sought to bring fun and joy to the world through his music.

Pump It Up: Collecting Elvis Records

So you wanna be an Elvis record collector? Unless you already have the start of an Elvis record collection from your past or from a parent or other relative, starting cold is difficult. You have to do your homework and you have to love the vinyl—even if you started on CDs. You'll also want a turntable, to delight in that wonderful needle-on-vinyl sound, but if you're really in it for the collecting, *playing* your records is not something you'll want to do too often. Of course, the closer to mint condition a collectible is, the greater its value.

Record collecting is not just about the music—you can hear much of it on tapes and CDs now—it's also about audio history and antiquities. This chapter will let you know what to expect in record collecting, and walk you through collecting other types of Elvis memorabilia.

Four-Step Program

Here's a summary of how I'd attack record collecting if I were you. Approaching the hobby this way will enable you to reassess your commitment along the way and decide if you want to go for the gold.

Step 1: Buy an up-to-date price guide. Go to the Antiques and Collectibles section of a bookstore and look for one of the following guides (or something similar):

➤ *The Official Price Guide to Records* or *The Official Price Guide to Elvis Presley Records and Memorabilia*, both by Jerry Osborne and published by House of Collectibles

➤ *The Price Guide to 45 RPM Records*, by Tim Neely and published by Krause

➤ *The Goldmine Price Guide to Collectible Record Albums*, by Neal Umphred and published by Krause.

Read the introductions carefully to get a handle on what general knowledge you'll be dealing with. Figure out the rating systems. Peruse the prices.

Step 2: Find a vintage record store. Almost any city has a few, or has flea markets with record dealers of varying quality, and big cities like Los Angeles and New York have *many*. Compare the prices with those in your price guide. If there's no store near you, check out mail-order lists, such as the Elvis Presley Unique Record Club, run by Paul Lichter (602-984-5026). You might even want to subscribe to *DISCoveries*, a magazine for record and CD collectors (800-334-7165).

Step 3: Specialize in one area of collecting. After that you can branch out. Maybe you want to concentrate on albums or even a narrower category, such as movie albums. (I'll get into your options in a moment.)

Step 4: Talk to a collector. Pick his or her brain. If you don't personally know anyone who collects records, you can always call one of those 800 numbers located in the advertising section of your price guides to try to find a friendly soul who will answer your questions.

Going for Gold

Don't be afraid to ask questions of pros! They probably won't care if you're not as knowledgeable as they are. Most collectors are passionate about their hobby and will probably be happy to help you—and talk your arm off. It's better to risk seeming ignorant than to get ripped off.

Oh, one other piece of advice. Go treasure hunting. Check those attics! Talk to family and friends. Someone might just have a trunk of dusty vinyl somewhere. And in that trunk there might be gold.

The three formats for vinyl records are *singles*, extended players (*EPs*), and long players (*LPs*). Some early Elvis 10-inch releases were designed to play at 78 rpm. Early releases were mono or monophonic; stereo eventually became the norm. Here's a quick rundown of the terms you need to know:

➤ A **single** record is a seven-inch record, usually with an "A" side and "B" side, designed to play at 45 RPM (revolutions per minute). These are the ones with the big hole in the middle that used to be in most jukeboxes.

➤ An **EP** or "extended player" is a seven-inch record designed to play at $33^1/_3$ RPM.

➤ An **LP** or "long-play" is a 12-inch record designed to play at $33^1/_3$ RPM.

➤ A **mono** or "monophonic" record is a system of sound reproduction using a single channel for transmission. Early record players were all monophonic.

➤ A **stereo** or "stereophonic" record is designed to be played on a system of sound reproduction using two channels for transmission. The music is separated into two different speakers to create a live effect.

There are separate listings in most price guides for changes in label design, such as from "Mono" to "Monaural" to "Orange." Also, different pressings are identified—there may have been dozens of different pressings (or stampings) of a record during a period when only three different label designs were used. Record covers have to be matched appropriately with different pressings—there were variations in cover designs of the same records too, with changes coming with re-issues. Keep in mind that there are separate prices for the actual records, covers, outer stickers, inner sleeves, and inserts.

To understand some of the variables, study record-production procedures. Collectors get confused by errors in stamping, for example, making it difficult to determine when a record really was made. In some instances, a printing error makes a collectible unique and even more valuable. Special promotional markings—such as "Dee Jay Copy"—might add worth to a record.

The Word

The term **mint** is applied to objects not marred or soiled. The only truly mint records are those never even opened, much less played. If played even once, they are **near mint**. Good quality basically means no scratches or warping.

For the Record

In 1956, a Cincinnati used-car lot had a special promotional offer: A salesman would break 50 Elvis Presley records in a customer's presence if the customer purchased a car. Take *that*, Elvis! Bet any participating sales people or customers wish they had those records now!

Return to Sender
So you found an Elvis record in your aunt's attic in near-mint condition. It's listed at $200. Think you're automatically $200 richer? Don't count on it. If you find a collector who has to have that record, you might get that price or more. But dealers expect to make a profit, so unless you find someone very hungry, expect to get half or less of its listed worth.

The grading system generally used for records includes the categories *mint, near mint, very good,* and *good.* Mint records are rare. Few Elvis fans stashed records away in their wrappers and never played them. Near mint is generally the best you can hope for. Very good usually means a collectible is worth half to two-thirds the near-mint price. Good condition means only about 10 to 20 percent of the near-mint price. Glancing through a record price guide, you might see a range of $3.00 for one near-mint item to $400 for another.

Pricing is a fluid process, relating to availability and demand. People who determine prices look at developments like the private sale of collections, auction sales, record convention trading, retail pricing, and personal want lists.

The King's Jewels

In some instances, record companies made test pressings to check out the quality of a recording or to hurry copies to a radio station before the record officially was released. They also used acetic acid and cellulose compositions to make acetates of a song that could be used for promotional purposes, but were not designed for repeated use.

If you should be so lucky to locate a test pressing or acetate (such as through a relative who used to work for a record company) of an Elvis song unreleased in any other form, you have a potential gold mine. The most valuable acetate to turn up to date was the personal recording 18-year-old Elvis made of "My Happiness" and "That's When Your Heartaches Begin."

Here's another gem. Remember I told you Elvis appeared on the cover of *TV Guide* the week of September 8-14, 1956, because of his appearance on *The Ed Sullivan Show* on Sunday, September 9? Above his photograph was written: "The Plain Truth About Elvis Presley." To promote the event, RCA and *TV Guide* collaborated on a promotional recording—an interview single—500 copies of which were to be mailed to radio stations. Along with the records were sent a list of questions that DJs could ask before playing the prerecorded answers. The records were to be returned to RCA. Several months later, the British magazine *Reveille* offered the interview by mail order, "Elvis Presley: The Truth About Me." The interview has been bootlegged. A different edit of the interview exists on the 1979 record *Elvis: A Legendary Performance* (RCA CPL 1-3082). The original pressing—one of the 500—is a valuable collector's item.

The Price Guide to 45 RPM Records by Tim Neely has a $1,000 (and above) list for sought-after records. The top three Elvis 45s are "I'll Be Back" (RCA Victor 4-834-115DJ)—a one-sided promo record with the special designation "For Academy Consideration only"—valued at $8,000; "Such a Night"/"Never Ending" (RCA Victor 47-8400DJ)—a white label promo—valued at $5,000; and "Good Luck Charm"/ "Anything That's Part of You"(RCA Victor 37-7992PS)—a special picture sleeve for Compact 33-Single record.

> **The King and I**
> "We do not tolerate Elvis Presley records at our dances, or blue jeans or ducktail haircuts."
>
> —Orren T. Freeman, high-school principal in Wichita Falls, Texas

Honor the King: Tribute Records

In the beginning, many criticized, banned, or even smashed Elvis records. But that sure changed. Indications of the impact Elvis has had on other musicians' lives can be found in the number of tribute songs and albums recorded of his music or that reference him in lyrics. By 1987, more than 1,000 songs had been written about him around the world (more than double written about The Beatles by that year); since that time there have been hundreds more.

One type of tribute is performing an entire album of Elvis songs. There are at least 12 albums by little-known performers entitled *Tribute to Elvis* or *Tribute to Elvis Presley* in which they sing Elvis songs. Some try to sound like Elvis and are part of the impersonation phenomenon.

Here are some more notable tribute albums:

> **The Word**
> A **tribute** single or album is a release containing a song or songs specifically praising an artist and/or his/her music. Primarily, a tribute record refers to a release in which the artist is actually covering the songs done by the original artist.

➤ Pat Boone released an album in 1964 entitled *Pat Boone Sings Guess Who?*

➤ A great tribute album is *King Does The King's Thing*. Albert King, the renowned blues artist, released it in 1969. He sings a great "Don't Be Cruel" and other classic early Elvis tunes.

➤ Check out Scotty Moore's album *The Guitar That Changed The World* from 1964—if you're lucky enough to find a copy.

➤ Another must-find album is the *Class of '55*. In this 1986 release, Elvis' peers— Johnny Cash, Carl Perkins, and Roy Orbison—reference the King and sing his songs.

Some notable performers who've referenced Elvis in the lyrics of songs include: The Beach Boys in "Do You Remember" (*All Summer Long*, 1964); James Brown in "That's Sweet Music" (*People*, 1980); Bob Dylan in "Went To See The Gypsy" (*New Morning*, 1970); Billy Idol in "Don't Need a Gun" (*Whiplash Smile*, 1986); John Lennon in "God" (*John Lennon Plastic Ono Band*, 1970); Little Richard in "King of Rock and Roll" (*King of Rock and Roll*, 1971); Talking Heads in "Cities" (*Fear of Music*, 1979); and U2 in "Elvis Presley and America" (*The Unforgettable Fire*, 1984).

An Honor...Sort of: Novelty Records

A *novelty* record is one that has special interest for collectors because of its humor or because of its unorthodox approach to the subject matter. There are many different kinds of novelty records, especially when it comes to Elvis. One kind of novelty record is one done in a foreign language (generally tributary in nature). For example, there's a four-volume series entitled *Elvis Hits in Deutsch*, released in 1985-86.

The Word
A **novelty** record is a release with special interest for collectors because of its humor or because of its unorthodox approach to the subject matter. With regard to the Elvis phenomenon; with foreign-language interpretations of his songs; or with imitations of his songs by impersonators...

Another type of novelty record is one with humorous songs *about* Elvis, such as the album *Elvis Presley for President*, with songs such as "I Dreamed I Was Elvis," and "I Want Elvis for Christmas." Some, such as "Elvis and the Outer Space Looters," are truly bizarre. A humorous cut about Elvis called "Ed Sullivan Self Taught" on George Carlin's comedy album *FM & AM* qualifies this record as Elvis novelty.

The musical *Joseph and the Amazing Technicolor Dreamcoat* has an Elvis-style number called "Song of The King" with references to "Don't Be Cruel," "All Shook Up," and "Treat Me Nice"; that makes it an Elvis novelty record for dedicated collectors. Paul Simon's *Graceland* also qualifies as a novelty record because of the album and song title.

Albums presenting Elvis material in other styles might also be considered Elvis novelty records—Brazil's "Rock Samba Tribute to Elvis" by Lee Jackson is an example. Songs that reference some of the oddities of Elvis' life, death, or cult status also qualify as novelty releases—an example is the Australian band Nick Cave & the Bad Seeds' 1985 gothic-punk album *The Firstborn Is Dead*. Get the reference? The title refers to Elvis' twin, Jesse Garon, as does a song from the album, "Tupelo."

Secrets and Lies: Bootlegs and Counterfeits

You've heard the word bootleg before, right? What does that have to do with illegally sold music? The word *bootleg* comes from the days when bootleggers (who illegally sold alcohol or other goods) would hide their ill-gotten spoils in the leg of a high boot. In the 20th century, a bootleg album has come to mean a record, tape, or even CD that contains music taken from various sources (such as a live concert or a studio vault recording) and illegally sold without the artist's (or copyright-holder's) permission.

All successful recording artists have been bootlegged at one time or another. Bootleggers rationalize that it's a form of flattery to the artist and that they are serving a public need, providing fans with little recorded tidbits they can't find anywhere else. The artists themselves tend to hate bootlegging because a) They make no money for their work, b) They have no control over the quality of the product, and c) The recordings might embarrass them, since they probably aren't up to snuff. A few performers—notably The Grateful Dead—do not share this view; they regard private recordings (note: the word bootlegs is *not* used here) as part of sharing in the live experience of the band.

Bootlegs of Elvis' outtakes, live performances, or rehearsals are certainly prevalent today. More than 60 have been marketed by a number of different labels.

Some are not worth the fuss, with cuts inferior to official releases. Others, however, are unique, offering special glimpses of Elvis. For instance, if you can get ahold of the album *Forever Young, Forever Beautiful*, released in 1978 by Memphis Flash Records and recorded at Elvis' friend Eddie Fadal's home in Waco, Texas in 1958 (which Elvis visited with Anita Wood, the radio and TV personality and his main pre-Priscilla flame), you can hear Elvis playing piano and singing to other people's recordings.

Counterfeit records are made to look like the originals. Some appear on the market from time to time, and the serious collector should study the telltale signs. Counterfeits are not in high demand among collectors, but they have a certain novelty appeal.

The Word
A **bootleg record** is a recording not available on a standard release. This may include concert performances, rehearsals, studio outtakes, or demos. Bootlegging is illegal, although so rampant that many artists don't bother going after the culprits anymore.

Return to Sender
The Elvis phenomenon is so huge and Elvis records so sought after that Elvis bootlegs and counterfeits, especially the early ones, are not worthless, but have intrinsic value themselves. Imagine the appeal of such products 50 years from now!

A singer by the name of Jimmy Ellis sang on several records under the Orion for Sun International, after Shelby Singleton bought out the label from Sam Phillips. Ellis sounded a lot like Elvis. His first record was "That's All Right (Mama)"/"Blue Moon of Kentucky" (Sun 1129), released in 1974. No artist was credited, leading the public to believe that it was outtakes of Elvis' famous 1954 session. RCA filed suit, and Sun had to list the singer.

Ellis also made several records in 1978-79 after Elvis' death under the name Orion. He recorded the songs "Cold, Cold Heart"/"Hello, Josephine" (Sun 1141); "Be-Bop-a-Lula"/ "Breakup" (Sun 1151); and "Don't Cry for Christmas"/"Dr. X-Mas" (Sun ?). Some fans speculated that Orion really *was* Elvis and that he was still alive. Go back to your constellation in the sky, Orion.

Still another attempt by Shelby Singleton to trick the public was a 1978 album called *Duets* (Sun 1011) listing the artists as Jerry Lee Lewis and Friends, but once again the Elvis sound-alike is Jimmy Ellis. The 1979 album *Trio* (Sun 1018) had Ellis singing with Jerry Lee Lewis, Charlie Rich, and Carl Perkins.

These records might have some value as novelty items, but there was only one King.

The Modern Approach: Buying Elvis on CDs

The future is now. Compact discs have pushed aside other technologies. If you're into the music for the music's sake and not into records as collectibles, CDs are a good way to go. Some CDs of Elvis' early material have lost something in the remastering; the Sun sound should be heard as it was recorded—in monaural, not stereo—but hey, it's still Elvis.

Your ears will be very pleased with these CD offerings:

➤ You might start with Elvis, *The King of Rock 'n' Roll—The Complete 50's Masters*, a five-CD set, released in 1992 (RCA Victor CD 2030-66050), including an informative booklet about the cuts.

➤ For a sampling of movie material, try *Burning Love (and Hits from His Movies)*, released in 1987 (RCA/Camden CADI-2595).

➤ If you want Late Elvis live, buy *Elvis Presley, As Recorded at Madison Square Garden* (RCA Victor CD 7863-54776-2).

But don't just listen to me. Head for the nearest Tower Records or wherever you buy your CDs and see what they have in stock. Check out the discography in the back for more complete listings.

Between the Sheets

To me, sheet music for any Elvis song has special meaning and interest. Collectors who venture into this area of Elvis memorabilia generally target original sheet music of the most famous songs, such as "All Shook Up," "Blue Suede Shoes," "Burning Love," "Don't Be Cruel," "Heartbreak Hotel," "Hound Dog," "Jailhouse Rock," and "Mystery Train." But there's also a demand for some of his lesser known, but odd songs, such as from movies—"Ito Eats" (*not* an O.J. Simpson trial reference!) and "Yoga Is As Yoga Does." Sheet music collecting is not particularly expensive; expect to pay between $25 and $50.

Going for Gold
Sheet music signed or inscribed by Elvis himself makes it worth more, of course. To find an original signature of Elvis' on anything is like finding buried pirate's gold; his reproduced signature is the norm. After all, he was a busy man—too busy to be stuck in a room signing his name thousands of times.

A Major Commitment

Collecting records is a long-term commitment. It's not something you do on impulse, then lose interest. A collection is built up over the years and nurtured. You have to sustain the interest. You have to care for your investment. You need a safe place for storage, where dust won't collect and where heat won't do damage. You are taking on the responsibility of preserving treasures for future generations, so don't take it lightly. Imagine yourself going into a relationship—a marriage (and to hell with your other marriage). Now that I've given you this warning, just do it!

The Least You Need to Know

➤ Collecting Elvis' records is a huge (and enjoyable) business.

➤ Record collecting is a precise art; take your time, don't act on impulse.

➤ You're taking a risk when you pay top dollar for Elvis collectibles—guard yourself against being cheated.

Thanks for the Memories (and Memorabilia)

In the field of rock-and-roll collectibles, there's Elvis and The Beatles, and then there's everybody else. What's nice about collecting Elvis is that you can become a serious collector investing in Elvis-related items, or you can just start gathering new, reasonably priced items that strike your fancy.

Background Check

In 1956, Elvis Presley Enterprises was formed by Bob Neal and Elvis to market Elvis-related products in conjunction with Special Products, Inc. When Colonel Tom Parker came aboard, it was disbanded. In 1956, Parker hired Special Products, Inc., of Beverly Hills, to market Elvis' images. Colonel Parker and Elvis established Boxcar Enterprises in 1974 to oversee all merchandising of products bearing his name, not including films or

The King and I

"It's still Elvis and the Colonel, but now, it's Elvis and Vernon Presley and the Colonel. Elvis didn't die. The body did. We're keeping up the good spirits. We're keeping Elvis alive. I talked to him this morning and he told me to carry on."

—Colonel Tom Parker, one week after Elvis died

records. (Incredibly, the bottom line on the complicated deal between Boxcar and the Presley Estate meant that Tom Parker would receive 50 percent of all moneys made worldwide on Elvis merchandise.)

Two days after Elvis' death in 1977, Parker had Vernon Presley sign over global rights of merchandising Elvis-related products to Factors, Etc., Inc., with half of their share going to the Colonel, 25 percent to Factors, and 25 percent to the Elvis Presley Estate. The 1981 ruling ended Parker's role and turned the rights over entirely to the estate. A new company—also called Elvis Presley Enterprises—currently handles merchandising for the estate. Elvis Presley Enterprises licenses companies to manufacture Elvis-related products.

Your Elvis Room

What's an *Elvis room*? You may have one underway and not even know it. This a special room dedicated to Elvis, where photographs, records, books, and memorabilia are on display. For some it's a museum of special objects. For others it's a shrine.

That is to say, you start small with an Elvis room. Choose a special corner (repaint it with a favorite Elvis color). Hang a picture of Elvis (on black velvet might be nice) and build from there. Flashing neon lighting might work. Place the Elvis objects you already own. Then add to your special place over the weeks, months, years, and decades. If your Elvis Room starts overflowing, make it an Elvis house!

For the Record

If you want to claim you're the world's biggest Elvis collector, you'll get stiff competition from a woman named Robin Rosaan. She's collected Elvis merchandise since she saw the King on television as a little girl, then saved her pennies to buy her first Elvis 45 rpm record. Today she has over 40,000 Elvis objects, thought to be the largest Elvis memorabilia collection outside of Graceland. She saw Elvis in concert 72 times and was known to Elvis and his entourage, and has been to numerous Candlelight Services at Graceland. Her collection is featured in the book *All The King's Things: The Ultimate Elvis Memorabilia Book* (1993; Bluewood Books, San Francisco).

Buyer Beware

If you buy Elvis memorabilia as an investment and hope to make money, be wary of its condition. In collectibles, after authenticity, three things matter: *condition, condition, condition*. Avoid the battered and tattered unless you just *must* have a particular item to complete a set or for nostalgia's sake.

As to *authenticity*, if you're hoping to get an authentic Elvis Presley signature, you might have a rough time of it. Through much of his career, Elvis employed people to sign names on photos and other items, so it's difficult to know which are real and which aren't. Still, it's a good thing he had help—he did, after all, have music to make.

Everything but the Kitchen Sink

There are many ways to become a collector of Elvis memorabilia. One way is to go for any Elvis-object you can afford, old or new, and put together an Elvis room as I described earlier. Another is to become a serious collector and buy objects as investments—to hopefully sell someday for a profit. Another is to start small and put together a collection of new objects of a specific nature. Whatever route you choose, prepare to be over-whelmed, at least at the start, because there is an enormous amount of Elvis memorabilia out there.

There are literally thousands of Elvis-related objects available. Here's a list to familiarize you with the wide array. This is not a catalogue of new items; nor is it a price guide of vintage items—I've indicated some you can work from. Keep in mind prices vary dramatically between the new and the old. If new, expect to pay 25 percent more than what you'd pay for a similar object without Elvis' name or image. If vintage, the price varies dramatically depending on condition and availability. That's where a price guide comes in.

If you decide to collect, take it slow so you don't feel overwhelmed. Sure we'd all love to own at least one item from each category, but you can't always get what you want. This is a plan for a lifetime of dedication, not for a few days of impulse.

Going for Gold

If you want a catalogue of Elvis-related items currently available from Graceland, send away for a catalogue at Graceland Gifts, 3734 Elvis Presley Boulevard, Memphis, TN 38116 (or call 1-800-238-2000). It's published four times a year.

➤ **Address books:** Graceland sells one with a picture of Elvis in his gold suit.

➤ **Autographs:** Original autographs can go for thousands; reproduced autographs add some value to other objects.

➤ **Afghans:** To be used as a wall-hanging or a throw rug; or simply wear the image of Vegas Elvis over your shoulders.

➤ **Belt buckles:** The King was into big fancy belt buckles. You can find replicas. Or you may find one with his name and/or image.

The King and I
"No one has ever lost money on Elvis Presley."

—Vester Presley, Elvis' uncle (Vernon's brother)

➤ **Binders:** For school kids and organized adults.

➤ **Books:** You might want to check the appendix for more info. Some books are worth collectors' gold. *The Elvis Presley Story*, edited by James Gregory with an introduction by Dick Clark, published in 1960, was sold through ads in magazines for 35 cents. It's now worth as much as $50 if you should happen to spot a mint condition copy in a used bookstore.

➤ **Boxes:** A small cedar box with Elvis' image is available; a good place to store jewelry.

➤ **Bumper stickers:** Buy two, one to collect, the other to display. I've seen the TCB logo; "Memphis: Elvis Presley Blvd."; "Rocking and Rolling with Elvis"; "I Love Elvis"; and "Elvis Lives."

➤ **Buttons:** There are hundreds of different Elvis-related buttons with Elvis' image, name, or his song titles on them. Early ones are collector's items. One optical-illusion button from the 1950s that shows Elvis in two different poses depending on how you look at it is a real find. Remember the "I Like Ike" buttons? Well, there's an "I Like Elvis" one, too.

Going for Gold
Since 1991, collectors of Elvis-related items have had a price guide to go to—*Elvis Collectibles* by Rosalie Cranor, published by Overmountain Press. Thumbing through this book will help you get a handle on what to expect in the buying and selling of Elvis stuff. Another title is *The Official Price Guide to Elvis Presley Records and Memorabilia* by Jerry Osborne, published by House of Collectibles. *The Elvis Catalogue: Memorabilia, Icons and Collectibles* by Lee Cotton (Dolphin, 1987) is an earlier source.

➤ **Candles:** Elvis devotional candles can be bought at the Graceland Candlelight Service. They can be burned wherever and whenever you like, though.

➤ **Candy bars:** In 1956, a candy bar named "Love Me Tender" was marketed. Now a bar in its wrapper can bring you $100.

➤ **Checkbook covers:** A good place to start your collection because you'll have to go here a lot.

➤ **Clock:** The original—and most valuable—Elvis clock came out in 1992. This one features a nine-inch cutout of Elvis from his appearance on *The Milton Berle Show*, outlined by a neon tube. As the hands of the clock move, so do his legs into different dance moves.

➤ **Comic books:** Elvis would be happy to know he turns up from time to time as the subject of comic books because he enjoyed reading about other superheroes.

➤ **Computer accessories:** Screen savers and mouse pads; yes, Elvis can be part of your cyber-life. Have his image come up on your screen when your computer's at rest.

➤ **Cosmetics:** No, not from the same jars Elvis himself used, but products bearing his likeness. The first Elvis-related cosmetic appeared in 1956—Elvis Presley Lipstick with colors having names like "Hound Dog Orange" and "Heartbreak Pink." You'll probably have to raid someone's Elvis room to locate a tube. A more recent line of products is the Elvis Presley Love Me Tender Bath Products from 1985, including a bubble bath and milk bath. You might find one of the gold plastic bottles with the painting of Elvis. Elvis Cologne was marketed in 1991 "For All the King's Men," with a free Elvis mug, from Trends, Inc. In 1992, The King Cologne appeared from Elvis Fragrances, Inc. Both colognes are still available.

➤ **Decanters:** Whiskey decanters sculpted like Elvis were made in the 1980s.

➤ **Dolls:** The first Elvis doll appeared in 1957. This 18-inch-tall Elvis is dressed in a plaid shirt, blue jeans, and blue suede shoes. It originally sold for $3.98. Now it could be worth thousands. In 1994, a line of Elvis dolls appeared—two with different 1950s looks and a third in black leather as he appeared in his "Comeback Special" in 1968. *Elvis: The Paper Doll Book* offers different cutouts of the King and costumes. Written by Jim Fitzgerald and illustrated by Al Gilgore and published in 1982 by St. Martin's Press, it is now considered a collector's item.

➤ **Flags:** The Confederate flag with Elvis at the center of the crossed stripes is quite a sight.

➤ **Games:** An Elvis game was marketed in 1957 ("A Party Game for the Tender of Heart. See what the Elvis Presley game predicts for you … Love, Romance, Marriage.") A real find if you're so lucky. Check your attics!

➤ **Gold records:** Today one can buy a facsimile of one of Elvis' gold records, frame and all. It looks just like the real thing. It should. It costs over a hundred dollars—and is available from Graceland Gifts in Memphis!

➤ **Guitars:** An Elvis plastic guitar was made in the 1950s, and although it's not a quality musical instrument, it's worth (with the alligator pattern carrying case) $1,200 to $1,800. And one of Elvis' earliest guitars, the Gibson J-200, is still made today; it's not a collectible, but it was, along with the Martin D-28, Elvis' instrument of choice.

Return to Sender

There are licensed manufacturers of Elvis products authorized by Elvis Presley Enterprises. For example, the National Historic Mint in Westbury, New York, makes a commemorative Elvis medallion. If you or I were to try to make a medallion or some other Elvis product, we can be sued.

➤ **Hats:** There are more than 20 styles of baseball hats, some authorized by Elvis Presley Enterprises, some not. A favorite one has the TCB ("Taking Care of Business") logo with the lightning bolt.

➤ **License plates/license plate holders:** One variety is a replica of a Tennessee plate and says "1-ELVIS." Another says: "That's Rock N' Roll: ELVIS." Don't forget how much Elvis loved cars!

➤ **Jackets:** Warm-up style silk or nylon jackets are available with Elvis' image and/or name on them. Denim jackets can also be found with embroidered portraits of Elvis. One is a copy of the tour jacket designed for a tour scheduled just before his death: It says "Elvis—In Concert" and has a TCB logo.

➤ **Jewelry:** Replicas of the TCB pendant are a fan favorite. I like the dog-tag bracelets and anklets from the 1950s and '60s.

➤ **Magazines:** If possible, dig out of those old stacks the 1963 *TV & Movie Screen,* in which Elvis answered questions from readers; or the August 15-21, 1981, *TV Guide,* with Elvis on the cover and the article "The Day Elvis Died." There are many others that, if they're in good condition, can be worth a lot of money. One item I'd love to get my hands on is the December 1987 (No. 12) monthly English language edition of *Pravda* magazine—formerly the official Soviet newspaper—which has Elvis on the cover. An article inside analyzes Elvis as both a conqueror and a victim of the American way of life.

➤ **Lighters:** Zippo has the licensing to make a commemorative lighter.

➤ **Magnets:** Isn't it appropriate to have Elvis refrigerator magnets near your junk food (maybe you'll consider turning your kitchen into an Elvis room).

➤ **Mailbox:** You can purchase an Elvis mailbox to let your thing for Elvis be known in the neighborhood. And think how orderly the universe will seem when you get your first returned letter with "Return to Sender" stamped on it.

➤ **Masks:** There have been many versions of Elvis masks from cheap to expensive. You've probably seen many of them on Halloweens past.

➤ **Medallions:** Medallions evoke royalty. Some have the King's image; some have the TCB logo. A 1956 medallion that reads, "I Want You, I Need You, I Love You-Don't Be Cruel-Hound Dog-Heartbreak Hotel" sells for about $200.

➤ **Mugs:** Get an additional jolt from your tea or coffee. And ladies, this allows you to bring Elvis close to your lips.

➤ **Music boxes/mechanical figures:** A number of music boxes have been built over the years featuring Elvis songs. The most-used song is "Love Me Tender." There's also a mechanical figure of Elvis made from die-cast steel and plastic, which has him performing on a stage. It's made in Japan—they've done a good job.

➤ **Paperweights:** A Graceland souvenir paperweight looks stately on your desk. An Elvis bust is a little more personal.

➤ **Patches:** Like buttons, a host of patches with Elvis' image and favorite logos.

➤ **Pens and pencils:** If buying an Elvis pencil, get at least two—one to sharpen and use, the other to keep intact.

➤ **Phonographs:** Two models were sold by RCA in 1956. "The Elvis Presley Autographed Special" (model 7EP45) is a four speed portable Victrola and was sold with a double EP of eight tracks, including "Blue Suede Shoes"—all for $32.95. The deluxe version (model 7EP2) has an autochanger and was sold with a second record, the album "Elvis Presley—Perfect for Parties."

➤ **Photographs:** If a relative happened to snap one of Elvis that's unpublished, it can be worth a lot of money to a publisher or collector, but I say don't sell it. Put it in an Elvis photo album and spend hours gazing at it.

➤ **Pillows:** An Elvis pillow manufactured in the 1950s is listed in price guides at $500 to $700. You can understand why a fan would pay so much to put his or head down next to Elvis every night.

➤ **Plates:** The Bradford Exchange (1-800-541-8811) offers a number of Elvis commemorative plates that I've seen being sold on television. The plates are $8\frac{1}{2}$ inches in diameter and feature full color paintings of Elvis.

➤ **Playing cards:** There are a number of different varieties. One deck has 54 different photographs of Elvis, and yes, some with a poker face.

➤ **Pocket knives:** A knife appeared on the market in the 1980s with a picture of Elvis and the inscription "Elvis Presley, King Of Rock'n'Roll, 1935-1977."

➤ **Postcards:** A fun way to go. There have been hundreds over the years, reproducing early and late photographs. Order some, put Elvis stamps on them, then send them to a fictitious address to get that "Return to Sender" notice. (My favorite Elvis cards are those featuring the wonderful '50s photographs by Alfred Wertheimer.)

➤ **Posters:** A 1978 poster "Elvis: The King Lives On" was the best-selling poster of 1978. There are numerous others that have sold well over the decades. Movie posters (called one-sheets—the kind you see behind glass at your local theater), and lobby cards are a good way to specialize if you're a movie buff too, but originals can be pricey with one-sheets going for at least $200. Concert placards can be valuable items too with the pre-Army ones the most prized and most expensive, starting at $300.

➤ **Prints:** The Franklin Mint offers a framed print of Elvis entitled "Elvis The King" with the official seal of Graceland. Price tag: $200. Still interested? If so, contact The Franklin Mint, 2710 Franklin Center, PA 19092.

281

➤ **Puzzles:** Put together a thousand pieces of this Springbok puzzle and what do you get? Why, "Elvis, The King."

➤ **Scarves:** Silk scarves, the kind Elvis tossed to the crowd in his '70s concerts, can be bought. These, of course, are not anointed with his sweat.

➤ **Sculptures:** Ceramic busts of the King's head are available. One plaster-of-Paris variety is life-size. It's like Vegas Elvis is right next to you. Elvis figurines can be hot items, too. One set from the 1950s is a pair of bookends.

➤ **Socks:** Wear Elvis memorabilia on you (or just drape them over a chair in your Elvis room).

➤ **Soda cans:** Called an "art can," this 12-ounce aluminum can decorated with an image of Elvis shakes when you turn it on. It says "All Shook Up" on it.

For the Record

The story goes that Elvis came up with the idea of the song "All Shook Up" from his favorite soda, Pepsi. Fact or apocraphy? We'll never know—but it does sound great.

➤ **Spoons:** Eat your breakfast cereal with Elvis spoons. One spoon available has an emblem on the handle with Elvis in his black leather outfit. Wheaties and Elvis—a great way to start your day.

➤ **Stamps:** See the section coming up.

➤ **Stationery:** You can write a love letter to Elvis with special Elvis stationery. You can also find diaries and notebooks.

➤ **Stickers:** Stickers are a fun and inexpensive way to go. You can keep them intact or you can fill up an Elvis Presley notebook with them.

➤ **Street signs:** Copies of the Elvis Presley Boulevard sign are for sale as souvenirs of Memphis. They're full size with white lettering on a green background.

➤ **Stuffed animals:** Can you guess the two main kinds? Why, hound dogs and teddy bears of course. What else?

➤ **Tickets:** Tickets to concerts scheduled for after Elvis' death are valuable if you can get a fan to part with his or hers; I've seen them for sale at around $100. Ticket stubs are worth much less, usually under $50. A June 8, 1956, Shrine Auditorium concert in Los Angeles has the King's name spelled as "Alvis Presley," making them extra valuable.

➤ **Ties:** There are many styles, most showing a close-up of his face. I like the wide satin ones. An Elvis bolo tie from the 1950s is worth $150 to $250.

➤ **Toilet seats:** Didn't I say everything but the kitchen sink was available when it came to Elvis memorabilia?

➤ **Toothpick holders:** One variety exists so far. It says "Elvis Presley 1935-1977." Used Elvis toothpicks are rare and worth millions. (Kidding, just kidding!)

➤ **Towels:** Ladies, take a bath, then wrap Elvis around you.

Return to Sender
So you think you can buy Elvis' sweat? A product on the market from Maiden Jestz, Inc. since 1985 is a vial of what's supposed to be Elvis' sweat. It isn't, of course. Elvis Presley Enterprises has tried to block its sale, but the stuff can still be found at novelty stores.

➤ **Trading cards:** Bubble gum cards were sold in 1957 and 1978. Colonel Parker had a hand in both. The 1978 cards were licensed by Boxcar Enterprises and manufactured by Donruss, Inc., in Memphis. The latest attempt was the Elvis Collection in 1993 (minus the gum). An intact original bubble-gum card counter display from 1956 is worth at least $1,200.

➤ **T-shirts:** But of course what's America without T-shirts. And there are many with Elvis' portrait on them. Sweatshirts too—one collector's item is the "Elvis Tour '88" sweatshirt with a chronology of sightings on the back.

➤ **Wallets:** The money spent on Elvis wallets in the 1950s was well worth it—now we're talking a dollar value of $250 to $350.

➤ **Wallhangings:** Different tapestries can be found with images of the King. The material most closely associated with him is black velvet: Images of Elvis in day-glo paint on black velvet are a favorite collector's item and can be found on the walls of most Elvis rooms.

Return to Sender
So you think items that once belonged to Elvis or were held by Elvis never come on the market anymore? As recently as 1993, the guitar Elvis played to Ann-Margret in the film *Viva Las Vegas* was sold at a rock memorabilia auction in San Francisco. The price tag? A mere $22,000.

➤ **Wands:** The "Find Elvis" wand is an eight-inch Lucite tube with a clear viscous liquid in which glitter is suspended along with a tiny picture of Elvis and his car. They were first marketed in 1992.

➤ **Watches:** There are many varieties with Elvis likenesses. If you're well off, you might be able to purchase a watch Elvis actually owned at an auction. His 1969 Mathey-Tissot watch is worth at least $6,000 today.

➤ **Wine:** Yes, there's an "Always Elvis Wine." (And do we care that Elvis didn't drink wine?) Hard to find—perhaps commando raids on people's wine cellars. If you want to just see them, four bottles are on display, but nor for sale, at the All Elvis Shop at the International Marketplace at 2330 Kalakaua in Hawaii. The wine, incidentally, was a white Italian, called blanc d'oro (white gold).

Quite a list, isn't it? And I could go on and on. I suppose you're wondering what my favorite Elvis collectible is—a ticket stub to a Las Vegas concert. My price guide says it's only worth $15, but talk about memories!

For Stamp Collectors

Are you a philatelist (stamp collector)? Or do you want to start your Elvis collection for a mere 29 cents?

In 1992-93, Elvis received a lot of attention because of the U.S. Postal Service's issuing of a commemorative Elvis 29-cent stamp, the first of the 14-part Legends of American Music stamp series. This was more controversial than you'd think. Some people protested the idea that America would honor someone who died of an overdose—Elvis, still the center of the storm. In any case, the first step was to organize a design competition. After the field narrowed to two designs—one with Elvis as a young rockabilly performer, the other as an older Vegas performer—the public was asked to choose between a Young Elvis image, designed by Mark Stutzman of Mountain Lake, Maryland, and an older image designed by John Berkey of Excelsior, Minnesota.

On April 6, 1992, yellow ballot cards appeared in post offices around the country. In more than 50 locations Elvis impersonators appeared with them, reminding people to vote.

At 7:36 a.m., on June 4, 1992, Priscilla Presley announced the winner at Graceland—Young Elvis. Postmaster General Anthony Frank gave the final count—851,000 votes to 277,000. A 71-year-old woman by the name of Pat Geiger was flown in by the Elvis Presley Estate for the occasion—since 1984, she had spearheaded the drive for an Elvis stamp.

With all the fuss about the U.S. stamp, in July Publishers Clearing House marketed a limited-edition series of nine Elvis stamps from other countries. Other countries hadn't waited so long to honor the King philatelically.

For the Record

The first Elvis Presley postage stamp was issued by the Caribbean island of Grenada. It's hard to believe, but Grenada honored the King in 1979, 13 years before the U.S. got its act together.

In November 1992, the Postal Service sent a promotional brochure to those people whose addresses they had received during the earlier polling—order now for the January release: an Elvis Stamp Sleeve and Sheet of Stamps for $11.60; an Elvis Commemorative Album with a block of four mint stamps for $19.95; a Limited-Edition Elvis Print for $14.95; the "First Day" Ceremony Program with an Elvis stamp and a Graceland cancellation for $5.95. Or one could have *everything* for $44.95.

The U.S. Postal Service was in the Elvis memorabilia business! Talk about a stamp of approval for the Kid with the Sideburns. And why, you ask, is the Post Office so interested in Elvis? According to George Alevizos, one of the country's preeminent philatelists, "Commemorative stamps are enormously profitable for the U.S. Postal Service because— and this may seem, at first blush, counter-intuitive—people don't use them. They collect them. Thus, there is little or no liability to the Postal Service (i.e., they don't have to deliver a letter) other than the printing cost. Because the Elvis commemorative was, by far, the largest seller in U.S. Postal history, it is also, by far, the most profitable stamp ever issued anywhere, with profits certainly in excess of $100 million." Not to mention that people still have to buy stamps for their mail. Once again, as with all things Elvis, everybody—including our public institutions, made money on the King.

On January 8 (Elvis' birthday), at Graceland, Postmaster General Marvin Runyon officially released 500 million Elvis stamps for sale. Jack Soden, CEO of Elvis Presley Enterprises was on hand, as was Mark Stutzman, who had designed the winning image. The first-day issue had a stamp of the gates at Graceland on the postcard. The Postal Service also released a booklet entitled *Elvis Presley,* about Elvis' contributions to music. Priscilla attended and so did Lisa Marie in her first major public appearance. In post offices around the country, some 1,200 Elvis impersonators performed to mark the occasion.

Return to Sender

The U.S. Postal Service had planned that Graceland issue the first Elvis stamps on January 8. But it had mistakenly sent a shipment of stamps nearly two weeks early to Amarillo, TX. The Amarillo post office sold out their stamps in late December. Collectors should realize that the true first-day issues were from Amarillo, not Graceland. Elvis must have been in Texas that day.

Elvis fans and collectors are ingenious. Many of them sent letters to made-up names and addresses in the hope that the letters would be returned to them with the official postal mark: "Return to Sender—No Such Number." Talk about life imitating art!

Soon after the issuing of the stamp, Graceland Gifts put out a catalogue of items with the Elvis stamp reproduced on them, from baseball caps to earrings to music boxes to oven mitts to spoons.

The Once and Future King

Studying, listening to, and collecting Elvis is more than about keeping past memories of Elvis. It's also about keeping your own past alive as well. And it's also about remembering the birth and growth of rock and roll, about how America and the world was changed by Elvis and all that followed.

The cover of the 1960 album His Hand in Mine.

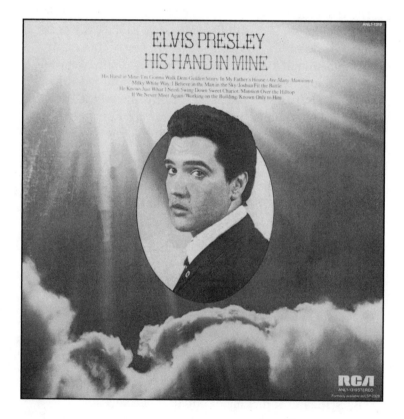

But there's something else to collecting Elvis. It's about future memories. Living with collectible Elvis and sharing your collection provides experiences now that you can enjoy later. Turning a younger person on to Elvis with your passion (demonstrated by your collection), and then seeing that person listen to Elvis and discover the magic in his music, is a very satisfying experience. You've passed something on that can enrich another life. Isn't that what Elvis was really all about?

The Least You Need to Know

➤ Elvis collectibles are some of the most sought after of all rock and roll collectibles.

➤ There are more different Elvis collectibles than for any other entertainer.

➤ The "young" Elvis stamp was the largest selling, most profitable commemorative stamp in history.

➤ Elvis collectibles range from buttons to toilet seat covers to wands (probably even to the kitchen sink).

➤ When buying Elvis memorabilia, check for authenticity and condition.

State of Grace

And now, it's time to start planning your own pilgrimage to the Holy Land: Memphis, Tennessee—Elvis Presley Boulevard—and, the home of the King, Graceland. When you think of Elvis, you probably imagine him, if not on-stage or on-screen, at his beloved Graceland.

Elvis and his folks, Gladys and Vernon, moved into Graceland on April 10, 1957. This is the place Elvis always wanted to be on holidays. This is where he died, and it was also where his funeral was held. Graceland has also been a center for Elvis controversy and fan communion: It's where Elvis was re-interred following rumors of a plot to steal his corpse from Forest Hill Cemetery and hold it for ransom, and it's the shrine where Elvis devotees flock. Graceland may be the second most famous house in America, after the White House.

In this chapter I'll talk about Graceland, what it meant to Elvis, what it means to his fans, and what it tells us about the King. I'll also give you practical information about getting to Graceland and how best to enjoy your visit. If you haven't visited already, you'd better get packin'.

Going to Graceland: Not Just a Vacation, a Pilgrimage

On November 27, 1977, the Meditation Garden—Elvis' gravesite—was opened to the public. The rest of Graceland opened on June 7, 1982. (Rather than sell Elvis' beloved home, Priscilla Presley, acting for her daughter Lisa Marie, decided to make the mansion and grounds a permanent memorial to the King.)

It's always rewarding to visit Graceland, but the annual Elvis Week, celebrated during the seven days prior to the anniversary of his death on August 16, offers the most intense Elvis experience one can have. This all-Elvis week includes performances, lectures, contests, parties, dances, non-stop Elvis shopping opportunities, celebrity guests, and much, much more. If you don't like crowds, don't even think about attending Elvis Week.

Going for Gold
The Elvis International Forum is the licensed magazine recommended by Graceland—and by me. A full-color, quarterly publication, it covers all things Elvis and is a bargain at $19.95 ($29.95 foreign). To get your subscription, call 1-805-379-4012.

Highlighting Graceland's semi-religious nature is the powerfully emotional Annual Candlelight Service (first sponsored by the Elvis Country Fan Club of Austin, Texas), which is held annually on the anniversary of the King's death, August 16th. Typically, as many as 10,000 fans show up at Graceland for the service. In 1987, on the 10th anniversary of his death, more than 50,000 fans came to remember him. Elvis Presley Boulevard is closed off and devotees carry candles through the Meditation Garden to Elvis' grave. The service begins at 10 p.m. and lasts until 5 a.m. There's no better way to experience the emotional attachment people feel to Elvis than to participate in the Candlelight Service.

Graceland's famous gates.

Help Me Information, Get Me Memphis, Tennessee

The southern portion of Bellevue Street, also known as Highway 51 South—the stretch from the Memphis city limits to the Mississippi border—was renamed Elvis Presley Boulevard in 1971.

Here's the official information on Graceland's address, schedule, hours, admission, and reservations.

Address: 3764 Elvis Presley Boulevard, Memphis, Tennessee 38116.

Schedule: Open 7 days a week, March-October; closed Tuesdays, November-February; closed Thanksgiving, Christmas, and New Year's Day.

Hours: 8 a.m. to 6 p.m. during the summer; 9 a.m. to 5 p.m. the rest of the year.

Admission: I recommend the guided "Platinum Tour Package" as the best way to see Graceland; the tour includes the mansion, the Sincerely Elvis Museum and all other Graceland attractions. The cost is $18.50 for adults, $16.50 for seniors, $11 for children 7-12 and is free for children 6 and under. Parking: $5.00

Reservations: Suggested. Call (800) 238-2000.

Return to Sender
Don't bother trying to sneak a souvenir street sign from Elvis Presley Boulevard. So many people had the same idea that the city of Memphis stopped replacing them. You can buy them in most Graceland gift shops.

Remember, travelers, Graceland is busy, busy, busy. I would recommend getting there early in the day (take advantage of the unusual 8 a.m. opening.) Allow at least a whole day to do everything comfortably, but more if you can swing it.

How Far to Graceland?

In planning your trip, remember flying will get you there faster, but driving—a pink Cadillac would be perfect—will make it feel more like the mecca it really is.

For the Record

Elvis' best-known car, his famous 1955 pink Cadillac—which he gave to his mother—was originally blue; Elvis had it painted "Studebaker pink. It was Elvis' second Caddy, the first, a secondhand '40s sedan, burned up while Elvis, Bill Black, and Scotty Moore were criss-crossing the South in 1955."

The distance to Graceland from ...

Atlanta	371 miles
Boston	1,296
Chicago	530
Cleveland	712
Denver	1,040
Detroit	713
Houston	516
Indianapolis	436
Kansas City	451
Los Angeles	1,817
Miami	1,018
Minneapolis-St. Paul	826
Montreal	1,332
New Orleans	390
New York	1,100
Philadelphia	1,000
St. Louis	285
San Francisco	2,125
Seattle	2,290
Washington, D.C.	975

Graceland, Inside and Out

Graceland stands on $13^3/_4$ acres. It was originally a farmhouse built in the early 1860s on 500 acres in Whitehaven by publisher S.E. Toof of the *Memphis Daily Appeal*, who named it after his daughter, Grace. The present building was built in 1939 by Dr. Thomas and Ruth Moore Thomas, niece of Grace Toof. It was constructed of Tennessee and Mississippi limestone in the Georgian colonial style, with Corinthian columns on the front portico.

Ruth, their daughter, a professional musician, sold Graceland to Elvis. She had been letting the Christian Graceland Church use it for services.

When Elvis bought Graceland, it consisted of the two-story house, a barn, and a small smokehouse. He renovated the buildings and grounds extensively, painted the exterior blue and gold—the mansion positively glows at night—and added on the Trophy and Jungle Rooms. He built a stone fence and wrought-iron gate, other outbuildings, a carport, a swimming pool and bath house, a garden, and a racquetball court. Graceland would ultimately have 23 rooms—eight of them bedrooms—plus eight full bathrooms and four half-baths.

The Word
Grace is defined in the dictionary in a couple of ways appropriate to Elvis: 1) The quality of being attractive, especially in movement, manner, or design; and 2) God's loving mercy toward mankind. Grace seems perfectly appropriate for the dream home and final resting place of Elvis Presley.

For the Record

Paul Simon sings about redemption on his album *Graceland*, which won the Grammy for Album of the Year in 1987. His song "Graceland" won a Grammy for Record of the Year in 1988. Simon admits imitating Elvis in hairstyle, clothing, and stage performing early in his career, though the song Graceland was more *inspired* by Graceland than *about* it.

Enter the Gates

The wall surrounding the estate of Graceland is made from Alabama fieldstone. It's sometimes referred to as the "Graffiti Wall" because visitors write sentiments to Elvis on it. A crew cleans the wall regularly with a pressurized water system, allowing for a new round of messages. From the book *Dear Elvis* by Daniel Wright, here's a sampling:

In the great divide between a life with meaning and one without, there is Graceland. —D.B.

You wouldn't have liked the way Caddies look today, anyway. —Mary Lou

The big men wear long sideburns in memory of Elvis and tasty snack cakes.

It's OK to love Elvis' music, but you shouldn't worship him. The only way to get to heaven is through ~~Jesus Christ~~ Jerry Lee Lewis.

The wrought-iron gates at Graceland, among the most famous in the world, show two guitar players and musical notes. Elvis used to wander down to the gates to sign autographs, pose for photos, and chat with fans. Now, on each anniversary of his death, thousands of fans gather at the gates to honor the King's memory and hold the Annual Candlelight Service.

Living It Up

The bisque-colored living room—where his funeral was held—has mostly white furniture with a long couch and two arm chairs. The long, black, gold, and glass coffee table matches the "sunburst" clock, hanging on the mirrored wall over the marble fireplace. An open doorway to the music room is flanked by stained peacocks.

The King Will Be Dining In

For most of Elvis' time at Graceland, the dining room had a blue, white, and gold color scheme (as it is today), but in 1974, it was redone in red. Red curtains were also sometimes added at Christmas time, since this is where Elvis had the tree set up—behind where he sat at the head of the table and in front of the picture window. Wall mirrors give the room a larger feel.

Dinner at Graceland was usually served at 9 or 10 p.m. (although Elvis' eating schedule was erratic). Elvis and his friends sometimes used the dining room to play poker.

Music in Grand Style

In the gold-curtained music room stood a piano (three different grands or baby grands over the years). Elvis was a pianist as well as a guitar player, and often entertained friends and family in this room. The wall mirror was moved here from the Presleys' house on Audubon Drive where they lived before buying Graceland.

Couch-Potato Heaven

A total of 16 television sets were spread throughout Graceland at the time of Elvis' death. Three of them were wall-mounted in the TV Room, as Elvis liked to watch three sporting events at once. (Elvis had also heard that President Lyndon Johnson watched all three networks simultaneously—and what's fit for a president is certainly fit for a King.)

The TV Room also held stereo equipment. A built-in jukebox played Elvis' collection of 45s. His album collection was also in this room, including gospel, R&B, country, pop, jazz, classical, and opera. The hi-fi equipment in the TV Room was wired to speakers throughout Graceland.

A panel near the bar opened to reveal a movie projector, which was operated from an adjoining projection room. Elvis had a collection of feature films and home movies, as well as 16mm prints of all his own films.

The room was decorated for the last time in 1974 with predominantly chrome and glass themes. On a wall painted in yellow, white, and blue is a lightning-bolt design which Elvis used in conjunction with his TCB logo.

A vinyl yellow bar was used in entertaining company. "Company" for Elvis meant family, local officials, musicians, and women—especially women. You might say that in many cases the vinyl yellow bar was a fueling station on the way to the bedroom upstairs, but I'll get into the women thing later.

Return to Sender

Now folks, remember to mind your manners when visiting Graceland. Don't expect to see Elvis' bedroom. Don't expect to be served fried peanut-butter-and-banana sandwiches. And don't make fun of the Elvis impersonators—no matter how lame their appearance, they have feelings too.

Home Office

The office, with metal furniture very typical for the 1950s, was run by Vernon Presley with a staff of secretaries. It was largely used for household business and to answer fan mail. (Colonel Tom Parker had his own office in Madison, Tennessee.)

Elvis had both green and red telephones throughout Graceland; green for a multi-line system and red for an intercom system.

For the Record

Elvis held a famous press conference from Vernon's desk on March 8, 1960, about his Army tour in Germany. The desk is therefore associated with the King (wrongly thought by some to be one of his "thrones"). But this was truly Vernon's domain, where he ran the day-to-day business of Graceland.

Rack 'Em Up: The Pool Room

Elvis bought the professional quality pool table about the time he bought Graceland. The cue stand is a converted Edwardian-style hat and umbrella stand. The stained-glass lightshade over the pool table is Tiffany.

The walls of the Pool Room were decorated in 1974 with more than 350 yards of fabric, mixing European and Asian themes.

Elvis' favorite games were 8-Ball and Rotation; a skilled player, he more than held his own in competition with friends.

Elvis the Wild Man: The Jungle Room

The Jungle Room is an add-on, built in the mid-1960s. It started as a screened-in porch, then was closed in as a den, with paneled walls and carpeted floor and ceiling. They say Elvis spent 30 minutes picking out the furniture for the Jungle Room (but whether that's remarkably fast or remarkably slow, they don't say). The wood-and-fur armchairs reminded Elvis of Hawaii. A mirror has an exotic feathered frame. The wooden bar is carved in animal and totem figures. Elvis had an indoor waterfall built out of stone.

Because of the Jungle Room's great acoustics, Elvis used it as a rehearsal room as well as for recordings, including much of the material for the album *Moody Blue*. (RCA parked their equipment truck in the backyard and ran wires to the Jungle Room.)

For the Record

Fox Mulder (as played by David Duchovny) of the hit series *The X-Files* is a huge Elvis fan. In one episode he announces to his female partner Scully (Gillian Anderson) that he is going somewhere on his own on a spiritual quest. We next see him in the Jungle Room at Graceland wearing shades and posing like the King.

Trophy Room: Big Room, Hall of Gold, and Time Line

Elvis originally stored his gold records in the TV Room. What became known as the Trophy Room was an add-on patio, once used for parties and briefly as a "slot car" track—toy racing cars. It was redone as a place to hold Elvis' awards and memorabilia, and now consists of the Hall of Gold (with cases holding Elvis' gold records); a wall display, known as the Time Line, tracing Elvis' early years in photos and documents; and the Big Room, which contains music and Hollywood memorabilia, including clothing, scripts, guitars, keys to cities, letters, honorary badges, and guns.

Upstairs at Graceland

The large staircase off the hall under the cut-glass chandelier leads to Graceland's second story. Unfortunately, it's off-limits to visitors. If you could go up there, you'd see Elvis' master suite, including the bedroom, wardrobe rooms, bath, and office, as well as Lisa Marie's bedroom and bath (where he died).

Elvis made many grand entrances down the stairs to greet guests. Before his funeral, his body lay in state in the hall at the foot of the stairs.

Smokin'!

During most of Elvis' time at Graceland, the historic brick smokehouse, once used to cure meats, was utilized for storage. For a short time, however, Elvis and friends used it as a gun firing range, standing outside and firing at a target inside.

Racquetball Anyone?

In 1975, advised by a doctor to exercise more, Elvis constructed a 2,240-square-foot Racquetball Building. A lower lounge has furniture, a piano, a half bath, and a glass wall for viewing the racquetball court. An upper lounge has furniture, a pinball machine, a bar, and weight-lifting equipment. Located upstairs is Elvis' private dressing room, with a shower, bath, Jacuzzi, and massage table, plus a second dressing area for friends (off-limits to visitors).

The Racquetball Building also has a special display area, with 110 gold, platinum, and multi-platinum albums and singles, posthumously awarded to Elvis on August 12, 1992, the 15th anniversary of his death, by RCA and the Recording Industry Association of America. In addition, RCA presented a nine-foot, etched-glass trophy, recognizing Elvis as "the Greatest Recording Artist of All Time."

Whose Barn? What Barn? My Barn!

The beautiful wood barn, now painted a stately white, was part of Graceland when Elvis bought the property. He used it as a stable for horses and mules.

His favorite horse was a golden palomino quarterhorse named Rising Sun. For a time, "House of the Rising Sun" was written on the barn door. Another favorite was a Tennessee Walking Horse named Bear.

Return to Sender
Graceland's swimming pool is shaped like a tear drop, not a guitar as many fans believe.

Sharing Elvis' Thoughts: Meditation Garden

The Meditation Garden (sometimes referred to as "Meditation Gardens"), surrounded by a circular brick wall with a columned walkway and a fountain at its center, was built in 1963 as a place of retreat for Elvis. It's come to be a place of pilgrimage for Elvis devotees. On October 2, 1977, the bodies of Elvis and his mother were moved to Graceland from Forest Hills Cemetery by his father. Vernon and his mother Minnie Mae (known as Grandma Presley) have also since been buried there. Although Elvis' twin Jesse Garon still rests in Tupelo (at an unmarked grave in the Priceville Cemetery), there is a plaque honoring him. The Presley family monument—a statue of Jesus with two angels—was also brought to the Garden from Forest Hill Cemetery.

The inscription Vernon Presley wrote for his son's grave marker goes as follows:

He was a precious gift from God
We cherished and loved dearly.

He had a God-given talent that he shared
with the world. And without a doubt,
He became most widely acclaimed;
capturing the hearts of young and old alike.

He was admired not only as an entertainer,
But as the great humanitarian that he was;
For his generosity, and his kind feelings
For his fellow man.

He revolutionized the field of music and
Received its highest awards.

He became a living legend in his own time,
Earning the respect and love of millions.

God saw that he needed some rest and
Called him home to be with Him.

We miss you, Son and Daddy. I thank God
that he gave us you as our son.

The front of Graceland as it appears today.

Graceland Stores

Collecting Elvis memorabilia is part of what you want to do, right? Then check out the stores at Graceland. Here are just a few of the things you'll find:

➤ Elvis Threads: Elvis-style clothing, jackets, sweatshirts, T-shirts, hats, and so on.

➤ EPs and LPs

➤ The 50% Off Gift Shop

➤ Gallery Elvis: Original artwork, limited edition collectibles, jewelry

➤ Good Rockin' Tonight: Books, posters, CDs, audiotapes, videotapes

➤ The Gotta Get to Memphis Gift Shop

➤ The Graceland Gift Shop

➤ The Graceland Photo Shop

➤ The Relive and Magic Museum and Gift Shop

Prices in these stores may run a little higher than mail outlets handling Elvis memorabilia (see Chapter 24), but they are well-stocked and you can be confident that every product is approved by Elvis Presley Enterprises. Plus, there's something empowering about buying Elvis memorabilia at Elvis' own special corner of the universe.

The Elvis Presley Automobile Museum

Return to Sender
The pink Cadillac in front of the Automobile Museum never belonged to Elvis—it was a salad bar at the King's Heartbreak Hotel Restaurant in Memphis. Graceland decided to renovate it and place it in front of the museum. Thousands of people have their picture taken next to it, making it perhaps the world's most-photographed car.

Across the highway from Graceland, several doors down from the Visitors Plaza, you'll find the Automobile Museum. The extensive collection of Elvis' cars and motorcycles includes the most famous car in the world—the pink 1957 Cadillac Fleetwood 250, known as his mother's although she didn't drive or even have a license. Other vehicles: a purple 1956 Cadillac Eldorado convertible, 1971 and 1973 Stutz Blackhawks, a white 956 Continental Mark II, a white 1971 Mercedes Benz 280 SL Roadster, and a black 1975 Dino Ferrari 308 GTT4 Coupe. You can also see 1957 and 1976 Harley-Davidson motorcycles.

The museum has a movie theater designed as a drive-in theater and named after a real one—Highway 51 Drive-In—which shows clips of Elvis movies. There is also a mock-up of a '50s-style gas station with two pumps.

Flying High at Graceland

In 1975, Elvis purchased a Convair 880, built by General Dynamics of San Diego, California. The cost: $250,000. Remarkably, customization cost over three times the purchase price, $800,000. (Elvis named it the *Lisa Marie* and changed the registration number to N 880 EP.) It sports the famous TCB logo. Elvis referred to the *Lisa Marie* jet as "Hound Dog One" and "Flying Graceland." It sat 28 lucky folks. You, too, can have the good fortune to be able to hang out a bit in this elegant steel tube—it's open for viewing.

Also in 1975, Elvis purchased a JetStar, built by Lockheed of Georgia, registration number N 777 EP. Elvis nicknamed this craft "Hound Dog Two." This smaller jet sat 10. You can tour this plane too.

"Sincerely Elvis" Exhibit

The exhibit at Graceland's Visitors Plaza across the highway from the mansion is called "Sincerely Elvis" and includes numerous personal items once belonging to the King, from gold boxing gloves autographed by Mohammad Ali to stage jumpsuits.

For the Record

Mohammad Ali autographed his Everlast boxing gloves to Elvis thusly: (right) "To Elvis, My main fan."; (left) "Elvis, you are the greatest." He signed his name and added "Peace, 1973" on both gloves.

The Elvis Presley Museum

The Elvis Presley Museum sits across from Graceland at 3350 Elvis Presley Boulevard. It was founded by Elvis' friend, the singer Jimmy Velvet in 1979 and has among its collection six automobiles and a motorcycle, Elvis' family Bible, Elvis' wedding album, clothing and jewelry, and acetate recordings. A touring version of the museum travels to other towns.

Other Sacred Sites

There are numerous other places to seek out Elvis. You can feel marvelous in Memphis, terrific in Tupelo, knowledgeable in Nashville, lucky in Las Vegas, and enduringly committed to everything Elvis everywhere else.

Sun Studios and the Elvis Presley Statue

In Memphis, go also to Sun Studios at 706 Union Avenue. Sun was where the defining sound first came together; it is where the legend started.

The record label, Sun Records, was founded by Sam Phillips on Union Avenue in 1952, along with the Memphis Recording Service, in a building that previously housed a radiator shop. The studio was 30 × 18 feet and had a single piano. In the late 1950s, Phillips moved Sun Records to 639 Madison Avenue, from where he launched the Phillips International label. Shelby Singleton bought Sun Records from Phillips in 1969 and moved the company to Nashville. The original Sun Studios building came to house a plumbing company, then an auto-parts store. After Elvis' death, Grayline Tours restored the building, and it was eventually designated a national landmark.

Also in Memphis, you have to go see the Elvis Presley Statue, near the corner of Beale and Main in Elvis Presley Plaza (901) 526-0110. The statue, sculpted by Eric Parks and unveiled in 1980, captures the spirit of Elvis: the way he stood, the way he gripped a guitar, and the way he looked at you.

Lansky's, clothier to the King, is located at 126 Beale Street. Call for an appointment at (901) 525-1521. Not far from there is Alfred's at 197 Beale Street with Elvis memorabilia, gold records, and a model of Graceland.

Tupelo, MS: Almost Bethlehem

Of course, you should also make a pilgrimage to Elvis' birthplace—Tupelo, a Lee County town in the northeast corner of the State of Mississippi, about 100 miles from Memphis. (Elvis was in fact born in East Tupelo, which was annexed by Tupelo 13 years later.) At the time of his birth, the population of Tupelo and East Tupelo was about 6,000. Tupelo's population is now over 30,000 and growing.

The small house Elvis was born in, now 306 Elvis Presley Drive, was designated as a state historical site by the Mississippi Department of Archives and History on January 8, 1978. Nearby stands the Elvis Presley Birthplace Museum.

The Elvis Presley Park in Tupelo is a 13$^1/_2$ -acre park encompassing Elvis' birthplace and containing a chapel, a community building, and a swimming pool.

For the Record

When Elvis was asked what kind of monument, if any, he would want built in his honor in Tupelo, he answered, "A chapel for my fans to meditate in." He would posthumously get his wish with Elvis Presley Chapel. The 1,200-square-foot building, with redwood siding and 12 pews, was dedicated on January 8, 1979. Vernon Presley dedicated the family Bible and Colonel Tom Parker arranged the purchase of the organ.

Return to Sender

In the 1979 TV-movie *Elvis* (produced by Dick Clark Pictures after the King's death), Jesse's grave is depicted with a headstone. Not so. At the time of Jesse's burial, the Presleys were too poor to afford a headstone.

Another place of great meaning is the Priceville Cemetery, located three miles northeast of Tupelo on Feemster Lake Road, where Elvis' brother Jesse Garon was buried in an unmarked grave. Only a few people know where the exact spot is, although it is said to be near a tree. No matter—just being at the cemetery is enough for many fans to sense the spirit of Jesse.

Also worth seeing are other local sites relevant to Elvis' childhood, including: the fairgrounds, Lawhon Elementary School (140 Lake Street, East Tupelo), Milam Junior High School (720 West Jefferson), the First Assembly of God Church (now the First Apostolic Church of Jesus Christ,

206 Adams St.), the Lyric Theater at North Broadway and Court streets (the Strand Theatre no longer exists), Leake and Goodlett Lumberyard (105 East Main Street), Tupelo Garment Company, and WELO radio station.

Eat at the Elvis McDonald's, 372 South Gloser, south of Main Street for a unique slant on the familiar fast food. Stay at the Elvis Presley Lake and Campground, five miles north of his birthplace (off Canal Extended, north of New Highway 78) to get a sense of the countryside he saw as a child.

Nashville: The Country Capital Owes Elvis Big-Time

The story of Elvis playing the Grand Ole Opry is legendary. On October 2, 1954, young Elvis and musicians Bill Black and Scotty Moore played at the country music show at Ryman Auditorium in Nashville. The audience was less than enthusiastic and, afterwards, talent coordinator Jim Denny suggested Elvis "go back to driving a truck." But Ernest Tubb, the "King of Country Music" told Elvis "not to worry, you have done a fine job and the audience just doesn't know."

Elvis recorded in various Nashville studios over the years—from "I Got a Woman" on January 10, 1956, at RCA Nashville's studios to "I, John" on June 9, 1971. The *Elvis in Nashville* album (1988) includes some of his sessions there.

Elvis also repeatedly paid homage to his country music roots, even though the country music community saw him as a threat to their commercial standing in the early years (which he certainly turned out to be).

If you're serious about Elvis, visit the following places in Nashville:

➤ Car Collector's Hall of Fame, 1534 Demonbreun Street, on Music Row, (615) 255-6804. See Elvis' 1976 Eldorado.

➤ Country Music Hall of Fame, 4 Music Square, (615) 256-1639. See Elvis' Fleetwood Cadillac, clothing, instruments, and other memorabilia.

➤ Country Music Wax Museum, 118 Sixteenth Avenue South. Elvis not quite in the flesh.

➤ Grand Guitar Museum, 535 New Kingsport Highway, (615) 968-1719. Some of Elvis' guitars are here.

➤ Music Valley Wax Museum of the Stars, 2515 McGavock Pike. More Elvis in the wax.

➤ RCA Studio B, Roy Acuff Place and Music Square West. Elvis did most of his recording here.

Las Vegas: The Neon Capital Also Owes Elvis

Elvis first played Las Vegas on April 23, 1956, at the New Frontier Hotel, signed by the hotel's manager Sammy Lewis for four weeks at $12,500 a week and advertised as the "Atomic-Powered Singer." The Venus Starlets danced behind Elvis. The middle-aged audience did not quite "get" Elvis and the engagement was cut short after the first two weeks.

Elvis would return, but not for a long time. On July 31, 1969, he played the first of 15 shows at the International Hotel (now the Las Vegas Hilton), the final booking on August 28. These were his first live appearances in eight years and he set a Vegas record of 101,509 paid customers and a gross take of $1.5 million. He returned to Vegas every year for the next seven years; his final Vegas concerts were at the Hilton December 2-12, 1976. His shows sold out and business went up by about 10 percent all over Las Vegas whenever he was in town.

At the Hilton (*not* the Flamingo Hilton on Las Vegas Boulevard), if you're a celebrity, you can stay in the Imperial Suite on the 30th floor where Elvis slept and which he helped design. The cost? $2,000-plus a night. If you're not a celebrity, at least come see the bronze statue of Elvis and the bronze guitar at the Hilton.

Elvis' Vegas debut was at the New Frontier Hotel (now called the Frontier), located at 3120 Las Vegas Boulevard South. The hotel has since been redecorated and the Venus Room where he played in 1956 no longer exists as such. Still, you can sense the King's presence, so make reservations at (800) 643-6966.

One last note: If you want to get married quickly, go to Las Vegas. If you want to get married with the blessing of the King, do it at the Graceland Wedding Chapel at 619 Las Vegas Boulevard South. The cost? $150. As a bonus? you'll hear a half hour of singing by an Elvis impersonator. Find someone who'll marry you and make a reservation now at (702) 382-0091.

By the way, Elvis and Priscilla were married in a second-floor suite of the Aladdin Hotel at 3667 Las Vegas Boulevard South. You can try to rent the room, but it takes a certain amount of guesswork because no one can identify the exact room (or so they say). In any case, the phone number is (800) 634-3424.

For the Record

The 1992 film *Honeymoon In Vegas* has a delicious tribute to Elvis: in the film's finale, hero Nicholas Cage joins members of the Flying Elvises club as they skydive onto a casino parking lot. It's a hilarious sequence—hats off to screenwriter/director Andrew Bergman.

... and Beyond

Here's a list of some other Elvis museums and locations to visit. Maybe some are in your home state, but if not, don't let that stop you.

➤ **California:** Hollywood Wax Museum, Hollywood.

➤ **Florida:** Elvis Presley Museum, 5700 Highway 192, Kissimmee ($2^1/_2$ miles east of Disney World), (407) 396-859. Lots of Elvis stuff.

London Wax Museum, 5505 Gulf Boulevard, St. Petersburg Beach, (813) 360-6985. A wax Elvis.

➤ **Illinois:** World Tattoo Gallery, 1255 South Wabash Street, Chicago, (312) 939-2222. Every December there's a tattoo art exhibit on the King.

➤ **Mississippi:** Flying Circle G Ranch, Walls, (601) 781-1411. 163-acre ranch, once owned by Elvis, then called the Circle G.

➤ **Missouri:** Boomland, exit 10, I-57, Charleston, (314) 683-6108. Elvis cars and other memorabilia.

➤ **Nevada:** Sierra 76 Truck Stop, 200 North McCarran Boulevard, Sparks. Elvis' handguns and jewelry, plus photos.

➤ **Oregon:** Church of Elvis, 219 SW Ankeny Street, Portland. Artwork of the King.

Fantastic Museum, Redmond. Elvis memorabilia on display.

➤ **Pennsylvania:** Memphis Memories, Levittown. Even in Levittown, you can feel you're in Memphis during Elvis' heyday.

➤ **South Dakota:** Murdo Pioneer Auto Museum, 503 Fifth Street, Murdo, (605) 669-2691. Elvis car and motorcycle.

➤ **Tennessee:** Buford Pusser Home & Museum, Pusser Street, Adamsville, (901) 632-4080. Elvis memorabilia.

Guinness World Records Exhibition Center, Highway 414, Gatlinburg, (615) 436-9100. Photos and touring jackets.

Elvis Presley Museum, Highway 441, Pigeon Forge, (615) 453-6499. Elvis exhibits.

"A Salute to Elvis," Highway 441, Pigeon Forge, (615) 428-7852. A tribute to the King in the Memories Theater.

The World of Illusions, Highway 441, Gatlinburg, (615) 436-9701. An illusion of Elvis singing...or is it?

➤ **Texas:** Eddie Fadal's Museum, 2807 Lasker Avenue, Waco, (817) 776-5388. Elvis mini-museum.

➤ **Virginia:** Celebrity Room, 7515 Brook Rd., Richmond, (804)-266-3328. An exhibit in the Celebrity Room Restaurant.

Outside the U.S., you can visit the following:

➤ **Canada:** Elvis Presley Museum, Maple Leaf Village Mall, Clifton Hill, Ontario, (416) 357-0008. Elvis' and Priscilla's honeymoon Cadillac and more.

➤ **England:** The Elvis Presley Museum, 46 Tottenham Court, London. Opened by impersonator Vince Everett.

➤ **Sweden:** Elvis Presley Museum, on E-6 in Munkerdale (near Oslo).

Catch the Mystery Train

You've come a long way, by now. You've learned much about Elvis Presley, his roots, his music, his life, and his significance. Hopefully you've developed an appreciation for the man and his talents, and perhaps discovered the reasons behind his enduring fame.

Now's the time to complete your journey with a trip to Graceland! There's no better way to get in touch with the reality and the absurdity of Elvis than to visit his home, and surround yourself with the history, the memorabilia, and the memories right there in the place he loved best. Meet other Elvis fans, load up on Elvis gear, soak up the Elvis atmosphere.

Maybe I'll see you there!

The Least You Need to Know

➤ Graceland, located in Memphis, TN, was Elvis' home and refuge, and his proudest possession.

➤ Elvis is buried in Graceland's Meditation Garden alongside his mother, Gladys, his father, Vernon, and his grandmother, Minnie Mae.

➤ Arguably America's second most famous house, Graceland opened to the public in 1982 and is now one of America's most popular tourist attractions.

➤ Graceland is a must-see for Elvis fans, but there are many other Elvis-related sites worth visiting elsewhere in Memphis as well as in Tupelo, Nashville, and Las Vegas.

Elvis Chronology

January 8, 1935: Elvis Aron Presley is born to Gladys and Vernon Presley of Tupelo Mississippi. His twin brother, Jesse Garon, is born dead shortly before and buried in a shoebox in an unmarked grave.

January 8, 1946: Eleven year-old Elvis, who wants a .22 caliber rifle for his birthday, is given a six-string guitar instead.

September 12, 1948: Vernon Presley, jobless and perhaps one step ahead of the law for moonshining, moves the family to a tiny apartment in Memphis, Tennessee.

July 18, 1953: Elvis goes to Sam Phillips' Memphis Recording Service and cuts a four-dollar acetate record. Accompanying himself on guitar he covers two songs by The Ink Spots, "My Happiness" and "That's When Your Heartaches Begin." Marion Keisker makes history by turning on a tape recorder and capturing Elvis' first studio visit.

July 5, 1954: Elvis joins musicians Scotty Moore and Bill Black at Sun Studios to record several songs. Elvis is nervous and the session goes poorly. During a break Elvis picks up his guitar and tries to get loose, riffing on a blues tune by Arthur "Big Boy" Crudup called "That's All Right (Mama)." Scotty and Bill join in. Sam Phillips overhears the jam session and senses he's found gold, literally.

July 7, 1954: Phillips gives a local DJ, Dewey Phillips, a copy of "That's All Right (Mama)" and the flip side, "Blue Moon of Kentucky," to air on his *Red, Hot and Blue* radio show. Response is so strong that Dewey plays the record at least 14 times.

July 19, 1954: "That's All Right (Mama)" is released by Sun Records (Sun 209).

July 30, 1954: Elvis' first billed appearance (he's listed third) is with Slim Whitman at Overton Park Shell in Memphis.

November 20, 1955: Elvis signs a three-year deal with RCA Victor.

January 10, 1956: Elvis records "Heartbreak Hotel" at RCA's Nashville studios. By April it would be the nation's #1 hit, the first of Elvis' 14 #1 hits on the top 100.

January 28, 1956: Elvis (with Bill Black and Scotty Moore) makes his national television debut on the Dorsey Brothers' *Stage Show*. Elvis sings: "I Got A Woman," "Shake, Rattle & Roll," and "Flip, Flop & Fly."

February 15, 1956: "I Forgot To Remember To Forget" becomes Elvis' first #1 Country Best Seller (for two weeks).

March 11, 1956: Colonel Tom Parker becomes Elvis' official manager for a 25 percent fee. Parker manages him until Elvis' death, never again representing another artist.

March 13, 1956: Elvis' first LP, *Elvis Presley,* is released.

April 6, 1956: Elvis signs a seven-year deal with Paramount. Hal B. Wallis will produce. Elvis will do three pictures on a rising pay scale starting at $100,000 and capping at $200,000 per picture.

April 11, 1956: "Heartbreak Hotel" becomes Elvis' first million seller.

April 23, 1956: Elvis' plays for the first time in Las Vegas at the New Frontier Hotel (with comedian Shecky Green) and bombs. Colonel Parker cuts the engagement from four weeks to two. It will be Elvis' last appearance in Vegas for 13 years.

April 30, 1956: *Life* magazine runs the first story on Elvis in a national magazine.

May 11, 1956: Elvis moves into his first home at 1034 Audubon Drive in Memphis. It costs $40,000 and Elvis pays cash. He lives with Vernon and Gladys.

May 12, 1956: "Heartbreak Hotel" has sold 1,350,000 copies and is moving at the unheard-of rate of 70,000 per week. *Elvis Presley* becomes RCA's biggest-selling LP ever.

July 1, 1956: Elvis appears on *The Steve Allen Show*. He sings "Hound Dog" (to a basset named Sherlock) and "I Want You, I Need You, I Love You." He also does a skit with Imogene Coca and Andy Griffith and will later recall the show as one of the most embarrassing experiences of his career.

July 2, 1956: Elvis records for the first time with The Jordanaires at RCA's studios in New York City. They do "Hound Dog," "Any Way You Want Me," and "Don't Be Cruel."

July 13, 1956: RCA releases "Hound Dog"/"Don't Be Cruel." Ed Sullivan (who once said, "I wouldn't have Elvis Presley on my show at any time") signs Elvis to three appearances for $50,000, making him the highest-paid guest star on a variety show in television history.

August 20, 1956: Principle shooting begins on *Love Me Tender*, Elvis' first movie.

September 9, 1956: Elvis appears for the first time on *The Ed Sullivan Show*. An estimated 54 million people watch Elvis sing "Hound Dog," "Don't Be Cruel," "Ready Teddy," and "Love Me Tender." Not until The Beatles appear in 1964 will a larger audience watch a television show.

November 15, 1956: *Love Me Tender* premieres.

December 4, 1956: A historic recording session at Sun Studios includes Elvis, Jerry Lee Lewis, Carl Perkins, and Johnny Cash. The Million-Dollar-Quartet recordings are not released until 1987.

April 10, 1957: Gladys, Vernon, and Elvis move into Graceland. "All Shook Up" reaches number one on *Billboard's* Top 100 chart, beginning a run of eight weeks at the top spot, the longest of any Elvis song.

October 17, 1957: *Jailhouse Rock* premieres in Memphis.

March 24, 1958: Elvis is inducted into the United States Army.

August 14, 1958: Gladys Presley dies in Memphis of a heart attack resulting from hepatitis.

March 5, 1960: Sgt. Elvis Presley is discharged from the Army.

December 25, 1960: Sixteen-year-old Priscilla Ann Beaulieu, who Elvis met in November of 1958 while stationed in Germany, spends Christmas at Graceland.

October 23, 1961: The *Blue Hawaii* album hits the charts where it will stay for 79 weeks, including an Elvis record of 20 weeks at #1.

December 11, 1963: *Love Me Tender* becomes the first Elvis movie to be shown on television.

August 27, 1965: The adoring Beatles meet their hero at Elvis' Bel Air (Los Angeles) mansion.

May 1, 1967: Elvis marries Priscilla Beaulieu in Las Vegas.

February 1, 1968: Lisa Marie Presley, Elvis' only child, is born—nine months to the day of her parents' marriage.

December 3, 1968: Elvis appears before a live audience for the first time since 1961 in his own TV special on NBC.

July 31, 1969: For the first time since 1956, Elvis appears in Las Vegas, at the International Hotel.

September 20, 1969: Elvis' last #1 hit, "Suspicious Minds," is released.

December 21, 1970: Elvis visits President Richard Nixon in the White House and receives a federal narcotics badge with which he pledges to help fight the battle against drugs.

January 14, 1973: Elvis appears live around the world in a TV special, "Elvis: Aloha from Hawaii." It is the first satellite broadcast ever and is viewed by an estimated one billion people.

October 9, 1973: Elvis and Priscilla divorce.

December 31, 1975: In a concert at the Silverdome in Pontiac, Michigan, Elvis sets a record for a single performance with $816,000 in gate receipts.

December 12, 1976: Elvis' last Las Vegas appearance, at the Las Vegas Hilton.

August 1, 1977: A year after being fired by Vernon Presley, Red and Sonny West publish a book with Dave Hebler, *Elvis: What Happened?*, which reveals shocking details of Elvis' life and sends him into a deep depression.

August 16, 1977: At about 2:30 in the afternoon, Elvis is found dead in his bathroom by his girlfriend Ginger Alden. The official cause of death is listed as cardiac arrhythmia. In fact, Elvis has numerous drugs in his system, including codeine and barbiturates and most likely died of multiple drug ingestion.

August 18, 1977: Elvis is buried beside his mother in Forest Hill cemetery.

October 2, 1977: Elvis and Gladys' bodies are moved to Graceland.

April 11, 1979: *Elvis*, starring Kurt Russell, airs on ABC-TV, soundly beating *Gone With The Wind* and *One Flew Over the Cuckoo's Nest* airing the same night.

June 26, 1979: Vernon Presley dies of heart failure at 63.

June 7, 1982: Graceland is opened to the public for the first time.

January 23, 1986: The Rock & Roll Hall of Fame announces its first 12 inductees, including Elvis Presley and Sam Phillips.

August 16, 1997: Unbelievably, this marks the 20th anniversary of Elvis' death.

Elvis' Top Records and Awards

Albums

Top Ten

1. *Blue Hawaii*	(#1—20 Weeks)
2. *Elvis Presley*	(#1—10 Weeks)
3. *Loving You*	(#1—10 Weeks)
4. *G.I. Blues*	(#1—10 Weeks)
5. *Elvis*	(#1—5 Weeks)
6. *Elvis' Christmas Album*	(#1—4 Weeks)
7. *Something For Everybody*	(#1—3 Weeks)
8. *Roustabout*	(#1—1 Week)
9. *Aloha From Hawaii Via Satellite*	(#1—1 Week)
10. *King Creole*	(#2)
11. *Elvis is Back*	(#2)
12. *Elvis' Golden Records*	(#3)
13. *Girls! Girls! Girls!*	(#3)
14. *Elvis' Golden Records, Vol. 3*	(#3)
15. *Fun In Acapulco*	(#3)
16. *Peace In The Valley* (EP)	(#3)
17. *Moody Blue*	(#3)
18. *Pot Luck*	(#4)
19. *It Happened At The World's Fair*	(#4)
20. *Elvis In Concert*	(#5)
21. *Kissin' Cousins*	(#6)
22. *Girl Happy*	(#8)
23. *Harum Scarum*	(#8)
24. *Elvis - TV Special*	(#8)
25. *Elvis For Everyone*	(#10)

Singles

Number Ones on the Top/Hot 100
1. "All Shook Up"   (8 Weeks)
2. "Heartbreak Hotel"   (7 Weeks)
3. "Don't Be Cruel"   (7 Weeks)
4. "Teddy Bear"   (7 Weeks)
5. "Jailhouse Rock"   (6 Weeks)
6. "Are You Lonesome Tonight?"   (6 Weeks)
7. "It's Now Or Never"   (5 Weeks)
8. "Love Me Tender"   (4 Weeks)
9. "Stuck On You"   (4 Weeks)
10. "A Big Hunk o' Love"   (2 Weeks)
11. "Good Luck Charm"   (2 Weeks)
12. "Surrender"   (2 Weeks)
13. "Don't"   (1 Week)
14. "Suspicious Minds"   (1 Week)

Number Ones on the Country Charts
1. "Heartbreak Hotel"   (17 Weeks)
2. "Don't Be Cruel"   (7 Weeks)
3. "I Forgot To Remember To Forget"   (5 Weeks)
4. "Hound Dog"   (3 Weeks)
5. "I Want You, I Need You, I Love You"   (2 Weeks)
6. "All Shook Up"   (1 Week)
7. "Teddy Bear"   (1 Week)
8. "Jailhouse Rock"   (1 Week)
9. "Moody Blue"/"She Still Thinks I Care" (1 Week)
10. "Way Down"/"Pledging My Love"   (1 Week)
11. "Guitar Man"   (1 Week)

Number Ones on the Rhythm & Blues Charts

1. "Jailhouse Rock"	(5 Weeks)
2. "Treat Me Nice"	(5 Weeks)
3. "All Shook Up"	(4 Weeks)
4. "Don't Be Cruel"	(1 Week)
5. "Hound Dog"	(1 Week)
6. "Teddy Bear"	(1 Week)
7. "Loving You"	(1 Week)

Number Ones on the Easy Listening Charts

1. "Crying In The Chapel"	(7 Weeks)
2. "Can't Help Falling In Love With You"	(6 Weeks)
3. "I'm Yours"	(3 Weeks)
4. "(Such An) Easy Question"	(2 Weeks)
5. "The Wonder Of You"	(1 Week)
6. "You Don't Have To Say You Love Me"	(1 Week)
7. "My Boy"	(1 Week)

Number Ones on the British Charts

1. "It's Now Or Never"	(8 Weeks)
2. "All Shook Up"	(7 Weeks)
3. "Wooden Heart"	(6 Weeks)
4. "The Wonder Of You"	(6 Weeks)
5. "A Fool Such As I"	(5 Weeks)
6. "I Need Your Love Tonight"	(5 Weeks)
7. "Good Luck Charm"	(5 Weeks)
8. "Way Down"	(5 Weeks)
9. "Are You Lonesome Tonight?"	(4 Weeks)
10. "Surrender"	(4 Weeks)
11. "(Marie's The Name) His Latest Flame"	(4 Weeks)
12. "Little Sister"	(4 Weeks)
13. "Can't Help Falling In Love"	(4 Weeks)
14. "Rock-A-Hula Baby"	(4 Weeks)

continues

continued

15. "Jailhouse Rock"	(3 Weeks)
16. "One Night"	(3 Weeks)
17. "I Got Stung"	(3 Weeks)
18. "She's Not You"	(3 Weeks)
19. "Return To Sender"	(3 Weeks)
20. "Crying In The Chapel"	(2 Weeks)
21. "(You're The) Devil In Disguise"	(1 Week)

Most Weeks on the Top/Hot 100

1. "All Shook Up"	(30 Weeks)
2. "Hound Dog"	(28 Weeks)
3. "Don't Be Cruel"	(27 Weeks)
4. "Heartbreak Hotel"	(27 Weeks)
5. "Jailhouse Rock"	(27 Weeks)
6. "Teddy Bear"	(25 Weeks)
7. "I Want You, I Need You, I Love You"	(24 Weeks)
8. "Love Me Tender"	(23 Weeks)
9. "Loving You"	(22 Weeks)
10. "Way Down"	(21 Weeks)

Gold Records

1956

Singles	*LPs*
"Heartbreak Hotel"	*Elvis Presley*
"I Was The One"	*Elvis*
"I Want You, I Need You, I Love You"	
"Don't Be Cruel"	
"Hound Dog"	
"Love Me"	
"Love Me Tender"	
"Any Way You Want Me"	

1957

Singles

"Too Much"

"Playing For Keeps"

"All Shook Up"

"That's When Your Heartaches Begin"

"Teddy Bear"

"Loving You"

"Jailhouse Rock"

"Treat Me Nice"

"Don't"

"I Beg Of You"

EPs

Peace In The Valley

Jailhouse Rock

LPs

Loving You

Elvis' Christmas Album

1958

Singles

"Wear My Ring Around Your Neck"

"Hard Headed Woman"

"I Got Stung"

"One Night"

EPs

King Creole, Vol. 1

LPs

Elvis Golden Records

King Creole

1959

Singles

"(Now And Then There's) A Fool Such As I"

"I Need Your Love Tonight"

"A Big Hunk O' Love"

LPs

50,000,000 Elvis Fans Can't Be Wrong—Elvis' Gold Records, Vol. 2

1960

Singles

"Stuck On You"

"It's Now Or Never"

"A Mess Of Blues"

"Are You Lonesome Tonight?"

"I Gotta Know"

"Wooden Heart" (Europe)

LPs

Elvis Is Back

G.I. Blues

His Hand In Mine

1961

Singles

"Surrender"

"I Feel So Bad"

"Little Sister"

"(Marie's The Name) His Latest Flame"

"Can't Help Falling In Love"

"Rock-A-Hula Baby"

EPs

Elvis By Request

LPs

Something For Everybody

Blue Hawaii

1962

Singles

"Good Luck Charm"

"Anything That's A Part Of You"

"She's Not You"

"Return To Sender"

"Where Do You Come From"

EPs

Follow That Dream

LPs

Pot Luck

Girls! Girls! Girls!

1963

Singles

"One Broken Heart For Sale"

"(You're The) Devil In Disguise"

"Bossa Nova Baby"

LPs

Elvis' Golden Records, Vol. 3

Fun In Acapulco

It Happened At The World's Fair

1964

Singles

"Kissin' Cousins"

"Viva Las Vegas"

"Ain't That Loving You Baby"

"Blue Christmas"

LPs

Kissin' Cousins

Roustabout

1965

Singles	LPs
"Crying In The Chapel"	*Girl Happy*
"I'm Yours"	*Elvis For Everyone*
"Puppet On A String"	*Harum Scarum*

1966

Singles	LPs
"Tell Me Why"	*Paradise, Hawaiian Style*
"Frankie And Johnny"	
"Love Letters"	
"Spinout"	
"All That I Am"	
"If Every Day Was Like Christmas"	

1967

Singles	LPs
"Indescribably Blue"	*How Great Thou Art*
"Big Boss Man"	

1968

Singles	LPs
"Guitar Man"	*Elvis—TV Special*
"Stay Away"	
"We Call On Him"	
"Let Yourself Go"	
"Almost In Love"	
"If I Can Dream"	

1969

Singles	LPs
"Charro"	*Elvis Sings Flaming Star*
"His Hand In Mine"	*From Elvis In Memphis*
"In The Ghetto"	*From Memphis To Vegas / From Vegas To Memphis*
"Clean Up Your Own Back Yard"	
"Suspicious Minds"	
"Don't Cry, Daddy"	

1970

Singles	LPs
"Kentucky Rain"	*On Stage: February 1970*
"The Wonder Of You"	*Elvis: Worldwide 50 Golden Award Hits, Vol. 1*
"Mama Like The Roses"	*That's The Way It Is*
"I've Lost You"	
"You Don't Have To Say You Love Me"	
"Patch It Up"	
"I Really Don't Want To Know"	

1971

Singles	LPs
"Where Did They Go, Lord"	*Elvis Country*
"Only Believe"	*Elvis Sings The Wonderful World Of Christmas*
"I'm Leavin'"	
"It's Only Love"	

1972

Singles	LPs
"An American Trilogy"	*Elvis As Recorded At Madison Square Garden*
"Burning Love"	
"Separate Ways"	

1973

Singles	*LPs*
"Raised On Rock"	*Aloha From Hawaii Via Satellite*
	Elvis (RCA DPl2-0056[e])

1974

Singles	*LPs*
"Take Good Care Of Her"	*Elvis—A Legendary Performer, Vol. 1*
"It's Midnight"	

1975

Singles	*LPs*
"My Boy"	*Promised Land*
"T-R-O-U-B-L-E"	*Pure Gold*

1976

Singles	*LPs*
"Hurt"	*Elvis—A Legendary Performer, Vol. 2*
	From Elvis Presley Boulevard, Memphis, Tennessee

1977

Singles	*LPs*
"Way Down"	*Welcome To My World*
"My Way"	*Moody Blue*
	Elvis In Concert

1978

LPs

Elvis—A Legendary Performer, Vol. 3

Elvis and the Grammys

14 Nominations and 3 Victories (in BOLD)

1959

Record of the Year—"A Fool Such As I"
Lost to "Mack The Knife" (Bobby Darin)

Best Performance by a "Top 40" Artist—"A Big Hunk o' Love"
Lost to Nat King Cole ("Midnight Flyer")

Best Rhythm & Blues Performance—"A Big Hunk o' Love"
Lost to Dinah Washington ("What A Difference A Day Makes")

1960

Record of the Year—"Are You Lonesome Tonight?"
Lost to "Theme from 'A Summer Place'" (Percy Faith)

Best Vocal Performance, Male—"Are You Lonesome Tonight?"
Lost to Ray Charles ("Georgia On My Mind")

Best Performance by a Pop Singles Artist—"Are You Lonesome Tonight?"
Lost to Ray Charles ("Georgia On My Mind")

Best Vocal Performance, Male, Album—*G.I. Blues*
Lost to Ray Charles *(The Genius of Ray Charles)*

Best Soundtrack Album or Recording of Original Cast from a
Motion Picture or Television—*G.I. Blues*
Lost to *Can-Can*

1961

Best Soundtrack Album or Recording of Original Cast from a
Motion Picture or Television—*Blue Hawaii*
Lost to *West Side Story*

1967

Best Sacred Performance—*How Great Thou Art* (album)

1968

Best Sacred Performance—*You'll Never Walk Alone* (Album)
Lost to *Beautiful Isle of Somewhere* (Jake Hess)

1972

Best Inspirational Performance—*He Touched Me* (album)

1974

Best Inspirational Performance—"How Great Thou Art"
(from *Elvis Recorded Live On Stage in Memphis*)

1978

Best Country Vocal Performance, Male—"Softly As I Leave You"
Lost to Willie Nelson ("Georgia On My Mind")

Elvis' Top 40 Hits

Since the rock-and-roll era began in 1955, Elvis Presley recorded more than twice as many Top 40 hits than any other artist or group:

Artist	Top 40 Hits
1. Elvis Presley	107
2. The Beatles	49
3. Elton John	48
4. Stevie Wonder	46
5. James Brown	44

Elvis' Complete List of Top 40 Hits

Song	Debuted	Weeks	Highest Rank
A Big Hunk O' Love	7/13/59	10	1
A Fool Such As I	3/30/59	11	2
A Mess of Blues	8/1/60	23	2
Ain't That Loving You Baby	10/24/64	8	16
All Shook Up	4/6/57	22	1
Anything That's A Part of You	4/7/62	5	31
Anyway You Want Me	11/10/56	4	20
Are You Lonesome Tonight?	11/14/60	14	1
Ask Me	10/24/64	8	12
Big Boss Man	11/4/67	2	38
Blue Suede Shoes	4/28/56	5	20
Bossa Nova Baby	11/2/63	7	8

continued

Song	Debuted	Weeks	Highest Rank
Burning Love	9/9/72	12	2
Can't Help Falling in Love	12/18/61	12	2
Clean Up Your Own Back Yard	8/2/69	4	35
Crying in the Chapel	5/8/65	11	3
Devil In Disguise	7/13/63	8	3
Do the Clam	3/13/65	6	21
Don't	1/27/58	16	1
Don't Be Cruel	8/4/56	24	1
Don't Cry Daddy	12/13/69	11	6
Doncha' Think It's Time	5/5/58	2	15
Easy Question	7/3/65	6	11
Fame and Fortune	4/25/60	7	17
Flaming Star	4/26/61	3	14
Follow That Dream	5/19/62	7	15
Frankie and Johnny	4/9/66	5	25
Good Luck Charm	3/24/62	11	1
Guitar Man	2/28/81	3	28
Hard Headed Woman	6/30/58	14	1
Heartbreak Hotel	3/10/56	22	1
His Latest Flame	9/4/61	7	4
Hound Dog	8/4/56	23	1
Hurt	5/1/76	5	28
I Beg of You	2/3/58	7	8
I Feel So Bad	5/22/61	7	5
I Got Stung	11/10/58	12	8
I Gotta Know	11/28/60	8	20
I Need Your Love Tonight	3/30/59	10	4
I Really Don't Want to Know	1/20/72	8	23
I Want You, I Need You, I Love You	6/2/56	10	1
I Was the One	3/17/56	10	19
I'm Leavin'	8/14/71	2	36

Song	Debuted	Weeks	Highest Rank
I'm Yours	9/18/65	7	11
I've Got A Thing About You Baby	3/23/74	2	39
I've Lost You	8/22/70	3	32
If I Can Dream	12/14/68	11	12
If You Talk in Your Sleep	6/29/74	7	17
In the Ghetto	5/17/69	11	3
Indescribably Blue	2/15/67	4	33
It Hurts Me	3/14/64	4	29
It's Now Or Never	7/25/60	16	1
Jailhouse Rock	10/14/57	19	1
Kentucky Rain	2/21/70	8	16
King of the Whole Wide World	10/6/62	4	30
Kiss Me Quick	5/23/64	2	34
Kissin' Cousins	3/7/64	7	11
Little Sister	8/25/61	10	5
Lonely Man	3/13/61	2	32
Love Letters	7/9/66	5	19
Love Me	11/24/56	14	2
Love Me Tender	10/20/56	19	1
Loving You	7/8/57	13	20
Memories	4/12/69	2	38
Moody Blue	2/5/77	5	31
My Baby Left Me	6/9/56	3	31
My Boy	2/15/75	6	20
My Way	12/3/77	7	22
My Wish Came True	7/13/59	10	12
One Broken Heart for Sale	2/23/63	7	11
One Night	11/10/58	14	4
Peace in the Valley	4/29/57	1	29
Playing For Keeps	2/9/57	4	21
Poor Boy	1/5/57	3	24

continues

continued

Song	Debuted	Weeks	Highest Rank
Promised Land	11/9/74	9	14
Puppet On a String	12/4/65	6	14
Rags to Riches	3/27/71	4	33
Return to Sender	10/27/62	14	2
Rock-A-Hula Baby	12/18/61	5	23
Separate Ways	12/23/72	8	20
She's Not You	8/11/62	9	5
Spinout	11/5/66	2	40
Steamroller Blues	5/5/73	7	17
Stuck On You	4/11/60	13	1
Such A Night	8/8/64	6	16
Surrender	2/20/61	11	1
Suspicious Minds	9/20/69	13	1
T-R-O-U-B-L-E	6/2/75	3	35
Teddy Bear	6/24/57	18	1
Tell Me Why	1/22/66	3	23
The Next Step is Love	8/22/70	3	32
The Wonder of You	5/23/70	11	9
There Goes My Everything	1/20/72	8	21
Too Much	1/26/57	14	1
Treat Me Nice	10/21/57	6	18
U.S. Male	4/20/68	4	28
Until It's Time For You To Go	3/11/72	1	40
Viva Las Vegas	5/30/64	4	29
Way Down	7/16/77	12	18
Wear My Ring Around Your Neck	4/21/58	13	2
What'd I Say	5/30/64	5	21
When My Blue Moon Turns to Gold Again	12/29/56	4	19
Where Did They Go, Lord	3/27/71	4	33
Wild in the Country	6/19/61	2	26
Witchcraft	11/9/63	3	32
You Don't Have to Say You Love Me	11/7/70	8	11

Selected Bibliography

The following books when taken together will give readers a balanced, well-rounded and thorough portrait of the King. The one book to avoid at all costs is Albert Goldman's *Elvis* (McGraw-Hill, 1981), a tabloid gusher that is an embarrassment to the King's memory and contains wildly unsubstantiated smut (even proclaiming at one point that Elvis wore diapers!).

I'll begin with what I consider to be the three finest books on Elvis—those you *have* to read—then I'll include a selection of the best of the rest.

My Favorite Elvis Books

Guralnick, Peter. *Last Train To Memphis: The Rise of Elvis Presley*. Boston: Little Brown, 1994.

Peter Guralnick's wonderful book on the King (the first in a two-volume biography) is a graceful and insightful paean/analysis of the young Elvis, taking him from 1935 to 1958. Modern biography doesn't get any better. Guralnick also produced *Lost Highway* (Godine, 1979), which features profiles on blues, R&B, and country performers, with more powerful writing on the King.

Marcus, Greil. *Mystery Train: Images of America in Rock'n'Roll Music*. New York: Dutton, 1975.

Greil Marcus' seminal work on rock and roll may be the best book ever written on rock, and it contains a brilliant, beautifully crafted final chapter, "Elvis: Presliad," analyzing Elvis and the roots of his music with a particular emphasis on the King's interaction with Sam Phillips and Sun Studios. Don't miss it. Marcus also published *Dead Elvis* (Doubleday, 1991), a passionate, intensely personal look at the post-mortem phenomenon that is Elvis.

Marsh, Dave. *Elvis*. New York: Rolling Stone/Times Books, 1982.

The rock writer knows his stuff and this wonderful (and beautiful) oversized book contains some of my favorite writing on the King. Lucid and graceful, the book's deceptively simple narrative tells a compelling story of Elvis from the beginning to the end. It is a source of real pride that Marsh provided the Foreword to the book you hold in your hands.

The Best of the Rest

Clayton, Rose and Heard, Dick. *Elvis Up Close: In the Words of Those Who Knew Him Best.* Atlanta: Turner, 1994. Quote after quote chronicling Elvis' life.

Dowling, Paul. *Elvis: The Ultimate Album Cover Book.* New York: Harry N. Abrams, 1996. A nice way to track Elvis' recording career.

Dundy, Elaine. *Elvis and Gladys.* New York: Dell, 1985. The poignant, well-done story of the King's relationship with his mother, and his youth in Tupelo.

Esposito, Joe and Oumano, Elena. *Good Rockin' Tonight: Twenty Years on the Road and on the Town with Elvis.* New York: Simon and Schuster, 1994. Joe Esposito, road manager/Memphis Mafia man #1, was there almost from the beginning and writes revealingly and fairly about the long, strange trip he shared with Elvis.

Flippo, Chet. *Graceland: The Living Legend of Elvis Presley.* San Francisco: Collins, 1993. A big, beautiful book, the next best thing to going there.

Haining, Peter. *Elvis in Private.* New York: St. Martin's, 1987. Articles about Elvis published over the years in magazines; writers include women in his life, such as Priscilla, Linda Thompson, and Ann-Margret; musicians, such as D.J. Fontana, Roy Orbison, Chet Atkins, Rufus Thomas, and John Lennon; Memphis Mafia, such as Charlie Hodge; other friends and family; and even one by Elvis himself.

Hawkins, Martin and Escott, Colin. *Catalyst: The Sun Records Story.* New York: Aquarius, 1975. A nicely done look at Elvis in his Sun stage and other musicians who recorded there.

Hawkins, Martin and Escott, Colin. *Elvis: The Illustrated Discography.* London: Omnibus, 1981. A solid guide to Elvis' records: You have to know the music, though.

Hopkins, Jerry. *Elvis: A Biography.* New York: Simon and Schuster, 1971.

Hopkins, Jerry. *Elvis: The Final Years.* New York: St. Martin's, 1980. The two Hopkins biographies taken together are solid if unpretentious, and can be counted on to get the facts straight. Good work, which I admire and respect.

Krebs, Gary M. *The Rock and Roll Reader's Guide*. New York: Billboard Books, 1997. A comprehensive, critical bibliography of rock literature, with substantial coverage of books on Elvis Presley.

Life magazine. *Elvis: A Celebration in Pictures*. New York: Warner, 1995. The editors of *Life* magazine select photographs from the magazine archives.

Matthew-Walker, Robert. *Elvis Presley: A Study in Music*. London: Omnibus, 1979. An exhaustive evaluation of every song Elvis released.

Pierce, Patricia Jobe. *The Ultimate Elvis: Elvis Presley Day by Day*. New York: Fireside/Simon and Schuster, 1995. A detailed, solid, and altogether admirable chronology of Elvis' life.

Stanley, David with Coffey, Frank. *The Elvis Encyclopedia*. Santa Monica: General Publishing Group, 1994. A handy reference tool with revealing anecdotes. (And yes, the co-author is yours truly.)

Tharpe, Jac L. *Elvis: Images and Fancies*. Jackson, Miss.: University Press of Mississippi, 1981. Moving, informative, and decidedly un-academic essays on Elvis.

Thompson, Charles C. II and Cole, James. *The Death of Elvis: What Really Happened*. New York: Delacorte, 1991. As the title says, written by a television producer and a Memphis reporter. Excellent, careful reporting.

Vellanga, Dick with Farren, Mike. *Elvis and the Colonel*. New York: Dell, 1988. An unauthorized and revealing biography of the Colonel.

Wertheimer, Albert. *Elvis '56: In the Beginning*. New York: Collier, 1979. Stunning, priceless photographs from the very beginning of Elvis' career.

West, Red, West, Sonny and Hebler, Dave with Dunleavy, Steve. *Elvis: What Happened?* New York: Ballantine, 1977. This is the book that tormented Elvis before and after it came out fifteen days before his death. Powerful, scandalous, lurid, and, unfortunately, absorbing.

Worth, Fred L. And Tamerious, Steve D. *Elvis: His Life From A to Z*. Chicago: Contemporary, 1988. A massive encyclopedia, loaded with information.

What Might Have Been

In 1956, Colonel Tom Parker started a book entitled *The Benevolent Con Man: How Much Does It Cost If It's Free?* He reportedly turned down a publisher's offer—one of many for an autobiography—of a $100,000 advance saying, "Well, I guess I could let you have the back cover for that!" His intention was to sell full-page ads to appear between chapters for

$25,000 each; as always, no matter how tacky, Parker was attempting to extract every last dollar from his project. He never did finish the book. It's a shame that Parker, who died in 1997 and rarely gave interviews about his time with Elvis, never sat down and told his remarkable story. And what a loss…though would *you* have believed his side of the story?

Sharing The King with Others: Prominent Elvis Fan Clubs

Since the first Elvis fan club, the Official Elvis Presley Fan Club Worldwide, was founded in 1956, hundreds of others have started up. It is a loose fraternity with exact information difficult to keep completely up-to-date. Estimates of the number of fan clubs worldwide vary; my best estimate is about 500—and growing.

A good way to decide which fan club to join is to go to the Elvis International Tribute Week held in Memphis every August around Elvis' death date on the 16th. Graceland holds a special luncheon for fan club officers so they're in attendance (they wouldn't miss the memorial celebration anyway if they're serious about their clubs).

The Association of Elvis Presley Fan Clubs at 5320 53rd Avenue E, Lot Q-47, Bradenton, Florida 34203 will help you get oriented. And if you want to have your name included in lists from various fan clubs, write Elvis List, P.O. Box 306, Oshkosh, WI 54902.

If you're the organizational type, you can always start your own Elvis fan club. Graceland is happy to help out anybody who would like to create an Elvis fan club; give them a call at 1-800-238-2000.

Perhaps the best way to choose a fan club is geographically. Check the following list of prominent Elvis fan clubs to find one close to you if you want to facilitate getting to events and establishing friendships.

U.S. Elvis Presley Fan Clubs

Always Elvis
320 E. 42nd St. Suite 1918
New York, NY 10017
Attn: Ray Morton

Asian Worldwide Elvis Fan Club
1025 Blackhawk
Houston, TX 77079
Attn: Henry Newinn

"Burning Love" Fan Club
P.O. Box 265 RD#3
Okeman, OK 74859
Attn: Connie Meadors

C'mon Everybody Elvis Fan Club
16 Dennis Drive
Belleville, IL 62226-4902
Attn: Mike Brown

Elvis Affairs
3640 Hope Road
Cummings, GA 30131-8926
Attn: Leah Wray

Elvis Aron Presley "King Heads"
Fan Club
2 Milton Ave.
Clinton, MA 01510
Attn: Daniel McMahon

Elvis Connection
716 Broadway #11
El Cajon, CA 92021
Attn: Pat Clemins

The Elvis Connection
P.O. Box 45951
Madison, WI 53744-5941
Attn: Mary Danks

Elvis Country Fan Club of Texas
4912 W. Park Dr.
Austin, TX 78731-5536

The Elvis 4-Ever King Fan Club
P.O. Box 215
Leesville, SC 29070
Attn: Kaye Waters

Elvis Friends Hollywood
333 N. Screenland Drive #142
Burbank, CA 91505
Attn: Bobbie Cunningham

Elvis From Graceland To Raceland
5100 Laughlin Ave.
Louisville, KY 40214-2737
Attn: Deanna Wathen

Elvis On Capital Hill
640 Sixth St. N.E.
Washington, DC 20002
Attn: Mary Hinds

Elvis Presley Continentals
P.O. Box 568082
Orlando, FL 32856-8082
Attn: Sue Manuszak

The Elvis Presley Fan Club of
the Capital District, Inc.
P.O. Box 265 RD#3
Schenectady, NY 12406

The Elvis Presley Walk A Mile
In My Shoes Fan Club
512 Dixie Ave.
South Pittsburg, TN 37380
Attn: Jonathan Long

Elvis Today
P.O. Box 190693
St. Louis, MO 63119
Attn: Elizabeth Corona

Elvis Worldwide Memorial Fan Club
3081 Sunrise
Memphis, TN 38127
Attn: Will McDaniel

Exclusively Elvis Fan Club
6952 Chesnut Hill Church Road
Coopersburg, PA 18036
Attn: Rob Nekich

If I Can Dream
847 E. LeMarche Ave.
Phoenix, AZ 85022
Attn: Charla Volkov

Loving You Elvis Fan Club
5210 Larin Rd.
Arbutus, MD 21227
Attn: Ms. Marty Roberts

Loving You Elvis Fan Club
P.O. Box 444
Rolling Fork, MS 39159
Attn: Judy French

Memories of Elvis
5 Thomas St.
High Bridge, NJ 08829
Attn: Roberta Gooley

The Presley Connection
P.O. Box 68068
Prattville, AL 36068
Attn: Karen Couch

Return To Sender Fan Club
420 Roberts Cut-off #9
Fort Worth, TX 76114
Attn: Paul Monroe

Rising Sun Productions
P.O.Box 58091
Seattle, WA 98138
Attn: Sandel DeMastus

Sincerely Elvis Fan Club
3714 Boston St.
Midland, MI 48642
Attn: Debra Smith

Still The King In West Virginia
Route 1 Box 76
Roncverte, WV 24970
Attn: Dave Jones

"Suspicious Minds" Fan Club
P.O. Box 808
Crawfordsville, IN 47933
Attn: Mike Lovenduski

Then, Now and Forever
Box 161130
Memphis, TN 38116
Attn: Betty Hicks

Tribute To a King
P.O. Box 734
Jena, LA 71342
Attn: Billie King

Virginia Is For Elvis
710 Kingsley Road
Vienna, VA 22180
Attn: Priscilla Lynn

Worldwide Elvis Fans, Inc.
2095 Stivers
Bryant, AR 72022
Attn: Jennifer Sinele

International Elvis Fan Clubs

Elvis' Brazilian Friends
Caixa Postal 31.069
Eng. Dentro
Rio de Janeiro 20.730
Attn: Rosoleta Esteves

Elvis Capital of Canada Fan Club
547-3 Gilmour St.
Ottawa, Ontario
Canada K1R5L5
Attn: Marc Bruneau

Elvis Club Berlin
Landsberger Allee 200
Berlin 0-1156
Germany
Attn: Werner Strube

Elvis Cross The Mersey
43 Brownlow Raod New Ferry
Wirral, Merseyside
England L621AU
Attn: Terry Bellis

Elvis Land Fan Club
R. Rondonopolis 148 Cidade Alta
Cuba-MT
Brazil 78025-240
Attn: Jaqueline Manzano

Elvis Presley Fan Club
38 Maxwell Drive, Bridgewater
Tasmania 7030
Australia
Attn: Brian Bedford

Elvis Presley Fan Club of Tokyo
P.O. Box 5
Kaai, Tokyo 134
Japan

Elvis Presley International Fan Club
Bevelandsestrast 15A
3083 NA Rotterdam
The Netherlands
Attn: Luuk Bonthond

Elvis Presley Love Me Tender Fan Club
Kathu 8845
South Africa
Attn: Marlene Potgieter

Love Me Tender Elvis Fan Club
Str. Panselelor 2B1.446
Sc. A Etj.5
Apt. 29 Sector 4
Buccuresti, Romania
Attn: Carmen Bode

Sound of Elvis Fan Club of S. Australia
3 Reedbeds Credscent
Seaton 5023
Australia
Attn: Monika Leone

Elvis Words

Aron   Elvis' middle name, sometimes spelled "Aaron." The name "Aron" or "Aaron" is from the Hebrew *Aaron*, meaning "exalted."

bluegrass music   "Bluegrass" is a form of country music with an emphasis on traditional string instruments, such as guitar, banjo, mandolin, and fiddle.

Blue Moon Boys   An early name for Elvis' musical act with Scotty Moore on guitar and Bill Black on bass. The name was taken from the song "Blue Moon of Kentucky," which they performed.

blues   A musical form consisting essentially of notes from a scale with the 3rd, 5th, and 7th notes microtonally flattened in comparison with the standard major scale, and played in a 12-bar chord progression, and having lyrics typically dealing with the hardships of life and love. "Delta blues" refers to blues played on acoustic guitars and harmonicas, typical of the southern Mississippi River region. "Chicago blues" refers to an electrified version of the blues with a more driving rhythm, typical of urban areas.

bobby-soxers   Teenage girls in the 1940s and early '50s were known as "bobby-soxers" because they wore short white ankle socks. Elvis wasn't the first to wow the bobby-soxers, it was Frank Sinatra and later Eddie Fisher. Early in his career, some writers referred to Elvis' fans as "country bobby-soxers."

bodyguard   Being a "bodyguard" for Elvis meant more than just protecting his Royal Highness when he was out and about. It also meant being a gopher when the King was safely tucked away, running all kinds of errands, as well as being a buddy, partying with the King (one of the many perks of the job) and helping find girls for him.

bootleg   A "bootleg" record is a recording not available on a standard release. This may include concert performances, rehearsals, studio outtakes, or demos. Bootlegging is illegal, although so rampant that many artists don't bother going after the culprits anymore.

British Invasion   The term "British Invasion" refers to British soldiers on American soil in the War of Independence. It also refers to a time in popular music—in particular the mid to late 1960s—when a lot of the hits on the American charts were by British bands. The Beatles were the vanguard. Other bands included The Animals, The Dave Clark Five, Herman's Hermits, The Rolling Stones, and The Zombies. After this period, British bands regularly crossed the Atlantic to promote their albums in the U.S., as they still do today.

Chai   "Chai" or "chi" is both a Hebrew letter and word; it is a symbol of life itself. Elvis wore the symbol around his neck along with a Christian crucifix and a Star of David. When asked why, he responded, "I don't want to miss out on heaven because of a technicality."

country music   "Country" is a style of songwriting and singing popularized especially in the South and West and drawing on hillbilly music, cowboy songs, blues-style singing, and the vocal harmonizing common to church music.

Elvis   The name "Elvis" is derived from the Old Norse word *alviss*, meaning "all wise."

Elvis impersonator   Someone who dresses, sings, talks, and dances like Elvis as an entertainment act.

Elvis Has Entered/Left the Building   Expression originally used at Elvis concerts to stir fan excitement over Elvis' arrival. "Left the building" was used to deter fans from seeking Elvis out after the show. Today, the expression is used humorously in conjunction with Elvis sightings.

Elvisology   The official Graceland term for historical and statistical information on the life and career of Elvis.

Elvis Presley Enterprises   Formerly a company established by Colonel Tom Parker, Elvis Presley Enterprises is now the name of the marketing entity of the Elvis Presley Estate. It directs the running of Graceland as well as the licensing of Elvis products. Record royalties go directly to the Elvis Presley Estate.

Elvis Room   A room where Elvis memorabilia and collectibles are on display, or where a shrine is kept to Elvis.

Elvis the Pelvis   A June 1956 issue of *Time* magazine referred to Elvis as "the Pelvis," after which the phrase "Elvis the Pelvis" became widely used. Often (but not always) used as a derogatory reference, the expression was inspired by Elvis' sexual leg and pelvic movements while he performed on stage.

gospel music   "Gospel" is the popularized singing of religious songs—both church hymns and personal statements of salvation and conversion—typically with more than one voice singing in harmony.

Graceland   Elvis' primary residence for the last 20 years of his life, located in Memphis, Tennessee. It is now a museum.

Grand Ole Opry   A country music show in Nashville, Tennessee. In 1925, the show was first broadcast on a local radio station, WSM; from 1942 to 1974, it took place at Ryman Auditorium; since that time it has been held at the Opryland Auditorium. Elvis played the Grand Ole Opry in 1954.

Hillbilly Cat   An early stage name for Elvis.

hillbilly music   "Hillbilly" or "mountain" music is an early American form of folk music (i.e., music sung by common folks) or country music, based on 18th-century English and Scottish ballads and African American work songs and developed in the Appalachian Mountains in the 19th century.

holy rollers   A term applied to the devotees of fundamentalist religions because of their lively style of worship, including singing and dancing and trances.

I Am and I Was   Elvis reportedly spoke this enigmatic phrase under his breath at concerts during his final tour in 1977. Only people in the very front rows caught it. It has been interpreted in a number of ways—by some to confirm his faking his own death, and by others to confirm a divine purpose.

I Saw Elvis   In World War II, GIs were known to write "Kilroy Was Here" on walls in both Europe and Asia as a way of asserting the American presence. During the Persian Gulf War, the chosen inscription was "I Saw Elvis." Thinking about Elvis evidently helped them get through the hard times.

jam session   A musical improvisation around a loose structure.

jazz   "Jazz" is a form of music with a strong rhythmic understructure and solo and ensemble improvisation around the melody. Jazz draws heavily from the blues.

kit   The "kit" was a bag that went everywhere with Elvis during his later years. It contained different amphetamines and barbiturates, as well as a driver's license, $10,000 in cash, jewelry, and makeup.

Louisiana Hayride   A Saturday night country music show in Shreveport, Louisiana, broadcast on KWKH, starting in 1948. The Louisiana Hayride has been referred to as the "Junior Grand Ole Opry." Elvis first played there in October 1954 and appeared regularly in 1955-56.

manager   A manager oversees and coordinates the affairs of a business or a person. In popular music, that can mean a "promoter" of certain events; a "booking agent," who gets jobs; a "public relations agent," who attempts to influence the public's reaction to a performer; or a "press agent," who handles the media. (See also *road manager*.)

Meditation Garden (or Gardens)   A garden at Graceland built by Elvis as a place of retreat. Elvis' body was moved there in 1977.

memorabilia   An object that inspires memories of a person or event. The term is used interchangeably with "collectibles" because, in the case of Elvis, it seems all memorabilia is worthy of collecting for intrinsic value.

Memphis Mafia   The inner circle of Elvis' family, friends, bodyguards, and hangers-on; a shifting alliance of insiders. They have also been referred to as "El's Angels" and "Elvis Presley's Boys."

Million Dollar Quartet   On December 4, 1956, Elvis, Johnny Cash, Jerry Lee Lewis, and Carl Perkins ended up together in Sun Studios and participated in an impromptu jam session beginning with the song "Blueberry Hill" and going on for hours. The so called "Million Dollar Quartet" session was caught on tape by producer Sam Phillips. Because of legal complications due to Elvis' deal with RCA, results of the session—17 songs worth—weren't released until 1980 as a bootleg album. In 1981, Sun, RCA, and the Elvis Presley Estate released an authorized version. In 1987, a second bootleg album was released, adding 22 songs to the original 17.

novelty record   A "novelty" record has special interest for collectors because of its humor or for its unorthodox approach to the subject matter. With regard to Elvis, the term is applied to records with: comical interpretations of his songs; references to the oddities of the Elvis phenomenon; foreign-language interpretations of his songs; imitations of his songs by impersonators.

Operation Elvis   Despite every attempt to continue business as usual with a draftee like Elvis Presley, the Army had to take special measures to protect him, which they referred to as "Operation Elvis." They assigned personnel and vehicles to the task of handling fans at every stage of his service and deliver the tons of mail to him (500 to 1,000 letters and packages a day in West Germany).

payola "Payola" is the bribing of DJs (disc jockeys) and program directors to get artists airtime. Elvis is one of the few artists from his era (or any era) to hit the big time without the use of such disreputable methods.

pompadour The hairstyle that Elvis began sporting in high school is called a "pompadour," with the hair—*long* hair, for the times—brushed up and back from the forehead. Some kind of ointment, like pomade, is added to keep the hair in place. Elvis embellished his pompadour with a ducktail in back (also called a "DA" for "duck's ass"), and a spit curl hanging over the forehead.

pop music "Pop" refers to musical arrangements of songs with an emphasis on melody, not rhythm, and orchestral accompaniment.

road manager In the music business, a "road manager" oversees details of touring, including details of travel and lodging as well as dealing with the local folks providing a site for the concert. Much of the work takes place before the arrival of the musician to the concert location.

rockabilly "Rockabilly" is a musical style combining black rhythm and blues and white country (hillbilly) music. It might have been Dewey Phillips, the first DJ to play Elvis, who coined the term. On his Memphis radio show he often said: "Man, they're rocking country music. They're rockabillys."

rock and roll (aka rock'n'roll, rock & roll)   A style of music with elements of many other styles of popular music—in particular blues, rhythm and blues, country, and pop—with an emphasis on rhythm. The phrase itself was borrowed by DJ Alan Freed from the 1934 song by the Boswell sisters called "Rock And Roll," used as a euphemism for sexual intercourse. In the 1960s, the shortened form "rock" became widely used.

rhythm and blues (R&B)   "Rhythm and blues" is a kind of rock and roll, with electrified blues with a danceable beat.

shotgun house (shotgun shack)   A tiny, run-down house. The term is thought to come from the idea of a structure being so small that a bullet could enter the front door and exit the back door without hitting a thing.

sighting An "Elvis sighting" is when an individual claims to have seen the King alive and well today. Supermarket tabloids (and even a few books) have claimed they have "definitive" evidence of real sightings (e.g., photographs), but so far all of these can be attributed to doctored photos or shots of impersonators.

TCB "TCB" is the acronym for "Taking Care of Business." Elvis first heard the phrase on an NBC special, featuring Motown performers like The Supremes and The Temptations. Elvis decided to make TCB his motto and had special jewelry designed. The letters were mounted over a lightning bolt, probably based on the lightning symbol on the comic-book character Captain Marvel, Jr.'s costume.

tribute record A "tribute" single or album is a release containing a song or songs specifically praising an artist and/or his/her music. The term refers primarily to a release in which the artist is actually covering a song or songs done by the original artist.

Index

U-V

W-X-Y-Z